Understanding
Cairo

THE LOGIC OF A CITY
OUT OF CONTROL

David Sims

With a Foreword by
Janet Abu-Lughod

The American University in Cairo Press
Cairo New York

First paperback edition published in 2012 by
The American University in Cairo Press
113 Sharia Kasr el Aini, Cairo, Egypt
420 Fifth Avenue, New York, NY 10018
www.aucpress.com

Dar el Kutub No. 21626/11
ISBN 978 977 416 553 5

Dar el Kutub Cataloging-in-Publication Data

Sims, David
        Understanding Cairo: The Logic of a City Out of Control / David Sims.—Cairo: The
    American University in Cairo Press, 2012
            p.   cm.
            ISBN 978 977 416 553 5
            1. Cairo (Egypt)—Description and Travel   I. Title
            916.216

1 2 3 4 5   16 15 14 13 12

Designed by Adam el-Sehemy
Printed in Egypt

Contents

List of Maps   vii
List of Illustrations   ix
List of Tables   xiii
Abbreviations and Acronyms   xv
Acknowledgments   xvii
Foreword *Janet Abu-Lughod*   xix

Introduction   1
1   Imaging Cairo   9
2   Cairo is Egypt and Egypt is Cairo   25
3   A History of Modern Cairo: Three Cities in One   45
4   Informal Cairo Triumphant   91
5   Housing Real and Speculative   139
6   The Desert City Today   169
7   Working in the City   211
8   City on the Move: A Complementary Informality?   227
9   Governing Cairo   251
10 Summing Up: Cairo Serendipity?   267
Postscript: Revolutionary Cairo One Year On   275

Notes   297
Glossary   331
Bibliography   335
Index   347

Maps

Map		Page
0	Greater Cairo Base Map 2009.	xiv
00	Central Greater Cairo Base Map 2009.	xvi
1.1	Cairo built-up area in 1798 compared to 2009.	11
2.1	Greater Cairo topography, 2006.	27
3.1	Built-up area of Cairo in 1950 compared to 2009.	47
3.2	Greater Cairo in 2006: extents of the three cities.	48
3.3	Greater Cairo's formal and informal cities, 2005.	60
3.4	Greater Cairo peri-urban areas, 2008.	71
4.1	Informal areas of Greater Cairo by typology in 2000.	98
4.2	Recent informal development on desert land in the al-Suf and 'Atfih areas.	118
4.3	Large informal areas of Greater Cairo in 2008.	127
6.1	Greater Cairo: new town boundaries in 2009.	174
6.2	Sixth of October boundary expansion.	179
6.3	Greater Cairo's western desert in 2009.	180
6.4	Greater Cairo's eastern desert in 2009.	184
7.1	Greater Cairo: main formal industrial areas in 2007.	215
7.2	Distribution of establishments in Greater Cairo 1996.	222
8.1	Greater Cairo: metro lines 1–4.	234
8.2	Greater Cairo: regional roads and second Ring Road.	244
8.3	Greater Cairo expressways in 2007.	247

Illustrations

Figure   *Page*

1.1   Typical older housing in Qaytbay village.   23

1.2   Typical street in the Northern (Mamluk) Cemeteries.   24

2.1   Urban and rural areas of Giza's urban fringe according to the 1996 Census.   30

3.1   Part of Mohandiseen.   49

3.2   Public housing estate of 'economic' units, 1960s, Helwan.   51

3.3   Part of Madinat Nasr, developed in the 1970s.   53

3.4   Al-Nahda public housing estate.   54

3.5   Contrasting fabrics: Dokki versus Bulaq al-Dakrur.   58

3.6   Semi-structured informal area, part of the *shiyakha* of al-Masakin al-Amiriya.   61

3.7   Extensive infill between villages of Dar al-Salam and al-Basatin.   63

3.8   Informal expansion in al-Munira al-Gharbiya.   65

3.9   Informal infill between villages of Saft al-Laban and Kafr al-Taharmus.   67

3.10   Tenth of Ramadan New Town, started in the late 1970s.   76

3.11   Off-plan developments near pyramids of Giza, started in the late 1970s.   81

3.12   Population growth of component parts of Greater Cairo 1946–2006.   83

4.1   Informal housing construction off the Ring Road in al-Baragil, 2001.   99

4.2   Village-style informal buildings, al-Bashtil, Giza.   100

4.3   Recent classic informal buildings, al-Munira al-Gharbiya.   101

4.4   Recent classic informal buildings in Khusus,
            next to Ring Road.   101
4.5   New one-off tower blocks in Bulaq al-Dakrur.   102
4.6   One-off tower blocks on fringe of Bulaq
            al-Dakrur, 2009.   102
4.7   Informal one-off tower buildings in Dar al-Salam.   103
4.8   Evolution of different types of informal housing
            in 'Izbit Bikhit.   104
4.9   Slum pocket behind former Rod al-Farag
            wholesale market.   108
4.10   Tight living in old *raba'* type housing in 'Izbit Bikhit.   109
4.11   Informal development by converted agricultural
            strips in al-Bashtil, Giza.   113
4.12   Recent informal development on hillsides in
            Wadi Pharaon.   116
4.13   Contrasting urban fabrics over nine hundred years.   117
4.14   Two apartment units in an informal building in
            Manshiyat Nasir.   123
4.15   Three apartment units in an informal building
            in Zenin (Bulaq al-Dakrur).   124
4.16   Two apartment units in an informal building in Imbaba. 125
4.17   Horizontal expansion into agricultural land
            in the *shiyakha* of Helwan al-Balad.   135
4.18   Recent detail of informal area of al-Khanka.   136
5.1   Typical narrow lane, Bulaq al-Dakrur.   143
5.2   Older public housing blocks *circa* 1985 in
            Sixth of October.   154
5.3   Different public housing types, Sixth of October.   155
5.4   Demolished ground-floor shop in public housing
            in Sixth of October.   156
5.5   Example of Mubarak Youth Housing in
            Sixth of October.   157
5.6   Largely vacant public housing, al-Shuruq
            New Town, 2006.   159
5.7   National Housing Program housing blocks,
            Sixth of October.   161
5.8   Example of *ibni baytak* self-built housing,
            Sixth of October.   163

5.9   National Housing Program block under construction,
        Sixth of October.   165
6.1   Part of industrial zone of Sixth of October,
        started in 1983.   176
6.2   Panorama of part of Sixth of October.   177
6.3   Central spine of New Cairo in relatively built-up area.   178
6.4   Panorama of mature part of Sheikh Zayed.   182
6.5   Patchy development in al-'Ubur New Town.   186
6.6   Patchy development in al-Shuruq New Town.   188
6.7   Transport problems inside Sixth of October.   190
6.8   New Cairo on the way to the American University
        in Cairo campus.   191
6.9   Successful gated residential compound,
        al-Shuruq New Town.   193
6.10   New Cairo subdivision, zoned for four-story
        apartment blocks.   195
6.11   Still uninhabited New Cairo subdivision, zoned
        for multistory villas.   196
6.12   Sparsely inhabited subdivision, started in 1988,
        Sixth of October.   197
6.13   Off-plan villa subdivisions and gated compounds
        near Giza Pyramids.   202
6.14   Off-plan gated community al-Sulimaniya.   203
6.15   Off-plan government technology park, 'Smart Village.'   204
8.1   Passenger transport in Greater Cairo, 1971–98.   230
8.2   Minibuses competing for passengers, Munib.   231
8.3   Minibuses stopping for passengers at Ismailiya
        Canal Road off-ramp.   232
8.4   Informal public transport interchange on Ring Road.   239
8.5   Clogged main road serving north Bulaq al-Dakrur.   240
8.6   Narrow unpaved lane in very dense residential
        area, 'Izbit al-Matar.   241
8.7   Tuk-tuk repair shop, Waraq al-'Arab.   242
9.1   Government water main serving informal areas
        of Manshiyat Nasir.   258
9.2   Local sewers and house connections, 'Izbit Bikhit.   261
11.1   Informal construction in north Giza, October 2011.   281

Tables

Tables   *Page*

2.1 Urban Egypt Household Income and Expenditure
      Distribution by Decile (2004/2005).   40

3.1 Evolution of the Population of Greater Cairo and
      Its Component Parts (1947–2009).   83

4.1 Large Informal Agglomerations in Greater Cairo (2006).   115

6.1 New Towns around Greater Cairo.   172

Abbreviations and Acronyms

ADSL   broadband connection
AUC   The American University in Cairo
CAPMAS   Central Agency for Public Mobilization and Statistics
              [al-Jihaz al-Markazi li-l-Ta'bi'a al-'Amma wa-l-Ihsa'] (Arab
              Republic of Egypt)
CEDEJ   Centre d'Études et de Documentation Économiques, Juridi-
              ques et Sociales (independent French research center in Cairo)
CNN   Cable News Network
GDP   Gross Domestic Product
GOPP   General Organization for Physical Planning (affiliated to
              MHUUD) (Arab Republic of Egypt)
GTZ   Deutsche Gesellschaft für Technische Zusammenarbeit
              GmbH (a German federally owned sustainable
              development organization)
HECIS   *Household Expenditure, Consumption and Income Survey.*
              See Bibliography under Arab Republic of Egypt, Central
              Agency for Public Mobilisation and Statistics, *Household
              Expenditure, Consumption and Income Survey.*
HSUE   *Housing Study for Urban Egypt,* 2008. See Bibliography
              under United States Agency for International
              Development (USAID), *Housing Study for Urban Egypt.*
IAURIF   Institut d'Aménagement et d'Urbanisme de la Région
              d'Ile-de-France (French government organization)
IDSC   Information Decision Support Center (Arab Republic
              of Egypt)
IGN   Institut Géographique National (French government
              mapping agency)

ILD	Institute for Liberty and Democracy (Lima, Peru)
INTA	International New Towns Association (The Hague)
JICA	Japanese International Cooperation Agency (government organization)
MHUUD	Ministry of Housing, Utilities, and Urban Development (Arab Republic of Egypt)
NGO	Nongovernmental Organization
NHP	National Housing Program (2005–2011) (Arab Republic of Egypt)
NUCA	New Urban Communities Authority (Arab Republic of Egypt)
SEAM	Egyptian Environmental Affairs Agency: Support for Environmental Assessment and Management Programme
SME	Small and Micro-Enterprises
SPOT	Satellite images from Spot Image S.A. (website: http://www.spotimage.com)
SUV	Sports utility vehicle
UN	United Nations
UN-Habitat	United Nations Programme for Human Settlements
UNDP	United Nations Development Programme
USAID	United States Agency for International Development

Acknowledgments

Many people need to be acknowledged who helped with this book. Warm thanks go first and foremost to Janet Abu-Lughod, who enthusiastically supported the project and made very useful and detailed comments on the text. Next, many thanks are extended to Marion Séjourné for her collaboration in all the cartographical work. Sonja Spruit made valuable contributions with photographs and architectural drawings. Lila Abu-Lughod cheerfully and unstintingly helped with communications.

A number of people shared their knowledge with the author or were colleagues in the work upon which this book rests. These persons included Eric Denis, Ahmed Eweida and Sameh Wahba at the World Bank, Nick Warner, Elena Piffero, Hazem Kamal, Zein Abd Al-Azim, Muna El-Shorbagi, Olivia Kummel, and Hala Bayoumi at the Centre des Etudes et Documentations economiques et juridiques (CEDEJ).

Thanks and gratitude are extended to the people at Google Earth who gave the author permission to use their screen imagery of parts of Greater Cairo.

Thanks must also be extended to the Dutch-Flemish Institute in Cairo, which invited the author to give a lecture on informal Cairo in November 2006, on the basis of which this book project was conceived.

Finally, many thanks are extended to Randi Danforth, Miriam Fahmi, and Nadia Naqib at the American University in Cairo Press, and Lesley Tweddle, whose much appreciated efforts were essential for editing and producing the book.

Foreword
by Janet Abu-Lughod

Cairo is perhaps the city that above all others has captured the hearts of writers and inspired prose ranging from the journalistically sensational to the seriously scholarly. The best of the latter tries to reconcile the city's rich history of religious and political changes with what appears to be the persistent essence of its people's character. Especially challenging has been the task of describing the protean shape of the city as a coherent geographic whole, since Cairo's urbanized region has expanded (and sometimes contracted) over many millennia of political change without losing its centrality or coherence. The exponential growth of Cairo's population in the last generation has been matched by radical expansion of the metropolitan region's boundaries. New urban settlement areas have more than doubled the city's extent, absorbing the increased residential population at efficient densities, mostly within the fringe and northern zones.

All fans of Cairo will therefore welcome this new path-breaking book by David Sims, original in its arguments and richly documented with detailed data never before accessible to the general reader. It is clearly a major addition to the voluminous literature about Cairo, thankfully updating and indeed superseding two earlier holistic accounts of the city's social and spatial organization: those written by Marcel Clerget in the early 1930s and by Janet Abu-Lughod in the late 1960s. The sheer size of the city's population and the rapidity with which it has grown in the last century means that the conclusions reached by earlier generations of scholars and the detailed descriptions they crafted, no matter how accurate for their time, have long been in need of updating.

Clerget's sympathetic historical narrative, his excellent maps (many of them lovingly hand drawn), and his laborious extraction of raw census data, carried the history of the city up through the height of British colonial rule when a bifurcation of the population into 'natives' and 'local and foreign elites' was sharply reflected geographically in the contrast between the 'old' city and the 'new.' My own book carried the city's history through the overthrow of the figurehead king, the exuberant period of Bandung, Arab Socialism, the nationalization of the Suez Canal, and the construction of the high dam designed to provide cheap electricity for heavy industrial development. It was accompanied by high rates of rural-to-city migration and soaring rates of natural increase, only partially mitigated by significant land reforms to break up enormous feudal estates and by the state's ambitious plans to construct industrial zones and mass housing, largely in the northern fringe and on the Giza shore. During this period, sizable parcels of state, military, and *waqf* (religious endowment) land adjacent to the built-up city were still available for development into popular housing and, later, middle-class projects such as Madinat Nasr (Nasr City) and Mohandiseen. These additions, together with the departure of foreigners, helped expand the housing supply to keep pace with in-migration and high natural increase.

Even such ambitious progressive investments, however, were insufficient to build Egypt's military capacity to defend the country from hostile attacks. The tripartite invasion of Sinai by British, French, and Israeli troops in 1956 was turned back after U.S. objections, but this only postponed the humiliating defeat of Egypt in 1967, when Israel occupied the remainder of Palestine and the Sinai up to the Suez Canal, ending Nasser's optimistic dreams of political autarchy and modern socialism.

Where my narrative ends, David Sims's excellent analysis picks up, concentrating essentially on the period after Egypt's defeat in 1967 and the death of Nasser in 1970. And it far exceeds the studies that preceded it, both in posing more analytic questions and in its access to details that are only now technically available to the student of urban development—easier computer mapping of census data and, above all, Google Earth, through which the actual and gradual changes in land use (especially in the agricultural fringe) can be traced graphically.

Tracing the major changes that have occurred in the past half century, Sims demonstrates how the city has managed to function despite its mounting challenges, thanks to the patience and ingenuity of its people—recognized and admired by all of us who marvel at the special resilient qualities of 'our' city. Sims argues that Cairo has avoided the dysfunctional chaos and unplanned overcrowding of many Third World cities, thanks to an ironic combination of an authoritarian but relatively ineffectual state committed to developing new towns in the unlimited desert, and the tenacity and ingenuity of informally organized entrepreneurial investors (ordinary people) in building regular dense housing developments on contiguous farmland, despite firm (but unenforceable) government laws prohibiting the conversion of agricultural land into urban settlements.

His tightly organized argument, focusing directly on this fundamental problematic, allows the author to avoid the temptation to include all the fascinating tidbits of historical interest so irresistible to other authors. Instead, his book ruthlessly confines itself to the past forty years, makes full use of the relevant new information available, and is deeply enriched by the author's understanding of Egypt, gained in his thirty-plus years of experience as a skilled data analyst and as a sophisticated hands-on activist/planner in that country. The result is an analysis that is rigorously disciplined, based on a cautious reading of statistical and geographic evidence, and illuminated by insights gained from actual experience as a planning practitioner of development projects.

As Sims states clearly in his introduction, "the message which is developed in this book is that Cairo has generated its own logics of accommodation and development, and that these operate largely outside the truncated powers of government or are at best in a symbiotic relation with its weakness. For lack of a better word, these logics can be called 'informal.'" In contrast to Egyptian critics who deplore informal solutions, he argues that in Cairo, they work! Its population is relatively well housed; the metropolitan region has kept its compact shape of high density by contiguous additions and infill within and between existing villages; roads, buses, and informal transportation systems move people with flexibility; wasteful suburban sprawl has been avoided, because planned industrial zones and better-class villas and government institutions have been relegated to government-sponsored peripheral satellite cities.

The latter group, ambitious government planners, with official power to appropriate unlimited 'free' state/military desert land, put its efforts into designing a set of 'new towns' in the desert, far from the city's center. The state has made heavy investments in infrastructure (notably the ring roads around the city designed to reach these satellite towns and to extend water lines) and has offered generous incentives to joint industrial ventures and to private builders of upper-class villas, hoping that sites and services and minimal worker housing would be filled with workers and their families eager for employment in the new factories of the planned spacious new towns. However, the population anticipated to fill up these still mostly empty spaces has failed to materialize. Instead, workers must be bused in daily while their families prefer to remain in town.

At the same time, a set of ordinary Cairenes, using entrepreneurial ingenuity and inventing quasi-legal techniques of land-transfer contracts based largely on trust, have managed to circumvent government restrictions that have proven either weakly enforced or subject to bending with bribes. In the most recent decades, these small investors have added massive amounts to the metropolitan region's affordable housing supply on the agricultural fringe. By analyzing serial Google Earth aerial photographs, Sims documents the achievements of these 'informal planners.' He commends them for averting growing housing shortages, for absorbing 'excess' population growth, for controlling construction costs, and for facilitating gradually accumulated capital investments and owner-supervised construction.

It should be acknowledged that not all of these techniques for building at efficient densities can be applied automatically in other resource-poor megacities. This makes the study of Cairo's solution of limited value in the growing academic field of comparative global urbanization. However, it may be of special interest as a counter-factual, which enhances its value to comparative urbanists.

Some differences that distinguish Cairo from others are cultural: long-term adaptation to living peacefully in high-density settlements; strong family and neighborhood ties; tolerance for diversity; self-reliance and skill at quietly resisting oppressive government controls.

Some are situational: the years of oil prosperity in neighboring labor-short kingdoms in the 1970s and beyond, encouraged Egyptian men to migrate for higher wages, despite their reluctance (and restrictions on family admissions) to emigrate permanently. Excess wages were repatriated and some of these were saved to invest in land and dwellings.

Some, like terrain, are relatively unique: flat rectangular agricultural plots divided by canals for irrigation, which, after land reforms, were subdivided into small ownership plots. These irrigation canals became suitable, when covered, for narrow access roads to collective settlements, and served as templates to guide regular designs.

But one deviation is relatively unique: that is, the sharp but somewhat flexible division between the desert and the sown, for which Egypt has always served as an extreme example. Unimproved desert lands belong collectively to the state or to tribes that can defend them, because, unless irrigated, they have little value except for animal grazing. Ownership of the sown (or irrigated) space is always contested and policed because its value fluctuates with what can be produced on it. According to standard theories of land economics, conversion from agricultural to accessible urban uses creates irresistible profits, unless recaptured in taxes or otherwise regulated. Few other countries outside MENA can take advantage of this opportunity to make contradictory policies. Similar contradictions, however, may also exist in other rapidly growing cities of the South. The challenge is to find and exploit them.

In conclusion, David Sims has not only produced an original and unique case study of Cairo but an innovative model of methodological sophistication and a theoretical challenge to superficial overgeneralizations. Hurrah!

To Tanta

To Alexandria

Airport

Shubra al-Khayma

Heliopolis

Sheikh Zayed

Madinat Nasr

Sixth of October

Giza Pyramids

Maadi

To Fayoum

Helwar

0   30Km

Map 0. Greater Cairo Base Map, 2009.

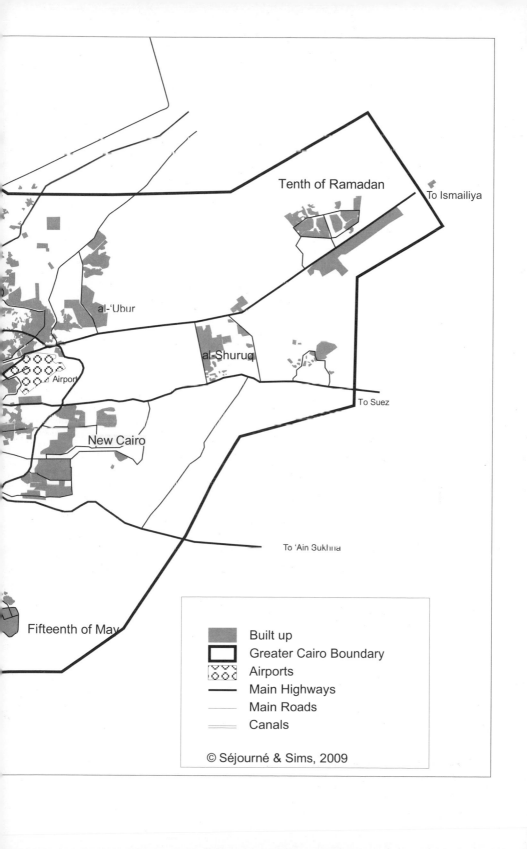

Tenth of Ramadan

To Ismailiya

al-'Ubur

al-Shuruq

Airport

To Suez

New Cairo

To 'Ain Sukhna

Fifteenth of May

Built up
Greater Cairo Boundary
Airports
Main Highways
Main Roads
Canals

© Séjourné & Sims, 2009

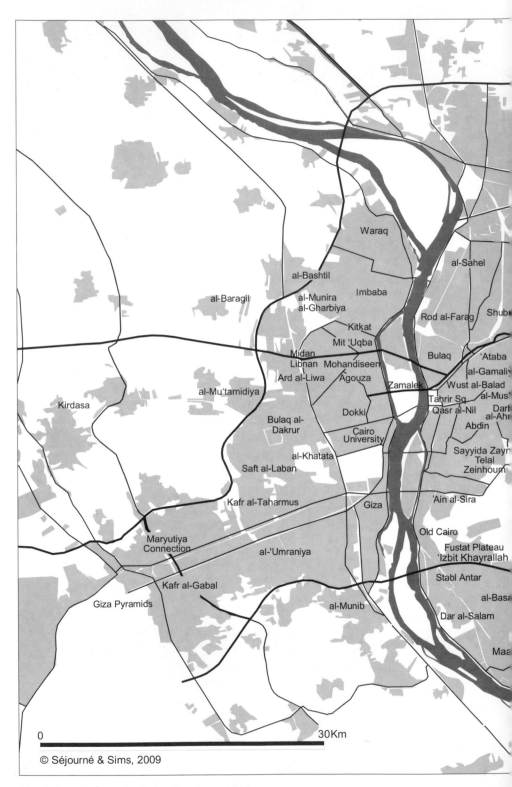

Map 00. Central Greater Cairo Base Map, 2009.

Introduction

Why try to understand a metropolis such as Cairo? Greater Cairo is certainly important as the home for over seventeen million people, as the engine of the Egyptian economy, and as the largest city in Africa (and, by some measures, the seventh largest in the world).[1] But an understanding of Cairo is crucial for other reasons. There is a need to move beyond the stereotypical generalizations that many are quick to apply to Third World megacities. There is so much clutter out there, so much cavalier commentary and superficial analysis, that it is frustratingly difficult for the simple realities of Cairo to emerge from the noise. Comprehending Cairo's urban realities is the subject of this book, which seeks to explain how it is possible for an apparently out-of-control Cairo to function and, in some ways, to function quite well.

Readers of this book who seek blinding insights or startling revelations applicable across the urban Third World may be disappointed. In fact, one of the points of this book is to show how easy it is to be superficial when tackling the subject of a huge city, and how facile it is to immediately and sweepingly confound it with the urban future of the planet. That over half the world is now urban, that it will inescapably become more so, and that almost all of this urbanization is a product of Asian and African countries, is tirelessly repeated these days. But it is precisely because cities such as Cairo are heralds of the planet's future that they need better, less cursory, and less prejudiced treatment.

Yet this book should have a certain universal appeal. It tries seriously to understand Cairo, and in doing so, it demonstrates an approach that can be applied to other cities. Our process has been to step back, take a bit of time, and proceed through the city's modern history, geography, built environment, transport, economy, and especially population, making doubly sure people count and are counted. The focus is on the last fifty years or so, a period of explosive growth in which the population has quadrupled and which has fundamentally changed the city forever. Within this process and at each juncture questions are constantly posed. What are current images and understandings? What is actually known and not known? And finally, does this or that aspect of the city work or not work, and why?

In the past decade or so there has been only a handful of attempts at putting the story of a contemporary non-western metropolis into a single treatment. *Maximum City: Bombay Lost and Found*, written in 2005 by Suketu Mehta, takes a look at Mumbai and, while certainly entertaining and informative, does so through a personal optic that seems to be preoccupied with class differences, police corruption and brutality, neo-fascist politics, and Mumbai's criminal world.[2] Rem Koolhaas tackled Lagos in a fifty-minute film released in 2003 called *Lagos/Koolhaas*, but this treatment is little more than a celebration of chaos, whose message is as much about Koolhaas as it is about Lagos.[3] On the more academic side, Ananya Roy produced *City Requiem: Calcutta* in 2003, which is an excellent narrative of many aspects of the city—politics, poverty, gender, and contested informality on the city's rapidly developing fringes—but in it the imperative to place her work within the fabric of western academic discourse is often overwhelming.[4]

Even looking back decades, there are precious few books that tackle cities in developing countries as a whole. Ironically, it is Cairo that has probably been better covered by serious treatment than any other non-western metropolis. Janet Abu-Lughod's *Cairo: 1001 Years of the City Victorious*, published in 1971, stands out in the literature as a much acclaimed and often referenced model of such an approach.[5] Her work was preceded in 1934 by Marcel Clerget's exhaustive and excellent if little-known work, *Le Caire: Étude de Géographie urbaine et d'Histoire économique*.[6] Our book, along with those of Abu-Lughod and Clerget, can be seen as punctuations or markers along both temporal and demographic continuums. Clerget was analyzing a Cairo that contained one million inhabitants in 1928, and Abu-Lughod was looking at a city that had grown to roughly four million inhabitants by 1966. The present book, another four decades on, is looking at the same city, whose population exceeded sixteen million inhabitants by 2006, another fourfold increase. These coincidental continuum markers dramatically underscore the reality of Cairo's exponential growth and the need for repeated investigations and updates.

Is modern Cairo out of control? The words chaotic, overcrowded, cacophonous, disorganized, confusing, polluted, dirty, teeming, sprawling, and so on, are quick to be used by foreign observers as well as Egyptians themselves. For the political leadership and most Egyptian professionals and academics, Cairo has become a *bête noire*, representing all that is backward and undisciplined, the antithesis of what modern Egyptian society should aim to be. For observers of global trends, Cairo is one of those places where it is fashionable to deplore the rising tide of 'intractable urban problems' associated with so many megacities in the Third World, and to see them as hopelessly out of control.

And in many ways Cairo is completely out of control, at least by the metric of western urban management. Two-thirds of the city's population now live in neighborhoods that have sprung up since 1950, devoid of any planning or control, and which are considered by officialdom as both illegal and undesirable. In contrast, there are vast extensions of the urban region that are completely planned and into which the state has poured more and more resources, but perversely these areas remain almost completely devoid of any inhabitants. Housing in Cairo is built, and property exchanged, in contravention of a host of laws; transport functions in strange and apparently contradictory ways; and hanging over all are near-dysfunctional and largely irrelevant bureaucracies. As one academic discussion of Cairo's 'master planning' efforts put it, "Greater Cairo has not been mastered or planned."[7]

Furthermore, superficially Cairo is a knot of contradictions. One of the most glaring is ostentatious wealth coexisting side by side with extreme poverty. In this sense Cairo is right up there with Lagos, Mumbai, or Mexico City—or at least would seem to be. There are huge SUVs and donkey carts, palaces and hovels, beggars and pampered youth. There are outrageously expensive weddings whose floral arrangements alone cost more than the average Egyptian earns in a lifetime. However, another of the city's contradictions follows directly on from this: for all the juxtaposition of wealth and poverty, Cairo is probably the safest large city on earth, at least in terms of violent crime. Yet another contradiction is that, even in a huge metropolis such as Cairo, one can still walk from the center of town and in less than two hours find oneself in the midst of verdant fields, sturdy farm workers, and placid water buffalos.[8] Another whole set of contradictions is to be found in the huge chasm between government pronouncements and realities on the ground, as we shall see in this book.

The contradictions of rich and poor are common to all Third World capital cities, where the poor and disenfranchised continue to multiply, where the thin layers of the rich and connected play out their fantasies, and where the state (whether hard, soft, high modernist, paternal, or some combination of all of these) continues to be at least partly irrelevant. But the message that is developed in this book is that Cairo has generated its own logics of accommodation and development, and that these operate largely outside the truncated powers of government or are at best in a symbiotic relation with its weakness. For lack of a better word, these logics can be called 'informal.'[9] Development literature, both donor and academic, is full of talk about informality, as any keyword search on Google will show. And informal urban development is now being recognized by many students of modern urbanism as one of, if not *the*, defining feature of the large developing world city.[10] To those wishing to uncover a hard anatomy of urban informality, one can only say, "Welcome to Cairo, where informality rules supreme!"

If there is a particular methodology to be found in this book, it is that a Third World metropolis needs to be seen as a sum of its people, their activities, and livelihoods, and the planner must ask where all of this is headed. We take as a premise that to understand such a place one needs to stand back and look at numbers: numbers of people, volume of investments, prices, land measurements, and so on, and ask how and why they are constantly changing. As Janet Abu-Lughod says, the "infrared lens of statistics" is needed to "separate the accidental from the essential."[11] Although it is valuable to focus on a particular locale or group of people or one of the myriad idiosyncrasies that Cairo hides, there is also a need to step back or above, put them in perspective, and determine the general context in which they emerge. All too often, when looking at a huge city, it is convenient to let tiny aspects dominate. While this approach may advance someone's particular agenda, it hardly contributes to understanding the city as a whole, and can introduce distortions that inflate triviality all out of proportion. As this book contends, there is a need to uncover underlying economic processes at work that shape the city and, parenthetically, frequently bedevil government planners, who ignore them in pursuit of their utopian dreams, and lawmakers, who assume that somehow legislation will automatically be enforced. It is these processes that, after all, help explain how cities may actually exhibit "order without design."[12]

Cairo is a moving target, as any dynamic city must be. This book was written in 2009, and it takes maximum advantage of the detailed results of the 2006 census (which appeared partially only in 2008) as well as of a number of very recent studies, theses, and reports. Inevitably, much of this data will soon be out of date as Cairo continues to grow and change. But hopefully the conclusions will not, since they are based on some fundamental traits and underlying driving forces that have shaped the city over the last five decades and continue to do so. Some of the policies and actions of government have had a definite impact, but rarely in the ways intended, as we shall see. And this disconnect between government pronouncements and reality continues in Greater Cairo, recent reforms and initiatives notwithstanding.

One of the challenges in writing this book has been to decide what should be included and what not.[13] To keep to the essentials of how Cairo works, in our book there is *no* discussion of Cairo's ethnic and religious groups (which get along quite well), crime (which is remarkably low), air pollution (extremely bad when there is no wind), or even solid waste collection systems (which are badly managed but include an efficient informal means for recycling). For each of the topics covered, there is a huge amount of information to draw on, and sifting and summarizing have been necessary to deliver what is hopefully only clear and essential. This having been said, by no means can the understanding of Cairo presented here be considered definitive. All representations of a city, especially a complex and dynamic city such as Greater Cairo, are approximations. This book is no exception. But we hope it advances an understanding of Cairo and how it works, knowing there is very much more that could be said.

This book was written in English, on the assumption that the main audience would be an international one. However, as many people have pointed out, for the book to advance the understanding of Cairo among those who actually count—in other words, decision makers in government and in the Egyptian intelligentsia—an Arabic version needs to be produced. This is very much the intention.

How to Use this Book

The organization of this book is straightforward. First, views of Cairo and ways in which it is imaged are summarized in Chapter 1, in order to show how reality is all too easily glossed over with facile portrayals and even sometimes, gleeful misconceptions. Chapter 2 puts Cairo into its Egyptian context, without which it is impossible for the reader to even begin to understand Cairo. Chapter 3 presents a history of modern Cairo by focusing on the development over the last half-century of its three component parts—the formal city, the informal city, and the desert city—and the relative weights of each. Chapter 4 expends considerable effort on dissecting the informal city and explaining both why it has become dominant and why it will inevitably continue to be so. Chapter 5 tries to untangle the confused picture of housing needs, housing markets, and the real-estate bonanza. Chapter 6 visits in some detail the new towns and desert developments around Cairo, since so much hope is placed in them by planners, local investors, and neo-liberal cheerleaders alike. Chapter 7 presents an overview of Cairo's economy and in particular the labor force, enterprises, and how informality dominates the livelihoods of many. Chapter 8 takes a look at transport and informality in Cairo, and Chapter 9 briefly sketches how Greater Cairo is governed, or is not. Finally, Chapter 10 tries to tie it all together.

A Definition of Greater Cairo

Just what is the extent of Greater Cairo, which is the subject of this book? Where to draw the boundaries of the metropolis is much debated, as is the case for virtually all megacities where boundaries need to be revised outward to keep up with urban expansion. To keep things simple, we take as the boundary of Greater Cairo that of the Japanese International Cooperation Agency (JICA) study area for Greater Cairo (see Nippon Koei Co. Ltd. and Katahira Engineers International, *Strategic Urban Development*, pp. S-1 and S-2). This is made up of three distinct sub-areas, listed below. The reader should know that in this definition and throughout the book we refer to the three governorates of Greater Cairo that existed prior to the administrative changes promulgated in May 2008, which created the two new governorates of Sixth of October and Helwan, carved partly out of Giza and Cairo governorates respectively.

1. Greater Cairo Proper

This includes all of Cairo Governorate, Giza City (part of Giza Governorate), and Shubra al-Khayma City (part of Qalyubiya Governorate).

These areas correspond to the main metropolitan agglomeration and to almost all of what the Central Agency for Public Mobilization and Statistics (CAPMAS) classified as 'urban' in the 2006 Census. The 2006 population of Greater Cairo proper was 11.7 million inhabitants.

2. Peri-urban Greater Cairo

This includes nine, mainly rural, administrative *marakiz* (districts) of Giza and Qalyubiya governorates. The *marakiz* of Qalyubiya are al-Qanatir al-Khayriya, Qalyub (including Khusus), al-Khanka, and Shibin al-Qanatir. Those of Giza are Giza, Imbaba, Usim, Badrashayn, and al-Hawamidiya. The 2006 population of peri-urban Greater Cairo was 3.9 million inhabitants.

3. Greater Cairo's Desert

This includes the eight desert new towns found around Cairo—Sixth of October, Fifteenth of May, al-'Ubur, al-Shuruq, Sheikh Zayed, New Cairo, al-Badr, and Tenth of Ramadan, plus other desert developments inside the Nippon (2008) study area boundary.[14] The 2006 population of Greater Cairo's desert was 602,000 inhabitants.

The totality of the extent of Greater Cairo is made by combining these three different spaces, equaling 4,367 square kilometers. This is sometimes referred to as the Greater Cairo region. The resulting boundary is shown in Map 0.

A Note on Sources

The sources for this book are many. It may be that there are more data, descriptions, and commentaries about Cairo than most non-western megacities. A main source is the Census of Egypt, and other outputs of the Egyptian government body responsible for the census, al-Jihaz al-Markazi li-l-Ta'bi'a al-'Amma wa-l-Ihsa'. This body also publishes in English under the name Central Agency for Public Mobilisation and Statistics, often known by its acronym CAPMAS. The Census of Egypt is a multivolume work that includes a Census of Population, Census of Buildings, Census of Establishments, and Census of Living Conditions. Other sources include newspaper articles, heavily obtuse reports found in the development literature, journalists' impressions, and academic theses and articles. Google Earth satellite images, that blessing and godsend to all who love and dissect cities, have been indispensable.

The author's personal experiences are also a prime source of information. The author has been based in Cairo for over thirty years and has worked as an urban planner and economist on numerous projects in Cairo and on studies about the city and its various facets. This has not only allowed access to much data but has also meant that 'getting into the field' has been a frequent task and, parenthetically, a great privilege. Having had to operate professionally as an independent consultant caught in the middle, with Egyptian government agencies on one side and foreign donors on the other, has been an uncomfortable but decidedly informative experience.[15]

It should be pointed out that many of the recent studies used in this book were produced by the author. Small parts of Chapters 2, 4, and 6 are condensed or revised versions of passages written by the author and listed in the Bibliography as: World Bank, *Arab Republic of Egypt: Urban Sector Note*. Vol. 1: *Urban Sector Update*, and World Bank, *Arab Republic of Egypt: Urban Sector Note*. Vol. 2: *Towards an Urban Sector Strategy*.

How reliable is the published information used in this book? All such information must be looked at with a critical eye, and in the text the basis of data is questioned when it is thought that the reader should form his or her own opinion as to their reliability. Since statistics coming from the Census of Egypt are copiously used throughout this book, the reader may wish to know how dependable these numbers are. As with any census, there are deficiencies to be found in terms of definitions, methodology, and geographical coverage. Also, the precise boundaries of census enumeration districts are somewhat confusing, especially in peri-urban areas.[16] Where housing unit or population numbers for a particular area may be over- or under-represented due to these deficiencies, this is noted. However, it should be realized that the Census of Egypt is a *de facto* census with a long tradition and a consistent approach. It first counts all buildings and housing units and then, on a particular night in the census year, counts all persons physically present in housing units. (For the 2006 Census, this was the night of 20 November.) This means distortions that could arise from considerations of what is a 'normal' or 'registered' residence are avoided, and also there is no double counting.

1

Imaging Cairo

Modern Cairo is certainly no backwater, judging by the amount of commentary that has been and continues to be poured out about it. The attention Cairo receives is found in books on Cairo itself, in articles, in television programs, on websites, in films on particular aspects of the city, and in works about Egypt and the Middle East, in which Cairo figures more or less prominently. Efforts range from serious journalism to guidebooks and travelogue impressions and from obscure academic material to obtuse development reports generated by aid agencies. There is also a large body of fiction whose stories are located in Cairo, some of it very good and well-known and some of it superficial and self-serving. Except for the fiction, most of the material is produced by western authors and institutions, and it is no exaggeration to say that the western optic, especially the Anglophone one, seems to predominate. Commentary on Cairo by Egyptians is rich and varied, but is found mostly in the newspapers, on television, and in local journals, rarely in books.[1]

Obviously, as a collective whole such sources can aid a reader in gaining an understanding of the city and how it works. But who has the time and patience to synthesize, even if information overload doesn't occur? In addition, the impressions gained are often superficial and sometimes completely incorrect, since 'out there' is a lot of material colored by preconceptions and myths. This can even be found in material that is ostensibly well-grounded in Cairo and its manifestations, but it is more often found in the copious transnational literature that throws in snippets about Cairo while advancing global truths seemingly valid across cities, across countries, and even across continents. There is too much of the need to neatly package and quickly extrapolate to the global, and in the process necessarily to stereotype, lose track, and objectify.

This chapter tries to set the scene, going through the most common types of imaging to which Cairo is subject. The aim is to inform the reader that there are numerous ways Cairo can be 'taken' and observed, and to provide a kind of gentle forewarning of some of the more common pitfalls and distortions found in the literature.

Cairo as History

The single strongest pull in the imaging of Cairo is probably the city's historical dimension. And Cairo certainly has a lot of history, over four thousand years of it if Memphis and the Giza pyramids are considered part of the city, and over one thousand years even if Cairo's history is considered to have begun only in the Fatimid era. In fact, it could be said that there is a whole industry, curiously dominated by American and French scholars, which looks just at Islamic Cairo. It even seems sometimes that the most important commentator on Cairo is the fourteenth-century chronicler and urban observer Ahmad ibn 'Ali al-Maqrizi.

It is worth remembering that, although Cairo certainly has a proud historic past, at present the parts of the city that can be considered historic (that is, those that existed at the time of the French occupation in 1798) represent only a minuscule fraction of the whole. Currently the population of these areas (see Map 1.1) does not exceed 350,000 persons, or 2 percent of Greater Cairo's total of over seventeen million inhabitants. It should be added that the population of these small areas continues to decline, and if the government has its way, historic Cairo will soon become a sterile open-air museum with little else but theme-park embellishments and tourist shops.

Although historic Cairo is now an almost insignificant part of the modern metropolis, Cairo as history seems to trump the literature. In the last fifteen years three substantial books have appeared that look specifically at Cairo—André Raymond's *Cairo: City of History* (published in 1993 in French, and in 2001 in English), Max Rodenbeck's *Cairo: The City Victorious* (1998), and Maria Golia's *Cairo: City of Sand* (2004).[2] Each tries to see the city as a whole, and each includes descriptions of contemporary Cairo. Yet in each the historical emphasis is at the forefront, if not overwhelming.

Raymond's book is the most historic, devoting only one chapter of some thirty pages to Cairo's development over the 1936–92 period. And

Map 1.1. Cairo built-up area in 1798 (from *Description de l'Égypte*) compared to 2009.

this chapter is predictably named "The Nightmares of Growth." It concentrates on "galloping population growth," wholesale urban expansion on precious agricultural land, the "frenetic growth" of what had been genteel neighborhoods, the "near-paralysis of traffic," and deplorable infrastructure services. Raymond devotes only two pages to the phenomenon of informal or spontaneous settlements around Cairo, which flourish "without the help of any planning, in agricultural areas that one would wish to preserve,"[3] focusing instead on laments for the decline of the historic quarters and the ugliness of recent architecture. Raymond seems to see nothing good in recent developments, implying that his "city of history" is losing its soul. He concludes:

> But Cairo risks becoming an ordinary city, another example of the vast conurbations proliferating throughout the world. . . . The population threat is still present, poised to sweep away the fragile barriers that technicians and politicians have managed to erect to direct its flow. In the past demographic growth has been an asset to Egypt, giving it power, prestige, and authority. Today it is a mortal danger. Cairo long played the part of safety valve for Egypt's population growth. Tomorrow it could be its detonator.[4]

This gloomy assessment was published in 1992, when Greater Cairo had just eleven million inhabitants. Today it has over seventeen million and is still nowhere near detonating.

Max Rodenbeck's book on Cairo is also unabashedly historical, and the first two-thirds present a very readable and insightful historical timeline that starts in earnest with the Arab conquest of Egypt in AD 640 and the establishment of al-Fustat. The last third of the book covers modern Cairo since the 1952 Revolution, going through the rule of Nasser, Sadat, and Mubarak, and focusing on Egypt's changing fortunes and social dynamics and how they played out in Cairo. Religion and fundamentalism, political games, bloated bureaucracy, foreign aid, riots, Sufi *mulid*s, coffee houses, class hierarchies, the hopeless education system, garbage and the *zabbalin*, song and film, are all subjects for observation. Cairene kindliness, stoicism, humor, and wit in the face of economic stagnation and chaos rightfully claim pride of place. Rodenbeck offers few generalizations, but he does sit back and muse, quite accurately: "On the surface Cairo's ways of coping seem hopelessly tangled and sclerotic.

They can be maddening. . . . By and large, though, the city's mechanisms work. . . . In richer cities formal structures, rules, and regulations channel a smooth flow of things. In Cairo informal structures predominate."[5]

Rodenbeck never completely abandons the historic take on the city, even when discussing modern facets. He is clever at intertwining the old with the new. Thus Nasser's autocracy is compared with that of the Mamluks, modern Cairo's cavalier attitude to garbage is compared to a similar pharaonic nonchalance, today's rampant bribery is compared to legal knavery recorded on tomb reliefs from the New Kingdom as well as to medieval Cairo's corrupt judges and bribed witnesses, and present-day funeral obsequies are compared to both the pharaonic and Islamic preoccupation with death. These comparisons might help provide continuity in a take on Cairo that is more or less biographical, but it does not in itself explain how modern Cairo grows and works. For example, although the book was published in 1998 when almost half the city could be considered informal, the phenomenon of informal urban development and its ascendancy in Cairo's landscape is hardly mentioned, except in a quote from Asef Bayat on the informal city's style of "quiet encroachment" and a reference to the "higgledy-piggledy burrows of Bulaq al-Dakrur."[6] To Rodenbeck, as to many other observers, the hard life of the poor is found in an amorphous geographic landscape called "the Popular Quarters," which combine new informal Cairo with older tenement and historic areas.[7]

Maria Golia's book is less historic than either Rodenbeck's or Raymond's. In the preface she poses the question: "Some of us wonder, watching Cairo teeter between a barely functional glide and an irretrievable nosedive, what keeps this plane in the air? . . . How and why, given some of the most grueling, incongruous conditions imaginable, Cairo retains its allure and its people their sanity."[8] She aims at looking at "Cairo's broader present moment, its giddy equilibrium and unfolding contemporary nature," pursuing lines of inquiry about Cairo's millions and their "grace under pressure."[9] Golia bravely tries to do just that, but even so, she also cannot avoid the historical spin. One of her five chapters is devoted entirely to the city's history, and references such as "the arc of fourteen centuries" pepper the text.

At one point Golia asks "Perhaps today's greatest riddle is not so much 'where is Cairo headed?' as 'where is Cairo at all?' Is it in the old quarters, or the remnants of belle époque downtown, or in the new middle-class areas on the west bank, or in the satellite cities of the desert? Or is the real Cairo to be found in the myriad hovels in which most of the people actually live?" Except for her pejorative and incorrect description of informal Cairo as a collection of hovels, this is a good question! Unfortunately she doesn't really answer it, except to ask another question, which turns back to history: "Does a collective hallucination sustain the image of an ancient and venerable city when it is in fact disfigured with slums and crass consumerism?"[10]

Even Janet Abu-Lughod, who describes the orientation of her well-known 1971 book on Cairo as "social and contemporary rather than historical and architectural," seems unable to escape from being partly tied down by a thousand years of history.[11] Over one-third of her book is devoted to the Islamic and Khedivial city, up to roughly the time of the First World War. However, the rest of the book investigates the formation and growth of the "contemporary city," which roughly covers the 1920 to 1960 period.

Cairo as Nostalgia

Closely related to Cairo as history is the nostalgic view of the glories of a more recent past. There are many Cairenes as well as foreigners who look back to some perceived golden period, usually through a blinkered memory conditioned by revulsion at what Cairo has since become.

Actually, what is perceived as Cairo's golden period is in the eye of the beholder, and it is possible to ride through time on the back of this nostalgia. Although no one still alive remembers Cairo's *belle époque* (generally considered to have spanned the 1870 to 1925 period), there has recently been an outpouring of material about its architecture, enterprise, and social life.[12] This view is frequently combined with a stubborn nostalgia for the Cairo that existed before King Farouk was overthrown in 1952. Cairo has a surprising number of unabashed royalists who see the 1930s and 1940s as the heyday of a sophisticated capitalist Egypt untainted by the self-serving officers of Arab socialism. From time to time glossy retrospectives of royalty and their social life appear.[13] The fact that much of what is now ascribed to the Nasser regime actually had its antecedents under Farouk, such as rent control, social housing, and even the oft-maligned Mugamma' al-Tahrir, the central government services complex in Tahrir Square, downtown Cairo, is conveniently ignored. Moving to still more recent times, there are many who look back nostalgically to the innocence of the early revolutionary period, 1952–62, with the flowering of national pride expressed in cinema, song, prestige industry, and Cairo's undisputed primacy as the political capital of the Arab world; that is, a period before all those 'peasants' flooded into the city and ruined everything.

This nostalgia has translated into a number of attempts to preserve the patrimony of older buildings in the downtown area. In 2008 the façades of older buildings began to be renovated by Cairo Governorate and the Ministry of Culture's *al-Tansiq al-Hadari* ('urban harmony') division. At the same time an important developer quietly began to buy up some downtown properties of particular architectural merit. There are even brave if fitful efforts at revitalizing the cultural scene of *wust al-balad*. In one of the strangest manifestations of nostalgia, a couple of real-estate developers are now promoting exclusive gated communities that seem, at least architecturally, to be recreating belle époque Cairo.[14] Only in the fine print is it discovered that these projects are in bleak desert locations many miles from the city proper.

The important point about the nostalgic take on Cairo is that it is largely referenced to and compared with what Cairo is today. And this modern Cairo is perceived as the epitome of savage urbanism, which conveniently leads to the following take on Cairo.

Cairo as Monster and Unmitigated Mess

The Egyptian middle classes and intelligentsia, as well as a sizable slice of the foreign community, love to deplore what Cairo has become. Crowds and congestion, pollution, garbage, chaos, gridlocked traffic, horrendous architecture, and no green space, all are endlessly invoked to describe the mess that Cairo has become. To many, the main culprits who have led to Cairo's present mess are the rural migrants. It is they who have spoiled the genteel city and turned it into a grinding nightmare. As one commentator wrote in *al-Ahram al-iqtisadi* in 1990, "All the neighboring villages have become part of the capital, and instead of inculcating them with city ways and civilization, the capital has become sick with all the backward diseases of the Egyptian villages. It has become a greater village instead of a greater Cairo."[15] On at least two occasions there have been calls made in Parliament to control migration to the city.[16] In fact, for many cultural and professional elites, Cairo would have remained a civilized place, had it not been for those 'peasants' who keep on coming, bringing with them backward behavior unsuited to modern city living.

The fact that migration from the countryside to Cairo has for all purposes halted, and that if many Cairenes can trace their ancestry to the countryside, it is through the filter of two or three generations of totally urban living, counts for naught. The fact that many of the perceived ills of present-day Cairo—the traffic, the pollution, and the "earsplitting auditory stimuli"[17]—are caused by the small minority of the population who are car owners, is lost on those elite critics, all of whom themselves own cars but see their city as sullied by the 'uncouth peasant.'

Cairo as Part of the World of Slums

Among the many ways Cairo can be imaged is that of the typical exploding developing world metropolis. This is what many see as an increasingly unstable and unequal urban world where a vast disenfranchised humanity is warehoused in sprawling slums, and these slums are seen as volcanoes waiting to erupt, the combat zones of the future.[18] This imaging was helped by estimates that by 2007 the world had changed forever, with more people living in urban areas than in the countryside, and that the planet would never look back, firmly planted in a trajectory of an ever increasingly urbanized humanity. Such is the storyline that is becoming more and more prominent, especially in the literature on global trends. Perhaps the most popular of all is *Planet of Slums* (2006) by Mike Davis.[19] This book contains a wealth of anecdotal information and startling descriptions from the world's 'hypercities' but there is no doubt about its message. It paints an unrelieved picture of an unending exodus of surplus rural labor toward the city, of stagnant urban economies that cannot offer more than precarious marginal livelihoods and insalubrious housing, of predatory and exploitative urban elites and real-estate speculators supported by deeply corrupt governments, and of an ever expanding "hermaphroditic landscape" of partly urbanized city fringes groaning with environmental disasters. Always global in its optic, the book loves to generalize:

> Thus, the cities of the future, rather than being made out of glass and steel as envisioned by earlier generations of urbanists, are instead largely constructed of crude brick, straw, recycled plastic, cement blocks, and scrap wood. Instead of cities of light soaring towards heaven, much of the twenty-first century urban world squats in squalor, surrounded by pollution, excrement, and decay.[20]

Davis, as well as many academics, lays the blame squarely at the Washington consensus club, whose dictates of structural adjustment, retrenchment of the state, and liberal trade and economic policies have been "an inevitable recipe for the mass production of slums."[21] Whether or not this blame sits well can be long debated, but the imaging of injustice and doom is strong, evoking the kind of hand-wringing despair that readers normally reserve for global warming.[22]

Does Cairo sit comfortably within this picture? Does it form part of a new urban frontier that includes Dhaka, Kinshasa, Mumbai, Sao Paulo, Kolkata, Lagos, and so on? According to Davis, it certainly does. In fact, Cairo is referred to twenty-seven times in his book, second only to Lagos with twenty-nine references. Among the anecdotes tossed out about Cairo are environmental disasters, child labor, squatters, state repression, slum-dwellers, gated communities for the rich, housing crises, tomb-dwellers, and even the black-market trade in human organs.

Davis is only one of many writers who love to paint a dire picture of the world's megacities and at the same time to throw in colorful snippets about Cairo. A 2005 article quotes the president of the Washington-based Population Institute: "By 2050, an estimated two-thirds of the world's population will live in urban areas, imposing even more pressure on the space infrastructure and resources of cities, leading to social disintegration and horrific urban poverty."[23] The article goes on to describe the terrible situations in Jakarta, Dhaka, and Mexico City, but it also manages to throw in the following statement apropos of nothing in particular: "In Cairo, Egypt, the rooftops of countless buildings are crowded with makeshift tents, shacks and mud shelters. It's not uncommon to see a family cooking their breakfast over an open fire while businesspeople work in their cubicles below."[24] Just where is this "not uncommon" scene to be found?

Such images of Cairo, which instantly conjure up the cliché 'Third World megacity' try to inform the reader of an ominous and unrelenting megatrend with "gripping stories from globalization's frontline."[25] There may be something in the idea that there is a new twenty-first century global urban phenomenon, but to roll all of this into facile generalizations doesn't help anyone.

The Imperative to Refer to the Global

It seems as if much of the discourse on world megacities must point to, and be defined by, the global. This is happening with more and more regularity, especially from academics. It is as if you have nothing to say if you can't show that what you look at is relevant as a part of a new paradigm or huge global trend. Ignore the complexities of history, the nasty details, and the geographic specifics embedded in any city, let alone a city of millions and millions of people. And it certainly helps if you include cutting-edge vocabulary.

An anthology called *Cairo Cosmopolitan: Politics, Culture, and Urban Space in the New Globalized Middle East*, published in 2006, typifies the common academic imperative of linking any analysis of Cairo to global trends.[26] It takes as its starting point the scattered protests in 2003–2005 against the Egyptian state, which is "run in the interests of an elite, state-subsidized ring of Cairo-based capitalists who call themselves liberals or globalizers or democratizers because they facilitate foreign investment in the economic sphere, even as they insist on repression, the extension of the emergency laws, and police state practices in the political sphere."[27]

All but two of the twenty-two contributors are university academics or researchers at western institutions. It is understandable that their orientation is 'out there' in the wider world of scholarship, but how much do their writings advance an understanding of Cairo? It is stated in the introduction that "this city and this region cannot be easily contained or understood through the rigid categories of the past."[28] Well and good. But then the introduction goes on to claim that the book moves beyond old and worn visions and the "fabric of neo-orientalist or neo-colonial meta-narratives" about Cairo. In fact, the approach is called, a bit pretentiously, "the new Cairo School of Urban Studies."[29] It is not altogether clear just what this 'school' represents, since its aims are couched in sweeping terms: "This school represents an international research collective that asks new questions about cities and citizenship, elite domination, public policy, and subaltern politics . . . [and] hopes to disseminate new critical methodologies for qualitative social science as well as new perspectives on urban social movements, state forms, public policy, elite domination, and subaltern publics in the globalized Middle East."[30] Although claiming to be based on down-to-earth field work, the authors "hoped to begin to reveal complexity and by implication, to challenge the necessity of repressive, exclusionary, hierarchical processes of globalization, neo-colonialism, and authoritarianism in the urban and transnational context."[31] It is hard to see how the case studies of the volume meet this challenge, but it is certain that the book succeeds in ascribing to Cairo specific vocabularies drawn from higher academic circles.[32]

Actually, many of the papers in the anthology are informative, especially those that look at specific phenomena of Cairo and are not overly cluttered with academic global-speak. Particularly interesting is a contribution by Eric Denis and Leïla Vignal, mainly because they try to quantify what is being talked about.[33] Ironically, quantification and statistics are pretty much shunned by the 'Cairo school,' which glorifies purely qualitative analysis. The overwhelming impression of the book is not one of a school of thought or analysis, but an interesting collection of vignettes of modern, elitist life in Cairo plus a handful of descriptions of the city's subcultures, its spaces, and its cultural/historical oddities, and how the state loves to modernize and sanitize them.

A second volume from the "Cairo School of Urban Studies" called *Cairo Contested: Governance, Urban Space, and Global Modernity* appeared in late 2009.[34] Like the first volume, this is a collection of academic papers that delve into particulars of Cairo space and life, with an emphasis on contestation and conflict. Many of the papers are quite informative when they stick to details and specifics, as with W. Judson Dorman's piece on government aversion to slum clearance or Agnès Deboulet's description of the "infralegal" area of Dar al-Salam and the marginal community of Stabl 'Antar (Fustat Plateau).[35] Others rightly highlight the repressive excesses of the state toward, for example, trade unions and Sudanese refugees. But as a whole this volume is much like the first, loaded with academic jargon and an overfamiliar castigation of neoliberal globalization as the sole cause of so many of Cairo's ills. The inhabitants of Cairo's *'ashwa'iyyat* (informal urban areas) might be bemused to discover that their neighborhoods "are the products of neoliberalism" and even amazed that it is there "that the contested character of, and resistance to, neoliberal globalization finds expression."[36] Given the fact that "there is little consensus on a definition of globalization," one would have thought that use of the term might be a bit more circumspect.[37] In fact, it would be just as easy to replace the phrase 'neoliberal globalization' with the less emotive 'westernization' or 'modernization.' These trends have been around Cairo for many decades, and it is hard to see much new and startling in the fact that government sometimes connives with business elites to assist foreign penetration, and that existing power structures are able to absorb it, ally with it, and turn it to means of regime preservation and allows the favored few to make lots of money.

Of course, not all academic work on modern Cairo becomes hopelessly entangled with the imperative to see everything through global lenses and to describe it with obscure vocabulary. Perhaps the best scholarly work on contemporary Cairo is a doctoral dissertation by W. Judson Dorman.[38] Dorman examines the connections between the "logic of durable authoritarianism" and Cairo's neglectful governance, particularly by focusing on its inaction vis-à-vis the city's huge and dynamic informal neighborhoods.[39] He explains why the government has been unable to intervene at all effectively, showing that the "strong regime, weak state" relies on the very clientist mechanisms of political control and regime durability that constrain any ability to manage and guide the city's development. He spends considerable time analyzing various externally funded projects relating to Cairo's urban infrastructure, town development, and housing. In this he describes the interplay between the government and the aid agencies (and their consultants), demonstrating the obfuscation on the part of government officials, who feared that such schemes might threaten timeworn control formulae and unleash something unforeseen, in spite of the promises of significant external capital. In short, to Dorman, informal Cairo exists and even dominates, due in part to the exigencies of Egypt's particular form of authoritarian rule and its pathologies of urban management and planning, not because of some simplistic notion of financial constraints. What Dorman does not attempt in his thesis is to construct generalizations, to uncover constants of regional and global worth, or to deduce overarching megatrends of world import. Although for a doctoral thesis he must troll through "the international literature," much to his credit his thesis is solidly and single-mindedly grounded in his subject, which is Cairo.

Tomb Dwellers—What Tomb Dwellers?

Although it is a very minor aspect of city life, the preoccupation with those living in and among the tombs north, east, and south of Cairo's historic core illustrates just how easily one facet of the city can be blown out of all proportion and repeatedly misconstrued. At some point in the 1970s references began appearing to the large numbers of squatters that were invading and living in and among Cairo's oldest graves and tomb courtyards. The image was an exciting one, at least for journalistic purposes. The crush of urban malaise and the impossible housing crisis were painted as so dire that the marginal poor were being forced to live cheek by jowl with the dead.

Janet Abu-Lughod noted that according to the census of 1960 there were perhaps 100,000 inhabitants in the *aqsam* (census districts) that contain the tombs, although included in these zones were legitimate villages and neighborhoods, and subsequently some quarters were razed for new highways. John Waterbury flagged the phenomenon as becoming huge as far back as 1978, when he noted that the then Governor of Cairo proclaimed that one million persons were living in the City of the Dead.[40] In any event, the march of references in from the 1980s on was remarkable. In the more academic literature, we have Yahya Sadowski in *Political Vegetables*: "Housing shortages, endemic since the late 1960s, compel the poorest strata to seek shelter in the medieval cemeteries which surround Cairo."[41] Even the World Bank had to refer to the City of the Dead in its 1990 poverty analysis of Egypt. Referring to the housing problem and the 1986 Census, "It should be noted that the figures for marginal residential places in urban areas (61,000 units) seem to be grossly underestimated in the light of numerous press reports on the growing squatter population of the City of the Dead in Cairo."[42]

Over roughly the same period it seems there was an imperative for journalistic articles and books on Cairo and Egypt to include at least a passing reference to the awful images of the delectably named 'City of the Dead.' Thus we have Daniel Le Gac in *l'Envers des Pyramides*: "Le problème du logement est devenu tellement aigu que les cités des morts de Qait Bai et du Qarafa, à l'est de la ville, ont été progressivement envahies par des 'squatters' qui sont près d'un million a l'heure actuelle."[43] Many other references of a very similar nature can be found. Tony Horwitz, in *Baghdad Without a Map*, states, "The only other option was to take up residence in the City of the Dead, a Cairo necropolis whose above-ground tombs had become cheap housing for half a million people, many of them newlyweds."[44] Or Stanley Stewart in *Old Serpent Nile*: "The shortage of housing is so acute that the vast Cairene cemeteries, known as the City of the Dead, host a population of squatters thought to number a million. They eke out an existence in cardboard and tin shacks amongst the graves."[45] Or the *Independent* magazine in December 1990: "The poor have learnt to live among the ruins. More than half a million people have set up home in the mausoleums of the City of the Dead."[46]

Interest in the tomb squatters was not limited to the print media. Evidently Cable News Network (CNN) tried to film tomb dwellers in 1994, provoking an angry response from both inhabitants and the Cairo press.[47] Egyptian filmmakers have made at least three movies based loosely on the lives of tomb dwellers. Bahaa Jahin even penned a poem that begins:

A city burst at the seams
It spilled over onto its dead (. . .)
How curious you are, O Cairo!
With life and death bundled together, jumbled up/Inside you.[48]

There is no doubt that there are some families who live in Cairo's tomb cities. So just how extensive is the phenomenon? Are there half a million, one million, or even five million inhabitants, as at least one website has claimed?[49] Galila El Kadi published an article in the French journal *Maghreb-Machrek* in 1990. She used the 1986 Census to calculate the population of the *aqsam* (tomb districts), and came up with a figure of 179,000 inhabitants. A full-page article appeared in *al-Ahram* in 1992 in which the tomb areas were discussed and an official from Cairo Governorate was interviewed. This official pointed to "research by the French" (presumably Galila El Kadi's work with the Centre des Études et Documentations economiques et juridiques (CEDEJ)) and declared that in total the population of the tomb districts did not exceed 200,000, and that this included housing estates and villages that were embedded within the cemetery precincts.[50] Finally, it seems, some sense of reality began to appear.

A much more precise and realistic estimate of those living in the tombs is contained in Galila El Kadi's *Architecture for the Dead: Cairo's Medieval Metropolis*, published in French in 2001 and in English in 2007.[51] She charts the demographics of the tomb districts in total, showing that the population grew slowly from about 30,000 at the turn of the century to 67,000 in 1947, and 179,000 in 1986. More interestingly, she distinguishes between those living in ordinary modest housing found within or near the cemetery precincts (mainly a mix of older and newer apartment blocks in Qaytbay and al-Tonsi villages, but also scattered on the fringes) from those actually living in among tombs. The latter, the subject of all the years of media hype, were found according to her field research to number only 12,780.[52] This figure includes all of Cairo's old cemeteries except the Jewish cemetery in al-Basatin. It also matches the 1986 Census

Figure 1.1. Typical older housing in Qaytbay village, part of the Northern (Mamluk) Cemeteries, 2001. (Photograph by David Sims.)

of Egypt, which listed 13,419 persons as living in the *ahwash* tomb typology of housing in all of Cairo Governorate. In the 1996 Census this number actually diminished significantly to 7,930 persons, implying that the tomb-dweller phenomenon peaked in the 1980s. Furthermore, of these tomb-dwellers proper, at least half were private tomb guards, morticians, gravediggers, and their families, all of whose livelihoods were linked to directly to the cemeteries. In other words, the total number of inhabitants who had been forced to invade the tombs in despair of finding other housing did not amount to more than about 6,000 persons in the 1980s, and probably not many more now! This is quite a minuscule fraction of the half million or million inhabitants repeatedly mentioned.

This digression shows how easy it is to objectify erroneously a facet of the city, even romanticizing an aspect of poverty mixed with a slice

Figure 1.2. Typical street in the Northern (Mamluk) Cemeteries, 2010. (Photograph by David Sims.)

of history. The fact that the vast majority of tombs are privately owned and reverently kept exclusively for family burials obviously did not fit the myth. Nor did the fact that there are no 'invaders' or 'squatters' to speak of, among the few thousands who have actually moved into tomb areas. As anywhere in Cairo, there are well-articulated informal markets that assign rental values and key money for even a little scrap of land or a shed.

How many other misconceptions and gross exaggerations exist about Cairo, and indeed about other megacities? It is a sobering thought. Are there really 1.5 million people living crammed onto Cairo's rooftops, as Ahmed Soliman states?[53] Are there really, according to one website, one million street children in Egypt, the majority of whom are found in Greater Cairo?[54]

2

Cairo is Egypt and Egypt is Cairo

U nderstanding Cairo first requires a short look at Egypt. All too often the city is treated in the literature as a stand-alone metropolis, something disembodied that can be seen in isolation from the rest of the country and immediately compared to other world cities, ignoring the fact that Egypt is in many ways not a typical developing country. There are also a few widely held misconceptions about Egypt that need to be set straight, and this chapter gives a background sketch that will make Cairo more readable. It covers Egypt's unique geographical space, its population dynamics, the income levels of its inhabitants, and their standards of living. Also presented are brief discussions of Greater Cairo's importance in the national economy and also of how and to what degree the city's inhabitants differ from those in the country as a whole.

Context of a Unique Physical Space

Herodotus certainly got it right when he said Egypt was the gift of the Nile. The Nile Valley, which runs over 1,100 kilometers from Aswan in the south to the Mediterranean in the north, contains almost all of Egypt's population and is the locus of practically all economic activity. The valley varies in width from two to three kilometers at Aswan to twenty kilometers at Cairo, whence the Delta fans out to form a large, flat triangular plain. As Egypt receives no significant rainfall (except along the Mediterranean coast), all agricultural land is irrigated through gravity take-off canals from the Nile and its two delta branches, and this allows a very intensive cultivation throughout the Valley, with two to three crops per year. The total irrigated area within the valley is about seven million *feddan*s (area of land equaling 4,200 square meters) or three million hectares, roughly the size of the Netherlands.[1]

Cultivation ends and the desert begins abruptly both to the east and the west of the Nile Valley. In Upper Egypt and until Cairo, the valley is mainly confined within cliffs and escarpments, beyond which is the 'high desert.' But starting south of Cairo, the desert fringes have gentler slopes and the distinction between desert and cultivation is sometimes not so sharp. In all cases the desert is extremely arid and inhospitable, although at some points near to the valley, ground water (itself a result of the Nile's hydrology) can be extracted for agriculture and other uses.

Such a physical space is unique among nations. Many countries have desert hinterlands, such as the North African states, but in none is the desert so complete and abrupt and in none is it so extensive. In effect, Egypt's settlement patterns are extremely simple: linear south–north with a large triangular fan at the northern limit. That practically all of the country's population is crammed within this configuration means that compact and high-density living is the norm. And having an 'empty' desert a stone's throw from all this means that it is easy to provide unencumbered lines of transport and communications parallel to the dense ribbon of the Nile Valley, linking up the country and connecting also to the ports of Alexandria, the Canal Zone, and the Red Sea.

Cairo is very strategically located at the point where the Delta fans out northward, which helps account for its five thousand years of more or less continuous settlement. It is something of a choke point, since the Muqattam/Tura hills, only five kilometers east of the Nile, represent the northern extreme of the Nile Valley's confining cliffs. Directly west of the Nile is a relatively wide agricultural plain, beyond which the Western Desert starts. For the most part, this desert rises gently from the plain, except for low cliffs that define the Giza Plateau and its pyramid field and the Abu Rawash hills. Similarly, to the northeast the desert slopes gently upward, allowing for almost unfettered expansion along the Ismailiya and Suez road axes. (See Map 2.1.)

That the Nile runs directly through Greater Cairo presents the metropolis with an added advantage. The enormous volume of water flowing past Cairo makes tapping it for urban uses straightforward and inexpensive, especially given that the main elements of the metropolis are very close by and rarely more than ten meters above the river's water levels. Such an advantage, crucial to allow for continued urban expansion,

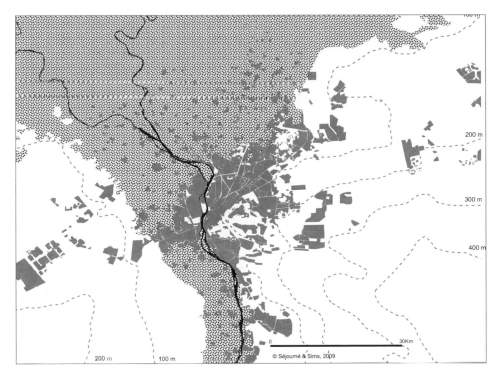

Map 2.1. Greater Cairo topography: agricultural areas, built-up areas, and desert areas with contours, 2006.

is something not all of the megacities of the developing world can be said to enjoy. (The water supply for Greater Cairo is taken up in Chapter 9.)

Thus, Cairo enjoys a uniquely favored physical space. It is at the southern apex of the Delta and is astride the country's main lines of transport and communications, which are improving rapidly throughout Egypt. It is tied to and confined within the Nile Valley, but it also enjoys almost unlimited opportunities to expand into an uncluttered desert both to the east and to the west. That is, in physical terms at least. As we shall see in Chapter 6, however, these desert opportunities have been wastefully exploited.

Egypt's Population

Egypt's population totaled 72.8 million inhabitants at the time of the 2006 Census and is estimated to be growing by 2.03 percent per year, which is substantial but below that of some other countries in the region.[2] For example, average natural increase rates of the Arab Maghrib countries cluster around 1.5 percent per year, whereas conversely those for the Arab Mashriq countries cluster around 2.8 percent per year. The rate of growth of Egypt has slowed, especially from the 1960s and 1970s when it peaked at 2.8 percent per year. Total fertility has also fallen from 5.3 children per female in 1980 to 2.9 in 2006. However, regional differences are significant, with total fertility in rural Upper Egypt estimated at above 4.5. Rates of natural increase in population (births over deaths) are relatively higher in rural and Upper Egyptian governorates, but the variations are not dramatic.[3]

Is Egypt firmly on the trajectory of demographic transition? In other words, will fertility levels continue to decline, with the population eventually reaching near-equilibrium? There is no consensus on this issue, and although UN population projections see a continued decline in fertility and in rates of population growth in Egypt, there are some indications that fertility rates have recently leveled off, which suggests that the resulting natural increase may remain stubbornly high for decades.[4] What is certain is that—even if overall fertility continues to fall—the momentum of higher birth rates from earlier decades will continue to work through the population pyramid, producing a large proportion of females of childbearing age, who will in turn contribute to higher numbers of live births. For this reason projections of Egypt's future population can vary widely, but it is certain that the population will increase rather steadily at least over the next two or three decades.

Egypt's Spatial Demographics and Its Levels of Urbanization
It is rare to find a report on Egypt's development that does not include a statement like "95 percent of the population lives on 4 percent of the land area," which often leads to images of relentless overcrowding in the Nile Valley and the Delta. It typically serves as the entry point to discussions of the imperative that Egypt expand into the desert. Certainly the valley strip and Delta are the home to almost all Egyptians and in spite of enormous efforts on the part of the government, population growth continues to concentrate almost exclusively within this area. In fact, census figures show that there has been a remarkably stable pattern of geographic distribution of the population over the period 1976–2006. The main concentrations of population—Lower Egypt with 36 percent and Upper Egypt with 29 percent—have remained largely unchanged over the last thirty-five years. Although Cairo Governorate's share of the population

has decreased slightly, this is more than outweighed by the increase in the populations of the adjacent governorates of Giza and Qalyubiya, large portions of which are now considered part of the Greater Cairo metropolitan area. To date, desert and frontier areas of Egypt have absorbed very few permanent settlers, whether in the new towns or in the newly reclaimed areas.

Throughout the Nile Valley and Delta, there is a very productive agricultural hinterland, all of which enjoys perennial irrigation. Most is made up of private small holdings, due to the land reforms introduced after the Revolution in 1952 and subsequent fragmentation due to inheritance. For example, for the country as a whole in 2005, the average size of a *muklafa* (agricultural land holding) was only 0.94 feddans or just over one-third of a hectare, and only 11 percent of holdings were larger than three feddans.[5] Agricultural holdings in Upper Egypt are even smaller and more fragmented than national averages. Throughout the countryside there is a dense fabric of hamlets, villages, 'mother villages,' and small towns. One of the striking features of rural areas is the large size of some village agglomerations, which can easily contain over 10,000 persons.

Other important features of Egypt's spatial system are the short distances and the reasonably good systems of transport and communications that bind and interconnect settlements in the Delta and Nile Valley. No village is more than a few kilometers from a sizable town, and movement to and from the main urban centers is quite efficient. Almost all roads connecting settlements are now paved, and levels of water, telephone, and electricity provision to rural households are reasonably high, even by international standards. The 'interconnectivity' of the Egyptian countryside and its cities is helped by the north–south linear structure of transport and settlement south of Cairo, the use of major transport corridors in the near desert that skirt heavily settled areas, and the fact that practically all human settlement in Egypt is situated on very flat topography. The compactness of settlement patterns and the close proximity of cities to one another mean that the concept of 'isolated' is restricted to frontier and far desert areas. For example, well over two-thirds of Egypt's population is within a three-hour drive of Cairo.

What is Egypt's rate of urbanization? Official figures report that in 2006 a total of 42.7 percent of Egypt's population was urban.[6] This percentage had grown slowly but steadily from 34 percent in 1947 to 44 percent in 1976, remaining 44 percent in 1986, then declining slightly over the 1986–96 period, and finally, remaining virtually unchanged over the 1996–2006 period. Can it be that Egypt is the only developing country in the world where the urban portion of the population has recently declined or remained constant? The answer is an emphatic no, and such an aberration points directly at the problem of the definition of urban areas in Egypt. The census records urban and rural populations according to an arbitrary administrative definition of an urban place. Urban areas considered to be either (1) urban governorates—limited to Cairo, Port Said, Suez, and Alexandria; (2) a few agglomerations that have been declared 'cities' and have a city council; and (3) the capitals of rural districts *(marakiz)* and capitals of rural governorates. This definition has no relation to the size of the agglomeration's population or its importance as an urban area. As a result, the official urban population of Egypt has been located largely in the same geographic space for decades.[7] In reality Egypt is already overwhelmingly urban, with estimates varying widely depending on the definitions adopted. Bayat and Denis carried out an analysis of the 1996 Census and, using the

Figure 2.1. Urban and rural areas of Giza's urban fringe according to the 1996 Census. (Prepared by David Sims.)

definition of urban places as contiguous settlement agglomerations of more than 10,000 inhabitants, calculated that Egypt was then at least 67 percent urban, residing in 628 urban places.[8] Other definitions of urban places would result in even higher levels of urbanization in Egypt. For example, if the U.S. Census definition—any incorporated settlement over two thousand persons—were to be applied, then Egypt's population would be well over 90 percent urban.

There are two main types of recent urbanization patterns that have been missed by census enumerations. The first is overspill from urban centers into village agglomerations in the agricultural hinterland: this could also be called spontaneous urbanization of agglomerations on the periphery of the large cities, in larger villages, and in small towns. The phenomenon can be traced, for example, in the significantly higher annual growth in population in officially rural areas surrounding secondary towns in the recent past. To illustrate, over the 1986–96 period, the city of Beni Suef in Upper Egypt grew at an annual rate of only 1.23 percent, whereas the rate for the surrounding rural areas was 4.02 percent, and the city of Mahalla al-Kubra grew at only 0.93 percent annually, compared to its surrounding rural areas which grew at 2.25 percent.

The second 'hidden' type of urbanization is the phenomenon of emerging small towns. Many small agglomerations in dense rural areas throughout Egypt have begun to reach well over ten or twenty thousand inhabitants, and their economic functions have begun to diversify away from purely agricultural activities. In fact, these 'urban villages,' or small towns, can be considered market towns and the loci of trade, small manufacturing, and services for the larger rural hinterlands, as well as the location for certain footloose enterprises.

The phenomenon of these emerging towns underscores an important point about the economics of Egypt's countryside. Even in the most 'rural' governorates, non-agricultural activities predominate. For example, census figures for 1996 show that in all rural Egypt, only 50.5 percent of working persons aged fifteen and above (8.40 million persons) were engaged in agriculture, fishing, and related activities. The rest relied on secondary and tertiary economic activities.[9] In 2006, in the predominantly agricultural (and poorest) governorate of Sohag, only 42 percent of employed persons were engaged primarily in agriculture. And in the rural governorate of al-Gharbiya in the Delta, the figure was only 33 percent.[10]

Dynamics of Internal Migration

In the middle decades of the twentieth century, and especially after industrialization efforts in the main cities, Egypt witnessed high migratory flows from rural areas to the cities, and in particular to Greater Cairo, Alexandria, Mahalla al-Kubra, and Aswan. This was the classic migration profile of a developing country, and it generated the imagery of a continuing stream of 'peasants' moving to the towns, bringing with them their particular lifestyles and bestowing upon Egypt's 'modern' cities a less desirable, rural character. However, as early as 1986, census figures showed that net rural-to-urban migration had diminished greatly. In an article in 1988, Frank Shorter demonstrated that, in fact, the population growth of Greater Cairo was practically all explained by natural increase and expanding boundaries, with net in-migration almost at zero.[11]

So what is the true picture of current internal migration in Egypt? First, it is important to realize that the Egyptian population tends to stay where it is. According to the 1996 Census, only 6.3 percent of the total population moved from one governorate to another in the previous ten years (and many of these moves were from one governorate to another inside Greater Cairo). As pointed out in a large household survey in 2008, there is little urban residential mobility, and only 18.8 percent of urban families changed residence in the previous five years. Most of these moves were within the same neighborhoods or city districts, and only a small fraction were between cities or governorates. The reasons for this low mobility are that housing choices are unaffordable to many, housing markets are partly dysfunctional, and for most Egyptian families, the move to a new location is a once-in-a-lifetime decision, usually at the point of marriage.[12] So whatever spatial development policies are espoused by government (new towns and agricultural settlements in the desert, stimulating urban growth poles and frontier settlements, and so on), historic migration patterns show that there is a tremendous 'stay-at-home' inertia, both within cities and within rural districts.

Interestingly, there are some significant movements in Egypt's population within the Nile Valley, but they have nothing to do with spatial policies. First, the bulk of migration to cities is urban–urban, usually in stages from smaller to larger towns. Rural–urban migration is limited, mostly occurring very locally to small emerging towns and *marakiz* from nearby rural areas. Surprisingly, this fact is unrecognized by some who still see massive rural-to-urban migration as a root problem. For example, in a 2006 article in the semi-official *al-Ahram* newspaper, the new 'desert backyard' initiative *(al-zahr al-sahrawi)* is described as having the objective of absorbing rural population growth and "limiting the massive internal migration from rural areas to existing cities."[13] And in an interview in 2009, the secretary general of the Integrated Care Society was reported as saying that halting the spread of informal areas in Cairo required a government plan to address the root of the problem, which stems from the constant flow of rural migration to Cairo.[14]

Second, for decades urban dwellers have been leaving the older urban cores in large numbers, mostly for fringe and outlying informal settlements. The causes are mainly the increasing commercialization of downtown space, the slow deterioration of much of the older housing stock, and, most importantly, urban core families seeking better accommodation in fringe informal areas. Such a trend was very noticeable in Cairo starting in 1966 and is still continuing, as is discussed in Chapter 3. The same movement out of city cores can be seen in Alexandria, Mansura, Tanta, Mahalla al-Kubra, and other secondary towns, although the scale is smaller.

Third, informal settlements in Egyptian cities, mostly found in peripheral and outlying areas, are huge and growing rapidly. This is very true for Greater Cairo, as is discussed in Chapter 3, and it is also the case in almost all Egyptian cities. The scale of the informality phenomenon in Egypt depends on how it is defined, and reports have come up with widely varying estimates. In 2008 a survey of 21,000 urban households[15] asked respondents whether they considered their neighborhoods to be informal, or *'ashwa'i*, as these areas are commonly known in Egypt. According to this self-definition, overall, 41 percent of Egypt's official urban population was living in informal areas. The highest incidence was in urban Upper Egypt, with 53 percent, followed by urban Greater Cairo at 44 percent, the urban Delta at 36 percent, and Alexandria at 34 percent. Only in the Canal Zone cities was the incidence much lower, at 24 percent. And these figures can be considered underestimates of the informality phenomenon, for two reasons. As the survey was conducted in official urban areas only, it did not capture any of the extensive informal settlements found around cities in areas that the census defines as rural. Secondly, *'ashwa'i* is a somewhat pejorative term, and it can be assumed that some respondents preferred not to classify themselves as such.

In contrast, migration to Egypt's desert has been practically insignificant, in spite of the government's longstanding national project of moving Egypt's population out of the narrow, crowded Nile Valley. This lack of enthusiasm for the desert on the part of Egyptians is very noticeable in the new towns around Greater Cairo, as is discussed in Chapters 3 and 6, even though these new towns are relatively close to the huge Greater Cairo agglomeration. And at the national level, the new desert communities have had even less demographic impact. In spite of the national program that began in the late 1970s and subsequently has soaked up a large portion of the nation's development budget, by 2006 the population in all of Egypt's new towns (twenty towns as recorded by the census) did not exceed 766,000 persons, or only 1 percent of Egypt's total population.

Similarly, Egypt's many large and prominently announced agricultural reclamation projects in various desert areas have failed to attract anywhere near their target populations. One factor is that most of these projects, even if successful, tend to be capital-intensive corporate enterprises, which, except during harvesting, need little labor. Another factor is that even where permanent employment is generated, workers find it much more practical and economical to leave their families back in towns and villages in the Nile Valley.

This last factor can also be seen in tourist developments in the Red Sea and along the Mediterranean. The tremendous growth in the resort sector over the last twenty years has generated considerable employment, but this is almost exclusively a temporary 'bachelor' labor force and has not led to any significant population shifts. Workers in the tourist villages and associated commercial and transport activities simply do not migrate with their families. For example, in a 2003 study of tourism and demographics in South Sinai, it was found that over 95 percent of the staff in tourist establishments were single males, who typically worked twelve-hour days, seven days a week in monthly rotations, with one week off back in their homes in the Nile Valley. Given low average salaries and the much higher living costs in coastal towns, bringing one's family was simply not economically feasible.[16]

Certain secondary towns seem to be attracting significant numbers of migrants, especially the cities of the Canal Zone. In Port Said, Suez, and Ismailiya there are free zones and industrial estates, and perhaps most importantly, there is considerable nearby vacant government land for the cities to expand into.

Does Greater Cairo Dominate Egypt?

In population terms Greater Cairo, at 16.1 million persons in 2006, represented 22 percent of Egypt's total inhabitants. Alexandria, Egypt's second city, had some four million inhabitants, and other Egyptian cities were relatively much smaller, with only Port Said, Suez, and Mahalla al-Kubra having populations slightly in excess of half a million persons. Thus, in population terms, Greater Cairo is certainly far and away the most important urban agglomeration in Egypt.

Greater Cairo is considered by many observers to be a 'primate' city, given its weight of numbers and the concentration of economic enterprises in it, including most national institutions.[17] For example, it has been said that Greater Cairo contains 55 percent of the nation's university places, 46 percent of hospital beds, 40 percent of pharmacies, 43 percent of public-sector jobs, and 40 percent of private-sector jobs.[18] Greater Cairo has captured, and continues to capture, a large share of national public and private investments and to attract business enterprises and higher-order economic activities. Partly, this is due to its role as Egypt's capital and main portal to the outside world. For example, as research carried out by Eric Denis and Leïla Vignal shows, in 2000, metropolitan Cairo accounted for 83 percent of all foreign establishments (including brands and franchises) found in Egypt.[19] Greater Cairo's dominance is also seen in the manufacturing sector. In 1996, of sixteen industrial poles or zones of manufacturing concentration found in Egypt, nine were to be found in Greater Cairo (including Sixth of October but excluding Tenth of Ramadan), and their cumulative estimated production value represented 57 percent of the nation's total. Alexandria, with four industrial poles, represented an additional 23 percent of the total.[20]

The use of the term 'primate' often has a negative connotation, implying that a country's largest city captures more than its share of investments and precludes the development of alternative urban and regional centers. Concepts of 'urban bias,' 'spatial distortion,' and 'regional disparities' are frequent adjuncts used to describe such megacities, with the implied need for correction through more investment programs in lagging cities and regions. Certainly there is an imbalance in Egypt, and Greater Cairo dominates. But in developing countries the primacy of one large megacity is frequently the norm, as a look at Thailand, Turkey, Iran, and other countries of roughly the same size as Egypt will show. And Egypt has Alexandria, currently with a population of 4 million inhabitants, which is growing almost as rapidly as Greater Cairo. Thus it is best to be cautious when looking at Cairo's dominance in Egypt and to avoid value judgments of what, after all, is the accumulation of long historical trends that are extremely difficult, if not impossible, to alter. In fact, recent thinking in economic geography has begun to describe such dominant primate cities in developing countries as being 'engines of growth' that pull the whole national economy along by performing those crucial higher-order functions that are indispensable in keenly competitive world markets. These huge cities are seen to live more in symbiosis than in tension with the rest of national economic space. True, Greater Cairo has more than its share of the country's affluence as well as an overrepresentation of ostentatious wealth, but any nation's capital is bound to display such a face.

Egypt's Labor Force

Egypt is part of the club of nations—over half the world—where demographic pressures have created a serious situation of surplus labor. In 2007 Egypt's labor force stood at 23.8 million workers, and currently it is increasing by almost one million per year.[21] The labor force itself is characterized by a high unemployment rate (officially reported at 8.9 percent in 2007, but considered by many observers to be very much higher) and a vast number of underemployed persons. The economy's ability to create formal employment has been limited, and more and more workers have found jobs in the huge informal enterprise sector, which is to a large extent an urban phenomenon, and which we discuss in Chapter 8. Traditionally, Egypt's main employment generators had been (a) the huge government, the military, and the public sector, (b) agricultural labor, and (c) emigration to work in oil-rich Arab countries. None of these sectors are expanding anymore. The formal private sector, upon which most hopes are placed, is expanding rapidly, but from such a small base that its ability to absorb significant numbers is limited.

The proportion of new entrants to the labor force among the unemployed has continued to climb, confirming that unemployment in Egypt is essentially a problem of youth participation in the labor market. Although the agricultural sector has been an important segment of the national economy, accounting for 29 percent of Egypt's total labor force in 2007, a recent study reveals that the demand for labor in agriculture accounted for just 5 percent of total national demand for labor over the 2001–2005 period, a strong indication of the sector's relative labor saturation.[22]

Employment in the Egyptian government and its public-sector companies was reported in 2007 to have reached 6.4 million persons, accounting for a huge 38 percent of the country's non-farm labor.[23] And this total does not include those in uniform in either the armed forces or the extensive security and police services. The bloated government sector is the result of a decades-long policy of guaranteeing jobs for those who complete secondary or university education, and although the state has, since the 1990s, made a conscious effort to limit additional government employment, it is still creeping up. Productivity in government service is notoriously low, salaries for the lower ranks are abysmal, many employees hardly show up for work, and many more have second and even third jobs. But landing a government job is still perceived as desirable for job security (and for some, rent-seeking and influence).

Education in Egypt
A particular feature of Egypt's labor market, indeed of the whole population, is the distortion in education levels due to the government's longstanding emphasis on higher education. Notwithstanding decades of government campaigns to eradicate illiteracy in the country, the rate still stands officially at 29.6 percent (22.3 percent for males and 37.3 percent for females), and an additional 12.0 percent are deemed to be able to 'read and write,' although they did not complete any schooling.[24] Unhappily, public primary education is universally so inadequate that many who complete it can barely sign their names; thus the real level of illiteracy is much higher than the official figures. Public secondary education is also very weak, hardly equipping the one million students who graduate each year with the kinds of skills required in the private economy. The depressing state of primary and secondary education in Egypt, with the particular system of private lessons on the side for those who can pay for them, is best summed up by a Cairo taxi driver, as reported by Khaled Al Khamissi:

> "The kids go to school and don't learn anything. The parents keep on coughing up for private lessons from the age of ten upwards. In the end the parents are penniless and the kids don't find jobs. . . . Today there's no industrial training that's any use or any agricultural training that's any use or any business training. And don't forget that kids, the poor things, expect the best and think they are well and truly educated, when they

don't even know how to read. The only thing they learn in school is the national anthem and what good does that do them?[25]

University education has been expanding very rapidly for decades, producing an ever larger pool of university graduates. This is definitely a case of quantity over quality, since universities are overcrowded, underfunded, and mired in a system of learning by rote. The numbers are staggering. By 2006, of Egypt's *total* population aged ten years and above, 9.6 percent had a university degree or higher. (In Cairo Governorate the figure was 21 percent, the highest in the country.)[26] And of Egypt's total labor force in 2007, 17.0 percent had a university education or higher. The number of those enrolled in both public and private universities was 1.96 million in 2007, twice the number registered ten years earlier.[27] This inexorable expansion of higher education may seem laudable at first glance, but the result is an ever-expanding army of ill-prepared degree holders without jobs and with little hope of finding any. For example, of those officially considered unemployed in Egypt, 700,000 or one-third of the total have university degrees and another 1.2 million are high school graduates. In fact, the rate of official unemployment is directly related to educational status: less than 1 percent of illiterates in the labor force are officially unemployed, but this figure rises steadily with educational attainment, reaching 15 percent for secondary school graduates and 17 percent for university graduates.[28]

The point is that the labor market is vastly oversupplied with degree holders poorly qualified for jobs in the formal private sector. Modern businesses complain that they cannot find well-educated staff, even at salaries that are several times the norm. But the 'educated' unemployed now represent a formidable interest group, and the government feels compelled to soak them up in government employment, in land reclamation schemes for graduates, or in various business loan programs, the largest of which is run by the Social Fund for Development.

Greater Cairo is no exception. In fact, the surplus of degree holders in the labor force of the capital is higher than elsewhere, as is the overproduction of university graduates. For example, in 2007 an enormous 46 percent of the officially unemployed in Cairo Governorate had university degrees or higher.[29] Greater Cairo contains four huge public universities—Cairo, 'Ain Shams, al-Azhar, and Helwan—whose total combined enrollment in 2007 was 906,000 students, and an additional

83,000 students attended private universities. Ten years earlier, the total number of university students in Greater Cairo was only 499,000.

Living Standards, Household Incomes, and Poverty

For any understanding of Egypt (or Greater Cairo for that matter), it is extremely important to have a basic knowledge of Egyptian living standards and prevailing trends. Anecdotal information and personal experience tend to emphasize manifestations of the extremes—grinding poverty versus outrageous wealth—but such information remains just that, perceptual and anecdotal. The quantification of the population's incomes, expenditures, and poverty are not just academic exercises, for they enlighten and put into perspective any optic on how the masses live.

Egypt scores quite highly on many basic quality-of-life indicators, especially when compared to other developing countries. For example, in 2006 the national rate of infant mortality (aged one year and less) was 19.3 deaths per thousand, a rate that has been declining steadily (it was 37.8 per thousand in 1990).[30] This compares very favorably with the average infant mortality rate for Africa in 2007 (86 deaths per thousand) and for Asia (48 deaths per thousand). Also, in 2007 the life expectancy at birth for Egypt was 69.5 years for males and 74.0 years for females, quite respectable figures.[31]

How much do Egyptians earn and how much do they spend? And how does this compare to other countries? In the CAPMAS *Household Expenditure, Consumption and Income Survey* of 2004–2005 (HECIS), a large representative sample of households was interviewed repeatedly, offering reasonably accurate figures on family expenditure and income.[32] For all Egypt, the median household income, that is the income level at which half of households earn more and half less, was reported to be LE992 per month.[33] Note that 'income' here includes all sources, including wages, self-employment, property income, cash transfers, and the imputed value of non-cash income such as agricultural products. Since the median household had 5.2 persons, this allows the calculation that the median household member lived on LE6.35 per day or, using exchange rates at the time, $1.10 per capita per day, an extremely low figure that would seemingly put Egypt among the very poorest countries on earth. But the cost of basic living in Egypt is low. To compare it with other countries, economists have constructed 'purchasing power parity' coefficients, which would raise this per capita figure to $2.47 a day, were this income to be spent in the USA.[34]

Thus in these terms, according to the World Bank, in 2005 over 40 percent of Egyptians lived on less than two dollars a day, but only 3.8 percent lived on less than one dollar a day. Family incomes are significantly lower in rural areas than urban areas (official definition). Whereas the overall poverty rate for Egypt in 2005 was 19.6 percent, the rate for rural areas was 26.8 percent and that of urban areas was only 10.1 percent.[35]

Some would say that these median income figures for the Egyptian family are far too high, especially if one considers prevailing salaries in the economy. These days a worker in a private-sector factory normally earns LE350 to LE500 per month for long workdays. The starting salary for a government employee is LE295, including bonuses. The entry salary for a professor at a university is LE750 a month. In informal service establishments, an assistant will be glad to earn LE300 per month. The list can go on and on, and it is difficult to reconcile these common wages with family incomes generated by the CAPMAS survey, even assuming some families have more than one bread earner. While debate goes on about income statistics, in overall terms it can certainly be said that the average or median Egyptian family struggles to make ends meet. And it must be repeated that these statistics refer to 2005, before Egypt began

Table 2.1: Urban Egypt household income and expenditure distribution by decile 2004/2005 (LE per month)

Decile	Household Income		Household Expenditures	
	Minimum	Maximum	Minimum	Maximum
First (lowest)	0	533	0	487
Second	533	678	487	598
Third	678	797	598	702
Fourth	797	908	702	800
Fifth	908	1,046	800	909
Sixth	1,046	1,199	909	1,037
Seventh	1,199	1,397	1,037	1,205
Eighth	1,397	1,699	1,205	1,451
Ninth	1,699	2,371	1,451	1,988
Tenth (highest)	2,371	-	1,988	-

Source: Calculated from annual urban household expenditure and income by twenty bands, from the CAPMAS *Household Expenditure, Consumption and Income Survey* of 2004–2005 (HECIS), preliminary results.

to experience tremendous and continuing inflation in the prices of basic consumer goods.

The median income only relates to what the household at the fiftieth percentile earns. How is this income distributed? Table 2.1 presents the 2004–2005 CAPMAS income distribution into deciles for urban households. This shows how much each tenth of urban households earns and spends per month, with the median income at LE1,046 per month and median expenditure at LE909 per month. What these statistics show is that urban income distribution is in general very shallow. That is, the differences in household income between poorer and richer deciles is not so sharp. In fact, there is a bulge or clustering of households located around the median. For example, at the twentieth percentile monthly income was LE678, and if this figure were only doubled to LE1,356, it would encompass a full 70 percent of all urban households. Certainly there are those who are desperately poor and there are those who are very wealthy, but the bulk of urban households have low to moderate incomes that cluster within a relatively narrow range. Such shallow income disparities are rare in developing countries. Economists have devised gini coefficients to measure overall income inequality, and for Egypt in 2005 this coefficient stood at 32, showing a more equitable income distribution than the average for the Middle East and North Africa, which stood at 37. For Latin America, the gini coefficient was a very high at 57.[36]

For urban households, the *Housing Study for Urban Egypt* (HSUE) (2008) provides more detail on household incomes and consumption for urban Egypt, and it is also much more up to date than the CAPMAS survey.[37] Income data from this survey confirmed the fact that urban household income distribution is shallow and fairly equitable, with the middle 60 percent of households earning between LE740 to LE1,350 per month. But it also shows that many livelihood indicators are sensitive to income. For example, as one moves from the poorest quintile (the first) to the richest quintile (the fifth), the rate of illiteracy drops dramatically, and the percentage of persons living in informal areas also drops, but less steeply. Conversely the incidence of university education shoots up from 6 percent in the first quintile to 41 percent in the fifth quintile, as does housing area per capita, which jumps from only 13 square meters in the first quintile to 40 square meters in the fifth. The percentage of households owning specific durable goods also increases dramatically. Nearly zero percent of households in the first quintile own a private car, but this rises to 32 percent for the fifth quintile. In other words, although income disparities in urban Egypt may not be acute, richer households enjoy higher living standards, especially the richest 20 percent of households.

How many Egyptians are poor? In Egypt the subjects of poverty, poverty levels, and incidences of poverty have recently gained increasing attention, and some would say increasing confusion, as carefully set out by Sarah Sabri.[38] At the national level, the portion of the population living below the nutrition-based poverty line was estimated at 16.7 percent in 1999/2000 and 19.6 percent in 2004/2005.[39] These poverty levels are much lower than in many other developing countries, but it is best to be careful with such figures. In any event, poverty in Egypt is certainly endemic and may be increasing.

In Egyptian cities, poverty is not notably concentrated in particular geographic areas. A few small and marginal urban pockets with high concentrations of the desperately poor exist, but most poor families are found mixed in with lower- and middle-income families in a wide number of older core neighborhoods and in the vast informal areas. Even in older upper-class neighborhoods, a small percentage of poor families may also be found. Conversely, in most informal areas, a percentage of well-off entrepreneurs, traders, and professionals can be found. This mix of income groups or 'income heterogeneity' in geographical space is something that sets Egypt off from the situation in many developing countries, where high concentrations of exclusively poor and destitute inhabitants can be found in huge slums, and in contrast the rich tend to cluster together in exclusive residential enclaves. This subject is taken up for Greater Cairo in Chapter 4.

Profile of the Average Household in Greater Cairo

To set the scene for the rest of the book, it is useful to chart the main features of the average household in Cairo and, to put it into context, compare it with national urban averages. Most of this information comes from the 2008 Housing Study of Urban Egypt, the only data set that disaggregates national data to allow a separate look at Greater Cairo. In fact, it provides one data set for Greater Cairo proper, which means all of Cairo Governorate, Giza City, and Shubra al-Khayma City, and another data set for peri-urban Greater Cairo, which relates to nine *marakiz* of Giza and Qalyubiya governorates that are part of Greater Cairo.[40]

First of all, the average household in Greater Cairo proper is better off in terms of income and expenditure than the national urban average, and that of peri-urban Greater Cairo is significantly below the urban average. Thus, Greater Cairo proper had an average per capita annual income in 2008 of LE4,324, versus LE2,804 for Greater Cairo's peri-urban areas and LE3,555 for all of urban Egypt. This is mainly due to the concentration of higher-income families in Greater Cairo proper, which raises the average, and also due to the relative poverty in peri-urban Greater Cairo. For example, the percentage of households in the highest urban income quintile was 29.4 percent in Greater Cairo proper versus only 10.0 percent in peri-urban Greater Cairo (and 20 percent for all of urban Egypt).

The higher living standards in Greater Cairo proper are reflected in statistics on household assets. For example, 14.9 percent of households in Greater Cairo proper owned at least one private car, versus only 3.0 percent in peri-urban Greater Cairo and 9.3 percent in all urban Egypt. Household possession of mobile phones was 73.5 percent, 57.7 percent, and 60.3 percent respectively. Household possession of a personal computer was 30.6 percent, 10.3 percent, and 21.8 percent respectively. And household possession of an air conditioner was 14.4 percent, 2.2 percent, and 8.3 percent respectively (which is remarkably similar to the pattern of private-car ownership).

Even with these differences, the bulk of households in all three categories are quite similar in basic terms, with almost the same household size, age/sex distribution, literacy, labor force participation, and unemployment rates. And, for example, in all three categories the ownership of a color television was near-universal (above 95 percent of households). In other words, if one were to exclude the richest households, which are heavily concentrated in Greater Cairo proper, the standards of living would not vary much between Greater Cairo proper and all of urban Egypt. On the other hand, socioeconomic and especially income characteristics of households in peri-urban Greater Cairo suggest somewhat lower living standards compared to those of Egypt's general urban population.

3

A History of Modern Cairo: Three Cities in One

To understand how Cairo got to where it is now, it is best to start in the middle of the twentieth century, roughly in 1950.[1] (See Map 3.1.) At that time the city had just emerged from its wartime restrictions and the literal as well as figurative hangovers of the massive Allied Forces armies. Cairo was bursting at its seams, since large migrations from the countryside had already commenced, while all urban projects had been frozen by the war. The metropolis contained roughly 2.8 million inhabitants, less than one-sixth of the number today, but the population was expanding at over 6 percent per year.[2] Due to the free-spending ways of the Allied armies, the city's economy had enjoyed a boom. Cairo's already significant industrial base soon started to expand rapidly, as bourgeois industrialists began to invest heavily in consumer industries protected by high import tariffs. Basic infrastructure was in place—in terms of roads, Nile bridges, railways, and trolley lines; and also in terms of water and wastewater systems, and power grids. And Cairo was not lacking in professional and business classes, a sizable but declining portion of whom were non-native. In effect, Cairo was poised to expand at a scale never before seen in its history.

In the lead-up to the war Cairo had already begun spilling out of its historic, traditional town and the European sector (today's downtown, also called Khedivial Cairo). This expansion occurred mostly to the north along two axes: Shubra/Rod al-Farag and al-Wayli/Heliopolis/'Ain Shams.[3] To the south of Cairo, the agglomerations of Maadi and Helwan were small isolated satellites, and across the Nile there was very little development, restricted to urban quarters near the traditional villages of Giza and Imbaba. The historic town to the east

45

had not expanded physically but continued to absorb more and more migrants, including most of the poorest. These prewar trends toward urban expansion were a prelude to Cairo's postwar explosion.

In this chapter we take up the story of Cairo's urban development from 1950 by focusing on three distinct morphological phenomena or urban forms: (1) the continuing growth of the formal city, (2) the emergence and explosive expansion of the informal city, and (3), beginning in the late 1970s, the crafting of the modern desert city. As will be seen, each urban form contains its own causes, rules, and norms, and although there have been some blurred and overlapping edges between the formal and informal cities, each of the three forms is fundamentally physically and legally separate.

A fourth form of urban development could have been added and called the peri-urban city. This development occurred on what was originally a rich agricultural plain dotted with villages and small towns, mostly west and north of Cairo proper. This area, in the governorates of Giza and Qalyubiya, has increasingly been enveloped into the megacity of Greater Cairo. But since, with very few exceptions, this mode of development began and continues to operate under informal norms, it has been treated as part of the informal city.

The Formal City

In 1950 virtually the whole of Cairo could be considered as formal. That is, up to then, the modes of city formation had been mainly legal, in the sense that they were real-estate projects and land subdivisions that conformed to the laws and government controls existent at the time. It is worth mentioning that most legislation controlling urban development and construction had been introduced in the 1940s, in particular the very strict laws on land subdivisions that imposed high European standards, making private land development much more difficult and expensive.[4] One might say "But what about historic Cairo, with its narrow and winding streets and jumbled mix of monumental and decrepit buildings? How could this part of the city be considered formal?" The answer is simply that, during the periods of its development, which extended over almost one thousand years, there were no controlling legislative frameworks, and thus, strictly speaking, its evolution was 'formal.'

In 1950, where did the poor and working classes live? They were either crowded into the historic or medieval city precincts or in tenement buildings found in such inner districts as Bulaq, Sayyida Zaynab, 'Abdin,

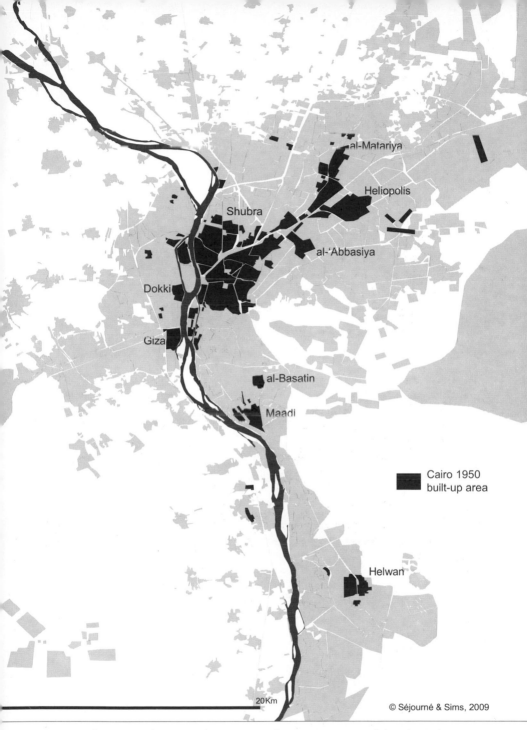

al-Matariya

Heliopolis

Shubra

al-'Abbasiya

Dokki

Giza

al-Basatin

Maadi

Cairo 1950
built-up area

Helwan

20Km

© Séjourné & Sims, 2009

Map 3.1. Built-up area of Cairo in 1950 compared to 2009. (From Maslahat al-Misaha (Egypt Survey Authority) map series 1:100,000, sheets 30/31 (1949) and 31/32 (1951)).

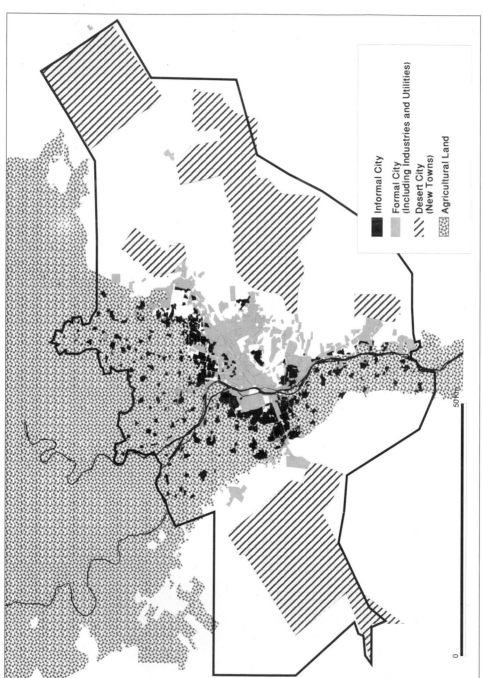

Map 3.2. Greater Cairo in 2006: extents of the three cities.

Informal City

Formal City
(Including Industries and Utilities)

Desert City
(New Towns)

Agricultural Land

0   50 km

and Misr al-Qadima. A few found accommodation within expanding nearby villages west of the Nile, such as Mit 'Uqba, Imbaba, and Giza. Some others were lucky to find affordable housing in the recently expanded urban quarters of North Cairo, the *aqsam* (districts) of al-Wayli, Shubra, Rod al-Farag, and Heliopolis.⁵ In most cases residential densities were extremely high, and living conditions were generally deplorable. For example, average densities for Cairo Governorate exceeded two

Figure 3.1. Part of Mohandiseen, originally launched as Madinat al-Awqaf in the late 1940s. Note tall buildings demarcated by shadows. (Image dated 2008, ©2010 DigitalGlobe / ©2009 GOOGLE.)

persons per room in 1947, and in inner districts such as al-Gamaliya, Bulaq, and Bab al-Sha'riya this rate exceeded 2.5 persons per room. As migrations to the city accelerated during the 1950s and early 1960s, most newcomers crowded into these areas, further exacerbating conditions. By 1960, in Cairo Governorate the average number of persons per room had increased to 2.3, and in some inner districts overcrowding was acute, with rates around, and even over, three persons per room.[6]

In the 1950s and early 1960s formal Cairo expanded substantially, mainly through the mechanism of state-sponsored subdivision projects in combination with private housing companies. The largest of these was in what is now Mohandiseen-Agouza west of the Nile. This project, originally called Madinat al-Awqaf, was started in 1948 and created out of roughly 800 hectares of agricultural lands held by the Ministry of Awqaf.[7] Other subdivisions and expansions launched at this time were smaller in scale, such as in al-Darrasa, Muqattam, Hilmiya, al-Zeitoun, and Helwan. Many were located in the 'Northern City,' which had doubled in population over the 1947–60 period to reach 1.6 million inhabitants, over one-third of Cairo's population.[8] With few exceptions (such as the Muqattam development) these new districts and neighborhoods were located directly on agricultural land next to the existing urban fabric.

Cairo of the 1950s witnessed Egypt's earliest experiments in what was to become a long and continuing love affair with state-subsidized public housing. The first law governing state-aided social housing was Law no. 206, issued in 1951. The first project was the Masakin al-'Ummal project in Imbaba, conceived in 1948 and only partly completed. It was aimed to house factory workers in modest two-floor attached units, each with its own street entrance.[9] Other public housing projects were launched around Cairo after the revolution in 1952 and into the 1960s, all of which were walk-up apartment blocks, initially of a maximum of four floors. The largest examples of such projects are to be found in the industrial suburb of Helwan and in al-Zawya al-Hamra', al-Sharabiya, and al-'Abbasiya, but many more smaller schemes were inserted in almost any vacant state-land pockets that could be found. By 1965 Cairo Governorate had constructed nearly 15,000 public housing units.[10] Most of these public housing units were very small (forty-five to sixty-five square meters) and were distributed to 'limited income' families and lower-ranking government employees. These units were designated *iskan iqtisadi* (economic

Figure 3.2. Public housing estate of 'economic' units built in the 1960s in Helwan. Note that most housing blocks have been extended horizontally by residents. (Image dated 2008, ©2010 DigitalGlobe / ©2009 GOOGLE.)

or affordable housing). However, in the 1960s the categories *mutawassit* (middle), *fuq mutawassit* (above the average), and *fakhr* (luxury) were also added, and these larger units tended to go to government officials and army officers.[11] In all cases nominal rents were charged, and the rental contracts gave the tenants and their heirs absolute and perpetual rights against eviction as long as rents were paid.

The 1950s also witnessed the creation of large industrial areas, most notably the iron and steel complex in Helwan (inaugurated in 1958), the cement factories in Helwan and Tura, and a number of textile and heavy industries in Shubra al-Khayma. These projects reflected the socialist regime's policy of rapid industrialization, so popular among developing nations at the time. Many smaller private factories also expanded in the 1950s, in particular textile works in Bahtim in Shubra al-Khayma, and in the smaller industrial clusters of al-Basatin (mainly building materials), 'Ain al-Sira (leather), and so on.

The June 1967 war put an abrupt halt to all of Cairo's formal urban expansion. Egypt rapidly shifted to a wartime economy, with controls on materials, foreign exchange restrictions, and a conscription that vacuumed up the labor force for the duration. Little of the government's budget could be spared for maintaining Cairo's infrastructure, let alone any new urban projects. This state of suspended animation lasted through the so-called War of Attrition and the October 1973 war, and its effects lingered until the 1977 Camp David peace negotiations.

In the mid-1970s President Sadat's *infitah*, or Open Door policy, took hold in Egypt and especially in Cairo. In a very short time local capitalist entrepreneurs began to reemerge, and Egyptian workers started to flood the Gulf countries and send back remittances. Imported goods, through exclusive local import agents, began to appear, as did foreign oil companies and banks. A real-estate boom began to change formal Cairo's landscape, with residential tower blocks, new hotels, and office complexes. Building controls seemed not to exist, and many landlords gleefully added several floors onto existing buildings. Infrastructure projects, mainly symbolized by the Sixth of October Bridge and flyovers, began to appear. The boom continued into the 1980s, with the introduction of the first metro line and new highways such as the Autostrad, and numerous subdivisions were added onto the existing urban layouts. Thanks largely to foreign assistance, long-neglected infrastructure began to receive attention. A completely revamped sewerage system began to be installed on both sides of the Nile, including the world's largest sewage collector, which runs under Port Said Street. Huge power plants as well as water treatment plants were installed, and even the dysfunctional telephone system actually began to work.

Madinat Nasr, a truly huge, 7,000-hectare concession on state desert land directly east of al-'Abassiya, became *the* formal city extension project, starting in the mid-1970s, and today it still contains lands to be developed. The project had been launched in 1958, but it only really took off after the 1967–74 war hiatus, mainly with government, parastatal, and

Figure 3.3. Part of Madinat Nasr, developed in the 1970s. Note tall buildings (over ten floors) demarcated by shadows. (Image dated 2008, ©2010 DigitalGlobe / ©2009 GOOGLE.)

cooperative housing projects, but also with numerous private building lots, government offices, the Cairo Stadium, the exhibition grounds, and even an industrial area. Although city plans stipulated a maximum of four floors, in no time fifteen-story residential blocks with commercial ground floors became the norm. Madinat Nasr, east of Cairo proper, reinforced the formal city's main growth in that direction. Other extensions—such as Nuzha, Madinat al-Salam, and 'Ain Shams—also added to the development weight of the northeast corridor.

In the 1970s and 1980s, formal Cairo's horizontal growth remained limited to the northeastern desert quadrant, and this has continued up to the present day. As discussed in the next section, any formal subdivisions on agricultural land were prohibited, which meant that the whole northern and western arcs of Cairo's fringe, those areas that would have been the most economically feasible and profitable for development and that had been earlier axes of expansion, were shut off. And already the state had adopted the new towns as the unique focus of its urban development policies, and had launched a number of these in desert locations around Cairo. In addition, rent controls continued to dampen severely any in-town real-estate investment.

Figure 3.4. Al-Nahda public housing estate, built progressively by Cairo Governorate 1985–95. (Image dated 2008, ©2010 DigitalGlobe / ©2009 GOOGLE.)

The government's penchant for subsidized public housing continued unabated, and in 1981 Cairo Governorate started the Madinat al-Salam project, located east of Heliopolis on flat desert land formerly held by the state chicken production organization. It, and the neighboring al-Nahda project, grew throughout the 1980s and 1990s, and today they together house over 150,000 inhabitants, some of whom were relocated from inner city locations due to urban redevelopment projects or building collapse. In fact, although there are no figures to confirm this, probably more than half of all public housing units built by Cairo Governorate in the 1980s and 1990s have ended up for resettlement, not for newlyweds and others just starting families as originally intended.

In 1982, the government, sensitive to the obvious run-down condition of existing public housing, adopted a policy of *tamlik* tenure for both existing and new public housing, whereby beneficiary families would pay modest monthly installments and eventually, after thirty or forty years, gain ownership of their units. Of course, these units continued to be heavily subsidized, and the hoped-for sense of ownership and improved maintenance has for the most part proven chimerical.

Over the 1982–2005 period Cairo Governorate (including its associated new towns) captured the largest share of public housing built in Egypt, at 463,000 units or almost one-third of all government-financed units. If the Greater Cairo governorates of Giza (ranked second, with a total of 104,500 units) and Qalyubiya (with a total of 58,000 units) are included, it can be calculated that Greater Cairo had benefited from just over 50 percent of all government housing production in Egypt from 1982 to 2005.[12] Even so, the HSUE (2008) calculated that only 5.1 percent of the households of Greater Cairo lived in government-built or financed units.[13]

In terms of population shifts in the formal city, the most startling aspect was the progressive depopulation of the older, especially historic districts in central Cairo. Such a trend was noticeable as far back as 1966 when, according to the census, six *aqsam* (central districts) had lost population. By 1986 this number had increased to eighteen districts. The exodus from central Cairo seems to have peaked in the 1986–96 period, when inner districts of Cairo Governorate lost over 500,000 inhabitants, a whopping 20 percent of their 1986 populations. These districts included historic areas such as Sayyida Zaynab, al-Gamaliya, al-Darb al-Ahmar, Bulaq, al-Muski, Bab al-Sha'riya, and Misr al-Qadima. Also included were downtown and older fringe areas such as Qasr al-Nil, al-Zahir, 'Abdin, Shubra,

Rod al-Farag, al-Sahel, al-Wayli, and even Hada'iq al-Qubba. In percentage terms the greatest losses were in the districts of al-Muski, Bulaq, and al-Gamaliya, each of which lost over 4 percent of its populations *per year*. In the 1996–2006 period, the trend continued, albeit at a slower overall rate. All of the inner seventeen districts continued to lose population, but the overall loss was 251,000 inhabitants over ten years, representing 12.1 percent of the 1996 population. Even the older Giza districts of Agouza (Mohandiseen) and Dokki recorded losses over the 1986–2006 period, although these losses were minor.[14]

The causes of such large population shifts out of historic and core formal areas were partly slum clearances for prestige projects in areas such as Bulaq and Rod al-Farag. But in most areas the main factor was the increasing commercialization of space and the conversion of housing into small factories, warehouses, and wholesale operations, especially in al-Darb al-Ahmar, al-Gamaliya, 'Abdin, and 'Ataba quarters, coupled with the slow deterioration, and even collapse, of much of the older housing stock. And where did most of these displaced urban core families go? As we discuss in the next section, most sought better accommodation and new lives in the informal city, whose huge expansions were taking place over precisely the same period.

In the 1990s and 2000s Cairo has witnessed a number of improvements and metamorphoses. Infrastructure has continued to be extended. The Cairo Ring Road was built in stages, the last of which (the southern arc running through al-Basatin) was not completed until 2001. More flyovers were built, as was the al-Azhar tunnel. The second metro line was completed and construction of a third line commenced. Telecommunications were much improved, and mobile phones were introduced in 1996, becoming ubiquitous in almost no time. For example, by 2008, in Greater Cairo some 76 percent of households had at least one mobile phone.[15] In addition, the decline of the downtown as the commercial center, already noticeable in the 1980s, accelerated, with most upscale establishments and offices opening or relocating to more prestigious quarters such as Mohandiseen, Heliopolis, Maadi, Zamalek, and Madinat Nasr. These areas also witnessed a new wave of higher-quality apartment block construction, partly due to the liberalized rent regime that was introduced in 1996. And in 1995 the formal city's belated love affair with shopping malls began, culminating with the opening of City Stars in Madinat Nasr in 2005.

In the last twenty years only a few new districts have been added or extended to the formal city. And almost all of these have been located on the eastern desert fringes of Cairo Governorate, mainly on concession lands of the nationalized housing companies. These extensions included the Zahra' al-Maadi subdivision and extensions to Muqattam, Nuzha, and especially to Madinat Nasr. Over the 1986–2006 period the population of Madinat Nasr increased by 401,000 inhabitants, expanding the 1986 population almost fourfold. Practically all of these subdivision developments were aimed at the upper-middle and investor classes.

There have been schemes mooted from time to time to relocate major activities, especially large government institutions, out of the central areas of formal Cairo, ostensibly to relieve congestion pressures. In fact, these ideas seem to come in waves. The first such scheme was hatched in the early 1980s to relocate government ministries out of Cairo to the new town of Sadat City, some ninety-five kilometers outside Cairo, off the Alexandria Desert Road. The first ministry set to make the move was the Ministry of Housing and Reconstruction, the very ministry that has proudly championed the new towns program over decades. But as the date for relocation approached, the ministry's employees actually threatened to strike, an unheard of action in Egypt at the time, and the relocation order was rescinded. Today, some thirty years later, the ministry still continues to operate out of its downtown premises off Qasr al-'Aini Street.

In 2007 a new wave of interest in relocating government offices took hold, and as of 2010 this project is still very much alive. A large piece of desert just inside the eastern arc of the Ring Road, which for decades has been an army camp, has been designated for a new government complex, which is supposed to house a large number of ministries to be relocated out of central Cairo.[16] This scheme seems to have considerable support, but it will be a colossal and expensive undertaking. Yet the underlying idea that moving government agencies outside central Cairo will somehow alleviate congestion is very popular in government circles and even among professional planners. Somehow the fact that doing so will dramatically increase person-trips throughout the main arterials of the metropolis, causing more systemic congestion, escapes notice.

Over the last twenty-five years there have been a series of attempts to cleanse formal Cairo of its more noxious and least attractive activities. In the 1980s the removal of car repair workshops from the downtown precincts gained momentum, and although new 'car repair cities'

Figure 3.5. Contrasting fabrics of formal and informal neighborhoods: Dokki versus Bulaq al-Dakrur. (Image dated 2008, ©2010 DigitalGlobe / ©2009 GOOGLE.)

were created within government housing estates in outer areas such as al-Salam and Manshiyat Nasir, few of the downtown workshops actually closed. Governors and the Egyptian Environmental Affairs Agency have repeatedly ordered the closing of polluting iron foundries and aluminum workshops in places like Shubra al-Khayma and 'Izbit al-'Arab, only to have to allow them to reopen 'temporarily,' since relocation schemes proved totally unrealistic. In fact, the Achilles' heel of efforts to rid central parts of Cairo of undesired activities has been, and continues to be, the inability of authorities to comprehend just how tied smaller enterprises are to Cairo's fabric. In terms of labor, markets, and inputs, and also in terms of industrial clustering of the mostly small and family-run businesses, proclaiming their wholesale transfer out into some far-flung desert location runs counter to economic logic. This has been the case of repeated attempts to remove 'Ain al-Sira's leather industries out to al-Badr New Town, and also of the long-held dream of relocating the garbage sorting activities and their associated pig farms out to remote sites off the 'Ain Sukhna Road. It is as if a simple, mechanical desert land assignment and the installation of some infrastructure will somehow entice small firms to operate many miles out of the city.

By 1996 the formal city had a population of 4.8 million inhabitants, and this had increased only slightly to five million by 2006. In effect, the formal city had ceased to absorb population, and there were precious few opportunities for its further physical expansion. Certainly, urban metamorphoses within formal Cairo are continuing, but to understand Greater Cairo's historical development and its present state of play, attention must be turned to the informal city and the desert city, the two urban forms that increasingly define the metropolis and are, paradoxically, absolute opposites.

The Informal City

In 1950 there were virtually no informal settlements around Cairo.[17] Where did the kernels of the informal city, which was to become so pervasive in Cairo, begin to appear? It is unfortunate that there is no recorded history of the germination of the phenomenon and the actors involved, but then, because of their marginal character and rather insignificant scale, informal areas did not generate academic or professional interest. Janet Abu-Lughod, a very keen observer of Cairo, whose main research covered the 1957–61 period, did not mention the phenomenon at all.[18] One can only deduce how these first areas began to blossom by looking at old maps, trying to read from the urban fabric one encounters today, and listening to elderly residents of these areas. It appears that there was no official resistance, even though these early informal subdivisions clearly contravened the subdivision laws and building code. Perhaps it was simply the fact that at the time the government was increasingly preoccupied with creating new socialist zones and prestige heavy industry, and it could afford to ignore a few marginal, unregulated developments on the periphery.

One can surmise from oral histories that a number of informal areas began their incipient growth in the early 1960s. Prominent examples on

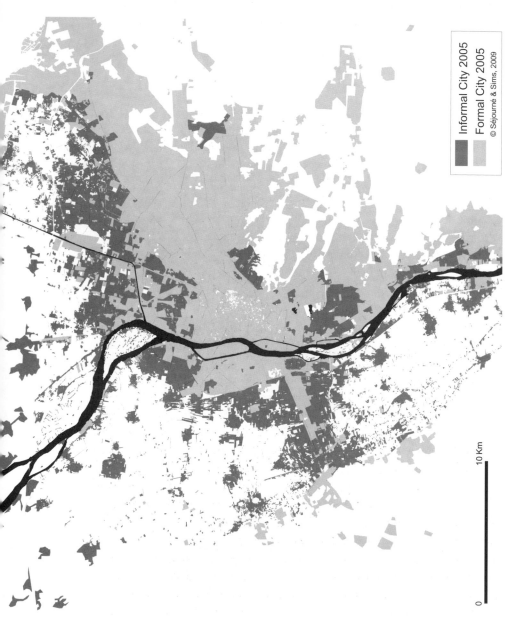

0   10 Km

Map 3.3. Greater Cairo's formal and informal cities, 2005.

agricultural land included al-Munira al-Gharbiya west of Kitkat, and Bulaq al-Dakrur and Ard al-Liwa, just across the railway tracks from Mohandiseen and Dokki. Certainly by 1965, parts of Bulaq al-Dakrur (especially the neighborhood of Abu Qatada) had become popular with students at Cairo University seeking the cheapest of accommodation. And it is certain that informal subdivisions on private agricultural land were starting in North Cairo in parts of al-Sharabiya, al-Wayli, and al-Zawya al-Hamra'. Informal occupancy of state land probably first appeared in Manshiyat Nasir, located in abandoned quarries just east of the northern Mamluk cemeteries and close to Fatimid Cairo. The first residents there had relocated from slum clearances in al-Darrasa and al-Azhar. Older residents of Manshiyat Nasir claim President Nasser himself ordered that a water line be extended to serve them in 1963, hence the name.

A perusal of satellite imagery of Cairo shows that, during the earliest emergence of the informal city, some residential subdivisions were created

Figure 3.6. Semi-structured informal area begun in the 1960s, part of *shiyakha* of al-Masakin al-Amiriya. (Image dated 2008, ©2010 DigitalGlobe / ©2009 GOOGLE.)

that exhibited some 'planned' features. That is, lanes were strictly parallel and there were occasional cross-streets, which implies that someone plotted the area in drawings and set it out. The building patterns within these blocks are however indistinguishable from those in classic informal areas, that is, small building footprints, 100 percent plot coverage, and little or no allocation for public open space or social facilities. Nor are socioeconomic markers, derived from the census, much different from those found in the informal city. Examples of these areas, almost all of which are in the Northern City, include residential blocks in Masakin al-Amiriya al-Ganub, Marg al-Qibliya, and Tulumbat 'Ain Shams. Can these areas be considered strictly 'informal'? Perhaps so, as the underlying agricultural field patterns in these areas were usually rigidly rectangular, and it could be that this order itself translated into subdivisions that appeared planned. But perhaps not, as the regularity and cross-streets seem suspiciously intentional and are of a scale that presupposes some official sanction. Such confusion underlines the fact that the knowledge of early informal development in Cairo is largely uncharted territory.

In any event, the first small appearances of informal settlements multiplied in various locations of Cairo in the 1960s and early 1970s, both on agricultural land and in the desert fringes. In most of the earliest cases, subdivision and development began in what had been agricultural land, frequently being grafted onto existing rural settlements. This helps to explain, at least to some extent, the lack of official reaction. Rural housing was not regulated (building permits were unnecessary outside city limits), so local administrations had a plausible excuse for overlooking what was already becoming quite evident. And the logic probably went: If some farmers want to sell off some strips of agricultural land piecemeal, this can hardly be construed as contravening the subdivision laws, which were meant for modern, proper housing areas.

Whereas during the war years between 1967 and 1975, all development of formal Cairo stopped, informal Cairo continued to grow, undoubtedly fueled by continued in-migration and the need to accommodate some of the one million people evacuated from the Suez Canal zone. Based on maps derived from 1977 aerial photographs,[19] quite substantial fringe areas must already have been largely subdivided and sold during the 1967–77 period. These included most of Dar al-Salam and almost all of al-Basatin, vast areas of al-Munira al-Gharbiya, and sections of Bulaq al-Dakrur, al-'Umraniya in southern Giza, al-Zawya al-Hamra', Matariya, 'Ain Shams,

Figure 3.7. Extensive, mostly informal infill between the villages of Dar al-Salam and al-Basatin: 1977 *(top)* and 2000 *(bottom)*. Note the Ring Road under construction in 2000. (1977 image from IGN 1:5000 series, 2000 from Ikonos satellite image.)

and Ma'sara. And significant expansion out from core villages in Giza also must have started, such as around Saft al-Laban, al-Bashtil, Kafr al-Gabal, and even al-Kirdasa. And Manshiyat Nasir continued to grow, aided by the relocation of a large *zabbalin* community there in 1972.

Beginning in 1974, domestic economic conditions in Egypt changed dramatically due to the liberalizations of the *infitah*. Most importantly, Egyptians were motivated—and allowed—to travel freely abroad. This coincided with the oil price hike of 1973 (and later 1979) that soon made neighboring countries, most importantly Saudi Arabia, Libya, and Iraq, awash with money and eager to hire all classes of Egyptians to do their work, particularly unattractive construction jobs. The earnings of these Egyptians soon found their way back into Egypt and began to create an unprecedented cash-based economic boom. Savings and remittances of these expatriate workers provided the main capital for the accelerated housing construction in the informal city, since it put serious investment money in the hands of the kinds of families who were attracted to live in informal areas. Not unreasonably, for many, the preferred choice of investment was in land, bricks, and mortar. The level of construction in the large fringe areas already established before 1977 rose to fever pitch. New buildings appeared and, equally common, vertical extensions were added to existing buildings. Also, new informal areas began to be created or extended from existing villages during this period, for example on agricultural land in Begam and Musturad (in Shubra al-Khayma) and Waraq al-'Arab, Kafr al-Taharmus, and al-Mu'tamidiya in Giza Governorate, and al-Marg in Cairo Governorate. According to Galila El Kadi's 1987 study, parceling of agricultural land in some fringe informal areas was carried out by subdivision companies that operated in a kind of semiformal world.[20] In parallel, new informal settlements appeared on state land, for example 'Izbit al-Nasr behind Maadi and 'Izbit Khayrallah on the Fustat plateau, and 'Izbit al-Haggana at Kilometer 4.5 on the Suez Road.[21]

In 1982, a much-quoted study commissioned by the United States Agency for International Development (USAID) concluded that over eighty percent of the additions to Cairo's housing stock over the previous five years had been supplied by the informal sector.[22] This report coincided with a considerable interest among foreign aid agencies (especially USAID, British aid, and the World Bank) in residential informality in Egypt as a potentially positive dynamic that could be harnessed to solve the country's housing problem. Among their advisors it began to

Figure 3.8. Informal expansion in al-Munira al-Gharbiya: 1977 *(top)* and 2000 *(bottom)*. Note that all canals have been filled to create main roads, and that minor lanes follow what were field boundaries. (1977 image from IGN 1:5000 series, 2000 from Ikonos satellite image.)

be recognized that informal processes, from land acquisition and sub-division to progressive construction and densification, fit well with the social and financial circumstances of the mass of Egypt's urban population. However, neither the USAID report nor the expert discussions had the slightest impact on Egyptian planners and policymakers. In fact, once the Egyptian government woke up to the informal phenomenon on its doorstep, its reaction was completely negative. Although the 1974–85 period could be called the heyday of urban informal development in Cairo, it was also the period when the state finally took notice of the phenomenon and began to proscribe it. Starting in the late 1970s, a series of decrees and orders made it increasingly illegal to build on what had been recognized as precious agricultural land, and parallel efforts were stepped up to preserve state lands from encroachment. Throughout the period in question, these proscriptions had little real impact, only making it more difficult for authorities to turn a blind eye and opening up a considerable business in petty bribes. There was little official commitment to tackle the issue, since it began to dawn on decision makers just how vast informal areas had become. For urban planners and the state alike, it was an unwelcome reality that hopefully could be wished away.

And wish away they did, by launching the national new towns policy in 1977. The new towns quickly came to dominate both Cairo's urban development discourse as well as its budgetary allocations. Regardless of the huge investments required and the dismal failure rapidly to attract residents, the policy of creating modern planned desert settlements was and is still offered by government as the ultimate solution and alternative to the phenomenon of urban informality.

Mapping analysis comparing 1983 with 1989 showed that, at least in terms of major *additional* new lands coming under informal urbanization, development had slowed, with fewer sizable additions to the large fringe developments, and a somewhat reduced level of activity around satellite villages.[23] How much effect government control was having is debatable, but certainly a contributing factor was the drying up of remittance income from Egyptians working abroad. World oil prices began to tumble in 1983–84, and host countries began to apply restrictions to Egyptian workers at about the same time. The Iran–Iraq War in the 1980s led progressively to the elimination of the Egyptian worker's best bet, Iraq. Another factor working to slow down urban informality was demographic. Starting in the mid-1970s, the population growth rates of Greater Cairo proper

Figure 3.9. Massive informal infill development between the villages of Saft al-Laban and Kafr al-Taharmus: 1977 *(top)* and 2000 *(bottom)*. Note that all canals have been filled to create main roads, and that minor lanes follow what were field boundaries. (1977 image from IGN 1:5000 series, 2000 from Ikonos satellite image.)

started to fall significantly. During 1961–75 Greater Cairo grew at an average of 3.1 percent per year, but this rate fell to 2.7 percent for the period 1976–86 and to 1.9 percent for the period 1986–96. Natural increase rates retreated slightly, but also migration to the city decreased dramatically.[24]

Although all new informal settlements or extensions started off without any public infrastructure or social services, as an area matured and the number of its inhabitants increased, needs became articulated and slowly authorities would give in and begin to provide basic services, at least in the larger informal areas. This was especially true in the 1980s and 1990s, when the utilities authorities in Cairo finally were able to improve and extend networks, partly due to foreign assistance. (See Chapter 9.) Of course, such infrastructure services were slow in coming, often substandard, and varied considerably from location to location. In addition, many of the minor water and especially wastewater lines were installed by neighbors themselves through *guhud zatiya* (self-help) efforts.[25] Public facilities such as schools were rarely provided in informal settlements, since in Egypt such services are only built on available state land, which was in most locales extremely hard to find.

On the level of both public awareness and government action, informal areas of Greater Cairo gained prominence in the 1992–93 period. The radical Islamic movements of the late 1980s and early 1990s became active in certain informal areas, offering some deficient services that the government should have provided. Suddenly these areas, termed *'ashwa'i* (meaning random or unplanned), gained notoriety as breeding grounds for fundamentalism and came to be seen as a threat to the security of the state. Most prominent was a fundamentalist cell operating in al-Munira al-Gharbiya, whose leader was called 'the Prince of Imbaba.' In response, the government began to step up delivery of much-needed infrastructure to these areas, with police stations figuring prominently.[26] Informal settlements all over Egypt were cursorily inventoried and sketch plans for infrastructure upgrading were prepared. In other words, the state only began to address the issue of informal settlements *after* their creation and maturation, and then in a rather ad hoc and small-scale manner.

One factor that had a temporary dampening effect on informal construction was a much stiffer prohibition of the phenomenon, embodied in two decrees issued in 1996. They stipulated that *any* new building on agricultural land and *any* urban construction without a permit would be severely punished through military courts, thereby avoiding the many well-established maneuvers familiar to lawyers in the civil courts. For a few years this dampened informal construction, both on agricultural land and in desert settlements around Cairo, especially in new, open spaces where contraventions were easily visible; but its main lasting effect seems to have been the sharp increase in the extralegal payments required to have authorities look the other way.

The Cairo Ring Road, started in 1985 and finally completed in 2001, sharply increased awareness of the informality phenomenon, as it skirted fringe informal areas of the metropolis. Ranking officials and middle-class drivers began to use the Ring Road, and to their consternation could see from their vehicles massive reddish-hued informal housing areas stretching far into the agricultural plain. This was especially true on the northern, western, and southwestern arcs of the Ring Road. No longer was the phenomenon out of sight, conveniently dismissed as a marginal aberration. In 2002 the then governor of Giza launched a demolition campaign that involved chopping off the ubiquitous concrete pillars pro-truding from the roofs of informal structures, intended to support future vertical extensions. However, his campaign never extended more than a hundred meters on either side of the Ring Road along its northwestern arc, and within a couple years all traces of his actions had disappeared.

In the year 2000, an attempt to quantify the informal development phenomenon in Greater Cairo was carried out for Hernando Desoto's Institute for Liberty and Democracy (ILD). This study, based mainly on map and satellite imagery and on the detailed results of the 1996 Census of Egypt, concluded that of the estimated 11.4 million inhabit-ants of Greater Cairo in 1996, some 7.1 million, or 62 percent, were to be found in areas developed informally since 1950, covering some 129 square kilometers. In other words, already *a majority* of the population and half of the residential surface areas of the metropolitan region were deemed to have been developed informally.[27] Another study, undertaken by CEDEJ and published in 2002, confirmed the dominance of informal areas in Greater Cairo and, importantly, looked at time trends. Compar-ing satellite images of Greater Cairo between 1991 and 1998, the study concluded that the net surface areas of informal settlements in Greater Cairo proper increased at an annual rate of 3.4 percent, and that the population in informal areas increased by 3.2 percent per year. This rep-resented an additional 200,000 persons or 42,000 families each year. In comparison, the annual population growth in formal Cairo was only 0.8

percent.[28] This study also showed how the forms of informal development had become much more nuanced. Few new areas on virgin land had been created; instead, the mode became more the infilling of agricultural pockets between informal buildings, and small accretions and additions to existing informal settlements and villages, along with the filling in and densification of informal areas on state-owned desert land.

In the decade since 2000 the informal city has continued to grow and absorb the majority of additions to Greater Cairo's population. The characteristics of the informal city and its dynamics are described in greater detail in the next chapter. However, before moving on to a brief history of the desert city, we need first to look at how the peri-urban parts of Greater Cairo, where current informal development is at its most active, have come to be developed and increasingly incorporated into the metropolis.

The Peri-urban Frontier

Although informal urban development is continuing at a somewhat reduced pace in and around Greater Cairo proper, since around 1990 its greatest advance is in what can be called Cairo's peri-urban frontier. This is the agricultural plain found both to the north and south of Greater Cairo proper, where there are long-existing and well-articulated rural settlement patterns and where a vibrant transformation is taking place. It is difficult to define precisely how far this peri-urban frontier extends, but for convenience it can be considered the nine rural administrative *marakiz* (zones) on the Greater Cairo periphery, where population growth has been significantly above the prevailing natural increase rates. In Qalyubiya Governorate these are Qalyub (including Khusus), al-Khanka, Shibin al-Qanatir, and al-Qanatir al-Khayriya. In Giza Governorate they are the *marakiz* of Giza, Imbaba, Usim, Badrashayn, and al-Hawamidiya.[29] (See Map 3.4.) All were originally flat, irrigated agricultural areas, although in Khanka (northeast of Cairo) some slightly higher, formerly desert land can be found. Settlements in these nine *marakiz* range from only five kilometers from the center of Cairo (in Giza directly west of the core), to between ten and twenty-five kilometers (where most of peri-urban development has taken place), to thirty-five kilometers at their most extreme extents both north and south.

In peri-urban Greater Cairo urban expansion has been and continues to be almost entirely polycentric in nature. That is, existing towns, core villages, and hamlets expand progressively through informal subdivision outward into the surrounding agricultural plain. Only in the northeast

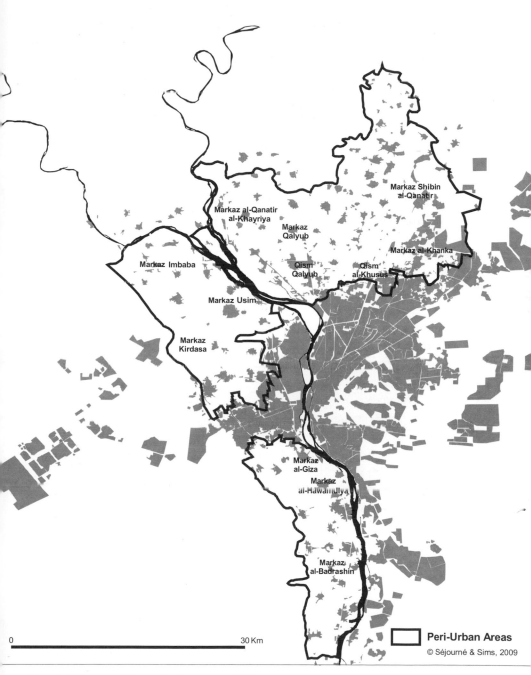

Map 3.4. Greater Cairo peri-urban areas, 2008.

quadrant of Greater Cairo (the Khusus–Qalag–Khanka areas) has this polycentric growth merged into what could be called a more or less continuous conurbation.

The 2006 population of the nine peri-urban *marakiz* of Greater Cairo can be estimated at 3.9 million inhabitants, representing 24 percent of Greater Cairo's 16.3 million inhabitants. The combined population of these areas has been growing rapidly, averaging 3.3 percent per year over the 1996–2006 period, an increase of over one million inhabitants. Practically all of this growth was and continues to be informal. During the same period, all of Greater Cairo grew at an annual rate of 2.10 percent. Growth in peri-urban areas had also been strong in the previous, 1986–96, period, when it averaged annual increases of 3.4 percent.

The rates of population increase have not been uniform throughout peri-urban space. For example, during the 1996–2006 period, the *markaz* of al-Khanka grew at a very high annual rate of 4.7 percent, whereas that of al-Hawamidiya was only 2.0 percent. Some particular locales increased at astronomical rates, particularly the rural *qism* of Khusus, which grew at 7.0 percent per year to reach a population of nearly 300,000 in 2006. In all of peri-urban Greater Cairo, eighteen village administrative units recorded annual growth rates in excess of 4.2 percent per year in the 1996–2006 decade, and together these units contained a population of 722,000 in 2006.

The main reason for the growing attraction of peri-urban areas can be said to relate to the array of affordable housing solutions that the mainly informal housing markets generate in these areas. Land accessibility and price are conducive to informal settlement creep and infill. Also, since development is largely out of sight, there is less prohibition on building on agricultural land than along the informal fringes of the core agglomeration of Greater Cairo. These two factors result in housing supply packages on the market that are more affordable, at least compared to other parts of Greater Cairo, especially for the bulk of lower-income families. Anything from a single room to a large flat or traditional rural house can be found on the informal market, either for rent or purchase.

Another attraction of peri-urban areas is the availability of affordable public transport systems and networks, which provide the needed mobility/access even from far distant settlements to other parts of Greater Cairo. Potential residents can and do calculate the trade-off between cheaper housing and higher expenditures on commuting. Furthermore, the local economies of existing peri-urban settlements easily accommodate incremental growth. Considerable employment and petty entrepreneur opportunities are generated within peri-urban villages and informal settlements themselves. Although public services and infrastructure may be lacking or over-burdened—and becoming more so in these areas—the situation does not seem to have got out of hand, so far at least. Finally, social cohesion seems to be good in peri-urban settlements, even with substantial numbers of new arrivals. This is partly due to the dynamic of informal settlement processes (which relies upon and works through social groupings), but is also simply because there are existing stable communities upon which to build.

Emergence of the Desert City

The desert around Cairo lies both east and west of the city proper. (See Map 0.) As mentioned above, the formal city had begun extending to the east into the adjacent desert plain from as early as 1905 with the Heliopolis suburb project as well as with the establishment of British army camps and depots in al-'Abbasiya and elsewhere in the 1920s. More recent formal extensions to the east included Madinat Nasr, Muqattam, Madinat al-Salam, Nuzha, and Zahra' al-Maadi. These were just that—extensions grafted onto Cairo proper—and until the late 1970s, the further, limitless desert to the east was hardly considered to have development potential. This eastern desert was mainly flat in the northern quadrant, but the topography was much more rugged east and south of Maadi.

Much the same could be said for Cairo's western desert. This desert area, seemingly without limits, was separated from Cairo proper by the agricultural plain whose width averages fifteen kilometers. Except for the pyramids area on the Giza Plateau, the Alexandria and Fayoum desert roads, various quarries in the Abu Rawash area, and the odd hotel or landowner's hacienda on the immediate desert fringe, the western desert was considered, until the arrival of the concept of the new towns, to be just one very large and empty backyard.

However, Cairo's vast deserts were *not* totally empty. From the time of the British occupation they proved excellent locations for military establishments. Most notable was the vast Heikastep camp extending from the Ismailiya Desert Road on the north to the Suez Desert Road to the south. This camp was established in the 1940s, and Cairo International Airport was carved out of its western section in the 1950s. After the 1967 war, the Egyptian military peppered Cairo's deserts with various camps, fortifications, air bases, air defense batteries, and factories, all part of its dispersal strategy. Thus, by the 1970s, Cairo's eastern desert was partly filled with large areas under military control, and even in the western desert, military and security establishments could be found near Dahshur and along desert roads leading out of Cairo. As we shall see, control of such lands by the armed forces was to be an important factor influencing Cairo's desert development.

The idea of developing the deserts around Cairo for urban expansion can be traced back to the 1956 Cairo Master Plan, and the concept was elaborated in the successor 1969 Master Plan. The latter, finally approved in 1974, concluded that Cairo's growth had already exceeded its "carrying capacity" and that the population of the metropolis should be limited to 9.5 million inhabitants. All excess population was to be directed to four satellite cities, two located in the eastern desert and two in the western desert.[30] Yet the real political commitment to developing Cairo's deserts derives from President Sadat's 1974 October Paper, itself a product of the euphoria following the successes of the 1973 October War. In this widely promoted document, Egypt's path to a modern future was sketched out, first by launching the economic *infitah*, and secondly by announcing a state policy of constructing desert cities throughout Egypt, thus shunting growth away from Cairo, Alexandria, and the crowded Nile Valley. The new towns were to be growth poles for alternative development and for decentralizing state institutions. They were aimed explicitly at attracting population, creating an industrial base outside the Valley, and attracting public and private investments, which dovetailed well with the economic Open Door policy.

It is important to note that even thirty years later, such a spatial policy for Egypt remains a central part of government thinking. As declared in 1990, the government perceived that "the old inhabited areas along the Nile valleys are no longer able to absorb the increasing population and that Egyptians have to conquer their desert land in order to ensure the sustainable growth of the nation."[31] An important affirmation of Egypt's desert development imperative was articulated by President Mubarak in an address given to both houses of parliament in 1996. After announcing the start of the massive Toshka land reclamation project near Aswan, the president declared:

> Leaving the narrow (Nile) valley and fanning out, in a planned and orga-
> nized manner, throughout the country, has become an unavoidable neces-
> sity. In view of these facts, the conquest of the desert is no longer a slogan

or dream but a necessity dictated by the spiraling population growth. What is required is not a token exodus into the desert but a complete reconsideration of the distribution of population throughout the country.[32]

In the 1970s, the concept of new towns in the desert generated considerable excitement among urban planners, higher state officials, and even Egypt's cultural elite. It was in these new desert settlements that the uncrowded, organized, and modern urban Egypt was expected to be established. And what a playground! For planners, the talk was of self-contained, balanced industrial towns economically independent of Cairo, designed on government-owned lands that appeared to be endless. Desert sites represented the planner's ultimate dream of a total blank sheet of paper, where town layouts would be constrained neither by topography nor existing urban realities. Concepts of low residential densities, separation of land uses, green belts, and integrated neighborhoods could be pursued with a vengeance. Egypt was going to be up there with the small group of nations, such as Brazil, Nigeria, and India, who were envisioning new capitals and new cities. In no time Egyptian planners and academics became part of the international conference circuit of new town associations.[33]

The first new town venture began in 1976 with the declaration by President Sadat of the intention to build from scratch a totally self-sufficient new town at a desert location about halfway between Cairo and Ismailiya, that is, supposedly far enough away to be independent from these existing urban poles.[34] To be called Tenth of Ramadan, the new city was to have a solid economic foundation based on manufacturing, and workers in the industrial enterprises were to reside in government-built housing blocks. A limited amount of middle-class housing was to be privately built in neighborhood subdivisions. Aimed at an ultimate population of 500,000, the design of the town was contracted by the (then) Ministry of Reconstruction to a Swedish consulting firm.

Even while Tenth of Ramadan was still on the drawing boards, other new town schemes, each to have a significant industrial base, were announced. (The locations of the new towns around Cairo can be found in Map 6.1.) Two of these were to be located near Cairo. The first was Sixth of October, west of Cairo at an isolated desert location about forty kilometers from the center of the metropolis, off the Bahariya Oasis road, and the second was al-'Ubur, to be located east of Cairo, about

مدينة العاشر من رمضان ● Ramadan City

Google

Figure 3.10. Tenth of Ramadan New Town, started in the late 1970s. (Image dated 2006, ©2010 DigitalGlobe / ©2009 GOOGLE.)

twenty-five kilometers from the city center, just north of the Ismailiya Desert Highway. Along with Sadat City and al-Amiriya al-Gadida near Alexandria, these cities were considered the 'first generation' of industrial new towns. In addition, another purely residential new town, Fifteenth of May, was to be developed in the near desert adjacent to the Cairo suburb of Helwan.

The industrial new towns enjoyed almost immediate success in attracting manufacturing. For example, within ten years of their establishment the industrial zones of Tenth of Ramadan had filled up and new industrial subdivisions had to be added to accommodate more factories. There was a similar rapid take-up of Sixth of October's huge industrial area. Such a glowing success of the industrial face of Cairo's new towns was due entirely to government incentives to attract private manufacturing, and government requirements that public-sector industries locate there. Serviced industrial land was offered at low, subsidized prices with long payment periods. Private enterprises in new towns enjoyed ten-year tax holidays, and the required permits and licenses were easily obtained. And for most foreign and joint-venture manufacturing projects, the Investment Authority would only facilitate approvals if these were located in the new towns.

The legislative and institutional framework for the new towns was formalized with the promulgation of the New Communities Law (Law no. 59 of 1979). This created the New Urban Communities Authority (NUCA) within the Ministry of Housing and gave it the right to declare special development zones on state-owned desert lands. Furthermore, the law gave NUCA the right to develop and sell lands within these special zones and to retain these revenues to finance further development. Such a right over lands was unique, something neither governorates nor ministries enjoyed. Law no. 59 of 1979 also stipulated that each new town would be managed by a town agency under NUCA, but that once developed, the new towns were to revert to municipal local administration under the relevant governorate. Incidentally, and symptomatic of where power actually lies in Egypt, this devolution of a new town to local governorate authorities has yet to occur anywhere in Egypt.

In 1980–81 a large study was commissioned by the then Ministry of Reconstruction, Housing, and Land Reclamation entitled *The National Urban Policy Study*, with USAID funding.[35] This study can be considered the only attempt in Egypt to have looked at the urban sector in its entirety. To meet national economic and social objectives, and also to limit the growth of Greater Cairo, it came up with a set of balanced recommendations that stressed the importance of directing scarce national resources toward stimulating the growth and economic competitiveness of existing urban agglomerations. Notably absent were recommendations to create dozens of new cities in the desert and to give desert regions the highest regional development priority. The study was not well received. The ministry never followed up on any of the recommendations, nor did it allow the circulation of the study's twenty-five separate reports. In effect, the new towns concept had already acquired an almost Messianic image in government and among the professional classes, and no American consulting firm's report was going to disturb this view.[36]

Although construction on the 'first generation' of new towns around Cairo had hardly begun, by the early 1980s the concept of satellite 'new settlements' around Cairo was launched, and this second generation of nine settlements was to be located in the desert both east and west of Cairo proper. These were to be dormitory suburbs of mainly subsidized public housing, aimed at absorbing Cairo's population increases, and they became cornerstones of the 1983 Master Plan for Cairo and were to be interlinked by the Ring Road. Although none ever materialized in their original planned forms, three have been amalgamated into New Cairo to the east and two into Sheikh Zayed to the west.

The 1986 Census revealed that growth of the residential population of the new towns around Cairo was proving to be exceptionally slow, in contrast to the rapid take-up of the industrial areas in Tenth of Ramadan and Sixth of October. The oldest new town, Tenth of Ramadan, registered only 8,500 inhabitants. Sixth of October had an insignificant 500 inhabitants. Only Fifteenth of May had any sizable population—24,000 inhabitants—and this was clearly due to its character as a purely residential suburb grafted onto the existing urban area of Helwan. Such figures did not at all dampen enthusiasm for the new town concept. Often heard was the statement that any new town takes time to be launched, and that 'sustained growth' was just around the corner, especially if investments and service projects in them were accelerated.[37] The results of the 1996 Census continued to deliver extremely disappointing population figures. Overall, the combined population of all these first new towns around Cairo registered less than 150,000 inhabitants, equivalent to an insignificant 1.1 percent of Greater Cairo's population at the time. Almost half of this population was to be found in Fifteenth of May, virtually an extension of Helwan, and another 48,000 inhabitants were located in Tenth of Ramadan, which due to its remoteness could hardly be considered part of Greater Cairo. Sixth of October had only 35,000 inhabitants.

In the early 1990s there was a fundamental shift in the concept of new towns and the associated land management policy. Up to this time, new towns had mainly been developed to attract the working classes through the construction of state-subsidized low-cost housing blocks, in addition to the provision of some middle-class land subdivisions. With the change of ministers and increasing criticism of the quality and aesthetic of social housing, a much more 'capitalist' mode of development was applied. First, the boundaries of existing new towns and settlements were dramatically extended, particularly for those cities around Cairo that were considered to have development potential. Huge tracts of subdivided land were sold at nominal, some would say give-away, prices to individuals. And large tracts were released, again at very low prices, to private developers. Three 'second generation' satellite settlements were amalgamated and boundaries extended to create New Cairo in the desert east of the metropolis, with a target population of two million. Also, two huge new settlements of Sheikh Zayed and al-Shuruq (both with target populations of 500,000 inhabitants) were created. Another new town, al-Badr, was begun at a very remote location off the Suez Desert Highway. Massive amounts of land in these extensions and new areas were sold throughout the late 1990s, mainly at prices that began to reflect some of the land servicing costs, but nowhere near full market values. This new land-disposal policy began to bring some welcome revenues to the NUCA and to the state treasury. Also, it signaled a fundamental shift, with new towns around Cairo evolving into the locations for the new middle classes and the rich. Gated communities, compounds, and upmarket subdivisions were launched. Yet, in parallel, the state continued to pour investment into subsidized public housing in the new towns around Cairo, creating more and more workers' housing estates.

All of this increased the geographical extent and sunk real-estate investments in the new towns around Greater Cairo, and created optimism for Cairo's desert city and an even greater amount of talk about these new towns as the face of modern Egypt. However, when the preliminary results of the census of 2006 were made available in late 2007, Egyptian planners and promoters of the new towns received a rude shock. Whereas the General Organization for Physical Planning (GOPP) had estimated in 2005 that the population of the new towns around Cairo had reached a figure of 1.75 million, the 2006 Census recorded only one-third of this figure, equivalent to only 3.7 percent of Greater Cairo's total population. Given all the construction activity going on, especially in Sixth of October and New Cairo, some planners and officials simply could not believe that population take-up continued to be so slow, choosing instead to doubt the validity of the census. The 2006 Census actually confirmed that investments in the new towns had been considerable, with a total of 409,000 housing units enumerated in Cairo's eight new towns. But an extraordinary amount of this housing was unfinished, stalled, vacant, or simply closed. The number of resident households enumerated was only 139,000, meaning that 63 percent of units were unutilized, or, put another way, that for every resident household there were three dwelling units available. Talk about dead capital![38]

It may appear puzzling that population growth in the new towns around Cairo has been and continues to be so slow, especially given that the government has built massive amounts of subsidized public housing in these areas. Over the 1982–2005 period more than 200,000 such units were built in Cairo's new towns. And under Egypt's National Housing Program (NHP), which aims to build 500,000 units in Egypt between 2005 and 2011, at least 208,000 of these units are earmarked for the new towns around Cairo. However, a very large portion of the current government-produced stock remains vacant or closed, and the same fate can be expected for units currently being built.

What went so wrong with the new towns around Greater Cairo, supposedly the vanguard of Egypt's desert development project? This is taken up in Chapter 6, which takes a closer look at the current state of play of the desert city.

It is important to realize that the desert city is not at all confined to its new towns, as large as they may be. Even more desert lands have been developed for various urban and suburban purposes. Although nominally all desert land is under state ownership and control, in the last thirty-five years huge tracts of desert around Cairo have been allocated and developed in what could best be described as a scramble to capture development rights on land that, at some point, is perceived as being extremely valuable, at least for speculative purposes. Both state and private-sector actors have been involved. The current status of these many 'off-plan' desert schemes is described in Chapter 6, but in the following paragraphs a slice of the history of the phenomenon is presented.

The oldest and perhaps most outstanding example of such desert land grabs is Hada'iq al-Ahram, or the Pyramid Gardens, subdivision, which began in the late 1970s. At that time a group of influential persons formed a housing cooperative and somehow gained development rights over a huge 420-hectare site along the Fayoum road just beyond Midan al-Rimaya. This site was just two kilometers from the Giza pyramids area, hence its name. The land was subdivided into large building lots. It is understood that when Anwar Sadat heard of the project, he ordered it cancelled, and for years it remained simply a collection of empty lots

Figure 3.11. Off-plan desert developments near pyramids of Giza, started in the late 1970s. (Hada'iq al-Ahram to the left and police officer housing at center.) (Image dated 2009, ©2010 DigitalGlobe / ©2009 GOOGLE.)

with only traces of a street network. However, slowly but surely, investors bought parcels from the original cooperative members and the construction of large villas and garden apartment blocks began. Today the site is perhaps half developed, utilities are in place, and land prices have soared to astronomical levels. The fact that the scheme is next door to the iconic Pyramids of Giza does not seem to bother anyone.

One way to gain control over desert lands around Cairo with future development potential was to create an agricultural land reclamation cooperative and obtain an assignment of state land from the Ministry of Agriculture. A very early example dating from 1978 was the Ahmad 'Urabi Land Reclamation Cooperative, located on 4,600 hectares north of the Ismailiya Desert Road. Members of this cooperative were high-ranking army officers, each of which was assigned a twenty-feddan parcel.

Most of these have either ended up as sumptuous suburban villa developments or remained vacant lots. Needless to say, agricultural output from
this project is practically nil.

Over the last four decades military and security-controlled desert lands
around Cairo have also been converted for urban uses. A large part of the
Heikastep camp was renamed Heikastep New Town in the 1980s, and the
army built a number of housing blocks for officers, although much of the
area of the new town remains relatively underdeveloped. Other officer
housing complexes can be found in locations in both the eastern and western deserts, and it seems that the majority of these cater more to security cadres than to the military. For example, a 3,000-unit housing-estate
project for police officers was built in the 1980s near Midan al-Rimaya,
on a raised portion of desert that now embarrassingly abuts the site of
the proposed Grand Egyptian Museum. Other examples include a large
police-housing complex constructed in the 1990s just off the entrance
road to Sixth of October. In addition, some desert military lands have been
handed over to other government authorities for various urban projects,
usually after very opaque negotiations. Still other military camps remain
under the control of the armed forces or security agencies, and they represent a kind of land bank for future urban development that will generate
huge profits for developers, whether private or government.

Looking at the history of desert development around Greater Cairo,
it is inescapable to suspect that much of this development represents an
opportunity for pure land speculation and windfall profits, especially for
state agencies and those who have influence with the government. This
speculative scramble for land in Cairo's deserts was noted as far back
as 1981 in the *National Urban Policy Study*.[39] In 1984, the Extension of
Municipal Services project carried out a 'land assembly' exercise to identify desert lands around Cairo for possible low-income urban-develop-
ment projects, only to discover that there was precious little land that was
not already held or claimed by the New Towns Authority, the military,
public-sector companies, government ministries, or housing and agricultural cooperatives.[40] In fact, it was found that many parcels were claimed
by more than one entity, that there was total confusion about boundaries,
and that documentation on desert land holdings was practically nonexistent. In the scramble to claim desert tracts, physical possession was all-
important, and in this the military and police usually trumped all other
competitors. Even the distinction between desert lands under the New

Table 3.1: Evolution of the population of Greater Cairo and its component parts (1947–2009)

Year	Formal Cairo	Informal Cairo	Peri-urban Cairo (mostly Informal)	Desert Cairo	Total Greater Cairo Region (GCR)	GCR Annual Increase (%)	Percent Informal in Cairo proper	Percent Informal in GCR
1947	2,400,242	0	586,038	0	2,986,280		0.0	10.2
1960	3,905,670	100,000	955,166	0	4,960,836	3.98	2.5	15.6
1976	4,610,326	1,969,000	1,374,317	0	7,953,643	2.99	29.9	38.1
1986	4,650,000	4,248,866	2,063,376	32,615	10,994,857	3.29	47.7	54.5
1996	4,807,632	5,436,477	2,857,468	149,992	13,251,569	1.88	53.1	59.7
2006	5,005,824	6,742,416	3,942,262	601,767	16,292,269	2.09	57.4	62.8
2009*	5,038,763	7,155,106	4,345,567	800,952	17,340,388	2.09	58.7	63.6

Source: Census of Egypt, various years: detailed results, combined with map and satellite image analysis by the author to distinguish informal areas.

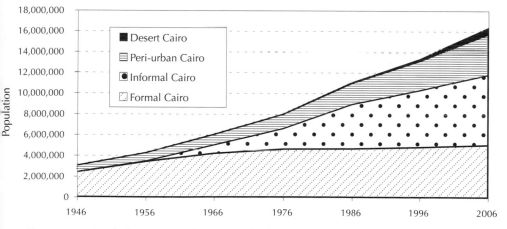

Figure 3.12. Graph showing population growth of component parts of Greater Cairo 1946–2006, based on Table 3.1.

---

* Estimate based on observed rates of increase 1996–2006.

Towns Authority and that of other claimants and entities was frequently blurred, leading not infrequently to disputes and protracted negotiations among different state actors.

Comparing the Three Cities

In this chapter we have spent some time looking at the different forms of Cairo's development over the last fifty years or so. Here, the focus is to summarize the evolution of each form and to compare results, especially in terms of population absorption. Table 3.1 shows best estimates of the populations of Cairo's distinct types of urban growth as they have evolved over the 1947–2009 period, based on census years.

In 1947, all of Greater Cairo's urban population—some 2.4 million persons—was contained in formal Cairo.[41] In addition, there were just over half a million persons in what now constitutes peri-urban Cairo, most of whom were in rural households engaged either directly or indirectly in the agricultural economy. From 1947 to 1960 Cairo experienced very high demographic growth averaging almost 4 percent per year, mainly due to in-migration. Formal Cairo gained 1.5 million inhabitants and the peri-urban areas almost 400,000. Informal Cairo was still practically nonexistent, although we have included a nominal 100,000 persons in this category, since informal development was just starting in 1960. We have also categorized most development in the peri-urban areas as informal.

In the sixteen years between 1960 to 1976 the informal city took off with a vengeance, increasing from practically zero to two million inhabitants, mainly in inner fringe areas that were to become, over the subsequent decades, enormous agglomerations, almost cities in themselves. Prominent examples include Shubra al-Khayma, Imbaba/Waraq, Bulaq al-Dakrur, al-'Umraniya, al-Basatin/Dar al-Salam, Manshiyat Nasir, and al-Marg/Khusus.[42] The population of the formal city also increased, but by a relatively fewer 700,000 persons. Few formal areas were being created over the period, due to Egypt's war footing after 1967, and already the very strong trend of depopulation of inner formal areas had begun.

Between 1976 and 1986 the expansion of the informal city was in its heyday, fueled partly by massive remittances from Egyptians working in the Gulf. In ten short years the population of the informal city had increased by 1.3 million, already nearing half Cairo's total population. The growth of the informal city's population was an incredible 8 percent per year. In contrast, the formal city virtually stagnated in population terms. It was not that there were no urban projects in the formal city (in fact, the *infitah* generated considerable real-estate investments), but these did not create much affordable housing. And at precisely the same time, the exodus from the inner formal city had reached its peak—with these areas recording an absolute decrease of over 600,000 persons, some 20 percent of their population. And where did these people go? Most moved out of their crowded and dilapidated housing and into new lives in the burgeoning informal city. Some also moved to large public-housing projects such as Madinat al-Salam, and other 'pioneers' moved farther afield into what were already exploding peri-urban villages. Although the new towns that made up the desert city had already been heavily promoted for a decade, their total population in 1986 was a tiny 33,000 inhabitants.

Over the 1986–96 period Greater Cairo as a whole witnessed a significant slowing of its population increase, registering only 1.9 percent annual growth, down from 3.3 percent in the preceding decade. Net in-migration to the capital region had almost ceased. The informal city continued to grow substantially, although at a slower rate than in the 1976–86 period, reaching over 5.4 million inhabitants and exceeding for the first time the population of the formal city. The formal city itself registered modest growth, mainly due to expansions and densifications of Madinat Nasr, al-Nuzha, Mohandiseen/Dokki, coupled with a reduction of the high rate of flight from its inner precincts (estimated at 'only' 300,000 inhabitants over the decade). In this period the rate of population growth of peri-urban Cairo exceeded that of the informal city for the first time, growing at a rate of 3.3 percent per year versus 2.5 percent per year for informal areas of Greater Cairo proper. The population of the new towns in Greater Cairo's desert increased to 150,000, still totally insignificant when compared to demographic increases in informal Cairo and the peri-urban areas.

The 2006 Census clearly showed that trends observed in earlier inter-census years were continuing. Overall, Greater Cairo increased to 16.3 million inhabitants, showing a slightly higher annual growth rate (2.11 percent) than in the 1986–96 period. The already massive informal city continued to grow, adding another 1.3 million inhabitants, but at a more sedate growth rate of 2.2 percent per year. Peri-urban Cairo continued to absorb huge population shifts—for the first time, over one million persons in ten years—and grew at a relatively high rate of 3.3 percent per year. The formal city actually began to show some expansion, adding

200,000 inhabitants and registering a 0.4 percent annual growth rate, its highest since the early 1970s. In the 1996–2006 period the desert new towns finally began to register as a blip on Cairo's demographic radar, absorbing 450,000 additional inhabitants and rising to almost 4 percent of Greater Cairo's 2006 total population.

Discussing population statistics may be a dry exercise, but these numbers for Greater Cairo tell a very important story. After all, ultimately a city is made up of its people, and how a megacity absorbs and accommodates them needs close examination. The results are startling, as can be seen in Table 3.1 and Figure 3.12. Over the forty-six years from 1960 to 2006 the informal city jumped from nearly zero to nearly seven million inhabitants, whereas the formal city expanded only very slowly, from roughly four million to five million inhabitants. Over the same period, peri-urban Cairo absorbed three million inhabitants, practically all of whom found accommodation in informal settlements. The desert city, for which planners and government had held out such hopes, absorbed only 600,000 inhabitants over these forty-six years. It is thus no exaggeration at all to say that almost all of today's Greater Cairo is the product of informal processes, that these processes are dominant, and that they will continue to dominate for years to come.

The informal dominance of Greater Cairo in terms of population absorption is found in all recent census decades. For example, in the 1976 to 1986 period just over three million persons were added to the population of the metropolis. Of these additions, over 95 percent were absorbed by the informal city or by informal settlements on the peri-urban fringe. In the 1986–96 period, of the 2.25 million inhabitants added to Greater Cairo, over 85 percent were absorbed informally. Even in 1996 to 2006, when one might have expected the modern desert city to begin to weigh in, of the 3 million additional inhabitants, a full 79 percent were absorbed informally.

One could say that the trend is in the right direction, with the informal share of population absorption decreasing slightly decade by decade. Yes, it is; but the absolute share of this absorption remains colossal and is still set to capture most additions to the population for several more decades. And these informal settlements have considerable weight of inertia, grounded in spatial configurations and sunk investments, and now housing the majority of Greater Cairo's inhabitants. They define the city's landscape and are set to absorb even more inhabitants, whatever the government decides.

Despite this reality, the government insists that the desert city should be Cairo's future, notwithstanding its dismal success to date. It is revealing to compare the planned physical space of the desert city to that of Greater Cairo proper. Using recent satellite imagery and other documentation, it is possible to calculate that in 2008, Greater Cairo (that is, the formal plus informal cities plus the peri-urban settlements) covered a total of 529 square kilometers.[43] This included all built-up areas and the few planned extensions to the formal city. In contrast, the areas already under development, allocated, or planned in the new towns around Greater Cairo cover an immense 1,200 square kilometers, or over two times the surface area of the existing built-up city.[44] And these desert areas do not include possible further extensions to the new town boundaries, nor do they include the numerous 'off plan' and random desert projects that seem to be proliferating very rapidly. Thus, in spatial terms, the desert city already completely eclipses all other forms of Cairo's development. The facts that in relative terms practically no one lives there, that Cairo's desert development generates more dead capital than live, and that it brings new meaning to the concept of a city's 'speculative fringe,' these are some of the subjects which are taken up in Chapter 6.

And what about the future and the expected population increases of Greater Cairo? Population projections made by GOPP and their Japanese consultants for the year 2027 show that Egypt's penchant for wishful thinking in development projections has not abated.[45] First, the calculations assume that the population of the Greater Cairo region will increase by 8.1 million inhabitants over the 2006–2027 period to reach 24.2 million persons. The overall annual rate of increase is assumed to drop from 2.26 percent in 2006 to only 1.61 percent in 2027, which would imply a dramatic demographic shift away from observed trends for Greater Cairo, and, parenthetically, an optimistic drop in the rate of Egypt's population growth. Secondly, the distribution of this population assumes that Cairo's new towns will absorb at least half this increase, rising to reach 6.5 million by 2027, a very optimistic scenario indeed. And the 'small towns and villages' in Giza and Qalyubiya governorates, which are roughly synonymous with peri-urban Greater Cairo and which are growing extremely rapidly, are assumed under GOPP projections to have practically stopped growing by 2027, their implied annual rate of increase dropping to only 0.9 percent per year. In other words, the long-hoped-for success of the new towns will somehow materialize, and the long-dreaded encroachment of informal development on agricultural land will somehow be stopped. Not only is this in contradiction of all past trends, it assumes population increases that have been occurring in peri-urban Cairo will be shifted entirely to the new towns. This implies that families now forming in peri-urban Cairo—who are among the poorest, and definitely *not* of the middle and upper classes—will almost all find preferred housing alternatives in the new towns.

Peering into Cairo's Future

Starting in 2008 the Egyptian government began spending considerable efforts to promote a future vision for Greater Cairo, with GOPP sponsoring a study called "Greater Cairo Strategic Planning 2050 Concept." Using a time horizon of over forty years, and some extremely optimistic assumptions about Egypt's demography and economic performance, government planners and their consultants have demonstrated in 'Cairo 2050' a continued penchant for the manufacture of unrealistic dreams. However, these dreams firmly reflect their wishes for Cairo to become a super-modern, high-tech, green, and connected city that can stand shoulder-to-shoulder with the metropolises in the world's most advanced countries.

The features that collectively make up the 'Cairo 2050' vision are truly amazing, both in their daring and in their cost implications, There are to be new universities, libraries, movie studios, and specialized hospitals and museums, all of the highest international standards. There are also to be technology and research centers, new hotel and conference districts, immense new boulevards and architectural focal points. A prominent feature will be huge green areas and recreational parks, both in the city's desert and in what are now the historic cemeteries and Nile islands. Downtown Cairo will be completely gentrified, and historic areas transformed into 'open-air museums.' Most government offices are to be relocated and concentrated into one large desert site. New central business parks are to be created on what are now poor neighborhoods. Huge office towers and hotels will spring up all along the Nile. The informal and shabby parts of Cairo are either to be removed entirely (with the inhabitants relocated to public housing in the desert or to new neighborhoods on agricultural land to be developed by private investors), or they are to be 'decongested' by creating wide roads and green corridors that cut through major informal areas. Millions upon millions of residents in informal areas will need resettlement.

It hardly needs saying that few of the schemes and projects of Cairo 2050 will ever see the light of day. The colossal sums needed to finance investments will simply not materialize, and social resistance can be expected to be fierce. In a way it seems that government planners enjoy going through a rosy design exercise in which they can conveniently forget the reality that is present-day Cairo and over which the government has so little control. It is much simpler to look so far into the future that nasty details need not besmirch the vision.

4

Informal Cairo Triumphant

From the previous chapter it should be abundantly clear that the informal mode of urban development in Greater Cairo has been dominant over the last decades, that it continues to be so, and that all trends point to its continued importance. Of the 17 million inhabitants living in Greater Cairo in 2009, a conservative 11 million or 63 percent inhabit areas that have been developed informally or extralegally since 1960, a few short decades ago. And a large majority of future additions to the population of the metropolis will inevitably be absorbed in existing and newly forming informal areas, especially those located in the peri-urban fringes.

Such a huge and important phenomenon deserves a special focus, and in this chapter we take a closer look at the informal city. While we aim to paint as accurate a picture of Cairo's informal areas and their underlying causes as is possible, it must be kept in mind that there are tremendous gaps in understanding informal urban developments in Greater Cairo and Egypt in general. It is striking that there is so little serious and factual analysis of what is in effect the main mode of Cairo's urbanization, and this neglect is symptomatic of the attitudes toward informality among Egyptian officials and academics. What little is known about these areas is mainly derived from projects and studies supported by international and bilateral donors, as will be seen from the references in this chapter.[1] And this knowledge is itself only piecemeal and incomplete; much of it is composed of circular references to the same shaky data. Perversely, even in this near information vacuum, prescriptive policies and plans on how to halt or otherwise deal with the informal city can be found both in government and among donors, as will be seen below.

Images of and Attitudes toward Informal Areas

If you purchase a map of Cairo, even the most recent, you will find the central areas of town, historic Cairo, and the usual known quarters such as Zamalek, Mohandiseen, Roda, and Dokki well covered, with inserts for Maadi and Heliopolis and even for New Cairo and Sixth of October. But most of these cartographic efforts totally miss the informal areas that make up the rest of the metropolis, either leaving them blank or sprinkling some names over an amorphous hinterland. As we have shown in Chapter 3, this 'rest' of Cairo is, paradoxically, where most Cairenes live and is, in population terms, the city's future.

Such omissions are not mistakes. The informal city is of little or no interest to modern Cairenes or foreigners who read maps, who need banking, travel, or business services, or who need to shop in high-end outlets. In the cognizance of middle-class Egyptians and most government officials such areas are definitely beyond the pale. Certainly, some may have heard of such places as Ard al-Liwa, Imbaba, al-Basatin, and so on—usually because they have servants or drivers or employees who live there—but it is rare that they will have a clue how to get there. Even architects and planners would be hard put to locate these informal areas.[2] Cognizance of the 'rest,' at least visually, improved with the construction of the Ring Road in the late 1980s and the Twenty-Six July Corridor in the early 1990s. These arteries are heavily used by private-car commuters as well as trucks and minibuses and so on. They became great eye-openers for the better-off classes, since it was not easy to ignore the brick-red and concrete expanses of informal housing stretching out on either side of the new highways.

Although the informal city has been around for decades and houses almost two-thirds of the population of Greater Cairo, in the minds of most comfortably established Egyptians 'ashwa'i Cairo remains a remote and marginal part of the metropolis. If thought of at all, the informal city is usually considered a repository of poverty, backwardness, crime, misery, and all that is wrong with Cairo. It is, in addition, a cancer that is gobbling up precious agricultural land. In films and books and journalistic articles such areas are portrayed, if at all, as sinkholes of unrelieved poverty and social deviation, or even breeding grounds for fundamentalist extremism and terrorism.

A film that opened in Cairo's movie theaters in 2008, *Hina maysara* (When Fate Calls), is typical of the genre. It uses a very run-down quarter as the backdrop to a plot full of gangsters, fallen women, social unrest, lost children, and police brutality. Although the film was promoted as an eye-opener into the *'ashwa'i* subculture and gave the director a chance to indulge in the usual moralizing about the state of Egyptian society, the locale used was in fact an old slum pocket of inner Cairo, which is totally atypical of Cairo's huge and relatively new *'ashwa'i* areas.

In 2007 a best-selling book called *Taxi* appeared, a very entertaining account of sarcastic, hilarious, and sometimes-depressing conversations with dozens of Cairo taxi drivers. The perceptive and sympathetic author, Khaled Al Khamissi, recounts taxi rides taken all over town. But only once in all his trips does he actually end up in an *'ashwa'i* area—Saft al-Laban, which is behind Cairo University Lecturers' City. His reaction was, well, typical of his class of Egyptians: "The place was a real monstrosity of an indeterminate nature . . . . I caught sight of a taxi from the city and I ran toward it to escape, after besmirching my face in this salad bowl of humanity."[3] And it should be pointed out that conditions in Saft al-Laban are not bad, at least compared to many of Giza's informal areas.

Some journalists positively love to report on the *'ashwa'i* phenomenon in Cairo, and articles have been appearing with regularity over the last twenty years. These pieces typically repeat the standard misconceptions, deplore the state of affairs, and assume a tone of moral superiority, blaming both the ignorant 'peasants' who flock to Cairo's 'slums' and the government authorities who continue to do nothing. Reading these journalistic pieces, it seems the usual narrative is to focus on a particular locale or disaster, then conflate this with the millions of 'the poor' who live in 'shantytowns and slums' around Cairo, and finally to fling out quotes from the usual 'experts,' who are only too ready to lecture and pontificate. The Duweiqa cliff collapse in 2008 became a godsend to such journalists and is a good example of this journalistic license. For them it was fortunate that the affected area of 'Izbit Bikhit was definitely poor and did include some shoddy dwellings hastily constructed by real squatters. This then set the immediate image of the dangerous, poverty-stricken shantytown, quickly to be generalized to all of informal Cairo.

A front-page article in *Al-Ahram Weekly*, which appeared just after the disaster, is typical.[5] The leap from the disaster area to the general was in the leader: "People die in shantytowns because shantytowns are there." In the first paragraph experts are being quoted. Housing expert Milad Hanna generalizes: "The poor are required to construct houses with cheap materials. They access electricity and water supplies in ingenuous[sic] but illegal ways. The dangerous buildings that result might provide temporary shelter but they are liable to collapse at any moment. The only question we need to ask ourselves, as a nation, [is] are we willing to seriously tackle the problem." The article then calls the *'ashwa'iyyat* phenomenon in Cairo "this most embarrassing of national fiascos," and states: "according to one *al-Ahram* pundit, the shanty towns encircling Cairo are but potential danger zones, ticking time bombs, nestling within Egypt's capital. They are areas beyond the control of the state and the authorities." Not to be outdone, in the same article a political sociologist makes a number of scary generalizations about *'ashwa'i* inhabitants: "They dream of living somewhere permanent. They live in one slum for a decade then move to another. There is no direction, no control. The slum dwellers are not city-dwellers in the proper sense of the word, they are not even citizens . . . . They tolerate rising heaps of refuse. They live beyond the regulations affecting the residents of the city proper. Indeed, some of these slums are inaccessible to outsiders. This is why we desperately need a comprehensive plan of action."

Reading generalizations such as these about Cairo's *'ashwa'i* areas, one cannot but wonder if such negative images of the 'other' serve as a necessary confirmation of the 'non-other,' that is, the modern middle- and upper-classes and self-styled urban elites. They can feel good by objectifying 'slum-dwelling' Cairenes as backward, living hand-to-mouth, undisciplined, and even barely human. This gives them space to pontificate, which is for some an opportunity to indulge in a little charity work or to form an NGO. It can even be said that there is a perverse undertone in these attitudes, a kind of barely disguised glee that "there, but for the grace of God, go I." This objectifying of inhabitants in informal areas and the necessary construction of 'the other' is well described in an essay by Diane Singerman.[5]

A slightly different, if again generalized, take on the informal city, one favored by some Egyptian academics and *mufakkirin*, is that these blighted areas are only symptoms of deeper ills in Egyptian society and government. The *'ashwa'i* phenomenon is perceived as 'disease,' which requires a fundamental 'cure,' or as is sometimes said, a cancerous tumor on the nation which requires radical surgery. This then opens the way to express one's personal opinions on what is wrong with Egypt. A paper presented by a Cairo University professor at a conference on urban upgrading in October 2008 is illustrative.[6] To paraphrase, a cure to the *'ashwa'i* problem must be complete and deep, and for this the root causes must be known. These, it turns out, are the lack of opportunities for most Egyptians to pursue an honorable life. Government seems only to help the elites, and for fundamental change to occur, absolute priority must be given to human resource development, that is, better education, which should be available to all equally. Such sentiments, expressed in the paper, are noble and many would certainly agree with them, but it is hardly correct to identify the *'ashwa'iyyat* as the symptom.

What are Informal Areas, What are Their Extents, and Where are they Found?

There are a number of definitions of what constitutes an informal or *'ashwa'i* area. Countless pages are written about definitions and classifications, and these are then revisited from time to time, even today.[7] Certainly there are different types or typologies of informal areas and their ages and conditions vary considerably from one area of Cairo to another, as we will see below. After all, the phenomenon is very diverse and heterogeneous. But to be preoccupied with concepts and vocabularies, even after the *'ashwa'i* phenomenon has been around for decades, is counterproductive to say the least.

The best definition of informal areas in Cairo is that they are the result of extralegal urban development processes that first appeared around 1950, and they exhibit a complete lack of urban planning or building control.[8] In fact, *al-manatiq al-gheir mukhattata* (unplanned areas) is now the preferred terminology used by GOPP. These areas were established and consolidated in contravention of a host of laws and decrees that either prohibited building on agricultural land or governed urban subdivisions and the requirement for a building permit to be issued for any structure. Physically, in informal areas there are few if any organized street patterns,[9] no public space reserves, and little or no land for public services such as schools, health clinics, or youth centers. Streets are commonly very narrow (two to four meters wide), except where canals and other public rights of way allow for the creation of main streets. Land parcels are generally small, averaging 80–150 square meters. Buildings have no side or back setbacks, and the whole parcel of land is built upon, except for narrow light- and air-shafts. Since there is no construction licensing, there is no restriction on building heights and this results, over time, in quite high net-population densities that can easily exceed one thousand persons per hectare. These physical features of informal areas allow for reasonably accurate delineations of them using high-resolution satellite imagery.

Using this definition of informal areas, what is the current magnitude of the informal city in terms of its population and area? Table 3.1 in Chapter 3 shows that in 2009, it can be conservatively estimated that a full 63.6 percent of Greater Cairo's population of 17.3 million inhabitants lived in informal areas. This equals eleven million persons. Of this total, about 7.15 million persons lived in the main agglomeration or 'Cairo proper' and another 3.84 million lived in peri-urban Cairo, that is, those mainly rural parts of Giza and Qalyubiya governorates that are contained within the Greater Cairo region. The informal city represents a much smaller portion of built-up Greater Cairo in square-kilometer terms, since population densities in these mostly compact areas are quite high and there are few nonresidential urban land uses to be found in them. It can be calculated that in 2008, informal areas, including those in peri-urban Cairo, extended over 205 square kilometers, which is 39 percent of Greater Cairo's built-up area of 529 square kilometers (excluding the modern desert developments).[10] Were the area of desert Cairo to be added to the calculations of what constitutes Greater Cairo, we would find that in 2008 the informal city, with 63 percent of the population, represented less than 17 percent of the total surface area of the metropolis!

Many maps delineating informal areas in parts of Greater Cairo have by now been produced, but it is symptomatic of the lack of knowledge of informality that the first known attempt only appeared in 1987, even though by then 'informal settlements' in the metropolis had already been amply discussed. This map, a series of very rough and schematic sketches of informal areas around Cairo, appeared in a book on informal areas written by Galila El Kadi.[11] Another map, showing informal areas in more detail, was prepared by the author in 1989 at the request of Frank Shorter, to accompany his article "Cairo's Great Leap Forward."[12] The map was hardly scientific and had to rely on old topographical maps and personal knowledge. The next cartographic exercise on Cairo's informal areas, in 1997, was also made by the author, this time for the ILD.[13] Again, this was hardly precise. It could be said that the first proper attempt was made by the author in 2000, again for ILD, in which not only were informal areas by their various typologies delineated on a map, but the areas and populations of these informal areas were estimated, based on the detailed *shiyakha* results of the 1996 Census.[14] Following this, in 2002 Eric Denis and Marion Séjourné produced a cartographic analysis that also delineated the extent of informal areas and added, for the first time, estimates of the growth of informal populations and areas based on comparisons of satellite images between 1993 and 1999.[15] Since then, a number of other general maps of informal areas have been produced, for example a map prepared by the Wilson Center in 2005, and also a composite map produced by Deutsche Gesellschaft für Technische Zusammenarbeit GmbH (GTZ) in 2009.[16] GOPP has recently produced several planning maps, which, while demarcating some informal areas within Greater Cairo, do not attempt to create a comprehensive map or to estimate seriously the populations of informal areas.[17]

The point of recalling this cartographic history is to show that knowledge of Cairo's informal areas, at least in mapping terms, has been restricted to modest efforts. However, there is a remarkable congruence among all the maps mentioned above of where informal areas in Greater Cairo can be found. No government agency has tried to undertake any serious spatial or demographic analysis of Cairo's informality, in spite of numerous, repeated, and still conflicting lists of the names of informal areas produced by GOPP, Information Decision Support Center (IDSC), and the Ministry of Local Development.[18]

Types of Informal Areas in Greater Cairo

The nature and characteristics of informal housing can be best understood by reference to the history of the phenomenon, which also helps explain the different subtypes and subareas. The best effort to date at classifying Cairo's informal areas can be found in the 2000 study of informal areas produced for the ILD.[19] Basically, the study showed that in Greater Cairo the vast majority, or roughly 83 percent, of informal settlements, measured by their areas, were found to be developed on what had been privately held agricultural land. Informal occupancy of state-owned desert lands was limited to about 10 percent of the total, and the remaining 7 percent of informal settlements were developed on agricultural reclamation land nominally controlled by the state. An updated version of this map is presented in Map 4.1. It should be noted that delineating informal areas can be challenging cartographically, since although there are some huge informal agglomerations that are easily bounded, there is in many other districts a confusing jumble of informal strips and blocks

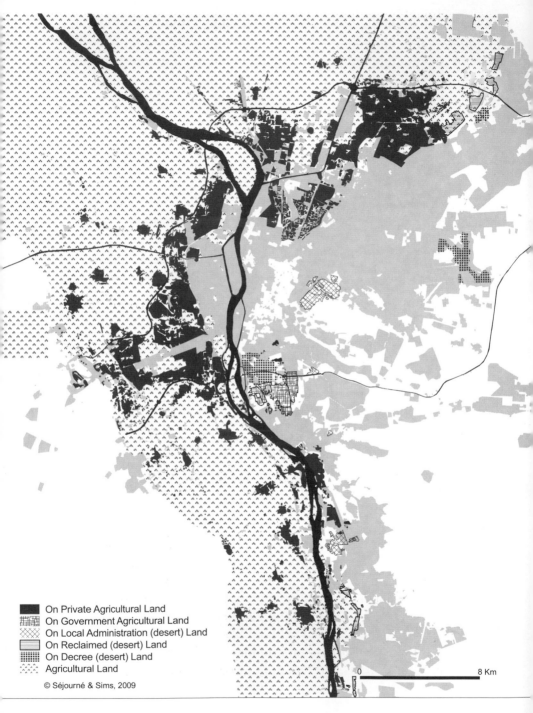

Map 4.1. Informal areas of Greater Cairo by typology in 2000.

On Private Agricultural Land
On Government Agricultural Land
On Local Administration (desert) Land
On Reclaimed (desert) Land
On Decree (desert) Land
Agricultural Land

© Séjourné & Sims, 2009

0   8 Km

Figure 4.1. Informal housing construction off the Ring Road in al-Baragil, 2001. Note the almost universal use of reinforced concrete frames and slab floors, with red-brick infill walls. (Photograph by David Sims.)

interspersed with agricultural parcels, factories, and other nonresidential land uses, blocks of public housing, and even some formal subdivisions.

Within each of these three main typologies lie many variations. Perhaps the most important variations are temporal. All informal areas began small, usually adjacent to existing agglomerations, factories, or villages, and they expanded incrementally and horizontally, and at the same time slowly densified. The original plots might be further subdivided and built on, other buildings would be built to 'infill' the remaining vacant lots, and buildings themselves would be progressively extended vertically as floors and rooms were added. Slowly, shops and other businesses would appear, and very slowly, basic infrastructure would be added. Thus a recently developed informal area may appear very rough, sparsely settled, and devoid of services, whereas a mature area several decades old may seem to be completely different, a very dense and vibrant area with relatively good utilities coverage and even some paved streets.

The Quality and Types of Informal Buildings
There is a misconception held by many Egyptian professionals, especially engineers, that informal housing is haphazardly constructed and

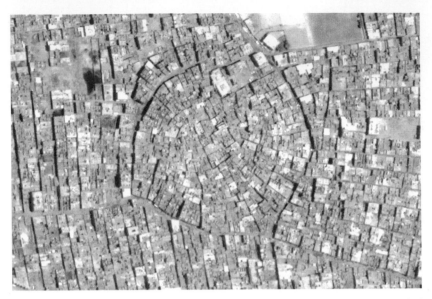

Figure 4.2. Village-style informal buildings (inside old village boundary) surrounded by later classic informal development, al-Bashtil, Giza. (Image dated 2008, ©2010 DigitalGlobe / ©2009 GOOGLE.)

liable to collapse. However, such precarious housing is almost unknown in informal areas. Since informal housing is overwhelmingly owner-built without use of formal contractors, it is in the owner's own best interest to ensure that care is taken in construction. In fact, one of the main features of informal housing construction is its high structural quality, reflecting the substantial financial resources and tremendous efforts that owners devote to these buildings. It is worth noting that in the 1992 earthquake in Cairo, practically all building collapses and the resulting fatalities occurred *not* in informal areas, but either in dilapidated historic parts of the city or in formal areas such as Heliopolis and Madinat Nasr, where apartment blocks had been constructed by (sometimes) unscrupulous developers and contractors.

At the risk of overgeneralization, it is possible to construct a list of informal housing types or categories as they existed in 2009.

First, there are the older, village-style informal structures, often dating back to the 1950s and 1960s. Typically, buildings of two to four floors were constructed, usually in stages, with load-bearing masonry walls and either slab concrete or wood floors. This type can often be found in, or next to, what had been villages on the agricultural fringes of towns that

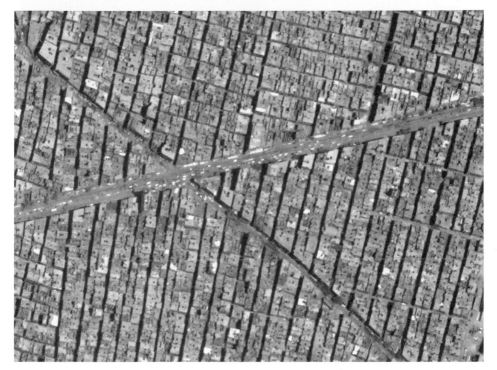

Figure 4.3. Recent classic informal buildings, part of al-Munira al-Gharbiya. (Image dated 2008, ©2010 DigitalGlobe / ©2009 GOOGLE.)

Figure 4.4. Recent classic informal buildings in Khusus, next to the Ring Road. (Image dated 2008, ©2010 DigitalGlobe / ©2009 GOOGLE.)

Figure 4.5. New one-off tower blocks in Bulaq al-Dakrur, off Feisal Street, 2009. (Photograph by David Sims.)

Figure 4.6. One-off tower blocks on fringe of Bulaq al-Dakrur, 2009. (Photograph by David Sims.)

Figure 4.7. Concentration of recent informal one-off tower buildings (identifiable by shadows) in Dar al-Salam. (Image dated 2008, ©2010 DigitalGlobe / ©2009 GOOGLE.)

have subsequently either expanded into larger informal agglomerations or have been engulfed by horizontal informal expansion. To a limited extent they are still being constructed in Cairo's peri-urban areas. Housing units in this category are generally small apartments, although some individual houses were built.

Second, there is what could be termed classic informal housing, and from the 1970s to the present, this type dominates. Buildings of this type are built with reinforced concrete foundations, frames, and floor slabs, with masonry (usually red brick) wall infill. Rule of thumb norms typically allow for ground plus five floors. Building footprints are normally 75–125 square meters, with one or two small apartments per floor (usually ranging from forty to eighty square meters per unit). Construction is almost always in stages, with floors being added as finances permit. Some owners will continue to add floors above the standard ground-plus-five if the building, usually overdesigned, can support them. Such

Figure 4.8. Evolution of different types of informal housing in 'Izbit Bikhit (Manshiyat Nasir), 2001. Note the single-story rubble-walled house with wood roofing in the foreground, the load-bearing masonry-walled building with concrete slab floors to the right, and finally the reinforced concrete frame building to the left. (Photograph by David Sims.)

higher buildings are becoming more common in areas under intense development pressures.

Finally, there is the recent phenomenon of speculative one-off towers, which began to appear in the late 1990s, especially dotting well-located inner fringe areas of Cairo. These buildings tend to have larger foot-prints (250 to 450 square meters), larger apartments, and more apartments per floor. Heights can reach fifteen floors. What makes this type unique is that the entire building is completed in a single stage, and apartment units are then put on the market for sale or rental. It is understood that groups of relatives or neighbors, mostly from Upper Egypt, pool their financial resources to rapidly construct and rapidly sell off units, realizing quick profits. In many cases the building owner some-how obtains a building permit or otherwise gains acquiescence from local authorities to allow construction. These buildings have become very visible parts of the informal landscape because of their height and their plastered and brightly painted exteriors. They are an indication that, in terms of Cairo's housing markets, there is a strong demand from certain segments of the lower- and middle-classes for substantial housing units that are well-located within the city, despite their situation in decidedly *'ashwa'i* areas. In fact, the housing units produced by this 'one-off tower' phenomenon in informal areas are competing very successfully on the market with recent attempts to introduce smaller, more affordable apartments in the new towns.

These three main types of informal construction are found in all informal areas of Cairo. However, in formerly desert sites such as Manshiyat Nasir and 'Izbit al-Haggana, one can still find quite humble single-story buildings constructed of rubble or brick and roofed in wood. Most of these buildings have either been replaced with the more substantial structures—or else, following what was in vogue in the 1970s, reinforced concrete columns were placed along the exterior of the building to support additional floors.

Quality of and Amenities in Informal Neighborhoods

Although all new informal settlements start off without any public infrastructure or social services, as an area matures and the number of its inhabitants grows, needs become articulated and, in most cases, utility authorities slowly begin to provide basic services. Metered electricity is usually the first network to arrive. Potable water networks serving individual buildings are usually next. Sewers, the most expensive of infrastructure services, are slowly and sometimes arbitrarily extended, with building owners required to pay hefty fees for individual connections.[20] Finally, in formerly agricultural areas, canals are filled in, and main roads created and sometimes paved. Schools and other social facilities are problematic since they require public land sites, which are extremely scarce. Overall, the provision of services to an area may take decades and will depend in large part on the proximity to existing utilities mains, the availability of state land parcels for public facilities, and also on the pressures a community can exert on local politicians.

Statistically at least, infrastructure service levels in Cairo's informal areas are quite good and not far from citywide averages. For example, the 2006 Census recorded near universal water, electricity, and sewerage connections for individual households in Cairo Governorate as a whole, with over 98 percent coverage for all three infrastructure services. The same near-universal coverage was reported in Cairo's main *aqsam* or informal districts, with over 97 percent coverage for all three. The same conclusion can be derived from the 2008 HSUE, which was able to distinguish between formal and informal areas. For urban Egypt as a whole, 98.3 percent of households in formal areas had water faucets within the housing unit, compared to 95.1 percent in informal areas. And in formal areas 95.0 percent of housing units were connected to sewers, compared to 87.5 percent in informal areas.[21]

Today the main problem with utilities and other services in Cairo's informal areas is that as populations increase, these services quickly become overburdened; over time such services can reach a crisis point. In many mature informal areas, water, power, and sewerage networks were extended rather haphazardly in the 1970s and 1980s, and they now must function for several times the original design populations. The results are voltage and water pressure drops, power and water cuts, and blocked and overflowing sewers. Similarly, public primary and secondary schools built at the same period in *'ashwa'i* areas must now cater to armies of kids, with the number of students per classroom frequently exceeding eighty pupils, even with double shifts.[22]

Roads and lanes in Cairo's informal areas are mostly in a deplorable state, although in some areas there are exceptions. Most main roads, if ever paved, have long ago reverted to dust and rubble, and smaller lanes were almost never paved. The 2008 HSUE reported that, for all of Greater Cairo proper, only 34 percent of residential buildings fronted on paved streets in good condition. For peri-urban Greater Cairo, the same figure was a pathetic 6 percent. And these figures relate to *both* formal and informal neighborhoods, so one can imagine what the percentages for informal areas alone might be.

Finally, although all residential areas of Greater Cairo are supposed to be served by garbage collectors and street cleaners, the state of solid waste management in the metropolis is of variable quality, even at the best of times. Upper-income areas are relatively well served, but in informal areas garbage collection is limited to metal bins, placed on main thoroughfares, which are only irregularly emptied. A common sight is a sea of garbage surrounding them. The situation is even worse in informal settlements on the agricultural fringes, where there is virtually no garbage collection at all. In these neighborhoods irrigation channels become the preferred locations for dumping, and it is not uncommon to see canals so clogged with accumulated rubbish that they appear to be solid ground.

In effect, the quality and levels of infrastructure and public services vary greatly from one informal area to another. As mentioned above, it is the older, more mature areas that tend to be better served. Also to generalize, 'ashwa'i areas that are found within established urban districts tend to be of higher quality than those located within village clusters and extensions into agricultural land. Thus informal areas found in the peri-urban frontier in Giza and Qalyubiya Governorates tend to suffer more. But in all informal areas public amenities could be vastly improved, and it is simply government neglect, and lack of sufficient investment in upgrading or extending networks and in building, equipping, renovating, and maintaining public facilities, which are to blame.

Slums: What Slums?

Contrary to common perceptions, there are practically no parts of the informal city in Cairo that exhibit the characteristics of the stereotypical 'Third World slum'—hutments, shantytowns, or *bidonvilles*. Only in small pockets, usually on public rights of way or in just-occupied desert areas, does one find the type of precarious construction that evokes the images of jerry-built slums that are standard in many parts of the developing world. As described in a case study on Cairo in the 2003 UN Habitat Report on slums, these areas can be called 'deteriorated slum pockets,' and they house only a tiny fraction, probably not exceeding one or two percent, of Greater Cairo's inhabitants. Furthermore, these slum pockets are very rarely to be found in Cairo's informal areas. They are mostly restricted to inner-city districts developed in the nineteenth and early twentieth centuries, such as parts of Misr al-Qadima, Hikr Sakakini in al-Wayli District, the huts in 'Ain al-Sira behind the leather tanneries, and those behind the old wholesale market in Rod al-Farag, and so on. "In every case the existence of these pockets is due to precarious land tenure situations which put in doubt the wisdom of serious housing investments, resulting in a very precarious type of housing which in turn attracted very poor families seeking the cheapest possible housing solutions."[23] Most of these areas are slated for removal and the resettlement of inhabitants, and some have already been converted to parks. It is these very rare degraded areas that are the preferred locations for films that claim to take place in 'ashwa'i areas.

Figure 4.9. Slum pocket next to railway line behind former Rod al-Farag wholesale market, 2003. (Photograph by David Sims.)

There are very poor living conditions in deteriorated buildings in some parts of historic Cairo, such as in al-Darb al-Ahmar and al-Gamaliya, but these are mainly isolated structures within areas that are vibrant and can hardly be called slums. In addition, in some informal areas, especially in Manshiyat Nasir and 'Izbit Khayrallah, people have built not only shacks but substantial houses, both above and below cliffs that present serious dangers. Such dangers became only too apparent following the collapse of limestone cliffs in September 2008 in Duweiqa/'Izbit Bikhit, which resulted in at least 120 deaths. Following this disaster the government established a national fund, which will remove and resettle all inhabitants in these dangerous areas.[24]

Another kind of slum area found in parts of Cairo, also very marginal, are made up of small, one- to three-room units of *masakin iwa'* (emergency housing) built by the government at various times to house welfare cases and those resettled from unsafe buildings. These areas also attracted poor squatters, who constructed shacks alongside, and sometimes on top of, this emergency housing. The main concentrations are found in Duweiqa,

Figure 4.10. Tight living in old *raba'* type housing in 'Izbit Bikhit (Manshiyat Nasir), 2001. Six families in six rooms with narrow central court and only one toilet. (Photograph by David Sims.)

a part of Manshiyat Nasir, and in Telal Zeinhoum. The Telal Zeinhoum area has already been completely redeveloped to a very high standard, and the Duweiqa emergency housing is slated for removal.

Security of Tenure in Informal Areas

The international literature on urban development and slums is full of discussions on security of tenure, since lack of security and fear of arbitrary eviction not only discourage investment in housing improvement but constitute the deprivation of a basic human right. The tenure insecurity facing the urban poor in such places as Addis Ababa, Sao Paulo, Mumbai, Bangkok, and Manila is rightly high on the agendas of international agencies and certain academics.[25] However, as with many facets of urban life, the situation in Cairo's informal areas simply does not conform to standard international wisdom. In fact, as carefully set out in an article published in

2002, in Cairo's informal areas the security of building owners, apartment owners, and apartment renters is remarkably good.[26] Protection against arbitrary eviction is very strong, mainly because the state maintains a policy of providing compensation or alternative accommodation for affected families, regardless of their documented property claims or lack of them. Clearing large informal areas for redevelopment is thus a very expensive undertaking for a chronically cash-poor government. And the threat of public disturbances and unrest makes local authorities reluctant to undertake removals without the agreement of citizens.[27] There have been forced removals from time to time in Cairo, but only on a very limited scale and almost never in large informal areas.[28] However, during the resettlement of inhabitants into new government apartments as part of clearances, abuses have been known to occur because of incompetence on the part of authorities, fraud on the part of citizens, or both.[29]

Even though practically *no* property owners in informal areas have clear, registered title to their plots of land, this does not at all limit their ability to sell properties at full market values through a number of quasi-legal and informal means, as will be explained in Chapter 5. This translates into a high level of security to invest, as evidenced by the massive and growing amounts of construction found in Greater Cairo's informal areas, even in districts that are clearly occupying state-owned land. Of course, property investments may be risky on the fringes of new informal settlements on state land, especially if the encroachments are on land that the government (or powerful private interests) perceives as having considerable value. But these risks are well known, and occupants are unlikely to make substantial investments until the area consolidates and there is a critical mass of population whose removal involves such a degree of cost, hassle, and political opposition as to make local authorities simply give up.

It should be added that security of tenure is also good for rental of housing units in informal areas. Those who rent, both under the old rent-control system and the new (post-1996) rent law contracts are rarely evicted by landlords. In cases of dispute, both the courts and local police invariably take the side of the tenant, even if there is no written rental contract. In addition, there is a deeply ingrained societal aversion to tossing a family out onto the street. This is not to say that evictions instigated by greedy landlords never take place, but they are rare, especially in informal settlements, where the sense of community is strong.

Who Are the Residents in Informal Areas?

Since those who live in informal areas constitute almost two-thirds of the current population of Greater Cairo, it does not require great mathematical powers to surmise that the average *'ashwa'i* inhabitant does not differ much from the norm for the city as a whole. But in spite of this fact, it is surprising how the misconception persists that informal settlements are zones of unrelieved poverty and misery. Census statistics and a number of socioeconomic studies show that most informal areas of Cairo contain households with a wide range of incomes and whose aggregate livelihood indicators are the same as, or not much lower than, averages for Greater Cairo. This was borne out in 2008 from a large random household survey of Greater Cairo proper, in which almost half of families said they lived in *'ashwa'i* areas. Although the median reported household income was higher in formal areas than in informal areas, and in formal areas there were higher representations of the rich (especially in the highest national urban income quintile, which contained almost 40 percent of Greater Cairo's formal households), there was a remarkable range of incomes in informal areas. In fact, the distribution of informal households by income quintiles in Greater Cairo proper was almost exactly the same as for urban Egypt as a whole.[30] Household income statistics were generated by the 2008 study for peri-urban areas of Greater Cairo, and these results also showed a wide range of incomes among families living in informal areas, although there was a higher representation in the lower income quintiles compared to national averages.[31] Parenthetically, these income statistics show that regardless of whether they live in formal or informal areas, the inhabitants of peri-urban areas of Greater Cairo are significantly poorer than those in Greater Cairo proper.

In other words, any single informal area is likely to contain a heterogeneous mix of inhabitants with a wide range of incomes. This heterogeneity is due to largely to an area's development over time. Many families built or acquired their units in informal areas in the 1970s with money from Gulf remittances, but circumstances did not improve and they now live in a kind of impoverished gentility. Many others, that is, those renting before 1996, are sitting tenants who enjoy near-perpetual fixed rent contracts. Others are building owners who make little rent from existing tenants and try to add more floors to improve their own family finances. Still others are proprietors of small businesses that have, over time, prospered—or not. In other words, every informal area exhibits both heterogeneity and a certain uniqueness due to historic chance.

Another misconception is that the residents of informal areas are composed of large families with lots of children, and that illiteracy is rife. Against this, the census of 2006 shows that the average household size for Cairo Governorate was 3.8 persons, while for the large informal areas of al-Basatin, al-Matariya, and Manshiyat Nasir, average household sizes were nearly the same, at 4.0, 3.8, and 3.9 persons respectively. And whereas for Cairo Governorate as a whole, 17.1 percent of inhabitants were under the age of ten, in the same three informal areas the percentages under the age of ten were only slightly higher at 19.6, 17.6, and 22.3 respectively. Also, whereas illiteracy was reported at 18.3 percent for Cairo Governorate as a whole, in the same three informal areas illiteracy rates were 20.4, 18.1, and 46.1 percent respectively.[32]

In addition, Cairo's informal areas are home to many micro-, small-and even medium- size enterprises, a vast sector that generates most urban employment opportunities throughout Egypt as a whole. Even in Manshiyat Nasir, one of the poorest informal areas in Egypt, one finds a mix of typical breadwinners, lower-ranking government employees, professionals, tradesmen, contractors, and so on, alongside some extreme hardship cases who live "*ala bab Allah*" (at God's gate). As was uncovered in a study carried out in 2001, over 55 percent of working inhabitants of Manshiyat Nasir found their livelihoods within the area itself.[33]

Current Dynamics of Informal Development on Agricultural Land

Agricultural land on the Nile flood plain is overwhelmingly held as private freehold property, usually in very small land holdings. On this land, which bounds the Cairo agglomeration on three sides, at least 80 percent of all informal development has taken place in the past, almost all ongoing informal development is now occurring, and practically all future informal expansion can be expected. The underlying causes of this phenomenon, which are embedded in the modern history of Cairo's growth and in Egypt's policies of urban development, have been sketched out in the preceding chapter. Here the focus is on identifying the specific factors that govern the dynamics of this type of informality as it operates today.

The patterns of irrigated agriculture around Cairo lend themselves to easy subdivision for building purposes. Agricultural holdings are very fragmented. They are more or less rectangular, and it is common for

Figure 4.11. Informal development by converted agricultural strips in al-Bashtil, Giza. (Image dated 2008, ©2010 DigitalGlobe / ©2009 GOOGLE.)

individual agricultural parcels to be as small as one *qirat* (175 square meters). Thus, subdivision is straightforward and the decision to sell/ subdivide can be made by a single owner. Multiples of holdings are normally arranged in *ahwad* (small irrigated agricultural plots), with strips separated by small irrigation channels. These channels become converted to the access lanes upon subdivision for building purposes. Larger irrigation canals and drains bound multiples of *ahwad*, and these have side reservations for paths and for canal cleaning. As development in an area intensifies, these are eventually filled in and become the main streets in an area.

Construction on agricultural land is guided by well-established technologies. Rule-of-thumb standards guide the design of foundations and structural elements, at least for the average modest building. Furthermore, temporary water and wastewater solutions can be found on-site, at least until networks are eventually extended to an inhabited area. Shallow tube wells are installed to tap the high groundwater, and *bayarat* (soakaway pits) are constructed to receive domestic sewage.

Even though irrigated agricultural land around Cairo is highly productive, its market value as building land is always many times higher, and this creates an almost irresistible incentive for farmers to convert their holdings if at all possible. A main determinant of prices for building land is the accessibility of the plot from existing settlements (with their services and economic life) and existing road networks that provide the link to the metropolitan economy. Plots on main roads always sell at a premium. Due to greater government restrictions on informal development in the last decade, another determinant of prices has become what can be called critical mass or 'safety in numbers,' whereby vacant plots within already-developing areas, and those adjacent to existing buildings, command higher prices because construction on them is less likely to be noticed by the authorities.

In most cases, subdivision and sale of agricultural land parcels for construction involves a straightforward transaction between the farmer-owner and end-purchaser, for which simple *'urfi* sales contracts are drawn up. A local *simsar* (informal real estate broker), who works on commission may be involved, as well a local sheikh or lawyer, who draws up the contract. Personal acquaintance and community-sanctioned trust are the main guarantees of these sale transactions. In some areas it is understood that middlemen, sometimes calling themselves land subdivision companies, will buy up larger parcels from farmers (and absentee landlords in a few cases) and resell them to individual builders.

It is important to realize that for the most part it is the individual or extended family that carries out residential construction. These owner-builders incorporate all the roles personally: they decide on a design, finance construction, purchase materials, contract labor, and dispose of units.[34] In these operations they rely on personal contacts and trust, and usually avoid formal written arrangements. Not only does this process reduce costs to a minimum: it ensures that the quality of construction is guaranteed by the owner-builders who have supervised it, and whose own families and relatives will in most cases be the end users. Building in stages is the key. Rooms and floors and finishings are added as finances permit. The negative side of this progressivity is that skeletal buildings and unfinished units are very common, especially in newer areas.[35]

Table 4.1: Large informal agglomerations in Greater Cairo (2006)

Name of Agglomeration	Estimated 2006 Population	Distance from City Center (km)	Area (km²)	Density (persons per hectare)
Imbaba-Waraq	851,000	6.5	9.19	920
Bulaq al-Dakrur	694,000	7.5	13.24	524
al-'Umraniya	690,000	9.8	9.39	735
al-Basatin/Dar al-Salam	805,000	9.1	6.80	1,183
Manshiyat Nasir*	451,000	4.2	2.96	1,925
al-Marg/Khusus	718,000	7.2	14.27	503
Shubra al-Khayma	945,000	9.0	13.87	681

*Manshiyat Nasir's population is derived from demographic estimates of the GTZ "Manshiet Nasser Guide Plan" (Existing Situation Volume, section 5, p. 4) rather than the census since there is a serious definitional problem with the *shiyakha* of al-Mahagar in the census and a resulting undercounting.

In older informal areas on agricultural land, most housing was built decades ago. These are now quite stable residential areas with only incremental building and occasional changeover of occupancy—much of which is among members of extended families or relatives. In these cases, informal rental or ownership tenure prevails. In newer areas and in new buildings in older areas, units may be put on the market either as *tamlik* (freehold ownership) or as time-bound rentals with substantial advance payments. It is understood that the market works quite well, with buyers and sellers meeting through informal networks and personal contacts. The newer, speculative tower blocks may advertise units with signs, but this is as far as media are employed. (See also Chapter 5 for a discussion of how housing markets in Greater Cairo operate.)

Current Informal Development on Desert Land

In the past, a few large areas of Cairo's desert were settled informally—mainly Manshiyat Nasir, 'Izbit al-Haggana, and the Fustat plateau—as have many other smaller areas and pockets on the desert fringes, which together represent roughly 10 percent by surface area of all informal areas around Cairo. The process of informal desert encroachment by individuals was a fascinating one, what with initial toehold settlements, shadow

Figure 4.12. Recent informal development on hillsides in Wadi Pharaon (Manshiyat Nasir, 2002). (Photograph by David Sims.)

land-markets, manipulation of patronage and police power, and the very important concept of critical mass, both to avoid demolition and also to attract the eventual delivery of at least some basic services.

Another fascinating aspect of informal development on state desert land is how urban fabrics are created. Streets, lanes, and building layouts are determined 'organically' over time through negotiation among settlers, the operations of informal land markets, and the common need for access and circulation. Obviously, the government has little or no say in the matter. The resulting local neighborhood patterns are remarkably reminiscent of, and even indistinguishable from, medieval urban fabrics in Cairo (as well as in other Middle Eastern cities). Figure 4.13 demonstrates this by comparing a satellite image of a medieval Cairo neighborhood dating from the eleventh century with that of a very recent informal neighborhood of Cairo settled in the 1980s on state desert land.

Today, opportunities for creating new informal settlements or expanding existing ones are practically nil around Greater Cairo. There is simply no more desert land that is easily accessible and does not already have a public enterprise, military, or other formal institutional claim on it. Furthermore, the more remote desert lands anywhere near Cairo are under

Figure 4.13. Contrasting urban fabrics over nine hundred years. *Top*: the Bab al-Wazir area of historic Cairo (developed in the eleventh century); *bottom*: Fustat Plateau area (developed in the 1980s).

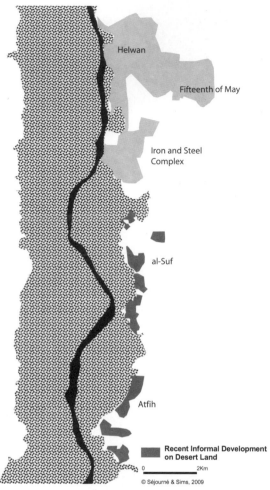

Map 4.2. Recent informal development on desert land in the al-Suf and 'Atfih areas.

the authority of the MHUUD or other state agencies, and these lands are now jealously protected against encroachment. (See Chapter 6 for a description of the new towns around Greater Cairo.)

Can it be said that the informal development of the desert around Greater Cairo has completely halted? To a large degree the answer is yes. However, in the desert verges south of Helwan, in al-Suf, and almost as far as 'Atfih, where there are existing rural settlements and some incipient agricultural land reclamation projects, informal encroachment and consolidation continues. (See Map 4.2.) These areas may be as much as twelve to thirty kilometers from Helwan and thirty-five to fifty-four kilometers from the center of the metropolis, but the attractions of cheap land for construction and for informal land speculation are substantial. Luckily for those investing in these areas, there is little or no development interest, at least so far, on the part of government or private developers. Using Google Earth images and making assumptions about normative densities, it is possible to calculate that the population of these strung-out informal settlements along the desert fringes south of Cairo may already have reached 200,000 inhabitants, and the settlements are definitely still growing.

Means of Financing Informal Housing

The production of 'classic' informal housing is a progressive and quite drawn-out affair, the pace of which normally relies on an extended family's ability to save and otherwise mobilize and pool financial resources.

The first step is to purchase vacant land. With modest parcels easily fetching in excess of LE500 per square meter today, an upfront payment will require marshalling, say, LE40,000 to LE50,000. This is a very large sum, which may take years to accumulate. Then construction begins, usually with the ground floor which will require accumulating as much as LE20,000 to LE40,000, again a struggle which can take years. The additional floors (and rooms) similarly require further savings and conversion of other assets over years.

What are understood to be the main sources of such finance? Many observers consider the single most important source to be savings, especially savings generated by Egyptians working abroad. (At least in the 1970s and 1980s these remittances were the main sources of finance fueling the informal sector.) Other important sources include personal loans (usually without interest and usually from relatives) and from *gam'iyat* (informal revolving credit groups). The conversion of other family assets, such as the selling of agricultural land, animals, jewelry, and so on, is also common. Another method, perhaps becoming more and more important, is the sale or rent of parts of a building to finance its further vertical expansion. This last point helps explain how it is possible for simple extended families to produce over time multistory structures that represent hundreds of thousands of pounds in investment.

There is no recourse to formal financial services in the informal housing sector. Informal property cannot be used as collateral for bank loans, nor can such property be mortgaged under the nascent mortgage system in Egypt (since the properties have no registered titles), and personal bank loans carry high interest and may require onerous personal guarantees. In a recent study of informal construction in three areas of Greater Cairo, finance from bank loans was mentioned as a source in only between 2 and 4 percent of those interviewed.[36]

In the case of the one-off speculative towers, which are becoming more and more common in informal areas, little is known about their financing mechanisms. In fact, it is surprising that virtually no studies have been undertaken of these huge investments, which are starting to alter the skyline of parts of informal Cairo.

Advantages and Disadvantages of Informal Areas

At risk of overgeneralization, it can be said that the advantages of living in an informal area outweigh the disadvantages, at least for the mass of

Cairenes for whom the struggle for a decent livelihood is a daily challenge. First, what are the advantages? Probably the most important is that housing in informal areas is reasonably affordable, and that there is a very wide range of choice. The 2008 Housing Study of Urban Egypt revealed that over the previous five years families moved into units in informal areas under all kinds of tenure arrangements. The single most popular was rental under the New Rent Law (in 37 percent of cases), a significantly higher percentage than found in Egypt's formal urban areas. The median monthly rent for these informal units was only LE200 in Greater Cairo proper and LE170 in peri-urban Greater Cairo, and these are quite affordable rents by any measure.[37] In the same period another 30 percent of families acquired ownership of housing units in informal areas, and for these it is interesting to see that about half purchased the unit, another third constructed their own units, and one-quarter inherited or were gifted the unit.[38] Of those that purchased an informal unit in Greater Cairo proper, the median purchase price was only LE45,000, compared to LE100,000 per unit in formal urban areas, a very significant difference. (The average price per square meter for informal units was LE666 compared to LE1,114 in formal areas of Greater Cairo.)

Another set of advantages of living in informal areas in Greater Cairo can be collectively called 'social.' Due to the very vibrant, albeit mostly word-of-mouth housing markets found in every informal area, families can locate near to other family members, kin, friends, and even those coming from the same part of Egypt. (In all of Greater Cairo, the 2008 HSUE reported that 57 percent of housing units were found through relatives or friends and another 12 percent through neighbors. In informal areas these percentages are undoubtedly even higher.) These close neighborhood ties or 'social glue' have many advantages not normally found in formal Cairo and, parenthetically, hardly ever in the new towns around Cairo. As reported in a 2009 GTZ publication, in informal areas the proximity to relatives helps in times of crisis, in daily chores such as child minding, and in flows of information on jobs and business opportunities. Since everyone in a dense informal neighborhood is likely to know the others, crime is kept down and even the hassling of girls is diminished, at least when compared to the more anonymous formal parts of Cairo.[39]

Any sizable informal area that has been in existence for some years will have a full range of shopping opportunities as well as personal services, most of which are provided by establishments that are themselves informal. Stiff competition and the bargaining skills of consumers keep prices at low levels. It must be noted that the high-density neighborhoods are particularly attractive to entrepreneurs, since they offer both a large clientele and a pool of labor within a walkable radius. The dense character of urban settlement thus generates business opportunities, while in turn this enterprise phenomenon makes living in these areas attractive. Many jobs can be found for residents of an area, whether being employed in a retail store, in one of the wide range of workshops (carpentry, metal working, repair, and so on), or in a myriad of transport, construction, personal care, and even information technology activities. As pointed out previously, in larger informal areas it is common for as much as half of the workforce to be employed within the area itself. (The subject of Cairo's informal economy is taken up in Chapter 7.)

In most informal areas, particularly in the huge, inner urban areas of Greater Cairo such as al-Basatin, Bulaq al-Dakrur, Manshiyat Nasir, and Imbaba, both residents and workers enjoy relatively easy access to central Cairo and to other formal locations within the metropolis through a range of cheap public transport options, as described in Chapter 8. Even those living in far-flung peri-urban settlements are served by informal minibus lines.

So much for the advantages.[40] The disadvantages of living in one of Cairo's informal areas are many, and can be divided into two types: those that result from the informal, uncontrolled urbanization process itself, and those that are simply due to government neglect. In the former case, the main problem is that streets and lanes are narrow and that buildings are tall and take up the entire plot of land. This is the inevitable result of an urban system lacking even the most basic of controls for the public good, and as a consequence space is exploited for maximum private gain. This means both sun and air are blocked from houses and street spaces, and this lack of sufficient light and ventilation is found throughout informal areas (and becomes worse as an area matures and floors are added). Although builders in informal areas have shown genius in providing at least some air and light through ventilation shafts and stairwells, there is only so much they can do. Also, the narrow lanes in informal areas mean that in many cases emergency vehicles can hardly pass, parking is an eternal problem, and the tiniest public green space or even trees are hard to find. These are serious microenvironmental and circulation problems in informal areas, for which there are no easy solutions.[41]

Figures 4.14, 4.15, and 4.16 present floor plans of typical informal housing units built in the 1960s and 1970s. These are located in Zenin (Bulaq al-Dakrur), Imbaba, and Manshiyat Nasir. The floor plans show how owner-builders have struggled to create small but affordable units with sufficient light and air in tight situations, where adjacent buildings preclude the use of external windows.

Other problems with informal areas—and they are many—have to do with government incompetence, neglect, and a simple lack of budgetary allocations. One of the most glaring is the poor quality or insufficiency of basic services or both, particularly in terms of infrastructure, playgrounds, and educational facilities. These are population-serving services, and they are almost always insufficient in one way or another, especially given the huge and growing populations they must cater to.

Another problem is the very poor vehicular access into and out of some informal areas, where there are frequently only a couple of narrow choke points, which can take more than an hour for a vehicle to traverse, as is the case in Munira al-Gharbiya and in Bulaq al-Dakrur. Also, what main roads exist within informal areas will in most cases be totally congested and completely unpaved, with stiff competition for very limited space between private cars, minibuses, pickup trucks, *tuk-tuk*s, petty traders, overflowing trash receptacles, storefront displays, and amorphous accumulated rubble. The flow of traffic in these essential arteries is chaotic and any discipline must rely on the civic-mindedness of drivers themselves, something that is in very short supply. One will almost never see even a low-ranking traffic policeman in an informal area, and definitely one will never see a traffic police officer.

The Informal Development Process: Personal Relations and Negotiated Norms in the Shadows of Bureaucracy

Government control over informal areas and attempts to prohibit illegal construction have increased in the last fifteen years, at least in the fringe areas of Cairo where they are most visible. Around smaller towns and villages that are within the urban orb, such control is still relatively lax. This increased surveillance has not at all stopped informal residential construction, but it has generated newer modes of construction and additional actors in the process.

First, construction—at least of the first floor of a structure—must be done quickly. Also, building in open areas where construction is easily

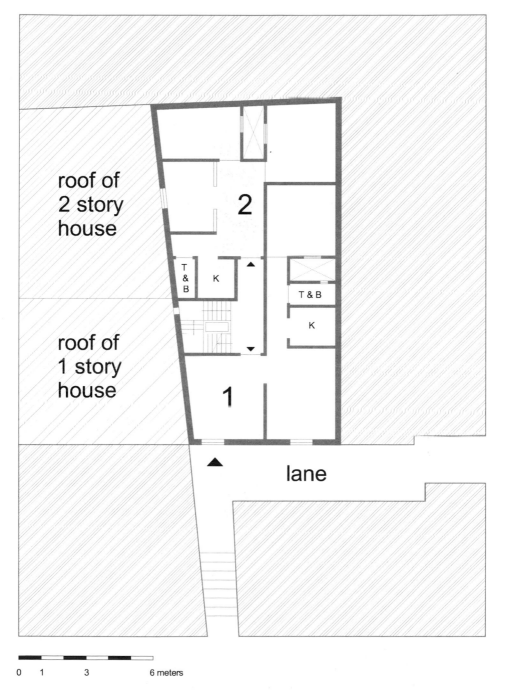

roof of
2 story
house

2

roof of
1 story
house

1

T
&
B

K

T & B

K

lane

0   1   3   6 meters

Figure 4.14. Two apartment units in an informal building in Manshiyat Nasir built in the early 1970s. Note it is blocked on three sides by neighboring buildings. Located on the third floor, unit 1 has a gross area of 52 square meters, unit 2 of 49 square meters (not counting air shafts).

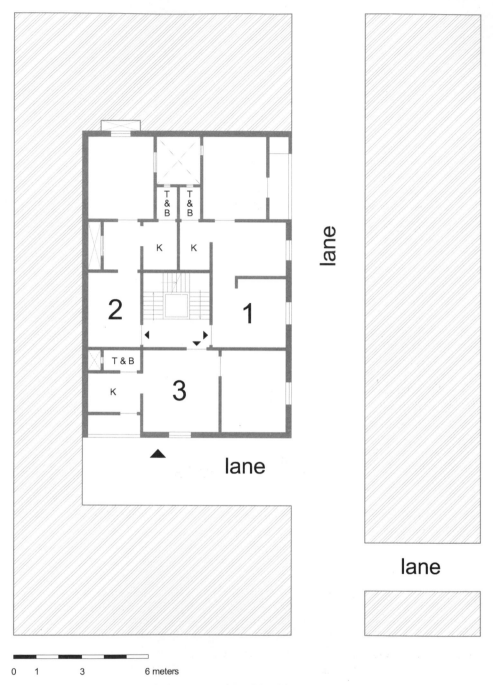

Figure 4.15. Three apartment units in an informal building in Zenin (Bulaq al-Dakrur), built in the late 1960s. Note it is blocked on three sides by neighboring buildings. Located on the second floor, unit 1 has a gross area of 41 square meters, unit 2 of 32 square meters, and unit 3 of 36 square meters (not counting air shafts).

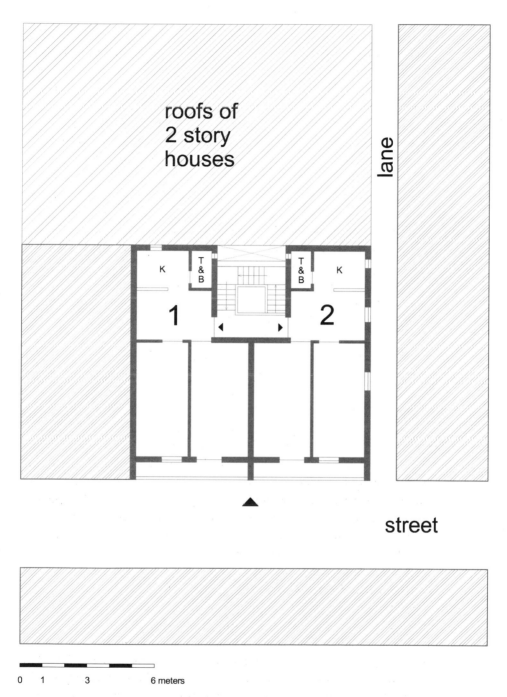

Figure 4.16. Two apartment units in an informal building in Imbaba (near Shari' al-Wahda), built in the early 1970s. Note it is blocked on three sides by neighboring buildings. Located on the fourth floor, both units have a gross area of 50 square meters (including balconies but not counting air shafts).

seen from main roads has become more difficult. In fact, local land prices put a premium on plots that are small, infill, and hidden within the built fabric. Second, there is a rising phenomenon of middlemen who specialize in overcoming and circumventing the control of government officials. These may be local lawyers or those who are called *muqawilin* (contractors) or *samasira* (agents). In a recent investigation of informal building processes in three neighborhoods of Cairo and Giza,[42] it was found that these middlemen were the primary organizers of construction in 37 to 41 percent of cases. These persons personally know the local officials from the *hayy* (urban administrative district), agricultural directorate, and/or utilities offices, and they know whom to ask for favors and how much a bribe will cost. Sometimes they may be elected officials in the *magalis* (local popular councils) or even members of parliament. They, especially the *muqawilin*, also have many tricks to avoid coming under the eye of control mechanisms. These may involve building on Friday and during the night, blocking access streets with vehicles, or even hiring local toughs to either prevent entry or create diversionary disturbances. Maneuvers may also involve building false walls to hide construction activity. They may also involve getting an official in the agricultural cooperative to declare the land unfit for agriculture, and other administrative chicanery, as well as the purchase of bogus permits.

It is not that such bribes, maneuvers, and subterfuges were unnecessary in previous stages of Cairo's informal development. But in an earlier age things were simpler, and it was usually the owner-builder himself who carried the burden. The upshot of this is that building an informal structure in sensitive areas today involves many more actors and has become much more expensive, which translates into higher prices for finished housing units, which in turn makes such informal development less affordable to those of limited income or modest family capital.

Cairo's Large Informal Areas

Up to now, we have talked about the informal city in the abstract sense, however diverse and heterogeneous. It is worthwhile to identify Cairo's most prominent and largest informal areas, each of which is a contiguous agglomeration or 'conurbation' of informal urbanization. The populations of these areas are estimated from the preliminary results of the 2006 Census at the census enumeration level (*shiyakha* or *qarya*),

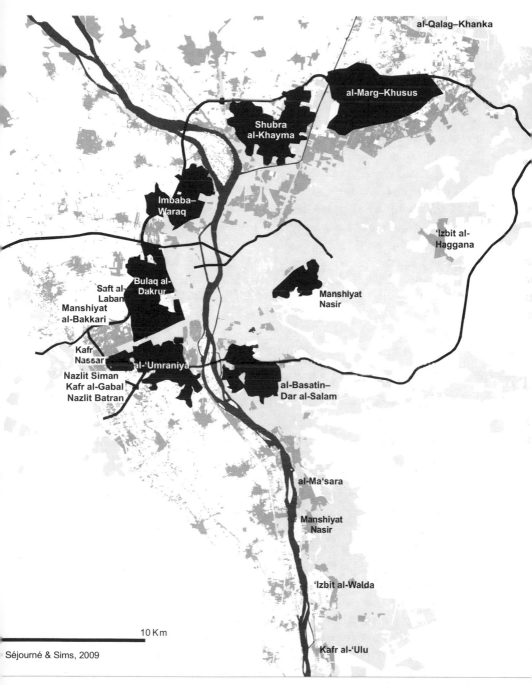

al-Qalag–Khanka

al-Marg–Khusus

Shubra al-Khayma

Imbaba–Waraq

'Izbit al-Haggana

Saft al-Laban

Bulaq al-Dakrur

Manshiyat al-Bakkari

Manshiyat Nasir

Kafr Nassar

Nazlit Siman
Kafr al-Gabal
Nazlit Batran

al-'Umraniya

al-Basatin–Dar al-Salam

al-Ma'sara

Manshiyat Nasir

'Izbit al-Walda

10 Km

Kafr al-'Ulu

Map 4.3. Large informal areas of Greater Cairo in 2008.

adjusted to exclude formal residential areas. The surface areas are also calculated, which allows estimates of residential densities expressed as persons per hectare.[43]

There are seven such large areas, all but one of which is now home to over 700,000 persons. Their locations within Greater Cairo are shown in map 4.3, and the details of each area are given in Table 4.1.

All together the 2006 populations of these seven areas totaled 5.3 million persons, or one-third of Greater Cairo's population at that time. As can be seen, they tend to form a ring or collar of inner fringe areas, quite near the epicenter of Cairo, varying from 4.2 to 9.8 kilometers' distance from Ramsis Square. The estimated residential densities range from 503 persons per hectare in al-Marg/Khusus to an extremely high 1,925 persons per hectare in Manshiyat Nasir. There is, as one might expect, an inverse correlation between density and distance from the city center. Even so, all of these areas can be considered as compact, dense, and containing a huge number of inhabitants. (It might be added that each of these informal areas is larger, in population terms, than any other city in Egypt except Alexandria. Also, each one of these areas, except Manshiyat Nasir, had populations in 2006 that equaled or exceeded the aggregate population of *all* the government's new towns in Egypt.) Some areas, especially Shubra al-Khayma, contain numerous factories and other nonresidential land uses, and all areas have quite vibrant local economies and are well integrated into the surrounding city precincts. In no sense are they 'no-go zones,' except perhaps for those of Cairo's paranoid upper classes. All seven areas are mature urban quarters, and population increases are now modest, in the range of 1.7 to 2.25 percent per year, considerably lower than rates in fringe areas of peri-urban Greater Cairo, where the average growth rate is 3.4 percent per year and where in some settlements annual growth rates exceed 6 percent.

These seven informal areas of Cairo are only the most prominent and best known. There are many other large informal agglomerations with populations well above 100,000 persons. The most important of these is the al-Qalag/al-Khanka area to the northeast, which is a coalescing conurbation with a very rapid population growth (in excess of 5.0 percent per year) whose 2006 informal population was at least 290,000 inhabitants.[44] If the Abu Za'bal area to the north were to be included, then this informal conurbation would today exceed 350,000 persons and will certainly top half a million by the next census in 2016.

Not to be forgotten are many other significant informal areas found within and around Cairo. These include, but are not limited to, the following: (1) the exploding village of Manshiyat al-Bakari in Giza, which alone had 108,000 inhabitants in 2006, and to which could be added some of the 180,000 inhabitants of adjacent Saft al-Laban and Kafrat Nasar; (2) the urbanized villages of Nazlat al-Batran, Nazlat al-Samman, and Kafrat al-Gabal near the Pyramids, which together had a population of 109,000 inhabitants in 2006; (3) the informal clusters in al-Ma'sara, which had a combined 2006 population in excess of 210,000 persons; (4) the villages and informal neighborhoods around Helwan including 'Izbit al-Walda and 'Arab al-Walda, Arab Ghunaym, and Manshiyat Nasir (not to be confused with the much larger Manshiyat Nasir located on Map 4.3), which collectively contained at least 220,000 inhabitants in 2006; and (5) the large informal settlement of 'Izbit al-Haggana in Madinat Nasr whose current population is probably in the range of 100,000 to 200,000 persons.[45]

Government Approaches to the Informality Phenomenon

When informal areas began to appear in the 1960s and expand in the 1970s there was little interest from either government or academics in what was at first a very marginal and not very visible phenomenon. In the late 1970s uncontrolled urban expansion on the Nile Valley's limited agricultural land became an issue, and this provoked a series of decrees and laws aimed at prohibiting further encroachments by informal housing. These had little effect, and in the 1980s and 1990s further attempts were made to legislate away the informal phenomenon, culminating in 1996 with the promulgation of two presidential decrees stipulating that *any* new construction on agricultural land and *any* urban construction without a valid building permit would be severely punished through military courts. These stern decrees had a temporary dampening effect, but the vertical and horizontal expansion of informal settlements soon resumed in Greater Cairo, albeit with higher 'extralegal transaction costs, that is, bribes. The military decrees themselves were revoked in 2005.

From time to time Cairo's local administrations have also attempted to discourage informal building by denying water, sewerage, and electricity connections to those who do not have building permits or otherwise cannot prove a building's legality. This has caused certain hardships, but usually connections will eventually be provided quietly, often encouraged by small bribes. And the local administrations themselves frequently reverse their prohibitory decisions for political expediency. As recently as August 2006, the Governor of Cairo announced that any building in violation constructed before June 2006 would be allowed to have utilities connections "as a temporary measure." In other words, this decree allowed virtually all buildings in Cairo Governorate to be connected up, previous banning orders notwithstanding.[46]

Ever since the informal urbanization phenomenon became visible in Greater Cairo, it came to be recognized in some circles that simple prohibition was insufficient and that the state should offer alternatives to informal housing expansion on agricultural land. Although there has been much policy talk about attracting the informal dynamic and channeling it out into the desert, and although there have been a number of schemes proposed and even designed with donor support, in or around Greater Cairo there have been virtually no successful pilot projects to date.[47]

In effect, since the 1990s the state has only begun to address the issue of informal settlements in Greater Cairo after the fact, and *in situ* urban upgrading of informal areas has become the main preoccupation of government as well as donors. The first such effort was in Imbaba in 1992–93, and involved the introduction of infrastructure that was lacking and the opening up of some roads by Giza Governorate.[48] In 1998, GTZ, in alliance with Cairo and Giza governorates, began upgrading exercises in Manshiyat Nasir and Bulaq al-Dakrur. These efforts involved a limited amount of capital investment for water, sewers, roads, and social facilities, combined with a considerable amount of technical assistance for studies, planning, training, community mobilization, and capacity building. The concept of community participation, always in vogue among international donors, has been a paramount dimension to these two projects, both of which continue more than ten years later, although focus is now limited to scaling up and general policy impact.[49]

In 1998 the area of Telal Zeinhoum, an older, deteriorated area of Cairo in Sayyida Zaynab district, became a model redevelopment project championed by the Egyptian Red Crescent, the Future Foundation, and the First Lady, with funding mainly from voluntary contributions by prominent businessmen. This project involved the demolition of all old structures and the rehousing of residents in new walk-up apartments surrounded by manicured gardens. The final phase was completed in 2009 and the different phases together saw the building of 2,400 housing units as well as a number of public facilities. Although the Telal Zeinhoum area had been a minor run-down inner-city area of squatters and crumbling emergency housing, and in no way could be considered typical of *'ashwa'i* areas of Greater Cairo, the state and its media have lost no time in declaring that this kind of showcase redevelopment is the model for dealing with informal areas.[50] Such an approach was repeated in some small informal settlements around Helwan in 2005 to 2007 called 'Izbit al-Walda and 'Arab al-Walda. This project was also championed by the First Lady and involved some very plush social services as well as roads and parks built by the Egyptian Army (and, it might be added, on land that had been an army camp).[51] Both of these projects are tirelessly lauded by the state media as successful approaches that show the commitment of government to solve the *'ashwa'i* problem, although it is more correct to say they are drop-in-the-ocean, expensive showcase efforts that are hardly replicable without the strong and continued interest from the very highest levels of political power.

A government project currently underway in Imbaba represents what is probably the most ambitious and large-scale venture at improving and restructuring an informal area of Cairo. The scheme, which first was considered in 2000 by the Ministry of Housing, is using the 74-hectare site of the disused Imbaba Airport to build a park, a major boulevard, and social facilities for the surrounding informal areas. Also being built on the site are public housing blocks that are to be used to resettle those in the path of street widening. If implemented as intended, this project will definitely benefit the huge surrounding informal areas where more than half a million people reside.[52] However, even if successful, this experiment is hardly an approach that is replicable, since in addition to being expensive, finding more prime sites embedded in Cairo's informal areas is well nigh impossible.

Whether and to what extent one considers that the state has officially recognized informal development and conceptualized approaches and strategies to deal with or stop the phenomenon, it is important to realize that state activities—mainly in the form of service provision (however slow) through traditional line agencies of government—have been considerable in informal areas, as discussed above. In fact, it could be said that there is a kind of 'organic' development operating—piecemeal, insufficient, and chaotic, always after the fact and limited—through local and national sectoral agencies. Roads eventually do get built, water and wastewater networks do get extended, schools do appear, and electricity does get provided to informal areas, just as they do in rural Egypt. It may take years, and even decades, but most informal neighborhoods of Cairo have been and are being served. (The subject of extension of basic infrastructure services in Greater Cairo is treated in more detail in Chapter 9.) If this is not state recognition, then what is? The residents of these areas may be disenfranchised and given pathetic funding priorities, but their very mass works in their favor. They do have some representation and some weight and voice, especially in local administrations, and this translates into a kind of pressure of numbers. Voting pools may work somewhat, but it is more the same kind of personal and informal relations and negotiated norms that ease the establishment and consolidation of informal areas and *also* allow the extension of public infrastructure and services, regardless of whether an area is considered illegal/informal or not.

It is important not to get carried away and to overly laud this quiet and piecemeal improvement of informal areas. The state's aggregate budgetary allocations to informal areas for infrastructure and services, on a per capita basis, whether through local authorities or line ministries, are truly pathetic. It is symptomatic of the embarrassing imbalance that such comparative budgetary exercises are never carried out. One has only to set levels of investments and the resulting services in informal areas, against what can be found in the new towns around Cairo, where almost no one lives and the few new inhabitants are likely to be decidedly well off. Or one can compare the level of investments in any informal area of Greater Cairo to those in a district like Zamalek, where it seems a street is hardly repaved and recurbed before the process starts over again, and where there are four government cooperative supermarkets, supposedly for limited-income customers, selling a wide range of fixed-price meats, canned goods, fish, fruits, and vegetables.[53]

If anything should constitute a scandal, it is this. One of the basic principles of urban development is that investing scarce public moneys in large and dense settlements and in areas adjacent to the city core would have a much higher impact on the welfare of the city as a whole than investing the same amount in faraway locations where demand is still sluggish or in areas already enjoying high levels of services. Government investments have much higher economic returns when the flow of benefits (such as clean water, good electricity, better transport, and better education) directly benefit a large number of people per unit of investment. This should be completely obvious. But it is symptomatic of where government priorities lie in Cairo that one can search high and wide and *never* find any calculation of per-capita investment allocations by geographic area of the city. This is true whether talking about sectoral allocations such as water and wastewater or education, or whether total investment budgets are being considered. In this vacuum, it is easy for decision-makers to continue to pour funds into grandiose desert schemes or into precious parts of the formal city. Informal areas of Greater Cairo, with almost two-thirds of the total population today, do not capture even a very tiny fraction of the city's investments in basic services.

Community in Informal Areas and Community Participation in Upgrading Projects

Grass-roots and community-based organizations are few and far between in Egyptian urban areas. Traditional community organizations tend to be limited to small informal associations based on a specific neighborhood or on the common rural origin of their members, and their activities are limited to assistance during special occasions such as weddings and funerals. Some also undertake small religious charitable works and some operate health clinics. There are also small registered *gam'iyat* (community associations), most of which were formed during the Nasser period among government employees and exist only on paper. In fact, the lack of locally based community organization in urban Egypt and apathy toward public voluntarism is something that is bemoaned by many.[54]

Starting in the 1970s, a number of national and citywide NGOs were formed and some became active in certain informal areas of Cairo. These NGOs were either large, service NGOs, usually with religious or international affiliations, while others were purely 'good works' charities with funds coming from donations. Since through the 1980s and 1990s more and more funds from international donors were being made available for NGO work, it is not surprising that there was an explosion in the number and scope of these associations. Many do serious work in poor and informal areas, although they tend to operate mainly in extremely deprived communities such as the *zabbalin* (garbage collectors). Few have activities in the large, mainstream informal areas of Greater Cairo. Another characteristic of these NGOs is that, with a few exceptions, they are run by the well-to-do, are very paternalistic, and can hardly be considered 'community-based.'

Various efforts have been made in some informal areas to encourage existing traditional neighborhood associations to take on more social service and developmental activities, and support has also been given for the formation of new local associations. In particular, the GTZ projects in Giza and Cairo governorates have had some success in fostering more organized community activities, although it has been difficult to cut through the prevailing apathy, and the ingrained belief among inhabitants that only the well-connected will benefit and that, anyway, social services are something the government should provide. It doesn't help that most of these community-building efforts employ elitist, top-down NGOs for the day-to-day work. In other words, attempts to build community in informal areas (or anywhere else in urban Egypt) is something difficult to sustain, and many are the initiatives that have dried up as soon as external funding stopped.

'Community participation' in slum upgrading projects has become almost a holy grail with development agencies, in which the emancipating potential of participatory approaches has an ability to 'empower' the marginalized. In Cairo, the single largest and longest attempt at participatory development has been undertaken by GTZ, first in the pilot areas of Bulaq al-Dakrur and Manshiyat Nasir starting in 1998, and later on more systematically in the governorate administrations of Giza and Cairo. This program, currently called the Participatory Development Programme in Urban Areas, has tried to foster true participation and community empowerment through a number of initiatives, struggling at the same time to overcome community apathy, lack of effective grass-roots community organizations, and the reluctance of official counterparts in local government. The results, as carefully analyzed by Elena Piffero in her 2008 PhD thesis, have been disappointing, to say the least. Here is not the place to go into the details of GTZ's participatory program in Greater Cairo, which has generated a whole corpus of studies, assessments, and evaluations, some of which are peppered with self-congratulatory and feel-good rhetoric. For those interested in the pitfalls of participatory approaches and their conceptual as well as practical problems, a reading of Piffero's excellent PhD thesis is highly recommended.[55]

The Future of the Informal City

Based on past trends, the informal city can be expected to keep growing, with an ever-increasing portion of Greater Cairo's inhabitants finding homes and livelihoods in it. Some mature informal areas have pretty much reached saturation, but in many others consolidation and incipient infill will continue for years. Most major horizontal expansion will inevitably occur on the peri-urban frontier on agricultural land in Giza and Qalyubiya governorates, although there are incidents of wholesale expansion in other areas (see Figure 4.17). In terms of direction of growth, it can be expected that the greatest expansion will be to the north-northeast along the al-Marg, al-Khanka, and Abu Za'bal axes, although other axes and clusters can be expected to emerge throughout peri-urban Cairo. Assuming that the observed 1996–2006 population growth rate for peri-urban Greater Cairo as a whole continues over the next decade, then by 2016 over 5.4 million inhabitants can be expected in this zone, and by 2027 this figure will exceed 7.5 million persons. And it may well be that actual future growth rates will exceed historical trends.[56]

Many will say that this will lead to an unacceptable loss of Egypt's precious agricultural land. However, informal expansion of Greater Cairo into the agricultural plain is extremely dense and efficient, and over the 2001–2007 period the JICA-commissioned Strategic Urban Development Plan for Greater Cairo calculated that agricultural land lost to urban expansion was only 2,300 hectares, or just 383 hectares per year.[57] Such a loss is almost nothing when compared to the tens of thousands of

Figure 4.17. Very rapid informal horizontal expansion, over eight years, into agricultural land in *shiyakha* of Helwan al-Balad: 2000 *(left)* and 2008 *(right)*. (Both images ©2010 DigitalGlobe / ©2009 GOOGLE.)

Figure 4.18. Recent detail of informal area of al-Khanka. Note that the majority of buildings are capable of extending vertically, as can be seen by the room walls and pillars on the roofs. (Image dated 2008, ©2010 DigitalGlobe / ©2009 GOOGLE.)

hectares being added each year for agricultural purposes in Egypt's many desert-reclamation schemes.[58]

There are two government initiatives that have been launched in the past few years, which might have some effect on informal areas in Greater Cairo. The first is the national Sunduq Tatwir al-Manatiq al-Ghayr Amina (Unsafe Area Development Fund), which was established in late 2008 under the prime minister's office and appears to be well financed. This initiative grew directly out of the Duweiqa landslide disaster and the resulting media frenzy, and it aims at redeveloping all dangerous informal areas in Egypt.[59] This is a limited approach that appears to be rationally thought out. For Cairo, it will mainly mean the redevelopment of cliff areas in Manshiyat Nasir and Stabl 'Antar as well as the removal of some slum pockets. Perhaps a total of 250,000 to 400,000 persons in all of Greater Cairo will be affected, almost all of whom will need to be resettled at government expense.

The second initiative is much more ambitious and, so far at least, not very well conceived. It is called the *tahzim* (belting or containment) strategy developed by GOPP in 2007 and 2008, and it aims to allow limited formal urban development on agricultural land around informal areas in order to contain further informal encroachment. Although this strategy represents a fundamental shift in government policy related to the urbanization of agricultural land, it has yet to be applied and will require planning and control mechanisms and institutions that still need to be articulated. Also, unless greatly relaxed standards of subdivision and building are allowed in these *tahzim* zones, there is the risk of creating yet more areas for private real-estate speculation and little if any affordable housing. In any event, this strategy has yet to become operational even on a pilot basis, and to quote a recent World Bank report that reviews the *tahzim* strategy, "the challenge is in the details."[60]

5

Housing Real and Speculative

On 25 May 2009, a third Egypt Housing Finance Conference was held under the interesting title "Affordable Housing in Challenging Times." Like the previous two housing conferences held in 2007 and 2008, it was organized by an events outfit called Euromoney Conferences, took place in the glitzy Semiramis Intercontinental Hotel, and was hosted by the Ministry of Investment and the Mortgage Finance Authority. A visitor arriving at the conference lobby was immediately assaulted by a bewildering array of booths with floor-to-ceiling displays and glossy brochures, all promoting housing schemes, almost all of which were to be located in the new towns around Greater Cairo. The standard imagery—which can also be found prominently on billboards throughout Cairo—almost jumped out at the visitor: the cute kids with smiling TV-perfect parents frolicking on a sea of very green grass, or an impossibly perfect villa, again on what appears to be an endless expanse of green, with slogans (always in English) such as "life as it should be," "cleaner, safer, and more beautiful environments," "built around people's desires," "healthy lifestyles combined with the comfort and security of gated communities," and even "innovative high street boutiques and iconic malls that attract the world's top brands." Most of the housing units on offer were either villas or luxury apartments and duplexes. It was impossible to find any apartment units under 150 square meters, and most were in the 200–375 square meters range.

The visitor could have been excused for being perplexed. Aren't we in Egypt? Isn't the conference theme *affordable* housing? The conference presentations and panel discussions did include such topics as "moving down the price pyramid" and "can good margins be made in the affordable housing market?" But these nods to housing affordability seemed to be just that—a kind of recognition that, in tough times, maybe going a little down-market might just find some customers who, in the halcyon boom times of 2006 and 2007, would have been ignored. Such a preoccupation with the high end of the housing market and the level just below it has been the hallmark of practically all new 'formal' housing for years, as can be seen in Cairo's new towns and also developments in Maadi, Madinat Nasr, and Heliopolis/Nuzha. In fact, this oversupply of expensive housing, and the speculative nature of it, has been one of the perplexing constants in a sector where 'real' demand is so far down the scale as to be almost a world apart.

The conference also presented another common feature of corporate housing in Egypt—its slavish imitation of western housing modes. The main real-estate developers in Egypt such as SODIC, Emaar Misr, Talat Moustafa, Rooya, and Orascom were all represented with their international vocabularies and global business styles, as were a few smaller developers.[1] Also represented in force were Egypt's four mortgage companies and the few Egyptian banks with mortgage windows. Given that only in 2001 were mortgage systems allowed in Egypt and that until now their mortgage portfolios remain minuscule, it is no mean feat that such mortgage institutions, with all the paraphernalia of western housing finance, should be so well established.

The conference also covered, at least briefly, the successes to date of the subsidized National Housing Program, better known as the president's Housing Promise, which was announced in 2005 and aimed to provide 500,000 low cost housing units over six years. Under its umbrella, central government, governorates, and private developers are producing 38-square-meter and 63-square-meter partly subsidized apartment units all over Egypt, with about half the total units going to the new towns around Greater Cairo.

The naive visitor to the conference might have come away with an image of a system where corporate producers dominate in close partnership with government, where modern housing finance mechanisms and securitization are well established, and where affordability and the concerns for housing those of limited incomes are being fully addressed. Unfortunately, such a visitor would be completely misinformed. If he or she were to move around parts of Cairo outside the new towns and the few upscale areas, another world of housing would have to be confronted. This reality, and how it functions in the shadows of infor-mality, is the subject of this chapter.

What is Known about How Cairo Houses Itself?

Up until very recently, there was little material on housing in Egypt. The subject was at best merely touched on by other development agendas and research interests, but nowhere treated as a sector in itself. What existed was based either on analyzing census results, on case studies, or on anec-dotal and impressionistic interpretations. In this light, it was very fortu-nate that a large, representative household survey of housing conditions and markets was carried out in 2008, one which covered all urban regions in Egypt, including Greater Cairo. This study, sponsored by the minis-tries of investment and housing, financed by USAID, and undertaken by a consultant team and a local research group, was called the *Housing Study for Urban Egypt* (HSUE).[2] Much of this chapter unabashedly mines the results of this study.

It is revealing that the genesis and justification for this study derived not from any imperative to understand housing systems and markets and to design better housing programs for urban Egypt's millions, but from a realization within USAID that its hefty technical assistance to Egypt's financial sector, under which was included substantial support for the nascent housing mortgage system and related institutions, was based on an almost shocking lack of basic understanding of how housing works in Egypt.[3] USAID's standard neoliberal viewpoint was that countries like Egypt simply needed to get their financial services, legislation, and institutions in order, securitize everything, and the private sector would perform to produce suitable housing that most people need and can afford. Well-targeted government subsidies would take care of the rest. As USAID's technical assistance unfolded and millions were being spent, embarrassing facts were beginning to emerge, and to its credit USAID accepted that there was a need to spend a couple of hundred thousand additional dollars to at least begin to know what was being talked about.

The 2008 HSUE itself has limitations. As a survey of households, it covered only occupied housing units; it did not include the huge amount of unoccupied, unsold, or unfinished housing and thus cannot be consid-ered a review of the whole housing stock or a report on current housing production and completion. Also, although statistically representative, it relied on the 2006 CAPMAS sampling study frame, which some observers consider to underrepresent marginal and newer urban areas and to have other flaws.[4] Finally, in order to be representative, the HSUE results are aggregated to the level of regions and thus cannot give any geographical refinement below this level.

Even so, the HSUE provides a wealth of information on housing that helps considerably to gain an overview of how Cairo houses itself. In the HSUE, Cairo is represented as two distinct regions—Greater Cairo proper and peri-urban Greater Cairo—and all results relate to these.[5] In 2006 the total population of Greater Cairo proper was 11.0 million inhabitants. Peri-urban Greater Cairo, the second region, covered the remainder of the population of the Greater Cairo region, about 5.1 million inhabitants. (map 3.4 shows the geographic extents of peri-urban Greater Cairo in relation to Cairo proper.) Peri-urban Greater Cairo contains what CAPMAS defines as both rural and urban areas, and is now the fastest growing area in Egypt in terms of additions to the population and has been treated in detail in Chapter 3.

Greater Cairo Housing Conditions—
Remarkably Good, Considering

The 2008 HSUE data, combined with the 2006 Census results, show that, in spite of low incomes and very constrained family resources, the mass of Cairo has become relatively well housed, at least when compared to other large Third World cities. In terms of size of housing units, number of rooms, basic utilities, and amenities, occupied housing units in Greater Cairo demonstrate a remarkably consistent and modestly good standard, on average. The overwhelming majority of housing units are small apartments in walk-up buildings that are structurally sound, and there are very few precarious structures. And, as perceived by inhabitants, the levels of satisfaction with housing as well as security of tenure are very high.

A few statistics underscore these generalizations and give a glimpse of how Cairenes are housed. In Greater Cairo proper, 92 percent of households live in apartment units. The median area of housing units is 70 square meters net (75 square meters gross). Only 24 percent of units exceed 90 square meters net in size, and only 9 percent are less than 40 square meters net. Only 6 percent of households lived in single rooms, and an insignificant number—0.1 percent—lived in 'precarious' units, that is, in shacks and structures not intended for residence. The average (mean) number of rooms per unit is 3.3 and on average a unit has two

Figure 5.1. Typical narrow lane in an informal housing area (Bulaq al-Dakrur, 2009) with very high ratios of building-height to street-width. (Photograph by David Sims.)

bedrooms. A full 92 percent of occupied units have separate kitchens, 94 percent have private baths with toilets, and 97 percent have access to water faucets inside the unit. Only 1.3 percent have no access to running water. The average number of units in a building is six and the average number of floors including the ground floor is five, with the median footprint of residential buildings being only 116 square meters. The average age of a building is thirty-two years.[6] An amazing 66 percent of all residential buildings are between three to five floors high, and only three percent have ten or more floors. Even though 44 percent of households in Greater Cairo proper are renters, tenure security is perceived to be high. This is reflected in the fact that a large majority of householders (91 percent) are not at all worried about the possibility of being evicted from their housing units. Overall, only 10 percent of householders expressed dissatisfaction with their current housing, and of these the most significant reason for dissatisfaction was insufficient living area.

Although these housing unit indicators are quite positive, the same cannot be said for those related to neighborhood conditions. The HSUE asked questions about the streets upon which residential buildings fronted, and the result is striking, if predictable, to those familiar with the city's large informal areas. For Greater Cairo proper, 50 percent of buildings faced streets with widths of 5.7 meters or less and 23 percent faced streets of less than four meters. In the Egyptian building code, the maximum allowed ratio of building height to street width is 1.5 to 1. By calculating this ratio for surveyed buildings, the 2008 HSUE revealed that only 23.7 percent of buildings in Greater Cairo proper had ratios equal or less than this, showing that the code's stipulation is widely ignored, even in 'formal' residential areas. The median ratio of building height to street width is roughly 2.2 to 1 and, in almost thirty percent of buildings, 3 to 1 or above. This reflects the very high residential densities for which Cairo is outstanding among world metropolises, but it also demonstrates that the quality of life for residents suffers as soon as they exit their housing units.

How do these general housing characteristics for Greater Cairo proper vary for the city's peri-urban areas, which contain almost one-third of the total inhabitants of the metropolis? In these areas, occupied apartment units also predominate, with 82 percent of the total; but a higher proportion, 11 percent, are either rural houses or detached units. Occupied housing units are slightly larger, with the median net area at 75 square meters (versus 70 square meters for Greater Cairo proper). Residential building footprints tend to be even smaller than in Greater Cairo proper, and on average with fewer floors. Over 90 percent of housing units have private kitchens, private bathrooms, and access to running water, but only 54 percent of units are connected to sewerage networks, in striking contrast to Greater Cairo proper where the figure is 98 percent. Also, street conditions are very poor, with only 6 percent of buildings facing streets that are paved and in good condition, compared to 34 percent in Greater Cairo proper. Overall housing unit conditions and also satisfaction with housing were found to be similar in the two areas.

Perhaps the single most important overall indicator of housing standards is the average number of inhabitants per room or the average area per capita. In Greater Cairo proper, the 2008 HSUE calculated this at 1.22 persons per room, or 1.6 persons per sleeping room.[7] Expressed another way, the net area of a housing unit per person was 23.8 square meters. While not anywhere near western standards (except perhaps in prime locations in Paris, London, and New York), such a moderate average measure of crowding allows one to conclude that Cairo's housing is remarkably decent. Compared to other metropolises of the industrializing world, such as Mumbai, where in 1990 the crowding rate was reported to be 4.7 persons per room, Cairo's housing seems positively spacious![8] This was not always so. In the 1960s, rates of overcrowding in Cairo were awful, and in many central areas rates exceeded 2.5 persons per room.[9] Also at that time, single-room units were reported to represent almost half of all units in Cairo.[10]

Of course, average figures can mask considerable variations, especially for lower-income households. The HSUE was able to calculate household incomes and to rank households according to income quintiles per capita, a standard process in household surveys.[11] This allowed analysis of how housing characteristics varied by the degree of poverty of the families residing in them. For Greater Cairo proper, the results were predictable, if not as extreme as might be imagined. In terms of crowding, the poorest 20 percent of households averaged only 11.2 square meters of unit space per capita, versus an average of 23.8 square meters for the whole population. This figure rises slowly to 22.9 square meters for the fourth quintile, then shoots up to 40 square meters for the fifth or richest quintile. Likewise, whereas for the poorest household quintile, over 22 percent of households lived in units of 40 square meters or less, only three percent of the richest families lived in such small units. In terms of number of rooms per unit, the variation by household income is not dramatic, with the poorest quintile living in 2.8 rooms per unit on average, rising slowly to 3.7 rooms per unit for the richest quintile. What this shows is that the higher income families enjoy much larger units but not very many more rooms, meaning that the average room size increases steeply with family income. Visits to informal and *sha'bi* (often understood to mean 'lower-class') housing confirm that room sizes can be tiny, with bedrooms of 2 x 2.5 meters being common. This demonstrates that housing production systems in Cairo are meeting mass demand by making a compromise between space and the number of rooms. This also helps explain how the primary indicator of crowding—persons per room—can be relatively good in Cairo. (See Figures 4.14, 4.15, and 4.16 for typical small-apartment unit layouts in informal areas.)

Other housing indicators that vary according to household income show that, although there is much to say about how well Cairo houses itself on average, housing remains a pressing concern for certain families and especially for poor, newly forming households seeking housing on the market, as will be shown in subsequent sections of this chapter. A simple statistic underlines this. The percentage of families living in one room is only six percent in Greater Cairo proper and 5.6 percent in peri-urban Greater Cairo. This sounds like a small number, but it translates to a total in 2008 of some 230,000 families or almost one million persons crammed into a single room, sharing beds and even sleeping in shifts. And these are not by any means the only ones who suffer from a lack of adequate housing.

Housing Tenure and the Rise of the New Rent Law System

During the Second World War, as an austerity measure, authorities in Egypt imposed a freeze on rents, which at the time affected mainly Cairo and Alexandria, the only cities where rental accommodation was widespread. Supposedly a temporary measure, this freeze was continued through to the Revolution in 1952 and beyond. In the late 1950s and early 1960s Nasser's regime, as a populist move, not only confirmed this rent control but actually decreed the reduction of rental values.[12] The upshot of this was that Cairo, by the 1990s, had a huge stock of housing under rent control, representing some 42 percent of all housing units in Cairo Governorate, with rents that had become, due to erosion by inflation, ridiculously small, and these fixed rents continue today.[13] Anyone living in Cairo knows someone who occupies a huge luxury flat in one of the downtown or older upscale areas and is paying as little as LE25 ($5) per month in rent. Even in modest apartments in older informal areas, most rentals remain fixed at LE10 to LE20 per month.

Obviously, such a holdover causes an amazing distortion in housing markets. Many are the ways, both illegal and quasi-legal, to circumvent them and realize the huge market value latent in rent-controlled units. But the control system remains remarkably rigid, mainly because it has created an enormous and influential group of people who continue to benefit from the system and in whose interest it is to see it maintained. The losers are, of course, the building landlords. Observers and housing economists have railed against the system for decades, pointing with despair to the run-down and even dangerous state of buildings where rent control predominates. But it is well known in government circles that the surest way to commit political suicide is to champion the removal of rent controls.

Fortunately, in 1996 a law was passed, which, although it did not abolish rent control on existing units, imposed a new time-bound contractual rent system for all units rented subsequently. This is popularly called the *qanun al-igar al-gadid*, or New Rent Law, and it has progressively become a prominent feature of housing markets in Greater Cairo, as will be seen below.

What today is the overall picture of housing tenure in Cairo? The 2008 HSUE gives a relatively good picture for Greater Cairo proper, showing that old rentals, that is, those under rent control, still predominate at 39 percent of the total. In second place are private units that are owned by the occupants, at 33 percent—and an overwhelming 92 percent of these are owned by a single person, usually the head of the household. Following this are 12 percent of all occupied units, which are held rent-free as gifts (usually from close relatives) or are provided by employers. Those units that are rented under the New Rent Law represent 10 percent of the total, which is a very significant number given that this type of tenure has only been in effect for twelve years. About five percent of all occupied units are owned through purchase from the government.[14] Finally, a tiny percentage of housing units in Greater Cairo proper—less than one percent—are either rented from the government or are rented furnished from landlords.[15]

The tenure picture of occupied housing in Greater Cairo proper varies significantly by family income. For ownership tenure, the richest household income quintile is overrepresented and the poorest slightly underrepresented. And an even greater distortion is found for gifted units, where there is a much higher concentration among the poorest income quintile households, and this diminishes as one moves up the income scale. On the other hand, those enjoying the rent control regime are found roughly equally in all income categories, as are those who rent units under the New Rent Law.

In peri-urban Greater Cairo the housing tenure situation is quite different from that of Cairo proper. Most striking is that only 13 percent of occupied units are under rent control (versus 39 percent for Cairo proper), that ownership is much higher (at 58 percent versus 33 percent for Cairo proper), and that rent-free tenure is also much higher (at 21 percent of all occupied units versus 12 percent for Cairo proper). These variations are logical, since peri-urban areas tend to be newer, poorer, and more subject to the informal or 'rural' mode of housing creation.

Affordable Housing: Rents and Prices in Cairo

'Affordable' is one of the most slippery words to be found in the housing literature. To an upscale developer, it may mean slightly smaller and less luxurious units, or less onerous down payments and installments, aiming to attract a slightly less affluent segment of the moneyed middle classes. But for analysts of general housing markets, affordability is usually measured by what the average or less-than-average household can afford to pay out of its income for a modest rent or can reasonably amass to purchase a unit, compared to what the market offers. Even here, difficult assumptions must be made, including what real incomes are and what percentage of income is considered reasonable for housing (usually 20 to 25 percent, although it is not unknown for 40 and even 50 percent to be allowed), what equity payments can be made, and what financing and systems might be actually available. In any case, most models of housing affordability derive from western practices, where steady, documented incomes are assumed, mortgage financing and credit are widely available, and a plethora of institutions and laws guarantee and protect the various parties involved.

Needless to say, in Egypt (and developing countries in general) such assumptions are difficult if not impossible to make. Egypt has only recently legislated a mortgage system: it remains minuscule, and it has yet to be seriously challenged in Egypt's courts. The framework of regulations, institutions, and services needed for a modern housing sector is very much in its infancy. As will be shown below, housing in Cairo remains largely a system in which personal, individualistic norms predominate, which the government hardly penetrates, and in which informal processes rule.

The results of the 2008 HSUE allow not only a good overall view of rents, housing unit prices, and market values in Greater Cairo, but they also permit comparisons of these with the incomes of those occupying the units. Two major and surprising generalized conclusions can be made. First, rents were quite affordable, even those subject to market forces, and second, unit purchase prices and perceived values of units were consistently modest and within the means of a large portion of households, assuming of course that these families can save or otherwise accumulate over time the required equity. The following paragraphs demonstrate this.

For Greater Cairo proper, the 2008 HSUE recorded the average purchase price for the median unit over the previous five years at LE100,000, or a per-square-meter price of LE923, with the median unit having only 105 square meters. In peri-urban Cairo this average dropped to only LE70,000 and the size to 76 square meters. In informal areas of Greater Cairo proper, purchased units were also similarly small and inexpensive, as is shown in Chapter 4. These averages were very far from what the organized or corporate private sector can offer today, where the cheapest flats are very rarely under 150 square meters and prices start at LE250,000. On average, the ratio of unit purchase price to annual household income for Greater Cairo as a whole was 4.5 to 1, almost half the ratio common in western countries, where a typical family can afford a unit whose value is eight times their annual income.

The affordability picture for rental units under the New Rent Law was even better. It is remarkable that the median market rent paid over the previous five years was reported to be LE200 per month in Greater Cairo proper and LE150 per month in peri-urban areas.[16] In terms of rents paid as a portion of household income, the overall median was 20 percent (and only 17 percent in peri-urban areas). Surprisingly, this percentage remained roughly the same for all household income quintiles. The rental burden on households was thus quite affordable, especially when compared to international norms. And it should be remembered that these were rents determined by market supply and demand, and did not include rents paid under the rent-control regime. (The median rent for units under rent control in Greater Cairo proper was a derisory LE30 per month.)

Perhaps the main message is that in Greater Cairo, with its huge housing stock and vibrant housing markets, diversity and choice dominate, affordable units are being supplied across a wide spectrum, and all of this has developed without any government intervention. Of course the system can't respond to the housing needs of desperately poor or vulnerable households, nor can it meet the marriage aspirations of all youth, but as a general picture housing affordability in Greater Cairo is not at all bad.[17]

How Cairo Houses Itself
How has it been possible for the city to turn housing conditions for the masses from one of overcrowding and misery into one of relative dignity, especially over four decades of tremendous population growth during

which Egypt's economic development has remained stubbornly anemic? To answer this question requires looking at the means of housing production in the city.

In Greater Cairo, housing is characterized by overwhelmingly individualistic, personal, and atomized modes of supply. It is individuals, families, and informal entrepreneurs who produce units and put them up for sale or rent (or, as in the case of the owner-builder, simply live in what they produce). Corporate and government production remain marginal. One might expect that this noncorporate system could be found in the countryside and in small towns, but that it dominates in the capital Cairo, with all its relative sophistication and assumed modern business penetration, is truly remarkable. For example, of all occupied units purchased in the previous five years in Greater Cairo proper, the 2008 HSUE reports that 78 percent were acquired from individuals or small informal developers. Only 17 percent were purchased from the government or public-sector entities, and only 8 percent were purchased from the private sector.[18] In peri-urban Cairo, housing supply figures were even more skewed toward the individual and informal modes, with 92 percent of all purchased units so supplied. In these peripheral areas, units acquired from the government represented only 2.5 percent of the total, and only 5 percent came from the corporate sector.

For rentals, the situation was even more inclined toward individual modes. In the five years up to 2008 in Greater Cairo proper, only 1.1 percent of all occupied rental units were supplied by private companies and only 2.6 were supplied by government entities. And in peri-urban areas over a similar period, government and private-sector supply of rental units was so minute as to be statistically zero. In other words, the landlord in market rentals in Greater Cairo is almost always another individual or family, usually also living in the same building, and often a relative or acquaintance. And it is rare that a landlord rents out more than a single unit, or at most two or three.

How Housing is Exchanged and the Rise of the New Rent Law

The personal, noncorporate mode also dominates how housing markets operate in Greater Cairo. For example, a large majority—74 percent—of those seeking units either for rent or purchase in the previous five years in Greater Cairo proper found them through word of mouth (from relatives, friends, neighbors, or co-workers) and another 20 percent found them through a *simsar* (a mainly informal, self-appointed real-estate broker operating in very localized markets). Only 4 percent found units through the media and other corporate forms of market information. For peri-urban areas of Greater Cairo, word of mouth was even more dominant, at 84 percent of all housing unit exchanges.[19]

The HSUE was able to look further into housing exchange and market behavior. Of all units moved into in the previous five years in Greater Cairo proper, 38 percent were rented under the New Rent Law, 18 percent were purchased on the market, another 3.5 percent were purchased from the government, and 15 percent were said to have been rented under the old law. The remainder were inherited, given as gifts, or provided by employers as 'in-kind privilege.' This means that only 56 percent of all units were exchanged in the last five years under free market conditions, the others being transferred through government bureaucracy or through personal relations and non-cash rewards. Of the units exchanged through the free market, *two thirds were under New Rent Law contracts*. Without any doubt this shows the emergence of market rentals as the new dominant mode of occupancy in Greater Cairo proper, the purchase of units on the market now representing only one-third of the total of market exchanges. For peri-urban Cairo, the situation is somewhat different. While New Law rents also dominated market exchanges in the last five years, in these poorer and more 'rural' areas, well over half of all units (65 percent) were exchanged outside the market, either through inheritance or as rent-free gifts, or were constructed by the owner-builder. This last category represented one-fifth of all exchanges, which demonstrates that the informal, owner-builder mode of housing construction is alive and doing very well, at least in peri-urban areas.

New Law rentals are virtually all contractual arrangements between individuals, with neither the corporate private sector nor government playing any role at all. The growing recent shift toward rentals under the New Rent Law may partly be explained by the inability of most families to accumulate the large equity needed for housing unit purchase, especially in increasingly hard economic times, but it also points to the fact that both landlords and tenants are acting rationally and that an efficient market system for housing exchange is emerging. This shift is occurring with practically no policy support from government and without any interest on the part of the corporate private sector.

Registered Property Titles: Who Needs Them?

From 1897 through the 1920s, most rural lands in Egypt, including those surrounding Cairo, were surveyed and mapped, and a cadastral registration system was set up. And in 1923 through 1940, cadastral mapping of most of Cairo's urban properties was carried out. In 1946 and 1964 two laws were issued that set out the legislative framework for the current property registration system in Egypt. The first, *al-sigill al-shakhsi*, or the Deed Law (Law no. 114 of 1946), set up the notary deed system (based on individual ownership), which covers most of Egypt. The second, *al-sigill al-'ayni*, or the Title Law (Law no. 142 of 1964), allowed the registration of property which was based on the property itself, although this system has never seen its coverage extend beyond a few rural districts. It is the Ministry of Justice that manages property registration through its *shahr al-'aqari* offices located throughout Egypt, and it is the Egyptian Survey Authority that carries out property surveying and inspection and is supposed to maintain cadastral mapping systems.

All properties (land and buildings) in Egypt are required to be registered under this legislative and institutional framework in order to be considered legally owned. In fact, there are penalties on the books for nonregistration, but these are never applied. The bureaucratic and clerical requirements of the property registration system are cumbersome and complicated, if not labyrinthine, and small *ikramiyyat*, or bribes, at the *shahr al-'aqari* offices as well as at the Survey Authority are normal events.[20] In order for a property transaction to be registered, a clear chain of title is required from the last time the property was entered into the registry, usually when it had been part of a larger agricultural land parcel. For all properties in informal areas of Cairo, and even for most formal properties, establishing this chain, which usually goes back unregistered for decades, is simply impossible. In 2005, a USAID project began, aimed at improving property registration for mortgage purposes, and an early finding was that the system of registry was hopelessly flawed. One report summarized the situation as follows: "The current condition of Egypt's real property registration system can best be described as onerous and complex for applicants, vastly underutilized, excessively bureaucratic and complex, misunderstood and unpopular with the public, and incapable in current form of promoting a real-estate mortgage finance market."[21]

The result has been that very few owners bother adhering to the property registration system, and over the decades the system has become less and less relevant. For example, a study by the ILD estimated that of a total of some 4.5 million dwelling units in Cairo existing in 1996, a full 57 percent were informal and unregistered and another 13 percent had once been registered but had devolved into informality over time. Only 27 percent could be considered formal, and of these only a fraction had been kept up-to-date in their registration.[22] Even the minister of justice admitted in 2005 that only 7 to 10 percent of properties in Egypt were registered.[23]

How then are properties in Greater Cairo transferred and how is ownership documented? The answer is that a number of quasi-legal or informal procedures have evolved that conveniently sidestep the official registration system and allow for relatively straightforward, quick, and inexpensive means to conclude a property transfer. These mainly use *'urfi* contracts, which are simple two-party sales contracts that should be witnessed by two persons. For many, these simple paper contracts are sufficient, but for more security it is possible to have these contracts endorsed in the courts under the *sihhat tawqi'* (contract signature confirmation) or the more stringent *da'wa sihha wa-nafadh* (petition for execution of a contract), either of which any lawyer can arrange for a small fee. Alternatively, the seller of a property can issue a *tawkil* (power of attorney) to the buyer giving him all ownership rights over the property, and then this *tawkil* can be endorsed, just as in the sale of a car, at a *shahr al-'aqari* office. Such systems of transfer are used not only by individual buyers and sellers, who dominate Cairo's housing markets, but also even by government agencies and private companies that are selling new units.

Even though in the last few years tremendous efforts have been and are continuing to be made to improve official property registration to facilitate the expansion of new mortgage-based housing finance, nevertheless the informal, sidestepping means of property transfer remain very much the norm. They are not perfect, and fraud is a remote possibility (such as selling the same property more than once), but for most people they are sufficient, since such systems minimize dealings with the government, depend more on personal relations and guarantees, are much less expensive, and are much more convenient.

Government Public Housing Programs[24]

Government-provided housing in Cairo (and in Egypt) has a considerable history, with the first project in Cairo constructed in 1952. A summary

Figure 5.2. Older public housing blocks *circa* 1985 in Sixth of October. (Photograph by Sonja Spruit.)

of this history is given in Chapter 3. In Greater Cairo the production of government housing has been substantial, representing almost 50 percent of all public housing units built in Egypt in the 1982–2005 period. Over this period a total of 523,000 units were built in Greater Cairo, including those erected in the associated new towns. However, the share of public housing production relative to the total number of housing units produced over the same period remains small, at roughly 10 percent.

Typical public housing in Egypt consists of four- to five- story walk-up blocks, usually with between two and four units per floor. Housing blocks are arranged in geometric patterns within the site. Different layouts and architectural combinations have been tried throughout the years, but in all cases an essential design feature is that all light and air for a unit comes through windows and balconies in the building façades. That is, there are no internal light and ventilation shafts. While such a system allows economies in the building design (fewer walls and less unusable space in a building), it demands wide spaces between buildings, which require landscaping and maintenance, and which in turn require larger land-per-unit ratios. The average land required per unit ranged from 39 to 115 square meters, with a clustering around 70–75 square meters in the new towns and, in general, lower averages for governorate housing. This results in

Figure 5.3. Satellite image showing a mix of different public housing types built between 1990 and 2000 in Sixth of October. (Image dated 2008, ©2010 DigitalGlobe/ ©2009 GOOGLE.)

rather low residential densities in most cases, lower than densities found in formal areas of Cairo and very much lower than prevailing densities in informal areas. Most observers would agree that government housing is, in general, of good structural quality. Of course, there are embarrassing cases of soil problems, bad foundations, or cheating contractors, but these are exceptions.[25]

Over the last twenty-five years there have been remarkably few attempts by planners in Cairo to introduce housing designs that deviate from the apartment block norm. As far as is known there have been no core housing schemes, no attached duplex or townhouse units, no purpose-built infill blocks, and, until very recently, no sites and services projects.[26] However, in the 1980s the concept of *hirafi* (artisanat) housing was introduced, notably in Madinat al-Salam and Duweiqa (both in Cairo Governorate). Standard apartment blocks were built, but with the ground floors devoted to workshops, whose owners and workers were to live in the apartments above. This concept had only limited success and has not been widely repeated.

Figure 5.4. Demolished ground-floor shop in public housing in Sixth of October. (Photograph by Sonja Spruit.)

A prominent characteristic of almost all government housing schemes is their large scale. Housing projects are laid out on wide, leveled super-blocks (parcels of land containing hundreds if not thousands of units). Attempts are almost never made to insert smaller groupings of buildings upon small sites of state land that might exist within existing urban fabrics. Also, shops are practically never built on the ground floors of government-built housing, in spite of the fact that it is extremely common for ground-floor residents in mature public housing areas to convert part or all of their units for commercial purposes.

Finishing of units in governorate housing is usually quite basic (cement wall rendering, cement tiles, basic internal water and power lines, simple wood doors and windows). Under the Mubarak Youth Housing Program (1997 to 2003), finishing quality improved noticeably, but then so did the comparable cost per unit. The same approach could be said to apply to on-site services and landscaping in housing estates. Some sidewalks and curbs, some paved parking, and street lighting have

Figure 5.5. Example of Mubarak Youth Housing in Sixth of October, built 1997–2000. (Photograph by Sonja Spruit.)

normally been provided. Under the Mubarak Youth Housing Program and in some recent governorate examples, much greater effort is made to landscape the estate areas.

The main problem with the quality of government housing is not in the finished product but in the level of operations and maintenance that follow. Civic responsibility and pride is rare, and operations and maintenance are perceived to be the responsibility of the local authorities. The overall functioning of utilities was considered good in a recent study of public housing units in Greater Cairo, but the state of roads, landscaping, and in particular cleanliness within and around buildings was judged by residents to be fair to poor, especially in older governorate-supplied units.[27] In spite of a handful of attempts over the years to mobilize residents in government housing estates, collective and voluntary concern for improving public spaces remains very much an exception to the norm.[28]

Until the launching of the National Housing Program in 2005, public housing in Cairo was quite affordable, with the monthly installment payments being within the means of all but the lowest income families. And no wonder, since units were all very heavily subsidized. For example, in the Mubarak Youth Housing Program (1997–2005) it has been estimated that the implied direct subsidy element represented 68 percent of total direct costs (construction, infrastructure, and overheads), and that this figure rises to 75 percent if indirect costs, mainly the associated land values, are included.[29]

The subsidies associated with public housing, and the subsequent and continuing drain on the state budget, not to mention the consumption of precious state-owned land, might have been palatable if the units built actually went to the poor and those in need. However, the system of targeting and allocation to families has, to put it politely, been rather hit-and-miss. Over decades the Egyptian government has relied on standard applications to begin the housing unit distribution process. National-level housing authorities and Greater Cairo's governorates announce that there is a housing program and accept filled-in *istimarat* (applications) from citizens. These applications are usually very straightforward and require payment of a nominal fee. Although, theoretically, new government housing is aimed at households with limited income, as far as is known there have been no attempts to target beneficiaries based on income or wealth thresholds, or to conduct means tests or social investigations. It is usually required that an applicant be living in the governorate in question and that he/she be married. Other criteria might apply, such as a statement that the applicant has no residential property. In any event, once an application has been screened and accepted, and the down payment deposited, the applicant is put on a waiting list. Once new units are available, they are distributed from the waiting list pool or, if demand exceeds supply, by *qur'a* (a kind of lottery draw). Even if an applicant is lucky, he or she will usually be assigned a unit many years after making the application, when his or her personal housing situation might be completely different. In all programs the allocation of units in a particular housing project is random, with valid applicants assigned units through lists. This leaves no way for a group of families to acquire units in the same building or area, and thus they cannot hope to bring with them even a fraction of the social networks and capital embodied in extended family or co-worker relationships. In effect, the 'application regime' is a bureaucratic means of rationing new subsidized units under a modicum of fairness, and there is little or no link with housing need or social requirements.

Figure 5.6. Largely vacant public housing in remote location of al-Shuruq New Town, 2006. (Photograph by David Sims.)

The public housing system is perhaps at its weakest when it comes to the issue of location. The reliance on vacant, cost-free public lands for the construction of subsidized housing in Egypt has caused and continues to cause serious distortions in attempts to match supply geographically with demand. In and around Greater Cairo, forty years of land allocations for public housing as well as for schools, health centers, youth clubs, state enterprises, megaprestige projects, and the armed forces has left precious little accessible state land, and as a result new housing schemes may be located in awkward, remote, or otherwise undesirable locations that are usually far from existing densely populated agglomerations. As will be pointed out in Chapter 8, in Greater Cairo residential location is of crucial importance, especially for the poorer segments of urban populations at which subsidized housing programs are theoretically targeted. Distance creates a serious direct (and rising) transport cost to all members of a family associated with living in remote housing estates. It is no wonder that vacancies in these projects exceed 50 percent of all units recently built, as is discussed below. There is already a serious transport crisis faced by the vast majority of residents in Cairo's new towns who do not own cars.[30] In these estates, government public transport is practically nonexistent and the private microbus system cannot provide convenient service, due to a lack of the necessary critical mass of customers. And heavily subsidized fuel prices, which, until 2008, have kept microbus fares affordable (at least for shorter distances) cannot be expected to continue forever.

Experience has shown that government housing estates that are remote and badly located (in terms of access from transport corridors and of proximity to popular and dense urban areas) tend to remain largely vacant and depressed for years, regardless of the success in distributing units. However, as Cairo's experiences in Madinat al-Salam and Madinat al-Nahda and also Masakin al-Zilzal in Muqattam show, reasonably-located and large government housing estates will, over time, fill up and mature, with both government and private-sector services eventually migrating to or near the area. In these cases it has been a matter of: (1) good location near a major urban corridor, and (2) an expanding critical mass of population that generates its own dynamic, much as occurs in the vast informal areas of Egyptian towns.

As we will discuss in Chapter 6, the new towns around Cairo have been planned on gigantic scales, and the NUCA enforces high development standards that lead to low urban densities. Furthermore, the mechanistic, wholesale approach to land assignments has resulted in a scattering of public housing estates throughout these vast spaces. Thus there is rarely any 'critical mass' of habitation that would attract private transport and services, and the distances between one part of a new town to another can be daunting, to say the least. Perhaps, if these new towns had attracted private investments in the manner and on the scale planned, they might have developed contiguous densities for logical urban systems, but in all new towns there are vast stalled property subdivisions that separate one area from another and have created public housing estates that appear as isolated islands.

The locational disadvantages of public housing in Greater Cairo, especially the more recent projects and those still on the drawing board, are much more serious than just a transportation problem. Families of limited income must struggle to make ends meet, and it is extremely common for the wage earner to also have a second casual job or a small business or both, and to have adult offspring working informally. The main sources of such supplementary income are to be found in the huge urban informal economy. If one lives in a remote government housing project, especially in the new towns, informal job and business opportunities are almost nil. As many studies have shown, casual and informal economic activities rely heavily on personal contacts and geographically specific markets. For someone living in a new town or isolated governorate housing estate, to access the informal economy will require such a daily transport bill as to nullify the income gained.

Any link between public housing supply and actual beneficiary need surviving from the *ad hoc* unit distribution system quickly disappears once a unit is allocated. Although usually prohibited, the rental or resale of public housing units by the beneficiary is extremely common, using the *'urfi* contract system or through *tawkilat* (powers of attorney.) There is a lively if underhand market in these units, with some buying up of

Figure 5.7. New remote National Housing Program housing blocks, Sixth of October, 2009. (Photograph by Sonja Spruit.)

apartments with a speculative eye for future resale. Units have been known to exchange hands even before the original beneficiary acquires his or her unit. In effect, public housing distribution has a roulette wheel nature, representing a potential highly subsidized windfall to those who eventually gain a unit, which can be either quickly or eventually realized through secondary markets.

Current Government Housing Policies and the National Housing Program

In 2005 the government announced a new National Housing Program (NHP), which aimed at building and distributing 500,000 affordable housing units over six years, to be located in the new towns and governorates and administered by MHUUD. Almost half of the units were to be constructed in Greater Cairo, almost exclusively in the new towns. As of mid-2009, most of the 500,000 units have been budgeted, and construction has at least commenced, and this is considered a great success by those in the MHUUD. All units under the NHP are either 63-square-meter standard two-bedroom units or 35–40-square-meter *al-ri'aya al-ula* (basic care) units for the very poor through rentals.

First, it must be emphasized that the NHP follows the previous supply-side approach to housing. It does not attempt to operate on the demand side, nor does it attempt to influence the wider urban housing market in Greater Cairo. But as a supply-side housing construction program, the NHP represents a departure from previous programs in a number of ways. It stipulates an upfront cash subsidy from the state budget (originally set at LE15,000 per unit, but now said to have been raised to LE20,000), rather than the more confusing interest-rate subsidies on soft loans for housing. For unit purchases, recourse is being made to mortgage finance under new laws and institutions set up since 2001. Beneficiaries seeking housing units are able to choose among different amounts of down payment and among repayment schedules, one of which includes an annual escalator clause of 7.5 percent on monthly installments. There is an explicit policy to include the private sector in the finance and construction of units, and around Cairo at least five companies have been allocated land to build and market units. Of these, the Orascom Hotels and Tourism Company is building the largest project, called Madinat al-Haram in Sixth of October. For the first time in decades, rental housing is included in the mix of units produced. Finally, a fundamental departure from previous public housing schemes is the introduction of the *ibni baytak* (Build Your Own House) program, a kind of sites and services approach that offers 150 square meters of serviced land upon which a unit of 63 square meters net can be built, with future vertical extensions allowed. This program, in which the beneficiary must build a standard unit within a year, with cash subsidies linked to progress in construction, has met with tremendous demand. Some 100,000 of the 500,000 units of the NHP are said to be under the *ibni baytak* program.

Another difference between the NHP and previous programs, and one that is much less popular, is that the units produced for sale to beneficiaries are not cheap. First of all, costs of construction have soared in the last few years, and the standard NHP unit, which had been assigned a nominal cost of LE60,000 to build, now is pegged at LE90,000 and even this is quite unrealistic. And it does not include the full cost of associated land or infrastructure. Furthermore, the requirement that finance for purchase be through the mortgage system, with interest rates ranging from 10.5 to 14 percent per year, means that monthly installment payments are quite high. Effective monthly installment payments for a unit are rarely below LE600 per month, even without escalator clauses. Given that the median

Figure 5.8. Example of *ibni baytak* self-built housing, Sixth of October, 2009. (Photograph by Sonja Spruit.)

family income in Greater Cairo is around LE1,000 per month, only about one-quarter of families are rich enough to meet these payments (on the assumption that 25 percent of income can go toward housing.) It is no wonder that in many NHP projects there is insufficient demand.

Another weakness of the NHP is that projects must be located on state land, which in Greater Cairo means the new towns and other remote desert locations. As has been described above, a fundamental problem with all subsidized government housing is the total reliance on state land and the resulting remote and isolated locations far from existing urban agglomerations. In this the NHP has not at all deviated from the flawed approach of past programs. In fact, it is inevitable that the problem will become worse. Although the NHP claims to have sufficient land available for its five-year production targets, such massive amounts of land can only be found in the furthest and most remote expansion areas of new towns. The transportation problems facing beneficiaries, and in addition the difficulties of economic survival and making ends meet, means that attracting the low-income families for which the NHP program was intended is far from assured, even assuming such families could afford the payments.

The targeted production levels of the NHP, at 85,000 units per year, may represent as much as one-fifth of national urban housing production. But there are no government efforts in the housing sector beside the NHP. There are no government policies that aim at improving how overall housing markets function, at reducing the high level of vacancies, at stimulating the private/informal sector to produce more affordable housing units, or at helping homeowners improve their housing. The new Unified Building Code does not reduce building and subdivision standards to make new housing more suitable and affordable, and in fact extends the building permit regime to every corner of Egypt, including rural areas. No efforts are being made to stimulate the completion and marketing of vacant units, of making the New Rent Law regime more user-friendly, or even in targeting the very poor and vulnerable through extending subsidies beyond the NHP into the larger market.[31] The Ministry of Investment is heavily promoting the new mortgage system for private developers, but if the mortgage-financed NHP units themselves are already unaffordable for the masses although subsidized, those of the corporate private sector will be totally beyond the reach of all but those who have very high incomes.

Housing Vacancies, Speculation, and Modern Real-estate Markets

Practically all observers of the housing scene in Cairo bemoan the high rates of housing vacancies. While there have been no surveys that allow an accurate counting of vacant and unoccupied units, an approximation can be made by comparing the number of households from the Census of Population to the number of housing units enumerated in the Census of Buildings. Using this rough measure, it can be estimated that in 2006 a huge 25 to 30 percent of units were presumably vacant.[32] Vacancies according to this measure were found to be high in all geographic areas of Greater Cairo, even in informal areas, but by far the highest were recorded in the new towns. Can it be that in Cairo, a crowded place that many would say has a housing crisis, almost one-third of the housing stock lies unused? Certainly anecdotal evidence and cursory observation show that vacancies are common in Cairo, but as always in Egypt, it is prudent to uncover just how statistics are derived. The

Figure 5.9. New National Housing Program public housing block under construction, Sixth of October, 2009. (Photograph by Sonja Spruit.)

figures on population and households can be considered reasonably accurate, but just what is a 'housing unit' according to the census? The census definition itself is vague, but based on informal queries at CAPMAS it becomes clear that enumerators in the Census of Buildings usually overestimate the number of units. First, whole unfinished buildings are included and their units are included in the counts, as long as outer walls are in place. In existing buildings, enumerators either take as fact what the building owner or *bawwab* says about the number of units, or, if they enter a building, they consider as a unit any door that leads off a stairwell or public corridor or roof. Given that in Cairo (and especially in the informal city) units are added to a building progressively, it is inevitable that half-finished units and even pure air (as long as there is a door) are included in the totals.

These over-optimistic ways in which housing units are counted means that global rates of housing unit vacancy derived from the census are much higher than in reality. Still, there is no question that Greater Cairo contains a huge number of unoccupied finished units, and there are a number of reasons for this. First, many rent-controlled units (which represent over one-third of all units in Greater Cairo proper) are unoccupied, the lifelong tenants having moved elsewhere. But they are under no pressure to relinquish the units, due to the absurdly low rents. Secondly, it is very common for a father, in anticipation of his son's marriage, to build or acquire a unit years and years before the event and simply leave it empty. Given serious inflation in building materials and the fact that there is little or no cost in holding owned units vacant, such a practice is a very rational one. For example, the HSUE gathered information about unoccupied units in buildings where sampled families lived, and in Greater Cairo proper it was found that the reason for an owner leaving a unit vacant was, in 69 percent of cases, "left for children when they marry." Why such owners do not rent these units out under short term contracts until the offspring's marriage is puzzling, and the best answer is that many landlords still do not trust the New Rent Law system and fear they will not be able to get the tenant out at the end of the contract period.

It is revealing that the HSUE reported that in another 16 percent of cases the reason for unoccupancy in Greater Cairo proper was "left as a long-term investment." This factor hints at what may be the real reason for the phenomenon of so many unoccupied units in Cairo, especially those in the new towns and in newer private-sector housing schemes. For decades, real estate and land have been the most popular forms of family investment. Property, especially land, is perceived in Egypt as always gaining in value, a better investment than banks, or the stock market, or investment in businesses, and the best hedge against inflation. Also, the holding of land and property for speculation does not incur any significant cost. Land taxes do not exist,[33] and Egypt's property tax regime is sparsely applied, poorly collected, and usually requires only tiny annual payments. Also, there are no municipal service taxes imposed on property. The result is that an owner incurs no cost for holding such 'dead' property. It is very common to find massive amounts of empty land in subdivisions, buildings half finished, empty private apartments, and vacant public housing units. This phenomenon is extremely common in the new towns and also in other desert subdivisions. The losses in economic terms are staggering, even if the financial return to the owner, at the time of resale, may be very positive.

Who speculates in housing? The answer is practically everyone who can. The logic goes, if one has some accumulated cash, it is best to put it in land and bricks and mortar. Many of those owners who keep units vacant for their sons also have an eye on the property as an investment, which might be sold in the future for a handsome profit. The phenomenon of speculative property investment is even common in Cairo's informal city and its peri-urban frontier, but its most glaring manifestations are found in the modern corporate housing sector, especially in the new towns. It goes a long way toward explaining the extremely high vacancy rates in these schemes and the huge disconnect between the real, utilitarian housing where Cairo's inhabitants actually live, and the modern corporate sector, which as we saw at the beginning of this chapter is so visible in the media and is the darling of the business elites. This sector's offerings are mostly unaffordable to all but the rich and those working in the Gulf, and their schemes are now scattered across most of Cairo's desert hinterland. This state of affairs is highlighted in the next chapter, where desert Cairo is presented as the chimera that epitomizes the modernist dream, and conveniently allows the state to ignore reality.

Summing Up

It should be clear that housing in Greater Cairo, as produced in the last forty to fifty years, has been remarkably affordable and of a good if modest standard, *on average*. The modes of this production have been almost totally through individual, family, and informal developers. The corporate sector has been practically nonexistent, and even government—pronouncements and huge subsidies notwithstanding—has played a only minor role in housing provision. The same can be said for housing exchange and housing markets, where again it is the individual and personal relations that dominate. Government control and taxing of housing and its markets has been only marginal. Even in the registration of residential properties and in systems of tenure security, government plays only a modest role. Nonetheless the perceived security of families in their homes is very high.

The explanation for this state of affairs is intimately linked to the dynamics of the informal city—and to the largely autonomous or organic (and extralegal) forms of urban land and housing development as already described in Chapters 3 and 4. It is as if the housing sector in Greater Cairo has developed without government, even in spite of it. How would Cairo's millions upon millions be housed if government plans and schemes had actually been followed and if the proscription of informal development had actually worked?

This is not to say that the housing picture is all rosy by any means. Finding an affordable housing unit is the main problem for Cairo's newly forming families and those wishing to marry, and many existing units, especially in informal areas, are small, crowded, and lacking in sufficient ventilation and light. Furthermore, many of the vulnerable, marginal, and destitute still live in deplorable circumstances. And the huge number of vacant units throughout many parts of Cairo, and especially in the new towns, represents an outright economic waste. Thus the 'good news' of this chapter is not at all an excuse for complacency when it comes to housing in the metropolis.

6

The Desert City Today

These days a visitor to Cairo could be excused for thinking that the surrounding desert was practically the only property game in town. Billboards and advertisements announce in glowing terms the schemes of private developers promising a quality of life in the desert that is the antithesis of the crowded, polluted, and noisy life found inside Cairo. There are big players, such as the Talaat Moustafa Group, with large developments such as al-Rehab City and now, Madinaty, "a world city in the land of Egypt," and SODIC, with its Beverly Hills compound and now, East Gate and West Gate; but there are many more smaller companies that offer luxury and serenity in gated communities and exclusive compounds. Also promoted are modern private hospitals, private international schools, and private universities. In addition there are the malls and shopping centers, the exclusive golf courses, the business parks, five-star hotels, amusement parks, car showrooms, and practically any kind of real-estate venture that could be found outside the average American city. There are also large subsidized government housing schemes underway, such as *ibni baytak* and Orascom's Haram City in Sixth of October. And many of the consumer goods found on supermarket shelves will have been manufactured in one of Cairo's new towns. The phenomenon of desert development around Cairo has provoked some political analysts to talk about "a new hybrid globalized Americano-Mediterranean lifestyle," which is "completely in tune with the parameters of economic liberalization and IMF-driven structural adjustment."[1]

Cairo's desert is the talk of large portions of Cairo's middle and upper classes: about someone who is thrilled with their new villa in a compound, or about someone else who is desperately trying to meet payments on land purchased in one of the new towns, or even about the tidy sum someone's maid has gained by selling the government flat she was lucky to acquire in al-'Ubur through the lottery system. Certainly, a perusal of the property section of the Friday edition of *al-Ahram* newspaper, or the free marketing paper *al-Waseet* gives the impression that real estate in the new towns and deserts around Cairo is by far the main preoccupation of Egypt's real-estate companies and individual buyers and sellers.

The image of the new towns, offering fresh promise and escape from that old, crowded Cairo and all its faults, is firmly established as part of Egypt's popular culture. As far back as 1984, a popular film called *Ayoub*, starring Omar Sharif was released.[2] It tells the story of an Egyptian expatriate businessman who returned to his homeland and, in an attempt to amass his fortune, strikes increasingly shady deals and rubs shoulders with the city's corrupt and influential business elite. Much of the plot turns on Ayoub's growing disgust at the wickedness that surrounds him, and he writes a kind of memoir (which gets him killed at the end of the film). His one ray of hope is his daughter, played by Athar al-Hakim, a bubbly university student who is engaged to a clean-cut and of course handsome youth. In a scene toward the end of the film, the young couple come up to Ayoub as he is sitting in the gardens of his sporting club and contemplating his past iniquities, and announce with gushing optimism that they have just found the perfect flat in Sixth of October, that they can now get married and, as is obvious to the audience, live happily ever after. This event, and the image of a clean, modern future in a new town far from the evils of Cairo, has been an oft-repeated theme of films, TV serials, and advertising.

For these reasons a closer look at desert Cairo is in order, not because any significant portion of Greater Cairo's population actually lives there, but because there is such a preoccupation with expansion into the desert as intrinsic to modern Cairo's future. In what follows we first look at the eight new towns around Cairo and their record of success to date, then examine the reasons for their continued slow take-up, then look at the host of other schemes that are spreading into yet more of Cairo's desert, and finally investigate what all of this means both for Greater Cairo and for the Egyptian economy.

The New Towns around Cairo

There are presently eight new towns that can be considered part of Greater Cairo: Sixth of October, Tenth of Ramadan, Fifteenth of May, al-'Ubur, al-Shuruq, Sheikh Zayed, New Cairo, and al-Badr.[3] These cities are part of Egypt's New Towns Program, which started in 1977, was codified under Law no. 59 of 1979, and is being implemented by the New Urban Communities Authority (NUCA) of the Ministry of Housing, Utilities, and Urban Development. Although the program is nationwide in scope and currently boasts some twenty new towns established throughout Egypt—and dozens more on the drawing boards—it is the eight new towns around Cairo that have captured most government investments and private capital and have attracted the most inhabitants. In 2006 the census recorded a combined population in these eight cities of 610,000 persons, and while this was less than four percent of the population of Greater Cairo at the time,[4] it represented over 80 percent of the population of all of Egypt's new towns. The other new towns have hardly developed at all, and it is only a slight exaggeration to say that Cairo's new towns *are* the national new cities program.

The eight new towns around Cairo and their main features are listed in Table 6.1, and their locations are shown on Map 6.1. Although population growth has been very disappointing compared to planned targets, these new towns have absorbed huge public investments over more than thirty years, and these investments are continuing and even increasing.[5] Infrastructure services—roads, sewers, water, street lighting, public spaces, landscaping, and treatment plants—accounted for most of these investments. Schools, housing, and other public buildings accounted for a smaller share, along with expensive access roads and utilities trunk lines needed to supply the new towns.

The physical layouts of all the new towns are quite similar. Both the original plans and extension areas are all conceived on a gigantic scale over empty and mostly flat desert tracts of state land, with staggering distances between the different elements and neighborhoods. Residential areas are designed at maturity in such a way as not to exceed very modest densities of fifty to seventy persons per hectare, and all such areas have as much as 60 percent of the land devoted to open space, green areas, playgrounds, and wide streets and boulevards. Generous land reserves for public services and green buffer zones are also designed into planning schemes. In the public housing estates, wide areas intended for parking and green spaces separate individual buildings. Residential street and block layouts conform to the western planner's standard street hierarchies, with main arteries buffered by

Table 6.1: New towns around Greater Cairo

New Town	Census Population 1986	Census Population 1996	Census Population 2006	GOPP Population Estimate 2005	2006 Census No. of Housing Units	2006 Census % of Housing Units Vacant	Area of New Town as of 2009
Fifteenth of May	24,106	65,560	90,324	180,000	36,434	35.1	16 km^2
al-Badr	-	248	17,172	60,000	21,381	71.1	52 km^2
New Cairo	-	-	118,678	302,000	108,220	64.1	351 km^2
al-Shuruq	-	-	20,983	62,000	27,764	79.2	42 km^2
al-ʿUbur	-	997	43,802	100,000	40,261	64.4	54 km^2
Sixth of October	528	35,354	157,135	500,000	142,244	62.8	413 km^2
Sheikh Zayed	-	-	29,553	48,000	32,876	68.6	38 km^2
Tenth of Ramadan	8,509	47,833	124,120	500,000	n.a.	n.a.	208 km^2
Total New Towns	33,143	149,992	601,767	1,752,000	409,180	62.8	1174 km^2
Total Greater Cairo	10,994,000	13,231,000	16,292,000	16,200,000	7,369,128	30.2	
% of GC Population in New Towns	0.3	1.1	3.7	10.8			

Sources: Arab Republic of Egypt. al-Jihaz al-Markazi li-l-Taʿbiʾa al-ʿAmma wa-l-Ihsaʾ. *al-Taʿdad al-ʿam li-l-sukkan wa-l-iskan wa-l-munshaʾat* [Census of Egypt] various years; for areas of new town concessions, calculated from GOPP maps and Google Earth.

open spaces, restricted access points into neighborhoods to discourage through traffic, and traffic circulation within neighborhoods limited to a confusing set of local street loops and bends.[6] Also in conformance to western planning norms, land uses are strictly segregated. In almost all neighborhoods commercial activities are limited to designated shopping nodes located, along with local services, into areas centered within the neighborhood block. Central commercial areas or spines exist within each new town, and it is in these zones that all larger office and retail establishments, as well as government offices, are intended to locate. And all industry and warehousing are restricted to designated zones far from residential quarters. While such planning norms may represent an ideal in western cities, they are questionable for an Egyptian urban culture that excels at diversity and compactness, and they are especially questionable in Cairo's new towns, where a harsh desert climate prevails and where all greenery will require copious irrigation *forever*.[7]

Industrial areas have been created in four of the eight new towns, and in three of these, Sixth of October, Tenth of Ramadan, and al-'Ubur, investments in factories and warehousing have been very significant. This is understandable, since cheap land and ten-year tax holidays have been provided to attract the burgeoning local capitalist sector, and the permit regime for foreign investors has meant that they have had no choice but to locate in the new towns.[8] The results have been dramatic, and by now the new towns around Cairo boast over 1,500 factories with a labor force said to exceed 200,000.[9] The main problem with these industrial areas from a planning point of view was that the labor force, which was intended to reside in the new towns, never materialized to any significant extent, in spite of considerable incentives. Today, vast fleets of buses and minibuses transport workers daily to these industrial zones from *sha'bi* neighborhoods of Cairo proper or from Sharqiya and Ismailiya. Also, due to structural problems within Egypt's industrial sector, even in successful industrial areas in the new towns, a large number of factories are closed, idle, or operating at a fraction of their capacities.

The location and boundaries of the eight new towns around Cairo are shown in Map 6.1. As can be seen, two of the towns are in the western desert, five are in the eastern desert, and one is attached to the southern suburb of Helwan. The boundaries shown derive from

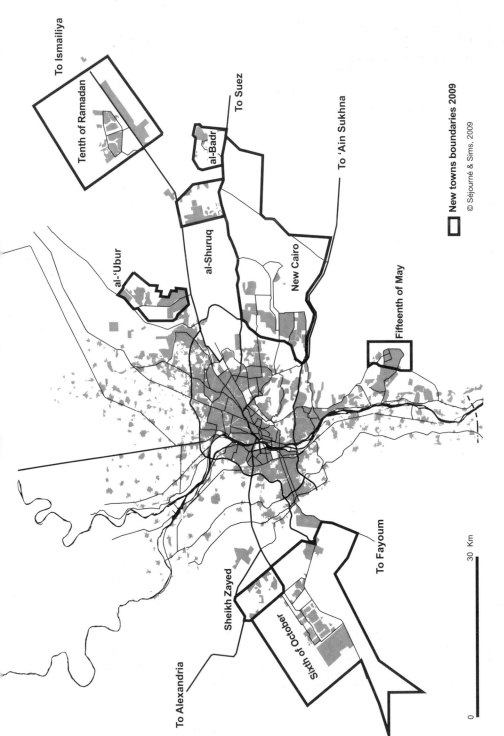

Map 6.1. Greater Cairo: new town boundaries in 2009.

New towns boundaries 2009

To Ismailiya

Tenth of Ramadan

al-Badr

To Suez

To 'Ain Sukhna

al-Shuruq

al-'Ubur

New Cairo

Fifteenth of May

Sheikh Zayed

Sixth of October

To Fayoum

To Alexandria

0   30 Km

information available in 2009, but it must be noted that the new town boundaries are not rigidly fixed. In many cases they have been redrawn from time to time to encompass additional virgin, government-owned desert land. In New Cairo and Sixth of October, this phenomenon of additional land incorporation has been very significant. For example, the area lying inside the boundaries of Sixth of October has been increased by a factor of at least seven over its original surface area, and this land accretion is symptomatic of the underlying rationale (or malaise if you will) of these new towns, as will become clear in this chapter. It would not be at all surprising if the 2009 boundaries are pushed further outward in the future, at least for the new towns that still have vacant desert land to incorporate.

The following paragraphs briefly describe each of the eight new towns around Cairo, with an emphasis on Sixth of October and New Cairo, since these are by far the largest, they can be considered the eastern and western anchors of desert development around Cairo, and they have had and continue to receive the greatest attention both from government and the private sector.

Sixth of October New Town

Sixth of October Town was launched in 1981,[10] was planned to have an ultimate population of 500,000, and was the first new town to be designed totally by Egyptian consulting firms. Like other first-generation new towns in Egypt, its original concept was for an industrial city with residential areas dedicated mainly for factory workers. The designs called for a large industrial zone to the west, a mix of public housing and individual housing subdivisions to the east, and a central commercial and office spine to interconnect the city. Sixth of October was located about thirty-five kilometers west of central Cairo on a large and flat desert site. Construction began in the early 1980s, but build-out and population growth have been disappointing, even though hundreds of factories quickly located in the town and there are now said to be between 40,000 and 60,000 jobs associated with these industries. In the early 1990s Sixth of October underwent fundamental changes. Boundaries of the new town were greatly expanded into the surrounding desert, and large chunks of land began to be allocated 'wholesale' to private-sector developers as well as many more individual building plots, land being sold at prices, which, although not near market rates, at least recovered

Figure 6.1. Part of industrial zone of Sixth of October, started in 1983. (Image dated 2006, ©2010 DigitalGlobe / ©2009 GOOGLE.)

a portion of the associated infrastructure costs. Attempts were made to attract flagship investments and signature brands, such as amusement parks, private universities, and a Media Production City.[11] By 1996, fifteen years after its launch, the population of Sixth of October had reached 35,000 and by 2006 the census registered 157,000 inhabitants, making Sixth of October the largest of all the new towns in population terms.[12] Even more substantial was the increase in housing units. According to the census, some 53,000 dwelling units in Sixth of October were recorded in 1996, and this jumped to 142,000 in 2006. However, as shown in Table 6.1, the occupancy of these units remained extremely low, with some 63 percent of units closed or vacant.[13]

Figure 6.2. Panorama of part of Sixth of October, 2009. (Photograph by David Sims.)

New Cairo New Town

New Cairo New Town is located just east of the Ring Road on a huge desert plateau. It was originally the site of three *mugamma'at 'umraniya gadida* (new settlements) that were launched in the 1980s as dormitory suburbs, each of which was designed eventually to house 200,000 inhabitants, mainly in public housing blocks. These three settlements were amalgamated into the design for New Cairo, which was officially declared a single new town in 1989. Its boundaries, even then, encompassed an enormous area of 13,000 hectares, and included the Mubarak Police City and Egypt's first golf course compound, called Qattamiya Heights. The urban design called for a huge east–west central commercial spine, some ten kilometers in length, and a large number of residential superblocks, each with central services and extremely ample open spaces and green areas. Notable was the exclusion from New Cairo of any industrial area.

Figure 6.3. Central spine of New Cairo in relatively built-up area, 2009. (Photograph by David Sims.)

Once New Cairo was established, there was a cascade of land allocations for three distinct kinds of developments—public housing estates, private developer compounds, and individual plot subdivisions, a mix similar to that found in Sixth of October and the other new towns around Cairo. New Cairo boasted a number of advantages, including excellent access via the Ring Road to the existing upmarket residential areas of Heliopolis/Nuzha, Maadi, and Madinat Nasr, as well as to Cairo Airport. In fact, New Cairo was quickly perceived as a very sought-after desert community, helped by the upscale image of Qattamiya Heights and, soon thereafter, al-Rehab City. This image was further enhanced by the establishment of a number of expensive private schools in New Cairo, as well as the purchase in the late 1990s of some 104 hectares by the American University in Cairo (AUC) as the site for its new campus. This new campus cost some $400 million, of which $97 million was a grant from USAID.[14]

However, as with the other new towns, development in New Cairo has been scattered over the city's huge landscape, and contains many empty desert tracts sprinkled with isolated projects. For example, up until mid-2009, the AUC campus, which began operation in 2008, had

Boundaries 2008
(470 sq km)

Original 1981 Boundary
(80 sq km)

0   10 Km

☐ Sixth of October Extension

© Séjourné & Sims, 2009

Map 6.2. Sixth of October boundary expansion.

an end-of-the-world feel. Students, faculty, and visitors alike had to traverse almost ten kilometers of mostly empty desert and nascent or stalled real-estate schemes, and it is sobering to think that the AUC site is itself actually in the geographic center of New Cairo as it is now defined.

By 2006 the population was recorded by the census at 119,000 inhabitants, but the number of housing units was 108,000, showing that, like Sixth of October, housing vacancies were very high, with over 64 percent of all units vacant or closed (Table 6.1).[15] And the official boundaries of New Cairo have been pushed ever further eastward into the desert. The huge Talaat Moustafa Group's Madinaty scheme, located off the Suez Road, some forty-four kilometers from the center of Cairo, needed to be grafted onto New Cairo, as were recent land allocations to the Heliopolis and Madinat Nasr housing companies and to Arab Contractors for its planned Future City. The result is that today, New Cairo's boundaries encompass an area of 264 square kilometers, which for comparison is *more than half* of the surface area of all existing built-up Greater Cairo

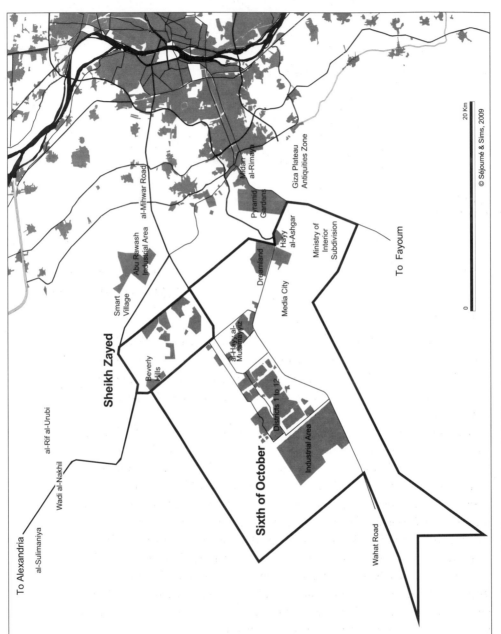

Map 6.3. Greater Cairo's western desert in 2009.

(which contains a current population of over sixteen million persons). By 2009, only sixty-eight square kilometers of New Cairo—at its eastern extreme—remained to be allocated, and plans for developing these areas are already well advanced.[16]

Sheikh Zayed New Town

Sheikh Zayed New Town is the only new town beside Sixth of October located in Cairo's western desert, and can be considered functionally as part of its larger neighbor. It was launched in 1989 on an area of thirty-eight square kilometers directly northeast of Sixth of October, and the 2020 population is targeted at 500,000 inhabitants. The site for Sheikh Zayed was originally earmarked in the early 1980s for New Settlements 6 and 7, and the area was also studied in 1984–85 to be the western location for the ill-fated Extension of Municipal Services Project.[17] In the end, the land of Sheikh Zayed was carved up into the three types of superblocks that are classic for the new towns—private developer compounds, public housing estates, and individual subdivisions. In 2006 the population was only 29,000 inhabitants, or less than 6 percent of its design target. Sheikh Zayed is a purely residential city, with no industrial area and only a smattering of schools and services, the most prominent of which is the relocated British International School in Cairo. Take-up has been slow, but perhaps better than in other new towns around Cairo, and it boasts some of the more prestigious private compounds such as Beverly Hills, Mena City, El Nada, al-Rabwa, and so on.

Tenth of Ramadan New Town

Tenth of Ramadan New Town was established in 1977 and was the first new town in Egypt. It was the prototype for the first generation of totally independent industrial new towns, and this factor influenced its location exactly halfway to the Suez Canal town of Ismailiya. Although it quickly attracted manufacturing enterprises, its population growth has remained anemic. It was originally designed for a population of 500,000, and this target has since been upped to one million inhabitants, but by 2006 the census registered only 124,000 inhabitants, a decidedly feeble population for almost thirty years of development. It should be pointed out that the inclusion of Tenth of Ramadan as part of Greater Cairo, as is common in studies by GOPP and others, could be questioned. At seventy kilometers northeast of the center of Cairo, the city is so far

Figure 6.4. Panorama of mature part of Sheikh Zayed, 2009. (Photograph by David Sims.)

away that its economic and social links to the metropolis are few, and in fact it was designed to be functionally independent. It is closer to the huge eastern Delta governorate of Sharqiya than to Cairo, and many of the workers in its numerous factories are bused in either from Bilbis or from Ismailiya. In fact, Tenth of Ramadan is nominally part of Sharqiya Governorate. Thus, for many observers, Tenth of Ramadan can hardly be considered part of Greater Cairo.

Fifteenth of May New Town

Fifteenth of May New Town was established quite early in 1980 on a limestone plateau directly east of the southern suburb of Helwan. It is unique among Cairo's new towns in that it abuts a well-established urban agglomeration, near to existing services, transport, and employment opportunities. Also, it is the only new town around Cairo whose development is mainly restricted to subsidized public housing blocks. For these two reasons Fifteenth of May enjoyed relatively rapid population growth and take-up of the subsidized units in public housing blocks. By 1996 the town already had 65,500 inhabitants, making it at the time by far the largest of Cairo's towns in population terms. In the late 1990s a second phase was launched, which extended the public housing blocks eastward and also included individual subdivisions to the north of the site. By 2006 the census registered a population of 90,000 persons and 36,000 housing units in Fifteenth of May. which by then extended over some sixteen square kilometers. At 'only' 35 percent, the city had by far the lowest unit vacancy rate of any of Cairo's new towns. However, the individual subdivision areas to the north remain a patchy affair of empty lots, stalled private construction, and only a few finished and inhabited buildings. In spite of this, more such superblocks are currently being planned for the city.

Al-'Ubur New Town

Al-'Ubur New Town, located some twenty-nine kilometers northeast of central Cairo, off the Ismailiya Desert Road, was intended to be one of the first of Cairo's new towns, and preliminary designs were being developed by GOPP as early as 1981 with support from GTZ.[18] However, none of these proposals was ever adopted, and as a result the town was designed mainly as a mix of public housing and high-standard individual subdivisions, with only one major private developer compound, which includes an amusement park, villas, and a large golf course. There was also an industrial and warehousing area on the southern part of the city. The boundaries of the new town had to be rearranged many times due to land-claim conflicts with both the military factories in the Abu Za'bal desert and the Ahmad 'Urabi Agricultural Land Reclamation Cooperative. In effect, implementation of the new town and construction of the first public housing neighborhoods only began in the late 1980s, and by 2006 the census recorded a population of al-'Ubur of 44,000 persons. This take-up is particularly disappointing in view of the town's excellent location, at least compared to other new towns, along the Ismailiya corridor, next to the existing large public housing estates of al-Salam and al-Nahda and also the al-'Ubur wholesale produce market (established with French assistance in 1988). In contrast to the feeble population growth, the industry and warehousing zone quickly filled up, mainly due to the good location and transport links within Greater Cairo. Such success led MHUUD to expand the city to the north to include another industrial area along the Bilbis desert road. Today al-'Ubur encompasses an area of fifty-four square kilometers, extending over thirteen kilometers in a north–south direction. The areas devoted to individual subdivisions are particularly large, representing twenty-five square kilometers or almost half the town's total area. These subdivision superblocks have stubbornly refused to mature or even take off. Virtually

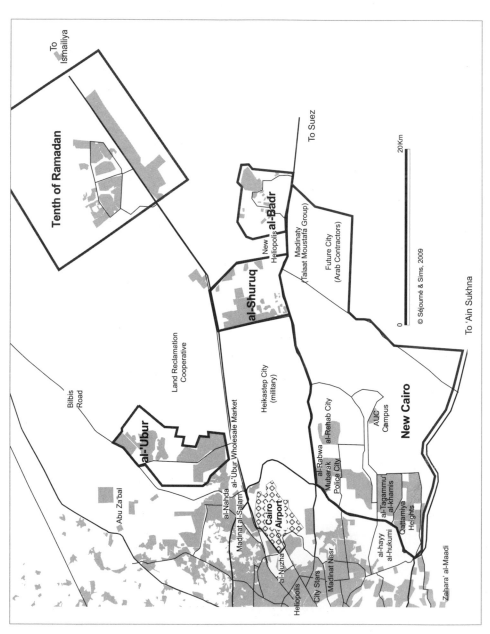

Map 6.4. Greater Cairo's eastern desert in 2009.

no one lives in most of these areas, which are characterized by the depressingly repetitive landscape of empty lots, bits of desert strewn with rubble, stalled individual structures, and a few buildings that appear finished on the outside but are uninhabited. The fact that there is only one significant private-developer compound in al-'Ubur (whose villa compound project itself seems largely stalled) is presumably because the town was never perceived as attractive for high-end residential development, being too close to the large *sha'bi* areas of al-Salam and al-Nahda.

Al-Shuruq New Town

Al-Shuruq New Town is located on a huge, flat, rectangular desert site over forty kilometers east of the center of Cairo. It covers forty-two square kilometers and lies between both the Ismailiya and Suez desert roads. The new town was only conceived in 1993 and caught many by surprise, as it had not been part of any Greater Cairo master schemes and seemed at first to be an unnecessary addition to Cairo's eastern desert, already boasting four new towns either established or on the drawing boards. In fact, its establishment was opposed, unsuccessfully, by many within GOPP as unwelcome competition to these other new towns. Yet the land within al-Shuruq was quickly allocated for the classic triple mix of public housing estates, private developer compounds, and high-standard individual subdivisions. None of the land was earmarked for industry or other economic activities, other than a few educational institutes and social clubs. The separate residential superblocks seem to have been randomly developed, and al-Shuruq today exhibits the all-too-familiar patchy development thrown over a huge landscape. The population, as recorded in the 2006 Census, was only 21,000 inhabitants, although all residential land in the town has been sold or allocated. With 28,000 housing units recorded in 2006, al-Shuruq had the highest unit vacancy rate of any new town around Cairo, at an astounding 79 percent. More than any other new town, al-Shuruq represents a very remote and purely residential commuter development, access to which depends exclusively on the private car.

Al-Badr New Town

Al-Badr New Town, which is the second most distant new town from Cairo, at some fifty-three kilometers from the center off the Suez Road, remains practically undeveloped although it was one of the first generation of industrial new towns, appearing in the 1982 Greater Cairo Master

Figure 6.5. Extremely slow and patchy development of individual subdivision area of al-'Ubur New Town. (Image dated 2006, ©2010 DigitalGlobe / ©2009 GOOGLE.)

Plan. By 2006 the census enumerated only 17,000 inhabitants, although the boundaries encompass a huge area of some fifty-two square kilometers. The government has built at least 16,000 subsidized housing units (giving a ratio of one resident per completed government housing unit in this city!).[19] Even al-Badr's industrial areas have attracted only a few factories, although for decades it has been the target of schemes to relocate noxious industries out of the central parts of the metropolis.[20] The new town has also been a favorite location to which to resettle families from slum clearance schemes, but most of these 'beneficiaries' have avoided it like the plague. Although heralded on a sign along the Suez Road as being "on the natural path of Greater Cairo's expansion," the town's stunted development to date could be summed up neatly as 'a city too far.'

Reasons for the Depressingly Slow Population Growth of the New Towns

Given the tremendous scale of both public and private investments in Cairo's new towns, their strategic locations on the desert fringes of Greater Cairo, and their huge land banks, which incur no land acquisition costs, why have the new towns around Cairo stubbornly refused to take off? Why have they not begun to absorb even a fraction of the planned target of at least twelve million inhabitants, as currently envisioned by GOPP? The answer is multifold.

First, in terms of attracting inhabitants, it is clear that these towns do not offer the kinds of housing, choice, and livelihoods that would entice even a small portion of the bulk of Cairene families, especially those who continue to crowd into the city's huge informal areas. The new towns around Cairo have been a main target of the government's various subsidized public housing programs, all of which are aimed at those of 'limited income.' NUCA alone has built 210,000 units from 1982 to 2005 in Cairo's new towns, representing over 80 percent of its total national production. Similarly, most subsidized housing projects under both the Cooperative Housing Authority and the Housing Development Bank, which together produced over 350,000 units nationwide in the 1982–2005 period, have been located in Cairo's new towns. And under the current National Housing Program, which aims to build 500,000 units all over Egypt by 2011, at least 40 percent are being located in Cairo's new towns.[21] Yet, as shown in Chapter 5, these programs rely on arbitrary methods of distribution of units, rarely relate to the needs of target families, attract considerable speculative intent, and result in housing units that are very poorly located and are only conveniently accessible by private cars. Seen this way, it is no surprise that vacancies in newer public housing units in Cairo's desert new towns commonly exceed 50 percent.[22]

Another factor that discourages the majority of Egyptians from moving to the new towns are the high standards and restricted uses imposed by NUCA authorities on private housing developers. Regulations limiting the density of population are extremely strict, and this, combined with the large unit sizes, forces the development of residential units that are very expensive and difficult to market. As a result, virtually all privately built housing units available on the market are completely unaffordable to the large majority of Cairo's households, even if finance were to be available—which, for most, it is not. Modest subsidized public housing

Figure 6.6. Satellite image of entire area of al-Shuruq New Town, showing patchy and discontinuous development. (Image dated 2006, ©2010 DigitalGlobe / ©2009 GOOGLE.)

units are commonly if extralegally resold in the new towns, but even these smaller units fetch prices that exclude the vast majority of Cairene families. Furthermore, in the new towns it is prohibited in most buildings to open retail shops, services, or offices. Workshops and repair shops are almost unknown, and even kiosks are discouraged.[23] These prohibited uses are precisely those that generate so much employment and so many business opportunities in Cairo proper. In effect, the vast micro and small informal business sector, which generates at least 40 percent of jobs in urban Egypt, is almost totally excluded from the new towns.

Perhaps the most serious problem facing the limited-income family who might choose to move to one of the new towns around Cairo is transport. In fact, poor transport services have for years been identified as one of the major obstacles to the development of Cairo's new towns. With the exception of Fifteenth of May and to a lesser extent al-'Ubur, all new towns around Cairo are many kilometers from the city's central areas or from any existing large urban agglomerations. As will be pointed out in Chapter 8, distance remains a crucial factor in Cairo's urban space. Location and mobility do count, and crucially. Good road links and rapid and affordable public transport are needed for the new towns to become fully integrated with the metropolitan area. Over the years, the government has made considerable efforts to develop major transport corridors out into the desert. In fact, the Ring Road, Cairo's most important artery, was conceived in 1982 mainly as a way to provide easy access to new towns and settlements located in both the eastern and western desert. Furthermore, al-mihwar (literally 'the corridor,' the axis road leading to Sixth of October City) was constructed under a crash program in 1998. In addition, a major highway link of 5.5 kilometers was built in 2007 from the far side of Madinat Nasr to the main entrance to New Cairo in the east. These corridors have improved general traffic movement to the new towns, but even though fleets of private minibuses, company worker buses, and some Cairo Transport Authority buses run on routes to serve the new towns, the lack of intercity public transit remains a serious problem. The long distances that must be covered represent not only a significant time loss, but more importantly they translate into transit fares that are hardly affordable to a struggling lower-income family residing in the new towns. There are a number of high-volume transport projects (bus rapid transit, light-rail, and super-trams) on the drawing boards that aim to improve public transport to new towns in both the western and eastern deserts, but the economic costs of such ventures mean that either these fares will be unaffordable to the masses or that they will need to be heavily subsidized.[24]

Even if somehow public transit to and from the new towns could be made convenient, fast, and affordable, movement *within* the new towns is and will remain an intractable problem. The issue is, again, distance. The new towns are planned on such astronomical scales that traversing from one part to another involves journeys that exceed most trajectories to be found within Cairo proper. For example, Sixth of October, with a current population of less than 180,000 inhabitants, encompasses an area of over four hundred square kilometers, an area almost as large as that of

Figure 6.7. Example of distances and transport problems inside Sixth of October, 2009. (Photograph by Sonja Spruit.)

all of Greater Cairo proper (see Map 00), which is home to some twelve million inhabitants! The distance within Sixth of October measures 19.5 kilometers in an east–west direction and 23.6 kilometers in a north–south direction. These distances are significantly greater than that from Tahrir Square in the city center all the way to Cairo Airport. And the original commercial spine of Sixth of October is almost seven kilometers in length, greater than the distance across central Cairo from Cairo University to al-Azhar Park.

These huge distances in Sixth of October are also to be found within the other new towns around Cairo, particularly in New Cairo, whose current boundaries encompass a colossal 350 square kilometers, which almost equals the extent of Sixth of October. The distances from one part of New Cairo to another are staggering. For example, those traveling to the American University in Cairo's new campus in New Cairo must traverse a distance of ten kilometers after exiting from the Ring Road, much of which traverses a bleak desert landscape sprinkled with new or stalled constructions. And the campus itself is actually located in the geographic center of New Cairo as currently planned.

Figure 6.8. Central spine of New Cairo on the way to the American University in Cairo campus, 2009. (Photograph by David Sims.)

Today public transport hardly exists *within* the new towns, and what services do operate are provided by private or informal minibuses that serve only the main concentrations of public housing estates or the main traffic nodes. The recent and popular phenomenon of *tuk-tuk* taxis, found in more mature areas of Sixth of October, may ease the problem somewhat, but again distances and low densities make the generalized use of this relatively cheap form of transport impossible. There are plans to create internal bus networks in some of the new towns, and these might be marginally feasible if trajectories traversed dense and well-populated areas that could support frequent private shuttle-bus services. But the scattered, leap-frog form of development so common in the new towns, plus the extremely low planned residential densities, means that any such services would need to be very heavily subsidized.

Of course, such tremendous distances to and within the new towns would not be a problem if everyone could rely on the private car, and if Cairo's road networks could handle the huge extra load. Certainly, most of those who live in the high-end residential compounds and some of those who work or study in the new towns will own cars, but the same cannot be said for those with more modest means. As will be pointed out in Chapter 8, only 11 percent of households in Greater Cairo presently own any kind of vehicle, and thus, for the large majority, car ownership will remain a dream for decades. Such a glaring fact somehow seems to escape many planners and higher-level government officials. Even a private-car commuter will have to think twice about the cost implications of living in a new town, as daily trips in excess of 120 kilometers are common, which translates today into monthly bills of LE400 for fuel alone, despite heavily subsidized gasoline prices.

New Towns as Successful Real-estate Ventures

Even if the new towns around Cairo have completely failed so far to meet the intended demographic targets, have they succeeded as pure real-estate ventures? Certainly, with all of the state investment and pro-motion, coupled with the ever-expanding surge in interest by modern private and even global capital, the new towns should at least have begun to exhibit some of the dynamic characteristics their promoters never cease to proclaim. Certainly, there are impressive amounts of scattered development going on in particular locations within the new towns, at least in terms of cement, bricks, and steel, and there are numerous if isolated examples of success. Yet even here there are fundamental flaws to the real-estate model of the new towns, most of which can be related to the poor management of development, especially how land is carved up and distributed, who gains, and for what purposes.

One basic flaw is the wasteful way land is allocated in the new towns and the frequent failure of these allocations to develop. Thousands and thousands of hectares of state land have been allocated for projects and sold to individuals and investors. In the early years, land prices were purely nominal, although recently, land prices have been set to at least partially recover infrastructure costs, or are sold through closed-envelope auctions. Terms of payment are very convenient, usually 10 percent down and the rest paid in equal installments over seven to ten years. Although sales contracts stipulate that a project or venture must be built within a set period (usually three years) or the site is repossessed, this condition is widely ignored. In fact, very few if any land allocations, whether to corporations or individuals, have ever been taken back throughout the history of the new towns. The results are very evident: all new towns around Cairo are characterized by empty lots, stalled construction, huge

Figure 6.9. Example of successful gated residential compound in al-Shuruq New Town. (Image dated 2006, ©2010 DigitalGlobe / ©2009 GOOGLE.)

empty concessions, and skeletal subdivisions. Not only does this represent a huge economic cost in underutilized prime land and associated infrastructure, it is hardly the image that NUCA is trying to project to visitors and potential investors.

In parallel, large parcels in the new towns have been (and continue to be) allocated at no cost for government and public-sector uses. Most of these lands have been used for the construction of public housing estates. Once built, these neighborhoods at least give the appearance of being fully developed, but vacancies are very high. Other large areas have been allocated to public enterprises, regardless of whether there is even any remote possibility that financing for the intended schemes will materialize.

Then there are the large private compounds. These mostly take the form of land allocations of 50- to 250-hectare blocks for the construction of integrated residential communities. A few of these—such as Beverly Hills, Hayy al-Ashgar, al-Rehab City, and the two al-Rabwas—have been well managed and aggressively marketed and, as a result, are quite successful. Such residential developments are mainly gated communities with extensive landscaping, swimming pools, sports facilities, and the obligatory golf course, and these stand out as prominent islands of success. But for every one of these there are several other similar land allocations to private developers that seem to have stalled or never got beyond the boundary wall. It needs to be remembered that the standard business model for most real-estate ventures in the new towns (as well as that for the corporate real-estate sector in general) relies heavily on what can be called 'buyer financing.' That is, normally a company secures a large land parcel from NUCA, pays the ten percent down payment, and prepares preliminary designs for the scheme (usually in phases), including the site layout with the all important green areas, playgrounds, and so on, as well as the apartment block or villa layouts. Immediately thereafter, the developer heavily advertises the units for sale.[25] Buyers are offered payment arrangements that usually include a reserve payment, a further payment upon signing a contract, perhaps other staged payments, another hefty payment upon receiving the completed unit, and then monthly or quarterly payments on the remainder of the purchase price over four to seven years. (These last post-possession payments rarely represent more than 20 to 40 percent of the total purchase price). The clever developer will use these sequence payments to finance most if not all construction as well as land purchase installments, relying only in dire need on bank loans. The point is that this form of buyer financing reduces to a minimum the up-front equity cost to the developer, but it means that the system attracts developers who have little experience or personal stake in the venture, so that finishing the project is not high on the agenda, and a lot could go wrong to delay and stall the project.

In the past there have also been huge land giveaways in the new towns, the largest and most controversial of which was Dreamland. Its history is illuminating. A huge 893-hectare parcel directly on the southern entrance to Sixth of October was sold to a prominent businessman in 1991 for the ludicrous sum of LE90,000, or one-third of a piaster per square meter. Eighteen years later, Dreamland, although it boasts an amusement park, a golf course, a five-star hotel, and residential compounds, still has over two thirds of the site completely undeveloped. And as has recently emerged in the press, the owner of Dreamland has been trying to sell off the remaining land on the open market to pay off huge debts incurred with state banks. When queried about this apparent scandal, the minister of housing leapt to the businessman's defense, calling him a heroic pioneer who helped make Sixth of October a success.

These various types of land allocations have created very patchy, discontinuous development in the new towns. In effect, there has been no logical sequencing of development. For example, lands in the original core of Sixth of October (Districts 1 through 12, the central spine, and the industrial area) were all rapidly allocated in the 1980s, practically one-off. There was no attempt to stage the development. Build-out proved very slow and patchy,[26] but instead of trying to densify and restructure the core areas, in the early 1990s, NUCA officials began to design vast new areas (in particular the *al-hayy al-mutamayyiz* (upscale or 'tourist' zone) directly

Figure 6.10. Example of slowly developing individual subdivision area in New Cairo, zoned for four-story apartment blocks, 2009. (Photograph by David Sims.)

east of the core city, with an area of 1,400 hectares) that were parceled for individual plots and for residential compounds. Lands in these areas were allocated in a wholesale fashion, again without any staging, and the result today is more patchy development with the odd successful project intermixed with massive empty spaces and stalled subdivisions. Such leapfrogging design of enormous additional city sectors in Sixth of October and their wholesale land allocation has continued into the 2010s.[27]

Any city, even a new town or suburban subcenter, needs to develop progressively out from its initial core. City managers know that once the core has taken off, immediate fringe sites gain in value and, if well planned, a rolling program of radiating land marketing will both maximize financial returns and promote dense and logical development. Such a logic has, unfortunately, been totally lacking in strategies to develop the new towns. A clever staging strategy was used by the Belgian entrepreneur Baron Empain to create Heliopolis, a very successful streetcar suburb of

Figure 6.11. Partly completed but still uninhabited individual subdivision area in New Cairo, zoned for multistory villas, 2009. (Photograph by David Sims.)

Cairo carved out of the nearby desert at the beginning of the twentieth century. Apologists for the new towns frequently point to Heliopolis as an example of how it is possible to successfully urbanize the desert, noting that at the time many thought the scheme to be foolhardy and that for years it remained a construction site. But whereas land development in Heliopolis was cleverly sequenced, the exact opposite is the unfortunate fact in the new towns.

The single most disappointing types of land development in the new towns are the subdivisions of individual land plots. These superblocks have been designed as residential subdivisions with large individual building plots that range from four hundred to one thousand square meters and include ample land for open spaces, circulation, and public services. Building specifications usually allow up to three- or four-story garden apartment blocks to be built on not more than 40 percent of the parcel's surface area (and prohibit commercial uses). These individual

Figure 6.12. Partly completed but sparsely inhabited individual subdivision started in 1988 in Sixth of October, 2009. (Photograph by David Sims.)

parcels were and continue to be distributed under an application system where plots are allocated by *qur'a* (lottery) if demand exceeds supply in a particular project. The successful applicant needs to pay only ten percent as down payment, with the balance of the land price spread over seven to ten years. There are the usual stipulations that timely land payments must be made, that the building permit must be issued, and that the building be completed within a set time period, but these requirements have been largely ignored or periodically relaxed.[28] In the last couple of years Housing Minister Ahmed al-Maghrabi has begun seriously to enforce building stipulations in some subdivisions in the new towns, and there is now a rush to finish buildings and plaster the outside façades. But because installing windows and completing interiors is not required, the results have been large 'Potemkin' neighborhoods that appear partly finished but in which it is rare to find habitable units and even rarer to find a single resident family.

In all of the new towns around Cairo these individual subdivisions, which generally make up between one-third and one-half of a new town's total residential area, have proven to be extremely slow to develop in terms of build-out and especially occupancy. Three such superblocks were studied in Sixth of October, and the results are startling: The oldest, on some 580 hectares started in 1984, was estimated by 2005 to have only 20 percent of building lots completed but with very low occupancy, 45 percent under construction or stalled, and 35 percent remaining vacant. The second, started in 1990 on some 180 hectares, had only 10 percent of lots built on and completed, 30 percent under construction or stalled, and a full 60 percent remaining empty. The third, started in 1997 on 576 hectares, had only an estimated 12 percent of plots either built on or under construction, with 88 percent of remaining lots still vacant.[29]

Such incomplete or stalled subdivision developments are extremely prejudicial to the success of the new towns. They are costly in terms of sunk investments and under-utilized infrastructure, they project a negative image, and they create gaping 'holes' in the city's overall urban fabric. Such past developments are bad enough, but it is understood similar individual subdivisions continue to be designed for newer extensions to Cairo's new towns. In fact, it appears that the continued large-scale release of such individual plots of land has become almost an obligation on the part of NUCA.

Current Strategies for Cairo's New Towns

Although the authorities have recognized that Cairo's new towns are in need of revitalization and replanning, it seems that what is being contemplated is, basically, more of the same kinds of development as in the past, all of it on truly grand scales. Recently a number of planning and revitalization studies have been commissioned by MHUUD for specific new towns, and while some of these contain good recommendations about the need for better management and more cohesive economic and transport strategies, most ideas focus on how to release and allocate yet more land, and none addresses the problems created by the enormous amounts of land already allocated or sold.

For example, strategies for New Cairo recognize that there is a dire need for the development of job-generating economic activities on the remaining 6,300 hectares of still unallocated land, all of which is far out in the desert, at least fifteen kilometers east of the Ring Road, ignoring the colossal 26,000 hectares in the city that have already been allocated, much of which remains underdeveloped or stalled. Plans for the remaining area call for a huge office and finance center on 3,780 hectares, an international health and curative complex on 550 hectares, an academic and research center on 350 hectares, an exposition and commercial complex on 500 hectares, and a sports and amusement complex on 800 hectares.[30] These clusters, the size of each of which completely dwarfs anything found in Cairo's central business areas and for which the word 'grandiose' is inadequate, are also to contain residential areas, complete services, and also vast green spaces. It is optimistically assumed that such additions will result in a population by 2027 in New Cairo of some 3.5 million inhabitants, representing a twentyfold increase over the current population in just eighteen years.

Strategies for Sixth of October similarly ignore the past and focus on new land developments on what little unallocated land remains within the city's boundaries, that is, some 5,000 hectares of new land compared to the roughly 30,000 hectares already allocated. It is interesting that although Sixth of October has a completely planned central commercial spine, this large 'downtown' area has hardly developed; and it is perceived that Sixth of October, including Sheikh Zayed, is in crucial need of yet another new town center that will give focus and structure to the disparate sections of the two towns and function as a high-end, globally branded commercial center and transport hub. One possible location would be north of Sixth of

October's old center next to Sheikh Zayed, and the other option would be a new central spine running along the Wahat Road. This second option, on almost 800 hectares, would require the reorganizing of some land assignments and the creation of green corridors and monumental focal points.

It should be added that current plans for the further expansion of Cairo's new towns, and especially that of Sixth of October and New Cairo, have had to incorporate colossal land assignments that recently materialized and were not at all part of the plans for the new towns. For example, a 2,900-hectare site along the Fayoum Road, planned as residential subdivision for Ministry of Interior police officers in 2001, has been tucked into the boundary of Sixth of October. This colossal area, which could easily accommodate a population of over 800,000 persons in garden apartment blocks, still remains empty desert. Only main roads have been bulldozed and only in one tiny residential neighborhood has ground been broken, although it is understood that land parcels there are being bought, sold, and resold at a rapid pace.

This grafting of off-plan land developments on to new towns is even more apparent in New Cairo. In 2005 Madinaty, an enormous integrated city development of the Talaat Moustafa Group, was launched and heavily marketed, located on a 3,800-hectare site off the Suez Road across from al-Shuruq New Town.[31] As if this were not enough, just south of this site another huge 3,000-hectare desert tract was recently allocated to Arab Contractors to develop yet another integrated complex to be called Madinat al-Mustaqbal or 'Future City.' This was reported to involve a deal whereby Arab Contractors, the largest contractor in Egypt and state-owned, would cancel the billions of Egyptian pounds of debt owed to it by the government in exchange for this land assignment. In addition, two large 630-hectare sites in the same area have been allocated to the recently privatized Madinat Nasr and Heliopolis housing companies as compensation for land taken by the government from within their original concessions, and it is presumed that these sites are earmarked for yet more exclusive residential development. The boundary of New Cairo has been redrawn to incorporate these land allocations, which together amount to over 8,000 hectares, and increase New Cairo's already huge area by about one fourth.

Will There Be Water for the New Towns?

Over the last twenty-five years particular efforts have been made by NUCA to bring water supplies to the new towns around Cairo, and this has involved installing new trunk mains to transmit water over long distances from the Nile or from existing networks. By 2007 water treatment plants had been constructed in Tenth of Ramadan (serving also al-Shuruq and al Badr new towns), Sheikh Zayed, Sixth of October, and al-'Ubur (serving also New Cairo). All together the capacities of these plants represented 22 percent of total water treatment capacities for all of Greater Cairo.[32] Due to the extensive landscaping called for in urban designs, as well as the popularity of swimming pools, golf courses, and gardens within private compounds, water consumption in these dry desert locations is extremely high. Although to date no serious water shortages have been experienced, some observers wonder whether water supplies will be sufficient once development accelerates, vacant housing is populated, and the very many projects and schemes on the drawing boards reach completion.[33] The water issue in the new towns is rarely discussed, and some observers wonder whether a water crisis is just around the corner. Very recently a study has been commissioned by the Ministry of Housing to design a new intake and transmission line that will service all the new towns east of Cairo (as well as parts of Maadi and Madinat Nasr extensions). This will be a colossal undertaking, which is said to be able to eventually supply eight million cubic meters per day to these areas. The wisdom of such a project can certainly be debated on economic and environmental grounds. Not only will much of this water go to golf courses, extensive green areas, and swimming pools, but most of it cannot be recycled and will end up lost forever in the desert. Also, because of the relatively high altitude of these desert communities,[34] simply designing the supply of electricity necessary to lift such huge quantities of water is proving a challenge.

Desert Cairo is Much More than New Towns

As mentioned in Chapter 3, the urbanization of the desert around Cairo is not at all limited to the New Towns. Although some 1,170 square kilometers of land have been planned, assigned, or allocated so far for new towns around Greater Cairo, representing a full 2.2 times the surface area of all existing built-up Cairo, still more massive amounts of desert lands, *separate from the new towns*, have been and continue to be acquired for urban purposes. Most of these projects are in contradiction to their original purpose or do not conform to the government's master plans. It is indicative of the scale of random desert developments around

Figure 6.13. Example of off-plan desert development near Giza Pyramids made up of villa subdivisions and gated compounds. (Image dated 2009, ©2010 DigitalGlobe / ©2009 GOOGLE.)

Cairo that already in 2005 the GOPP identified 282 square kilometers of urban residential developments that were not sanctioned by the 1997 Greater Cairo Master Plan, and that these areas were estimated to ultimately house over 3.3 million inhabitants.[35] And the GOPP map missed quite a few such 'off-plan' residential developments and did not count numerous nonresidential schemes in desert locations outside the new town boundaries.

Although, nominally, all desert land is under state ownership and control, huge tracts of desert around Cairo have been allocated and developed in what can best be described as a scramble by both state and private-sector actors to capture development rights on land that, at some point in time, is perceived as being extremely valuable, at least for speculative purposes.[36] The list of such projects is long and growing, in addition to the numerous land assignments that have been incorporated into the new town boundaries. For example, there are numerous

Figure 6.14. Part of the off-plan gated community, al-Sulimaniya, with a ninety-nine-hole golf course in a zone designated for agricultural land reclamation along the Alexandria Desert Road. (Image dated 2008, ©2010 DigitalGlobe/©2009 GOOGLE.)

far-flung suburban villa developments springing up along the Alexandria Desert Road starting at Kilometer 48. Examples include al-Sulimaniya (including a ninety-nine-hole golf course), Wadi al-Nakhil, al-Rif al-Urubi (which translates into 'European Countryside,' with separately themed large-lot villa neighborhoods called 'Bavaria,' 'Fransa,' and so on) and many other enclaves. These schemes are all on land originally allocated to private investors specifically for desert farm reclamation, and most were acquired from the Ministry of Agriculture and Land Reclamation at give-away prices.[37]

Other examples of off-plan developments in the western desert include the information-technology office park called Smart Village, the brainchild of the current prime minister, located just at the tollgate of the Alexandria Desert Road. Yet other examples can be found in the desert hills located between the old agricultural plain and Sixth of October, most of which are devoted to exclusive villa compounds that exhibit an

Figure 6.15. Entrance to off-plan government technology park called Smart Village, located at the beginning of the Alexandria Desert Road. (Image dated 2008, ©2010 DigitalGlobe / ©2009 GOOGLE.)

extraordinary concentration of swimming pools. And in the far eastern desert yet more residential enclaves, as well as private language schools, have sprung up along the Ismailiya Desert Road all the way to Tenth of Ramadan. In addition there is the still empty New Heliopolis development sandwiched between al-Shuruq and al-Badr new towns.

As if this were not enough, various well-located desert parcels lying along the Ring Road east of Cairo proper are being planned for yet more urban development. Most prominent among them is *al-hayy al-hukumi* (government zone), a recently launched scheme that envisions a new, high-end, government-office enclave-cum-prestige-shopping-malls, an urban megapark, and upscale urban residences, all to be located on 13.7 square kilometers just inside the Ring Road southeast of Cairo proper, on what had been an army camp. Some thirteen ministry headquarters (most of which are now found in the Qasr al-'Aini quarter and together will represent the transfer of at least 90,000 government employees), as well as the Parliament, the Shura Council, and the prime minister's office are to be relocated there, and a new metro line is to link *al-hayy al-hukumi* to Madinat Nasr.[38] And yet another ersatz 'downtown' urban center is being considered for a slice of land just inside the Ring Road within the Madinat Nasr land concession.

Desert Cairo—A Huge and Rising Oversupply on the Property Market?

It should be clear that desert Cairo contains a truly colossal amount of land and property and that this supply of real estate continues to be added to and expanded at an ever increasing rate. There are the land parcels and properties originally created in the new towns, plus huge new areas to being added to them, plus numerous off-plan desert developments that seem to multiply in number and scope every year. There are even plans to create more new towns around Cairo. The concept of the 'million person city' has recently appeared, and there is talk of creating these new towns in the desert west of 'Ayat, Sixth of October, and other desert locations on the far periphery of Greater Cairo. In addition, given past trends it is only a matter of time before the eastern boundary of New Cairo is pushed even further into the desert. Also, the second Ring Road project, which passes through remote desert areas south, east, and west of Greater Cairo, seems to have already generated stiff speculative interest in huge additional amounts of land, at least in the property sections of leading newspapers.

In fact, the conversion of raw desert land into marketable urban property seems to be the one constant in Cairo's desert story, the very disappointing record of past ventures notwithstanding. This begs the question, how can there be a continued sufficient market demand for all of this? Can the ever-increasing amounts of desert land being subdivided and marketed all find buyers, and can the myriad of urban projects actually be filled up?

This factor should cause serious unease among all those involved in modern desert real-estate development around Cairo. Standing back and looking at all the desert development schemes, both those within the new towns and those that are 'off-plan,' it is remarkable how similar they are. Residential development still dominates desert development, and practically all of the products—from super luxury villas to garden apartments, are aimed at the thin layers of the rich and high-income Egyptian families or at least the car-owning middle classes. Recently more and more large 'integrated' and 'urban center' developments have been launched, and all of these seem to offer much the same mix of office space, business parts, luxury hotels, world-standard hospitals and other international services, entertainment and leisure facilities, conference and exposition centers, and, predictably, high-end shopping malls and complexes, as well as yet more residential developments thrown in.

In effect, it seems as if all of these individual developments flung around Cairo's desert are competing for the same submarkets. And just how deep is demand? Will there be buyers for all of the leisure compound residential units that are planned and under construction, let alone those currently on the market? Can the new office parks and the millions of square meters of dedicated office space really be filled up with the modern global businesses being sought? Can the millions of square meters of commercial space aimed at high-end brand retailers actually be leased out, and will there actually be buyers for the luxury goods on offer?

For example, in the eastern part of Cairo there is presently only one commercial megacenter, City Stars in Madinat Nasr. This center, along with Dandy Mall in the west, today pretty much cover all of Cairo's current need for upmarket megamall retailing. But a review of real-estate projects under development in Cairo's eastern desert show that there are *at least* eight other new luxury shopping complexes planned either in New Cairo or in other eastern desert locations. And each of these is conceived to be at least as large as City Stars, with one named 'Park Avenue' being advertised as the "biggest retail destination in the Middle East."

It is indicative that neither the government nor the private sector is trying to quantify all this real-estate supply, both planned and under construction, to see if markets are or soon will be oversaturated. Private developers are extremely tight-fisted about divulging hard numbers about their schemes. Such an exercise just might generate a picture of such oversupply in the market, and a future scramble for thin demand, as to frighten even the most optimistic developers. And the competition is all the more stiff when one considers that additional supply on the market is coming from well-located developments in parts of Cairo proper—in particular along the Nile, in Zahra' al-Maadi, and in Madinat Nasr—which continue to witness the construction of new residential complexes, hotels, office towers, shopping complexes, and so on.[39]

Desert Cairo as the Speculative Frontier

Until now it seems that there continues to be 'real' demand for some of Cairo's desert development, at least in certain locations and in certain submarkets. That is, most of the tens of thousands of residential units and plots of land on the market continue to be bought.[40] For many private families with means (not to mention companies), the main purpose of purchasing land and buildings in desert Cairo is a means of speculative investment. It is perceived that moneys put into land, bricks, and concrete will be safe, incur no recurrent costs,[41] and will appreciate at rates higher than inflation. This helps explain the incredibly high rate of vacancies of completed housing units in the new towns. Alternative investment opportunities for family capital—the stock market, bank time deposits, businesses, and bonds—are either risky or generate only small returns that don't even match inflation. The intention may not only be speculative investment—the investor may reason that the housing unit could have a use in the future, as housing for sons or daughters, for example, but this purpose in many cases tends to be secondary.[42] This investment perspective goes a long way toward explaining both the past levels of property construction and vacancies, and the continuing rush to purchase land and property in desert Cairo.

The move of private and family capital into speculative real estate instead of productive investments and savings instruments is manifest not only in the new towns around Cairo. It is a phenomenon found throughout Cairo and Egypt, and is in fact a pervasive characteristic of developing economies in general and of Arab countries in particular. And the phenomenon is most apparent in capital cities, where there are both the highest concentrations of the wealthy *and* the most opportunities for such investment. All capital cities have their suburbs and enclaves where real-estate speculation is rampant, even in places such as Kabul, Damascus, Kinshasa, Sana'a, and Jakarta. Yet Cairo's desert represents a truly unique concentration of the speculative property playground within a major capital region, and it has absorbed and continues to suck up a huge portion of Egypt's speculative investment and family capital. In fact, the desire to invest in Cairo's desert, and especially to purchase new land parcels from NUCA, reflects a self-reinforcing speculative element. As long as speculative demand continues, the resale value of land and property will be high, which further encourages speculative investment.[43] Even public housing units in the new towns are subject to this phenomenon.

Is Desert Cairo a New Urban Development Paradigm or Just One Huge Investment Bubble and Patronage Vehicle?

Looking at the thirty-year history of the particular form of development found in desert Cairo and the continuing and even accelerating trend toward more of the same, the suspicion is inescapable that the real reason for the new towns and other desert projects around Cairo is to add to the speculative frontier, replenish the land resource needed for state patronage, and continue to create conditions for profitable private schemes with little or no utility value. This may sound like an overly severe conclusion, and it is certainly not a popular one. But the fact that more and more of Cairo's desert land continues to be converted into investment opportunities, in spite of the stubborn inability of even the older desert neighborhoods to reach anywhere near their potential, would seem to indicate that there are forces at play that have little to do with real urban expansion. All of this desert land is or was in the hands of government agencies, and it is government that has avoided any attempt to pause and reconsider where all of this desert development is leading, in spite of the heavy financial burdens placed upon it for required infrastructure.[44] Quite simply, there are too many pressures from special interests to capture some of this land resource and profit from it. It is revealing to see who gains such desert tracts. Either they are assigned wholesale to the well-known private corporate class, or to powerful state interests such as the police, or prominent public enterprises; or they are carved up and 'retailed' to citizens, many if not most of whom hope to make windfall profits out of resale.

Certainly, some development in Cairo's desert actually has a utility value. The many factories found in Cairo's new towns do churn out consumer goods and do provide employment. There are many satisfied middle- and upper-class families who swear by the quiet, uncrowded, and clean quality of residential life on offer in the desert compounds,[45] and there are some limited-income families who enjoy the subsidized apartment units built in the new towns. Even some of the commercial and service establishments that have located in the desert can actually be deemed successful. Yet, when looked at as a whole, it is the truly gigantic scale of Cairo's desert development and the resulting oversupply on the market, the patchy and disappointing record for most schemes, and the seemingly endless additions to it that compromise the whole experiment.

So what about the desert new towns as part of Greater Cairo? Will they ever succeed, if not on the grand scales envisioned, then at least as upscale suburban enclaves and clusters of modern 'beltway' enterprises? Only time will tell. Certainly the government can be expected to pour yet more resources into Cairo's new towns, and real-estate demand may continue to manifest itself, since speculative bubbles can be stubbornly durable. Also, it seems that MHUUD has finally discovered it can actually make huge profits through land sales in Cairo's new towns and indeed leverage more capital funds through bond issues.[46] It may be that MHUUD will impose some order on the land scramble and even begin to claw back some land upon which failed projects stand. Yet the trends are not promising.

Even if Cairo's new towns and other desert schemes do manage to register a certain success as suburban development, the basic issues remain. Desert Cairo will continue to be a financial drain on government budgets as more and more areas need to be served, as existing infrastructure, much of which has fallen into disrepair, needs renovation, and as the costs of operating and maintaining the new towns steadily mount. The drain on the national economy is even larger, especially in terms of the billions upon billions of pounds of both public and private sunk investments that are lying unfinished, unused, or abandoned.

Cairo's desert development seriously threatens the current compactness of the metropolis, probably the single greatest advantage of Greater Cairo as an efficient megacity, as explained in Chapter 8. There is already a tremendous explosion of vehicular travel required to traverse the huge new distances to and within Cairo's many desert developments, and this can only increase by orders of magnitude over the coming decades. Not only does this generate enormous new volumes of traffic throughout Cairo's already clogged arteries, it will represent a much higher level of fuel consumption for transport and also higher energy and water costs to maintain urban life in an inhospitable desert environment. This is very far from any idea of a sustainable city with a low carbon footprint.

Finally, it should not be forgotten that the original intention of the new towns around Cairo was to attract millions of ordinary Egyptians into the desert to deconcentrate Cairo and shift the city's urban expansion away from the agricultural plain. This, more than anything, is the failure of desert Cairo.

7

Working in the City

Greater Cairo is without a doubt the central pivot around which the nation's economy turns.[1] As with any megacity in a developing country, especially one that is also the nation's capital, Cairo captures more than its share of investments and higher-order economic activities, and it is where there is a disproportionate representation of the well-to-do and political as well as cultural elites. Whether or not this concentration constitutes an 'urban bias' or simply reflects urban economic logic can be long debated, but it is a given that is well understood.

What is less understood is how the nearly five million families in Greater Cairo gain their livelihoods. As pointed out in Chapter 2, it is becoming more and more difficult for the Egyptian economy to generate the jobs and economic opportunities needed to absorb the huge and growing labor force and to provide decent work. The population of Egypt is young, and unemployment and underemployment are chronic. Greater Cairo, where at least two hundred thousand persons enter the labor force each year, not counting others who come to the capital to seek new opportunities and new lives, is no exception. Most of these entrants into the workplace have few marketable skills that will land them stable jobs, and only a minuscule few belong to well-connected families. How do all these people cope? Especially, how are the armies of common people, poorly educated and with hardly any means to start a business, able to carry on and make a living?

This chapter tries to explain how Cairo's inhabitants work and survive in an environment that is, in many ways, stacked against them. First, the city's formal economy, and the jobs and opportunities it offers, is briefly described. Then the various kinds and shades of the informal economy are taken up, including a critical assessment of the ability of this huge sector to 'fill the gap' and to offer a future to Cairo's millions.

Jobs in Government

By far the largest single employer in Greater Cairo is the government. According to CAPMAS's *Statistical Year Book*, in 2007 there were 2.5 million employees in government agencies in Cairo Governorate alone, and this figure rises to almost 2.8 million employees in Greater Cairo as a whole. This total represents almost half of the country's total civilian government labor force (excluding those in uniform), and it underscores just how concentrated government is in Greater Cairo.[2] The figure for Cairo Governorate in 2007 showed an unexplained jump from 2005, when there were only 1.62 million government employees. Both of these figures seem very high when compared to Cairo Governorate's *total* labor force of 2.6 million, as reported in the census of 2006, but presumably this can be partly explained by the high number of employees working in Cairo's government offices but residing in Giza or Qalyubiya. If the 2007 figure can be believed, then government employment accounts for an amazing 49 percent of Greater Cairo's labor force, or 38 percent if the 2005 figures are used. Of course, many government employees have more than one job, so government dominance in the labor force is not as acute as the figures suggest.

Whatever the real figure, there is no doubt that government and public-sector jobs dominate Cairo's labor market. With thirty-two ministries, fifty central economic authorities, and eighty-nine service authorities, plus a myriad of local government offices in the three (since 2008, five) governorates of Greater Cairo, it could not be otherwise. Here is not the place to enter into the details and issues concerning government employment in Egypt, but the following points need to be understood. First, it could be said that to a considerable extent government employment has become a kind of colossal welfare program.[3] Salaries, even including bonuses and perks, are extremely low, especially lower-level entry wages, and the pay system itself is hopelessly bureaucratic.[4] Government employees have an entrenched reputation for underperformance, even though some lower-level officials, especially those who deal with the public, actually work very hard.

How does one land a government job? As with many aspects of the Egyptian government, the system is definitely opaque, and it is very rare that recruitment campaigns are launched or that vacant positions are announced. Usually it is only those inside a state organization who learn of possibilities, and then there is a scramble to amass the necessary papers of relatives or friends and get them to the official who matters. In any event, for over a decade there was supposed to be a freeze on new hiring, part of the government's policy of trying to shrink the bloated bureaucracy and the resulting continuous hemorrhage of the state budget.

The subject of government employment in Cairo cannot be closed without mentioning that some positions can be very lucrative. For those in government services who deal with citizens in need of documents, stamps, licenses, permits, and so on, petty bribes are common, and these can mount up over time to represent quite an income stream. Even heftier bribes are sometimes paid by people, such as those who want an inspector to look the other way while an illegal building is constructed. Thus, government employment, beside providing rock-solid job security and a certain prestige (at least in the marriage market), holds out the hope that an employee just might land at a desk or window through which the public desperately needs to pass. In fact, such 'gatekeeping' positions are understandably popular, and it is said that there is a secondary market, within particular government bureaucracies, which dispenses appointments to such positions against serious payments.

Jobs in Formal Manufacturing

By some accounts, Greater Cairo contributes to 57 percent of Egypt's total industrial production.[5] The industrial areas of Cairo's new towns (Tenth of Ramadan, Sixth of October, al-Badr and al-'Ubur) are home to over 1,500 factories and are said to employ almost 200,000 workers.[6] These factories, almost all of which are less than twenty-five years old, tend to be medium-size manufacturing and distribution concerns that employ fifty to two hundred and fifty workers, although a few large factories also exist. Most of these enterprises are privately owned, and quite a few are either Egyptian–foreign joint ventures or subsidiaries of multinationals. Most products are consumer goods. Starting salaries for semi-skilled workers are extremely low, and a monthly wage of LE400 ($80) for ten hours a day, six days a week, is the norm, at least in the garment factories. Although Egyptian labor laws theoretically protect workers from abuses, many are the tricks which employers utilize to enable them to fire employees at will and otherwise exploit them. In these remote new towns, companies usually provide buses to transport workers from and to various parts of Greater Cairo, and in addition to long working hours it is not uncommon for a factory worker to spend another two or three hours each day commuting.

Industries in new towns may be the most visible face of Cairo's manufacturing, but older industries continue to operate in various locations throughout the agglomeration, especially in Shubra al-Khayma, Helwan/Tura, and Abu Za'bal. These tend to be big heavy industries, the largest of which is the Egypt Iron and Steel Company in Helwan with 19,800 workers, followed by the Eastern Company for Tobacco (producing Egypt's favorite cigarette, Cleopatra) at the beginning of al-Haram Street in Giza with 12,300 workers. Almost all of these industrial plants were originally public-sector enterprises, although some have been privatized and others are slated for the same fate. Together these in-town factories employ over 60,000 persons.[7] Salaries are low but usually better than industrial wages in the new towns. There is a plan prepared by the Ministry of Trade and Industry to relocate almost all of these factories to new locations outside the city, but the costs of such moves will be colossal, and there is quite a history of unsuccessful attempts to get rid of the more polluting of these industries.

Greater Cairo's manufacturing is also carried out in thousands and thousands of small manufacturing enterprises situated in many neighborhoods of the city. In 1996 a total of 77,000 manufacturing establishments were enumerated in the Census of Establishments in Greater Cairo, with an average size of just under four workers. Although some of these enterprises can be considered formal, the bulk are definitely informal, as will be discussed below.

Jobs in the Formal Business Sector

The formal business sector, upon which the government pins so much hope as the way to generate jobs for the millions, has been growing rapidly in Greater Cairo, especially since the mid-1990s. There are very few reliable numbers to be found about its size or growth rates, but it seems still to employ only a small portion of the total labor force in the city, at least compared to the government and to the informal and small-firm sectors. The kinds of enterprises found in the formal business sector are many—hotels, restaurants, retail stores, banks, airlines and travel agencies, corporate offices, and real-estate agencies, not

Map 7.1. Greater Cairo: main formal industrial areas in 2007.

Tenth of Ramadan

al-Shuruq

To Suez

To 'Ain Sukna

Abu Za'bal

al-'Ubur

New Cairo

Airport

Fifteenth of May

Heliopolis

Madinat Nasr

Shaq al-Tha'ban

Shubra al-Khayma

Maadi

Helwan

Airport

Abu Rawash

Sheikh Zayed

Giza

Pyramids

Sixth of October

To Fayoum

0   30 Km

to mention embassies and foreign oil and gas companies, foreign aid administrations, and private schools and universities. The fastest growing subsector, and that in which the government puts so much faith, is information technology and services.

Recently, Egypt has introduced a number of reforms to improve the business environment—particularly in terms of starting a business, dealing with licenses, facilitating exports and imports, and registering property. Egypt seems to have scored quite well in these efforts, particularly in Cairo, according to a recent World Bank Report.[8] But these reforms benefit only larger, incorporated enterprises, which are statistically very few in Cairo. According to the 2006 Census of Establishments, of a total of almost 700,000 active, nongovernment establishments in Greater Cairo, only 2,036 had *shirka musahima* (limited liability share company) status. A full 92 percent of all establishments had no legal status: they were *fardi* (individual), that is, not registered under the Companies Law.[9]

It is possible, with a bit of generalization, to divide the job market of the private business sector in Cairo into two distinct segments. At the higher end are the much sought-after managerial and other white-collar positions to be found in such modern enterprises as banks, foreign companies, information technology services, and large Egyptian corporations. Starting salaries can exceed LE2,500 per month, and for some key skills such as software engineers, LE20,000 per month can be demanded. At this higher level a curious distortion in the city's job market is said to exist. Modern corporations are desperate to hire highly skilled managers and professionals (and almost invariably, good English is essential); they complain that finding these people is very difficult, and hence offer what, in Egypt, are astronomical wages. At the same time there are huge phalanxes of unemployed graduates, armed with multiple degrees and diplomas, who endlessly scurry around Cairo but who simply cannot find any position in their field, even at abysmal salaries.

The second part of the private-sector job market in Cairo, which is by far the largest in numbers of jobs, comprises the multitudes of clerical and menial positions in private establishments. These include drivers, maintenance men, shop assistants, office clerks, receptionists, tea boys, cleaners, and so on. Their salaries are very low; for example a female shop assistant will be lucky to earn LE300 a month, a driver LE600. Even young accountants, architects, and engineers will be happy with LE1,500 per month to start working in a private firm.

The private-business sector in Cairo, supposedly operating on market principles, hardly does so when it comes to hiring. In short, connections count. It may simply be that a clerk or driver petitions the boss to hire his son or daughter, or it may involve extended pressure through connected relatives for a worthless nephew to gain a managerial sinecure in a large Egyptian corporation. Certainly, some people are hired purely on merit, but with a total imbalance between supply and demand and scores of applicants lining up for every job vacancy, using every personal connection possible seems to be the standard approach to landing a job with anywhere near a decent wage.

The curious case of university professors and physicians, of which there must be tens of thousands in Cairo, must be noted. These professionals, who have spent years and years to become qualified, find themselves in an unenviable situation, where again supply totally outstrips demand on the job market. (See Chapter 2 for a discussion of the oversupply of the university-educated in Egypt.) A starting salary for assistant professor in one of Cairo's four public universities is LE750. Thus, to make ends meet, if he or she is an architect, engineer, or economist, he or she will either open a private office or try to gain employment with a consulting firm. Similarly, a medical doctor may have a secure if poorly paid position in a public hospital, but he or she will also need to open or work in a specialized private clinic or two. Thus, these professionals straddle both the public and private sectors, and, parenthetically, they need to carry more than one set of business cards.

Informal Work in Cairo and Small and Micro Enterprises

What is an 'informal enterprise' or the 'informal private sector?' While in the formal private sector "economic units are under indirect state control in the form of registration, regulations, and taxation, informal economic units are largely (but often not totally) free of both direct and indirect state control."[10] The word 'largely' is problematic, and it means that the boundary between formal and informal enterprises can be a fuzzy one. Hernando Desoto's Institute for Liberty and Democracy, which has investigated the nature of Cairo's informal enterprises in some depth, used the following definition: An informal enterprise (or extralegal enterprise, the terminology preferred) is one that has neither a business license nor a commercial or industrial registration, and does not keep regular accounting books, or pay regular taxes.[11] Thus there are degrees of informality, at least in the permit and regulation sense.[12] It should be pointed out that in Egypt, as in most developing countries, an informal enterprise is roughly synonymous with a very small enterprise. Normally, a distinction is made between agricultural and nonagricultural informal enterprises, and informal employment can be broken down into two types: informal wage employment (that is, working in a small, informal enterprise) and informal self-employment (that is, working for oneself, such as a street vendor).

To put the concept of informal economies into perspective, it has been estimated, based on data sets from developing countries, that informal, nonagricultural employment comprises 48 percent of all employment in North Africa and 65 percent in Asia. Calculations of the contribution of informal enterprises to national Gross Domestic Product (GDP) are less precise, but one study puts it at 29 percent in North Africa and 31 percent in Asia.[13]

Given the confusing definitions of what constitutes informal employment, it is difficult to come up with a precise figure of how many persons are so employed in Greater Cairo. It may be that 25 to 40 percent of all workers in the metropolis are mainly informally employed. Such figures must be treated with caution, since there is no clear-cut way to enumerate informal enterprises. Also, the same person can work both formally and informally.

What are the activities of informal enterprises? According to one rather dated but probably still valid study, in 1998 it was estimated that nationally, 38 percent of workers in informal establishments were engaged in various forms of trade, 31 percent in services, and 19 percent in manufacturing. Construction and transport represented only 5 percent each.[14]

As a rough proxy for informal enterprises, many observers focus on the small and micro-enterprise (SME) sector, usually defined as units employing from one to four employees including the proprietor.[15] But since an overwhelming majority of private enterprises in Egypt meet this definition, one is really talking about almost the entirety of private-sector enterprises and about 50 percent of their labor forces.

Just how extensive is Greater Cairo's SME sector today? In 1996 Cairo Governorate alone had a total of 310,000 active private establishments, of which 90 percent had four or less employees,[16] and of these, some 39 percent had only one single worker, in other words, the proprietor. All together, these SMEs employed 511,000 persons in 1996, or an average of only 1.65 workers per unit. It is possible to estimate that the number of such SMEs had grown from 279,000 to 348,000 in the period 1996–2006, an increase of 25 percent. While this calculation applies only to Cairo Governorate, it can be assumed that even faster growth of SMEs has occurred in other parts of Greater Cairo, especially in peri-urban areas. It is possible to conclude that in 2006 the total number of jobs generated by the SME sector exceeded 1.05 million in all of Greater Cairo.

These figures give some sense of the small, atomized, and personalized nature of the large bulk of private-sector establishments in Cairo. They also show that small and micro enterprises generate a huge amount of employment, that the phenomenon is firmly embedded in the private enterprise structure of Greater Cairo, and that the number of such establishments is increasing at a rate higher than overall population growth.

The advantages enjoyed by informal or extralegal enterprises are well known. Taxes are normally avoided. It is easy to enter into a particular market (required investment and working capital is small to minimal), working hours are flexible, and operating costs are low. However, there are also many disadvantages, both for the informal enterprise and for the informal self-employed. There is little or no job security, occupational health hazards may be horrendous, and, perhaps most importantly in Cairo at least, informal enterprises must pay bribes to keep operating.

Informal enterprises also have few sources of finance and credit, and the ways they mobilize capital are almost all through informal or family relations. One survey of informal enterprises in Greater Cairo discovered that 40 percent of them were financed by savings from previous work, another 25 percent were inherited or financed by inherited money, and another 13 percent by a combination of savings and loans from relatives and friends. Only 2.5 percent were financed, even in part, by bank loans.

Small Manufacturing Workshops

One important segment of the informal enterprise sector in Greater Cairo is made up of small manufacturing firms operating out of workshops in downtown and informal areas of Greater Cairo. Very roughly, these can be estimated to have numbered some 45,000 establishments in 2006, employing 200,000 persons. These small firms (average size four workers including the owner), produce a wide variety of intermediate and consumer goods, mainly plastic and paper products, metal items, car parts, furniture, processed food, footwear, and clothing.

Most of these manufacturing workshops are informal, that is, they can be considered illegal since they do not have and probably cannot obtain all the necessary permits. They are frequently prey to inspectors from various government agencies looking for bribes.[17] They also tend to use old and outdated technologies, do not keep proper records, and do not have any business plans. They have no access to finance or insurance and are not astute about market potentials. Most of their products are of low quality and low price. Mostly, skills are acquired through on-the-job training under the very common apprenticeship system. Furthermore, competition among similar manufacturing workshops is fierce, since it is very common for former apprentices to start up their own businesses. Finally, they are looked down upon by authorities.

A sampling of such workshop manufacturers, located in four run-down or informal neighborhoods, has been studied in detail over 1986 to 2004. The neighborhoods were Manshiyat Nasir, al-Gamaliya, Bab al-Sha'riya, and al-Matariya, and a total of 2,800 enterprises were covered.[18] These small firms mainly produced aluminum and metal products, textiles and clothing, furniture, foodstuffs, handicrafts, and shoes. It was found that there was a rapid increase in both the number of enterprises and workers in the 1980s. However, this boom came to an end in the early 1990s, partly due to overall economic stagnation in Egypt and also due to a flood on the local market of cheap manufacturing goods, either imported from Asia or produced by modern local industries. Such competition had a severe negative impact on the surveyed small workshops, yet their number managed to remain stable in the 1992–2004 period, with some closing and other new ones opening. The survival strategy of these firms was to reduce costs, mainly by decreasing the number of male laborers and by substituting more children and women. Those firms best able to adapt were those that produced intermediate handicraft products and were located in more central areas of the metropolis.

The Distribution and Concentrations of Establishments in Greater Cairo

Where were the 700,000 active private establishments, which together employed 2.5 million persons in 2006, to be found in Greater Cairo? The 2006 Census of Establishments tells us that 388,000 units were in Cairo Governorate, 200,000 in Giza, and 110,000 in Qalyubiya. Unfortunately, the detailed results of this census are not yet available, and it is necessary to refer to a study carried out for the Institute for Liberty and Democracy in 2002, which, although it used 1996 figures, gives a good picture of the then spatial distribution of establishments throughout Greater Cairo and one which probably has not changed much.[19]

Active private establishments were found throughout Greater Cairo in 1996. As is expected, there was a concentration of establishments in the downtown and central areas. But there was also a very significant concentration in some outer districts of the metropolis, as can be seen in Map 7.2. And almost all of these districts were either totally informal residential areas or primarily so. Thus al-Basatin, al-'Umraniya, Bulaq al-Dakrur, Imbaba, Waraq al-'Arab, Shubra al-Khayma (two *aqsam*), and Khusus/al-Marg contained very high numbers of private establishments, representing 40 percent of all establishments in Greater Cairo. These are also the main informal residential areas of Greater Cairo as described in Chapter 4, and such a relation is not simply coincidental. Not only do these areas contain very high concentrations of inhabitants, they are also the loci for a preponderance of population-serving establishments as well as a high proportion of informal enterprises, workshops in particular.

In these same areas the proportion of manufacturing establishments to the total was relatively high, usually exceeding 20 percent. In complete contrast, the more upscale areas, such as Dokki, Agouza, Madinat Nasr, and Heliopolis, contained almost no manufacturing establishments. But what is truly remarkable was the enormous concentration of manufacturing units in the historic areas of Cairo. The *aqsam* of 'Abdin, al-Muski, al-Azbakiya, al-Darb al-Ahmar, Bab al-Sha'riya and al-Gamaliya have very high concentrations of all three kinds of establishment, and in particular manufacturing firms. The highest concentrations are in al-Muski, with 125 establishments per hectare, of which one-third are manufacturing firms. This shows that the historic parts of town have become the preferred location for small and informal establishments, especially manufacturing units, where location within the metropolis is excellent, and where the full advantages of clustering and production chains can operate. The fact that these areas are terribly congested does not seem to matter.

The Self-employed and Living on the Margin
Beside work in informal establishments, many Cairenes find work as individuals outside enterprises. There are no firm figures, but one study estimates that in Cairo in 1998, 40 percent of the informally employed

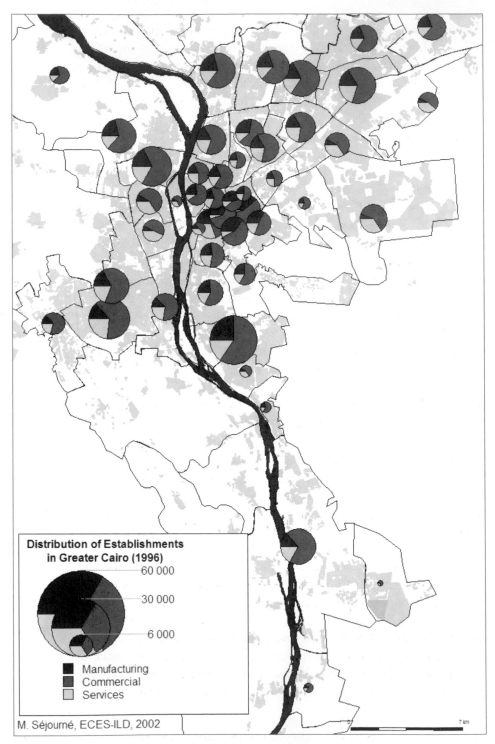

Map 7.2. Distribution of establishments in Greater Cairo 1996.

Inside image:

Distribution of Establishments in Greater Cairo (1996)
- 60 000
- 30 000
- 6 000

Manufacturing
Commercial
Services

M. Séjourné, ECES-ILD, 2002

7 km

worked outside any fixed establishment.[20] If this is true, then one could hazard a guess that these self-employed amounted to over 500,000 in 2006, or almost 10 percent of Greater Cairo's economically active population at that time.[21] These people can be seen in any street in Cairo and include vendors of vegetables, fruit, newspapers, clothes, prepared food, and other items. Their operations are carried out on carts or are found on sidewalks and practically any other public space. The streets of downtown Cairo sometimes seem to have become one vast bazaar of cheap clothing, shoes, and plastic toy vendors who keep one eye open for patrols from Cairo Governorate's utilities police. But there are also small armies of plumbers, carpenters, electricians, and painters who carry out repairs and remodel apartments. Then there are very large numbers of domestic servants and taxi, truck, and *tuk-tuk* drivers. In addition, there are a number of informal enterprises operating out of homes. Finally, there are car attendants and those who act as porters in commercial areas. Little other than anecdotal information is known about this huge number of workers since they largely escape coverage in the census and other statistical instruments.

Few of these self-employed make more than very modest and precarious incomes. But even worse off are the thousands who 'sell' paper tissues in the streets, scavenge for sellable trash, or wash cars. Then there are those who simply beg. Street children are recently said to have become a common phenomenon in Cairo. Whether this 'recent trend' is more due to the huge interest on the part of the media, aid agencies, NGOs, and social deviancy experts than to an actual increase in numbers, is difficult to say. Totally unsubstantiated estimates put the number of street children in Egypt at between 200,000 and one million, most of whom are presumed to be found in Greater Cairo.[22]

Attempts to Generate Informal Jobs and to Formalize the Informal

Ever since the 1980s, international aid agencies have been promoting ways to support informal enterprises in developing countries, mainly as a way to fight poverty and generate employment. Providing credit, raising skills, introducing better technologies, and extending business support services have all been part of their arsenals. Also featuring prominently are strategies to formalize informal firms by reducing and streamlining bureaucratic regulations, with the aim of reducing the costs and hassles of becoming formal.

Egypt has been a prominent target for these programs. Most activities have been aimed at rural areas, where poverty is considered to be the most acute. Even so, a number of forms of assistance have been extended to informal enterprises in Greater Cairo. For example, in what is considered one of the most successful programs of this nature worldwide, the Egyptian Social Fund for Development, through its Small Enterprise Development Organization, has extended massive amounts of credit, some to informal manufacturing enterprises to purchase new machinery, some to transportation operators to acquire minibuses—among other forms of credit.[23] Also, myriads of NGOs have begun setting up microloan programs, especially targeting the poor and women in informal areas. In fact, it is hard to find any donor organization operating in Egypt that does not have some form of assistance aimed at informal small and micro enterprises.

Yet whether and to what extent all of these efforts have been successful in generating new jobs and in combating poverty is hotly debated. The government has been very slow in removing and simplifying regulations associated with starting up a formal business and keeping it running. Informal business owners have also proven less than enthusiastic in joining such programs. And there are indications that improving and formalizing some enterprises does not necessarily generate an overall increase in employment, since these improved firms simply tend to crowd out less fortunate informal competitors.[24] Perhaps all that can be said is that in Greater Cairo, with its huge, complex, and diversified markets, assistance to informal enterprises is more likely to succeed than in rural towns and villages.

Optimism and Pessimism

Standing back and looking at how jobs are created and how people find work in Greater Cairo, one needs doses of both optimism and pessimism. First of all, the supply of labor will continue to outstrip employers' demand for the foreseeable future. Government employment simply cannot continue to grow, and there are not enough formal private-sector jobs being created, whether in manufacturing or services or trade. All the hope placed in the information technology sector, direct foreign investment, and the modern, global corporation as a means to provide decent work for Greater Cairo's millions is wildly off the mark. The SME and informal sectors have more and more filled the gap, and certainly, programs aimed at stimulating the sector and formalizing it have had some benefits in terms of job creation. But how long can informal employment, with its low remuneration and low productivity, remain the sponge that soaks up the unemployed? Informal enterprises and the self-employed exhibit incredible entrepreneurship, dynamism, and flexibility to adapt to changing market situations, and it just may be that a significant portion of these enterprises will become formal, improve productivity, and generate a whole new wave of employment opportunities. But will this be enough?

8

City on the Move: A Complementary Informality?

Every large metropolis lives by its transport. Much is said about information technology and the wired city of the future, where trips and the workplace are made largely redundant, but so far—even in the west—getting people and goods from place to place remains the key to a functioning city. Highways and bridges and streets and rail lines and metros are the blood vessels of the city, and these need to be kept flowing. Thus the question is: how is Cairo able to cope? How can a huge and growing urban agglomeration, one whose development is so chaotic and out of control, maintain even the semblance of a functioning transport system?

Of course, many would say that Cairo's transport systems do *not* function. In fact, it is hard to find a description of Cairo, however short, which does not manage to conjure up images of near-Armageddon when it comes to traffic, and to many a casual visitor the ensnarled streets rank only second to the Pyramids of Giza as the defining impression of the city. Visitors are shocked by the erratic and seemingly suicidal driving, by the nonchalance of meandering pedestrians, and by the seemingly perverse disregard for traffic rules. Among Cairenes, commentary on the daily odyssey of getting from A to B usually trumps talk of the weather, of politics, and of anything else. Horror stories abound of total paralysis, gridlock, two-hour standstills, and, most famously, of half-the-city shutdowns when the president's motorcade moves, an event that has become standard front-page news in the opposition newspapers. Add to this the rapidly growing private car ownership, total lack of off-street parking, the poorly maintained public bus fleet, and the random and arbitrary exercise of authority by the traffic police, and one could be excused for thinking that the city is about to shut down.

Is this true? As economists would ask, have the negative externalities of urban agglomeration—the congestion—come to outweigh the positive economic benefits of scale and proximity? Has Cairo reached that tipping point? Certainly the traffic can be awful, even horrific, and it seems to be becoming much worse.[1] And given the completely arbitrary approach of the Ministry of Interior toward traffic management and enforcement, plus the Lego mindset used to design elevated highways, on-ramps, lanes, curbing, and traffic intersections, it is a wonder that Cairo's transport functions at all.

But the city's traffic does move, and its transport systems do function, however chaotically. For example, the average speed of traffic movement in Greater Cairo is currently estimated at 15.8 km/hour, compared to 12.3 km/hour in Bangkok and 12.4 km/hour in Mexico City.[2] Prophesies of doom and paralysis for Cairo's traffic have been around for decades. Yet the city manages to lurch from one stop-gap measure to the other, a highway here, a bridge there, and one-way traffic systems almost everywhere. Thus the real question to answer is how does the city keep moving?

First, and perhaps most crucially, moving around Cairo is relatively easy because the metropolis is dense and for the most part *very* compact. According to the Japan International Cooperation Agency, Greater Cairo can be considered the most densely inhabited metropolis on earth, at 257 persons per built-up hectare, denser than the metropolitan areas of Lagos, Manila, Tehran, Jakarta, or Delhi.[3] Even higher density estimates of above 350 persons per hectare, are given for Greater Cairo, although some sources put Mumbai just ahead of Cairo as the world's most dense city.[4]

High density means that trips are mostly short. Over three-fourths of Greater Cairo's population live within fifteen kilometers of the center of Cairo (Ramsis Square), and almost half live within ten kilometers of al-Azhar. It is revealing that, according to a trip movement study in 2000, more than 36 percent of all journeys within Greater Cairo were on foot, up from an estimated 25 percent in 1970.[5] And this is in what is probably the least pedestrian-friendly city in the world. Obviously, high densities and compact urban development mitigate the load on transport systems and, perhaps more importantly, allow for the very high ridership of public transport systems that guarantees their frequent service and economic viability.

How did Cairo become so dense and compact, in spite of the centrifugal tendencies so common in large modern cities toward endless sprawl?

The answer is clear, as has been explained above in Chapters 3 and 4. It is the informal response to growing demand for habitation in Greater Cairo that has produced and continues to produce huge, dense and well-located neighborhoods that not only absorb most of the additional population but that also generate, within or in close proximity to them, most of the economic activities, jobs, and services these inhabitants need. It was not at all planned this way, and had the government's long-held determination to expand the city solely into its distant and extensive desert fringes been successful, it is hard to imagine how Cairo's transport, with all its faults, would be able to function, or at what costs.

High densities alone, however, cannot explain how the city's transport functions. There are an estimated twenty million person-trips per day in the metropolis by vehicle; some of these entail very significant distances, and it is estimated that such trips increase in number by almost 5 percent per year. To understand transport dynamics in Cairo, perhaps the most revealing feature is its evolving mix of types of vehicular transport, or 'modal split,' as transport engineers like to call it.

The Rise of the Private Microbus and Metro

Back in the early 1970s, when the population of Greater Cairo was just over a third of what it is today, the Cairo Transport Authority public bus system accounted for 62 percent of all motorized person-trips, tramways for another 15 percent, and suburban rail for 8 percent.[6] Thus, government modes of transport accommodated 86 percent of all vehicular trips, with the rest accommodated by metered taxis and private cars. At the time, the urban ballet of overstuffed, wheezing, sideways-leaning buses, near-riots at bus stops, and trains with as many people on the roof as inside, were some of Cairo's enduring images.

Sometime in the mid-1970s the first private, informal minibuses started to appear. In 1977, a law allowed the operation of eight hundred of these eleven-seat minibuses on a limited number of fixed routes. In the mid 1980s, fourteen- and eighteen-seat vehicles were also allowed, and by 1985 the number of private minibuses had jumped to 14,000 vehicles on 133 different routes. By 1998 the Giza and Cairo Traffic administrations reported that there were 27,300 minibuses running on over 650 routes.[7] Although more recent figures are unavailable, it is inevitable that the number of such minibuses has continued to rise, as have their routes, share of the market, and sophistication.

The importance of this mode of public transport, especially for the average citizen, cannot be exaggerated. By 1998 the minibus share of total vehicular trips in Greater Cairo had reached 28 percent, or a full half of all modes of public transport. The minibus network covers the whole agglomeration of Greater Cairo, expanding into areas, especially informal neighborhoods, where government buses do not penetrate. Whenever an area—even an outlying village—grows to a sufficient size, private minibus operators will lay on services. The flexibility of minibuses to serve all parts of the metropolis in response to demand goes a long way toward explaining the attraction of informal areas and their ascendancy in urban space. And studies have repeatedly shown that the minibus is the main form of transport for the poor. For example, in informal areas such as Imbaba and Bulaq al-Dakrur, the minibus represented 57 and 58 percent of all vehicular trips respectively.[8] The minibus is also very popular with women, since by this mode they can avoid what transport planners like to call the 'promiscuous nature' of some male passengers in the public buses and in the metro.

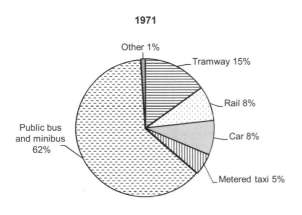

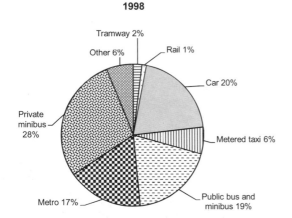

Figure 8.1. Fundamental shift in composition of passenger transport in Greater Cairo 1971–98. Note 'shared taxi' mode refers to the private minibus, 'bus and minibus' to the public bus system, and 'ENR' to Egyptian National Railways (Metge, *World Bank Urban Transport Strategy Review*).

The success of the minibus is due to its individualistic, minimally regulated, market-oriented modes of operation. Fares and routes are nominally set by the governorate traffic departments, but there is much leeway for individual operators to alter both of these. Current fares range from LE0.50 to LE1.50, depending on the distances involved. Most minibus owners have only one vehicle, which they either drive them themselves or 'rent' to other operators. Other owners may have two to five vehicles or mini-fleets. It is said that many of the owners are police officers, which helps immeasurably to resolve the inevitable control hassles to which minibus operators are subject. In all cases, it is common to keep the vehicles operating as much as possible, with drivers managing different shifts. After all, for many owners there are hefty monthly installment payments on their vehicles that must be met.

The minibus in Cairo is not a total success story by far. The individualistic, market-oriented modes of operation and minimal control also mean that the minibus is a major contributor to traffic congestion. Profit margins are very thin, and thus speed, low maintenance, and erratic driving are almost a necessity. Competition among drivers for passengers is very stiff, and along any route a driver will aggressively try to overtake his competitors to scoop up waiting passengers. In narrow streets this means it is in the leading minibus driver's interest to block

Figure 8.2. Minibuses competing for passengers, Munib, 2009. (Photograph by David Sims.)

Figure 8.3. Minibuses stopping for passengers on Ring Road at Ismailiya Canal Road off-ramp, 2009. (Photograph by David Sims.)

the general flow to prevent this. Add to this the fact that the minibus will stop anywhere to pick up or let out passengers, even on the city's most important arterials such as the Ring Road, and it is no wonder that traffic management consultants bemoan the minibus. As will be seen later, current plans see no role for the minibus in Greater Cairo's future public transport scenarios.

In addition to the minibus phenomenon, it is the progressive although delayed introduction of underground metro lines that has saved Cairo from complete paralysis. And had the original timetable for the implementation of the metro lines been adhered to, Greater Cairo proper just might, by now, be functioning as well as do the main capital cities of Europe. As it is, by 1998, with only one-and-a-half underground lines functioning, the metro already accounted for 17 percent of all vehicular person-trips in Greater Cairo and 30 percent of all public-transport trips.

Planning for Cairo's metro system was carried out in the early 1970s by the Ministry of Transport with French assistance. One north–south regional line from al-Marg to Helwan was proposed, as well as two urban underground lines, one from Bulaq al-Dakrur to Shubra al-Khayma, and the other from Imbaba to Salah Salim Street. Interchanges were planned within the central business district. The detailed design study, published in May 1973, foresaw the completion of the regional line by 1980 and the two urban lines by 1990, resulting in a total of sixty-two kilometers of networks.[9] The Ministry of Transport report actually suggested that a much faster implementation schedule could be adhered to, with all three lines able to be technically completed by 1981. However, the heavy financing needed to construct these lines was very slow in materializing due to the Egyptian government's other priorities, among them the new towns and *infitah* (Open Door) megaprojects. And in addition, the technical aspects of tunneling proved to be daunting, especially as there were no maps of existing water, power, and sewerage lines, all of which needed to be diverted. Some Cairo residents will remember the epic struggles in the 1980s to bore the first, 3.6-kilometer tunnel under the Tahrir area to link up the existing surface lines, a struggle that took five years and untold near-disasters.

As it was, the north–south regional line was opened only in 1987 and the second line was completed only by 1999, not including the extension to Munib, which was finished only in 2005. Construction of the first phase of the third line has recently begun on the al-'Abbasiya–'Ataba section. The alignment of this line has been radically changed from the original design, mainly because the Twenty-Six July flyover and the al-Azhar tunnel preclude using these axes. And the trajectory for this line has also been considerably extended. It is now planned to have two branches west of the Nile, one running the length of Gam'at al-Duwal al-'Arabiya Street and the other serving the huge informal areas of Imbaba and al-Waraq. In addition, after al-'Abbasiya, the line is expected to extend northeastward along Salah Salim, into Heliopolis and Nuzha, ultimately to terminate at Cairo Airport. Such an important line, with a total length of thirty-three kilometers, will greatly improve the movement of people within the metropolis and improve surface traffic circulation, but the first phase is not expected to be completed until 2010 and the whole line not until 2020. A fourth and even fifth underground metro line are on the drawing boards, but it is anyone's guess at what distant point in the far future these lines will materialize.

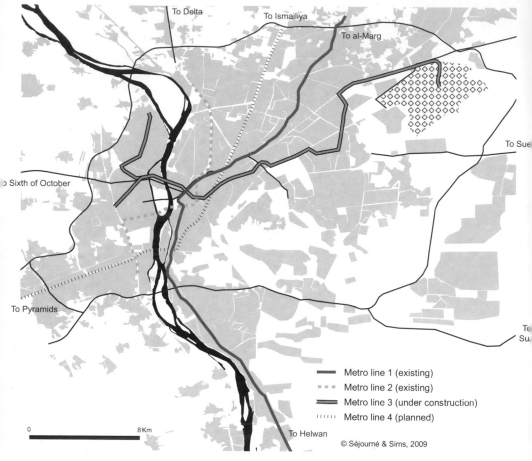

Map 8.1. Greater Cairo: metro lines 1–4.

The Private Car: The Avalanche to Come

To the casual observer visiting Cairo, it may appear that the private car is the main means of transport. Private vehicles clog all the main thoroughfares at peak times and well into the nights, especially in summer. Their numbers are such that parking is well-nigh impossible, not only in the main business areas but in many residential neighborhoods as well. And the casual observer would be correct to assume that private car ownership is increasing very rapidly, with the appearance of more and more fancy SUVs and luxury models, combined with legions of new small sedans and the ubiquitous Hundai Matrix. Sales of new vehicles in Egypt peaked in 2007 at a rate of 24,000 per month, over half of which end up on Cairo's already crammed streets.[10] An important factor contributing to the recent explosion in the numbers of the private car is the ease in obtaining car loans through monthly finance installments, which local banks love to promote and which have become the single most important form of consumer finance in Egypt.[11] And these new additions to the city's private car fleet have not at all replaced older vehicles. The Nasr 127s, 128s, and 133s, the Ladas, Peugeots, and so on, most of which are well over twenty years old, remain popular and have impressive resale values. A trip to the Friday private car market in Madinat Nasr or the Friday taxi market in al-Tonsi is instructive!

So, just how important is the private car as a form of transport in Cairo? As with many statistics in Egypt, there are contradictory figures on the number of cars and their usage.[12] But it is clear that, in spite of the avalanche of private vehicles one sees on the streets, Cairo remains a city where the private car is only a relatively minor mode of transport. According to the latest transport studies, in 1998 private cars represented only 20 percent of all vehicular person-trips in Greater Cairo, up from 8 percent in 1971. If pedestrian trips were included, this percentage for 1998 would drop to 14 percent of the total. Of course today the percentage will be higher.

It is revealing to look at the rates of private car ownership in the metropolis. According to a large household survey of urban Egypt carried out in June 2008,[13] it was estimated that in Greater Cairo proper (composed of Cairo Governorate, Giza City, and Shubra al-Khayma City and associated new towns) only 14.9 percent of households owned a private car. In peri-urban Greater Cairo (eight districts of Giza and Qalyubiya Governorates surrounding Greater Cairo) this percentage dropped dramatically to 3.1 percent. Taken together, for the whole metropolitan region it can be said that only 11 percent of households own private cars, or that almost 90 percent of households, equivalent to over 15 million persons, must rely on public transport or taxis to move within the metropolis.[14] In fact, there are millions of people in Greater Cairo who have never even ridden in a private car!

The private car is by far the major contributor to the traffic congestion.[15] The private car accounts for roughly two-thirds of all vehicles on the streets of the Greater Cairo region, with the remainder being made up of different kinds of buses, taxis, trucks, government vehicles, and motorcycles. In addition, it is the parking of the private car two- and three-deep that has clogged secondary and even main arteries—the term arteriosclerosis comes to mind—and has made walking on Cairo's streets a nightmare. Since 1982 the building code has required that buildings be constructed with one off-street car space per housing unit, but this stipulation is widely ignored and has had little positive effect.

Cairo suffers, as do many megacities in the developing world, from the avalanche of the private car. The economics of twenty-first-century development favor the rapid expansion of an urban middle class and a further concentration of wealth among the highest two to three urban income deciles. Whether this eventually leads to general trickle-down prosperity or not is much debated, but it is clear that these rising middle classes are hungry for private cars and are acquiring them with a vengeance.[16] If at present some 11 percent of Greater Cairo households possess a vehicle, this percentage can easily double in a few short years. Add to this the increasing phenomenon of families with more than one vehicle, presently at only 2.1 percent of Greater Cairo's households, and the situation can only get depressingly worse, and rapidly. The 2008 Nippon transport study estimates that the number of private cars in Cairo will grow at 5.6 percent per year, at least through 2022, equivalent to a doubling every thirteen years.[17]

Cairo has the density and compactness to support efficient, convenient, and cheap public transport, but the private car has trumped all. Way back in 1973, when only 7 percent of Cairo trips were by private car, sound recommendations were advanced by the Greater Cairo Transport Planning Study "to separate as much as possible public transport and private car movements by the creation of bus priority facilities . . . (and) to adopt, in general, a policy of restraint on private car movements in favour of public transport in and around the central business district."[18] Even more forceful recommendations were made in 1984: "If the authorities in Cairo confine their efforts to meeting the traffic crisis by attempting to improve conditions for the private automobile alone, the city risks writing a prescription for future paralysis."[19]

Since 1973 only a handful of halfhearted attempts have been made to prioritize surface public transport, and all have failed miserably. To the extent that it could be said that a transport policy exists for Cairo, it is one that by default accommodates general traffic, of which the private car is the major component, almost exclusively. Operating here in the minds of the political establishment is a preoccupation with 'modern' forms of car-based suburban living—at the head of which is the brave new world of the desert new towns around Cairo—combined with a kind of inverse class consciousness. Those with the means to have a new private car perceive themselves as part of a respectable upper class, which has the right to use and abuse its privileges, and everyone else is, well, simply out of luck. Who in the political establishment does not own one if not several cars, the more expensive the better?

The parking problem is reaching crisis proportions, and some would say it already has. It would be worse were it not for the system of *munadis*, or self-appointed car parkers from the city's underclass, who stake out their turf along all congested streets and operate on tips. They manage by pushing and shoving to maximize the number of cars that can be squeezed into any available space and will intercede with the police when necessary. Then there are the extremely large number of drivers employed by private car owners (hired full-time at between LE600 and LE800 month, not a huge expense) who spend much of their time simply hanging out and jockeying for the best parking spots. Finally, there are the private parking garage operators and *bawwab*s and their sons, who constantly shuffle cars around in the fronting streets. These people, numbering in the tens of thousands, serve the car owners well but only mitigate the overall chaos, and their maneuvers themselves can cause further congestion. Who has not been part of a huge tailback of cars caused simply by the decanting and rearrangement of cars in front of a large apartment building?

Motorcycles account for only a tiny fraction of the general traffic in Greater Cairo, which is in stark contrast to the situation in, for example, South and Southeast Asian megacities. Only 0.8 percent of households in Greater Cairo own a motorbike or vespa.[20] Were these two-wheelers more popular and used instead of the private car, the traffic situation, and especially parking, would dramatically improve. However, due to the common prejudice in Cairo that motorbikes are something fit only for the 'lower orders' and for take-out deliveries, it is hard to see how they might become more popular.

And what about the bicycle? Its use in Greater Cairo is almost nil, seemingly restricted to local delivery boys and the super-skilled but suicidal bread-distribution brigade. Even though in Cairo most distances are short, the geography flat, and the weather warm and dry, the bicycle is shunned by almost all. Again, class prejudices operate against its wider use, plus the perceived dangers of weaving in among general traffic and gulping very polluted air. This has not prevented the odd call for dedicated bicycle lanes and a policy of encouraging the bicycle, most courageously by Mohammed Al-Baaly in a 2005 World Bank essay competition entitled "Cairo—The Future Amsterdam of the Middle East?." Al-Baaly himself travels by bike from Dokki to Heliopolis almost daily, a distance of sixteen kilometers. It takes him less than half an hour to cover the distance by bike, whereas public transport would require one to two hours, depending on the congestion.[21]

Traffic Management, or the Lack of It

The class dimension of the private car infuses mundane aspects of traffic control in Cairo. The simple traffic *shawish* (police sergeant), or even the *amin al-shorta* (traffic officer), is likely to defer to the driver of a private car, especially one at the steering wheel of a sleek new SUV or Mercedes (who just might be a minister's son!), making enforcement of traffic or parking rules a joke. Every day there is the struggle to keep the traffic moving, but for every violation that is confronted, there are ten that are ignored.

In fact, traffic management, the responsibility of the traffic administrations of Greater Cairo's three governorates, has been and remains practically nonexistent. First of all, those in control are Ministry of Interior generals who have established an insulated subculture that hardly ever changes. Thus, vehicular control is limited to the random stationary checkpoints that simply look at licenses and registrations (and which themselves cause huge jams). There are no patrol cars to monitor moving violations, even the most erratic and dangerous. Traffic intersection lights remain completely manual, and the odd attempts at synchronized signaling have never lasted more than a couple weeks. Enforcing parking bans is completely arbitrary, with the dreaded winch and wheel-clamp teams gleefully pouncing on one tiny stretch of illegally parked cars, and then disappearing for lunch. Driving tests and car safety inspections at the city's traffic departments are a joke. In fact, the near-total retreat from any effective traffic management in the city is underlined by the recent preoccupation with turning all complicated intersections into pointless physical barriers and endless u-turns.

Time and again, transport experts have stressed that proper and universally applied traffic management could immeasurably improve traffic flows with little investment in new flyovers and other expensive hard

Figure 8.4. Informal public transport interchange on Ring Road, al-Mu'tamidiya, 2009. (Photograph by David Sims.)

engineering. A professor of transport engineering at Cairo University recently presented recommendations to improve Cairo's transport at an international seminar in Morocco, in which he stressed the usual call for better traffic planning, bus priorities, pedestrian zones, and integrated parking policies, and ended in a plea that transport management and planning actually be carried out by transport experts, rather than the current coterie of police generals.[22]

What defeats any attempt to enforce traffic rules is widespread petty corruption. It is no exaggeration to say that a simple bribe is the rule rather than the exception, and given the paltry salaries of policemen, such bribe taking is seen by them as a kind of just compensation or tax on the affluent. There are so many traffic laws on the books that it is almost impossible not to violate them on a daily basis, and a few pounds to a *shawish* is a much more rational approach than actually paying the fine or, what is infinitely worse, retrieving a confiscated car license or recovering a towed car. At the beginning of 2008 the new traffic law took effect, which dramatically increased the level of fines and added new and puzzling stipulations, such as requiring medical kits and yellow triangles in all cars. Without exception, every Cairo taxi and pickup driver is convinced that the sole purpose of the new law is to increase the traffic police's opportunities for bribes. In fact, the long-suffering Cairo taxi driver has been the main target of predatory police behavior.[23]

Transport for the Majority

For the large majority of Greater Cairo's inhabitants who live either in the huge informal areas or on the peri-urban fringes, transport is a constant struggle, and state interventions are completely absent. Although, thanks to the minibus and in some locations, the metro, public transport is available and relatively cheap, the congestion on the few main streets that penetrate informal areas is horrible, and street conditions are deplorable. The limited space on main thoroughfares in informal areas, such as Luxor Street in al-Munira al-Gharbiya or al-Zumur Street in Bulaq al-Dakrur, is sharply contested between minibuses and pickup trucks, pavement sellers, overflowing garbage receptacles, derelict cars, and random rubble. At times it can take well over an hour for a vehicle to penetrate an informal area or escape from it. In informal areas one will never see a traffic policeman or any traces of traffic engineering improvements, which contrasts sharply with the heavy presence of both

Figure 8.5. Clogged main road serving north Bulaq al-Dakrur, 2009. (Photograph by David Sims.)

the *amin al-shorta* and *shawish* in the city's main commercial areas and upscale neighborhoods as well as the frenetic repaving and repainting of streets and lanes in these prime areas. Any traffic discipline in informal areas comes from cooperative efforts among drivers themselves, something that is in very short supply in Egypt.

Even main streets in informal areas are often broken and potholed and periodically subject to overflowing sewage and burst water mains. According to the 2008 Housing Study of Urban Egypt, in *all* of Greater Cairo proper only one-third of residential buildings front on a paved street in good condition, another third front on a street with broken or lost paving, and the remaining third front on streets with no paving at all.[24] Obviously, street conditions in informal areas are much worse than the urban average.

For the five million or so inhabitants of Greater Cairo's peri-urban settlements, most of whom live in exploding villages and informal

Figure 8.6. Narrow unpaved lane in very dense residential area of 'Izbit al-Matar, 2002. Note that the length of this lane is 720 meters and there are no cross-lanes. (Photograph by David Sims.)

agglomerations, the transport situation is also difficult. Trips on public transport to the city center average one hour but can take up to two, either by minibus, or public bus, or through rides that combine conveyance by minibus with either suburban rail or the metro. Three intermodal exchanges have become extremely important, one at the metro terminus at al-Marg, another at Shubra al-Khayma, and the third at Giza South and Munib. And in peri-urban Greater Cairo, street conditions are even worse than in Greater Cairo proper. Only 6 percent of residential buildings in peri-urban Greater Cairo front on a paved street in good condition, one-third front on a street with broken or lost paving, and a colossal 60 percent front on streets with no paving at all.[25]

In both the large informal areas of the metropolis and in the peri-urban fringe, the *tuk-tuk* taxi has become a common feature of local transport in the last five years. These three-wheeled auto-rickshaws, imported from India, provide conveyance from the edge of an informal area to residences on even the narrowest lanes, and they offer an important service for inhabitants, at least for those who can afford the modest fares. The *tuk-tuk* is completely informal or 'extralegal.' For some reason the Ministry

Figure 8.7. *Tuk-tuk* repair shop in Waraq al-'Arab, 2008. (Photograph by David Sims.)

of Interior steadfastly refuses to register them, so most run without any license plates, and this seems tolerated as long as they do not appear on major roads but remain within informal enclaves. In what amounts to one of the few innovative moves ever made by local government, in some peri-urban city councils, for example in Qalyub City, officials have begun selling *tuk-tuk* drivers their own *maglis al-madina* license plates. The few commentators who remark on the *tuk-tuk* phenomenon usually concentrate on their negative side; that is, that most drivers are hashish-smoking twelve-year-olds, but as usual, this is more upper-class myth than fact.

Cairo's Regional Tentacles and Trucking

One aspect of Cairo's transport that can definitely be considered good news is the constantly improving highway connections between the metropolis and other parts of Egypt. As pointed out in Chapter 2, Cairo is supremely well located within the national space, and most major connecting corridors can run through desert areas where congestion (or what is sometimes called 'side friction') is not a problem. Although implemented and widened without any feasibility studies, these roads entering Cairo now provide an excellent network for intercity traffic movements. The six-lane desert toll roads to 'Ain Sukhna (130 kilometers) and Beni Suef (125 kilometers), built and run by the military, are prime examples. When and if the huge second Ring Road is completed, Greater Cairo will enjoy a fast and widespread regional network that many other megacities might well envy.

Except for the Alexandria Desert Road, with its many passenger cars traveling to and from Alexandria and the North Coast, these regional roads seem to be devoted mostly to goods transport. In fact, the enduring image of Cairo's gateway corridors is massive movement of all kinds of trucks carrying a bewildering variety of loads. From pickup trucks stuffed with crates of tomatoes to huge articulated trailers hauling gravel or containers, this is transport at its most basic. Some trucks are supplying the modern wholesale market in al-'Ubur (and to a much lesser extent the market in Sixth of October), others are servicing the industrial parks in the new towns and in Helwan, and still others are full of consumer goods for Cairo's millions. Accidents are a serious problem, and it is not advisable to drive on these highways at night. The new traffic law aims to ban trailer trucks, which according to the Ministry of Interior are the main cause of accidents. This is typical of the many convoluted logics of the

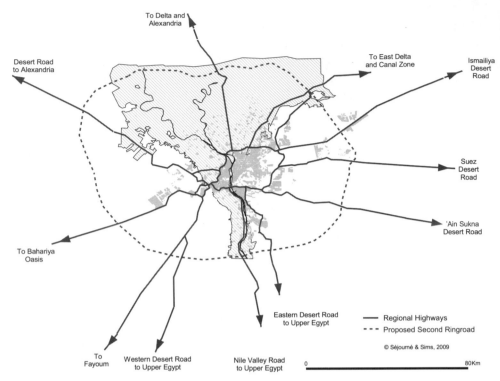

To Delta and
Alexandria

Desert Road
to Alexandria

To East Delta
and Canal Zone

Ismailiya
Desert
Road

Suez
Desert
Road

'Ain Sukna
Desert Road

To Bahariya
Oasis

Eastern Desert Road
to Upper Egypt

—— Regional Highways
--- Proposed Second Ringroad

© Séjourné & Sims, 2009

To
Fayoum

Western Desert Road
to Upper Egypt

Nile Valley Road
to Upper Egypt

0   80Km

Map 8.2. Greater Cairo: regional roads and second Ring Road.

law, which sees proscription as the solution instead of safety inspections. The fact that banning trailers will almost double truck traffic seems to have escaped the authors of the law.

Looking to the Future of Cairo's Transport

The prognosis for Cairo's transport is very bleak, due entirely to the inexorable rise in private car ownership and its uncontrolled use throughout the metropolis. Even so, there have lately been a number of initiatives that point to some welcome, and some not so welcome, improvements in the coming years.

Most welcome is the continued development of the metro system. Already it accounts for over 25 percent of all vehicular person trips in Greater Cairo and is used equally by the poor and the lower middle classes (but so far, by few of the car-owning rich). Yet the agonizingly slow construction of the third line and the pushing of the fourth and subsequent lines into the far future mean that the city will not enjoy the

244   City on the Move: A Complementary Informality?

transformational value of an underground metro system that leads to integrated public transport and away from private car use. If there was ever a national project clearly deserving of the highest political and funding priority, it would be a crash program to speed up the implementation of a complete urban metro network for Greater Cairo.

Following years of the decline of the street tram in Cairo, the government, with World Bank support, is planning the introduction of a modern 'super tram' with its own right of way to run from Heliopolis at the Kulliyat al-Banat tram station through Madinat Nasr and eastward to New Cairo. This line will serve the huge population concentrations of Madinat Nasr and will terminate in the northern part of New Cairo. Similarly, the new towns west of Cairo are scheduled to be linked with downtown Giza through either a rapid light rail (championed in the Nippon 2008 study) or a bus system on a dedicated high-volume busway running alongside the *mihwar* corridor (the cheaper option preferred by the World Bank). The terminus in Giza will be either at Midan Libnan or Cairo University.

Another improvement that has long been talked about is fare unification among the different means of public transport. At present, a passenger who uses more than one mode must purchase separate tickets, and this can be a significant financial burden that forces many long-distance riders to take very slow public or minibus lines over the whole journey rather than much faster multi-mode options. Transport planners have for years decried this very inefficient situation, but so far talk of reform has remained a topic only for consultant reports and conferences. An outside observer may wonder why the Cairo Transport Authority, the Tunnels Authority, the Heliopolis Tram Company, and the Egyptian Railways Authority, all of which are government entities, cannot cooperate on something simple like fares and transfers, but he or she would need to be educated in the peculiarity of most Egyptian government bodies, which persistently behave like small, separate fiefdoms, each jealously guarding its own turf. The Egyptian Railways Authority in particular is famous for this.

In addition to these schemes for public transport, there are a number of urban redevelopment projects and transport corridors on the drawing board to improve surface traffic. The most advanced of these is the redevelopment of the old Imbaba Airport site, where the Ministry of Housing has an ambitious plan to extend Ahmad 'Urabi Street north, to link with the Ring Road, and at the same time to construct a public park, schools, and other services, and relocation housing for the inhabitants of the huge informal area of al-Munira al-Gharbiya—as well as to allow a concession for private commercial development. Through expropriation, some of the roads inside Imbaba will be widened and inhabitants relocated. Many aspects of this project appear to be sound, especially the north–south arterial link and the intent to address Imbaba's huge deficit in services and to improve its awful internal circulation. However, the details of the plan are being kept as a "war secret," as the minister of housing has announced;[26] thus, as usual, government schemes only appear in the light of day when the bulldozers start work. Another urban corridor, sixty-three kilometers in length, is planned to run from Rod al-Farag across the Nile and directly westward, skirting heavily built-up al-Waraq, and onward across the agricultural plain to the new towns in the western desert. So far this scheme has not passed beyond the initial planning stages within the General Organization for Physical Planning, but the intent, much supported in the Nippon study and the NUCA, is to create yet another axis to serve the new towns and other developments in the western desert.

A number of city expressways and elevated highways are being contemplated that will interconnect arterials in and around the city proper. These are aimed at rationalizing traffic flows in the circumferential arcs of the congested built-up areas. However, some of these links have been planned for decades, and it is questionable whether there is the political will to allocate the huge funds and undertake the considerable property expropriations needed for these schemes to see the light of day. In any event, if all these expressways are built, they will blanket Cairo proper with a complex network of elevated arterials, almost exclusively to benefit of private-car circulation.

The construction of the second Ring Road, a truly colossal undertaking, has already begun on the southern arc fifteen kilometers south of Dahshur on both sides of the Nile. Although there appear to have been no feasibility studies, this scheme aims to encircle the whole Greater Cairo agglomeration, passing far outside Cairo's new towns, through Tenth of Ramadan and across the Delta on a Bilbis–Zagazig–Benha trajectory, finally intersecting with the Alexandria Desert Road, just south of Sadat City. Altogether, the length of this Ring Road will exceed 320 kilometers. It is understood that the northern alignment through the Delta is yet to

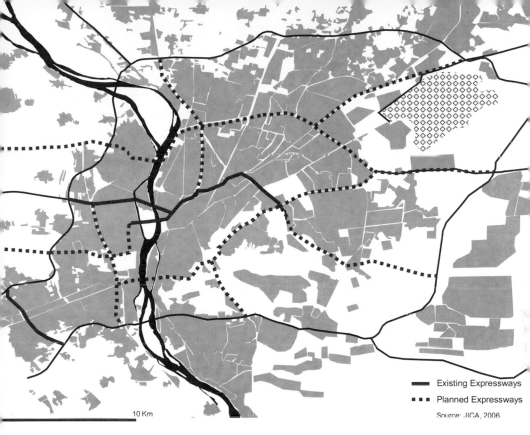

10 Km

Map 8.3. Greater Cairo expressways in 2007.

be finalized and may never be completed, but this has not prevented the
government from going ahead with the southern desert sections, which
are far easier to implement.

Another scheme that does not appear to have been the subject of prior
studies is the idea, advanced by the prime minister in January 2009, to
terminate all Egypt's trains outside Cairo proper. Thus passenger trains
from the north would all terminate at Qalyub City, some forty kilometers
from central Cairo, and those coming from Upper Egypt would terminate
at Munib. The intention is "to relieve the congestion on Ramses Square
and Giza and central Cairo in general," although logic would say that
such a measure would actually increase overall movements and would, in
addition, cause considerable inconvenience to passengers.[27] This idea may
never move forward, but it is a good example of the rather ad-hoc and ill-
thought-out approach of authorities toward Cairo's transport problems.

In 2008 a package of more systemic improvements for Cairo's
transport was advanced as part of a World Bank project that is under

preparation, and they seem, on paper at least, to be very welcome. Included is the creation of a metropolitan-wide transport authority "with adequately trained professional staff" to unify planning efforts and coordinate operations and investments of the various government entities responsible for transport in Greater Cairo. Other World Bank proposals include various public–private partnership schemes, among them private concessions for metered on-street parking (considerably more sophisticated and with higher parking fees than the current feeble system found in downtown Cairo) and also for off-street parking garages. And perhaps most importantly, the World Bank proposes expanding and improving traffic management and enforcement, noting that "the management of traffic in Cairo is among the worst of major cities in the world." Measures would include synchronized signal intersections, improved pedestrian ways, well-designed and managed bus stops, the extensive training of traffic police in modern traffic enforcement techniques, and the provision of modern equipment and vehicles.[28] It remains to be seen whether these good intentions, most of which have been proposed in the past, will ever materialize, faced as they are with an encrusted bureaucratic and rent-seeking culture that has so far confounded all attempts at reform.

But is There a Transport Policy to Serve the Majority?

With the exception of the excruciatingly slow extension of the metro system, it is clear that transport plans for Greater Cairo have two distinct biases. One is the preoccupation with making the desert new towns work, and the other is mainly to serve the private car. In fact, the two biases are intertwined, since the private car is, and will be, even more so, the main mode of transport for the new towns. But currently only 11 percent of the population of Greater Cairo have access to private cars, and only 4 percent live in the desert new towns. What about the 80-percent-plus who make up the overwhelming majority?

The preoccupation with making the new towns work has long been a key part of transport initiatives in Greater Cairo. The Ring Road itself, ninety kilometers in length and finished in 1994, had been intended mainly to provide access to the new desert communities around Cairo. The cancellation in the early 1990s of the segment that was to run south of the Pyramids, a triumph for the historical heritage crowd led by UNESCO, negated the 'ring' function and deprived Sixth of October of a crucial feeder.[29] In 1999, upon orders of the president, the long-term policy of not building new highways through agricultural land was discarded and *al-mihwar* (literally 'the corridor,' the axis road leading to Sixth of October City) was constructed in record time.

The preoccupation with the new towns continues. In addition to public transport investments in the pipeline to improve access east, to New Cairo, and west, to Sixth of October, the 2008 Nippon study postulated long-range transport strategies for the metropolis that assume rapidly increasing travel demand in these desert areas. These 'demand lines' are based on very optimistic assumptions about the success of the new towns, and they seem to imply that the future of the metropolis will be centered on eastern and western desert poles.

Any reading of planned surface transport improvements, including those that aim at better traffic management, confirms that there is an overwhelming bias toward the private car. Where is the strategy, so common in European cities, of restricting its usage in favor of public transport? It is depressing that one hears almost no voices calling for dedicated busways, for pedestrian priorities, for park-and-ride schemes, for congestion zones, for improving the river bus system, or for encouraging bicycle or motorbike transport. The only proposal related to the government-operated public bus system is progressively to privatize it. It is telling that the World Bank sees no future for the informal private minibus system as part of an integrated network, even though this mode of transport currently accounts for well over half of all public transport trips. And practically no one is talking about concerted efforts to improve transport and roads within informal areas, where the majority of the population lives.

In a way, time is short. Presently there are roughly 53 vehicles per 1,000 inhabitants in Greater Cairo. Compare this with 95 vehicles per 1,000 inhabitants in Tehran, 200 in Mexico City, 249 in Bangkok, and 301 in Sao Paulo, and one can see that inevitably Cairo will become swamped with cars whose owners will insist on their privileged use.[30] If the city is not quickly oriented to improved public transport modes to serve the large majority, building on its natural advantages of very high densities and informal systems, it is inevitable that Cairo will go the way of other major cities, and the private car will rule an increasingly dysfunctional and immobile metropolis.

9

Governing Cairo

How is a huge, complex, and dynamic city like Cairo governed? The short if cavalier answer is: not much. In previous chapters, various aspects of the city have been presented, and it should be apparent that some government actions have had an important impact on the city, but also that for every effective action or policy there has been a host of inactions, false starts, suspended initiatives, and pure negligence. Some actions have actually had consequences opposite to those intended, and for the most part there is a huge and pervasive gap between government pronouncements and legislation on the one hand, and implementation and enforcement on the other.

For those who are puzzled that a huge city like Cairo can function with little of what is usually associated with effective planning, municipal management, and local administration, this chapter quickly reviews the structures that are supposed to govern or at least guide Greater Cairo and establish some order. This analysis tries to show why most of the political apparatus dealing with Cairo simply doesn't work in the ways intended, and how, nevertheless, the city continues to function and evolve. In this, the concept is advanced of Cairo as the 'minimalist city,' one where only urban essentials are required to work, and the rest remains largely irrelevant.

The Nature of the Egyptian Government
Describing and analyzing the Egyptian government has long preoccupied political scientists and observers of the modern Middle East. These commentators have come up with a string of epithets such as 'strong regime, weak state,' 'political vegetables,' 'lame leviathan,' 'neglectful rule,' and so on, to summarize the particular form of rule exercised in modern Egypt.[1]

Perhaps Egypt best falls into the category first coined by Gunnar Myrdal in the late 1960s as a 'soft state,' that is, one good at perpetuating its own hold on power but largely ineffective no mater what policies it adopts.[2] The Egyptian government consistently projects itself and justifies its legitimacy as the prime agent of development, but with a huge, dispirited, poorly paid, and unmotivated civil service, with budgets that are never sufficient to finance ambitious plans, and with heavy doses of corruption, cronyism, patronage, and clientism, it is unable to mobilize its people or develop its economy in the ways it would want. The result, after decades of the same, is that the man in the street has learned that "the government is not there to better their lives; advancement is based on connections and bribes; the central authority is at best a benign force to be avoided."[3]

Such generalizations about the nature of the Egyptian government are perhaps a bit harsh, and they could just as easily be applied to a large number of governments in developing countries. Actually, the Egyptian state is quite solid and stable, has significant resources and rents, and has a huge, if centrally controlled, budget, which accounts for some 30 to 40 percent of the nation's Gross Domestic Product. Also economic reforms, initiated fitfully in the 1990s and with increased purpose since 2004, have improved the business environment, rationalized public finances, and begun to set up effective regulatory agencies.

So how does the 'soft state' operate in Greater Cairo? It should not be forgotten that Cairo is where central government is located and where practically all its top officials reside, so in a sense governing Cairo is inextricably intertwined with national policy and national aspirations. Whereas outside the capital local administrations might just have some real authority and can even innovate, in Cairo the eye of central government is all-pervasive, and local government is more than normally emasculated.

The Administration of Greater Cairo

Local administration in Greater Cairo is based, as in all of Egypt, on *muhafazat* (governorates). Up until 2008, Greater Cairo included all of Cairo Governorate plus parts of Giza and Qalyubiya governorates. According to two presidential decrees issued in May 2008, two new governorates—Sixth of October and Helwan—were carved out of Giza and Cairo governorates, and thus increased the total to five governorates wholly or partly within the confines of Greater Cairo. While such a radical and abrupt redrawing of governorate boundaries astonished many observers, the basic nature of local administration in Greater Cairo remains much as it has been for decades—that is, reliant on standard, top-down pyramidal structures.

Many attempts have been made to create more citywide local administrative structures, or at least coordination mechanisms, for Greater Cairo, but none have so far progressed beyond pronouncements in newspapers or proposals presented by various donors.[4] However, several urban systems in Greater Cairo operate as metropolitan-wide authorities under national-level ministries, particularly in such key areas as electrical distribution, water and sewerage, telecommunications, public buses, and the metro. These citywide institutions are taken up later in this chapter, and as will be seen, it may be that these system-specific, metropolitan organizations have in fact performed quite well, all things considered, and have consequently made a more unified local administration for Greater Cairo less of an imperative.

Governorates and Their Local Units

The three (now five) governorates that cover Greater Cairo are each presided over by a governor, who is appointed by the president, and who, according to the constitution, has presidential executive powers within his or her jurisdiction. The office of the governor is an important center of political power (and patronage), since under each governor is a huge bureaucratic apparatus and a small army of government employees. Each governorate has an impressive headquarters, controls considerable property, and operates under legislation that, on paper at least, gives it wide authority over local affairs.

Actually, the urban functions that are the exclusive remit of Greater Cairo's governorates are quite limited. These include solid waste management and street cleaning, public housing, local street paving and improvements, building control and permits, administration of cemeteries and mines, and upkeep and improvement of public gardens and public spaces. There is also a host of other functions whose responsibilities are nominally those of governorates, but which are in fact shared with national-level authorities. These include primary and secondary education (schools are built and staffed by the Ministry of Education), traffic control and vehicle licensing (run by the Ministry of Interior's traffic units in each governorate), and street lighting (tapped from the grids of the electrical distribution companies). Each governorate has ten to fifteen directorates or administrations that deal with these services, and others such as health centers, youth centers, and culture palaces, but again the main funding and staffing comes from the respective national ministries. Each governorate also has an environmental affairs unit, but its ability to regulate pollution-generating activities is limited and overshadowed by the Egyptian Environmental Affairs Agency, yet another national-level agency.

Under each governorate's housing directorate there are *tanzim* (urban control) functions and also a physical planning department. However, governorate planning units are overshadowed by the national-level General Organization for Physical Planning, are technically weak, and in any event have little to do, since land-use planning is mainly restricted to vacant state-owned desert lands. In Greater Cairo, the desert lands lying within a particular governorate's boundaries have been almost totally commandeered by central state organs like the NUCA, the military, and security services.

The governorates of Greater Cairo are, like all of Egypt's governorates, almost totally dependent on central government budget allocations and transfers. Typically, a governorate will depend on the central government for 80 percent of its total budget, and of the remaining 20 percent that comes from local taxes and fees, only a very small portion can be used by a governorate at its own discretion. And the composition of a governorate's annual expenditures, where around 55 to 70 percent goes just to salaries and perks for employees, and only 10 to 20 percent can be directed toward urban investments, underlines just how much governorates are beholden to and constrained by their huge staffs, have precious little leeway to launch projects, and thus have little chance to rise above the mundane day-to-day affairs of administration.[5] And it should not be forgotten that local government is, in financial terms, tiny. In 2007 the aggregate of all local administration funding in Egypt represented only 4.2 percent of the total national budget.

The urban areas of Greater Cairo are divided into *ahya'* (administrative districts).[6] Before the administrative changes in 2008, Cairo Governorate was made up of over thirty districts, Giza City had eight, and Shubra al-Khayma City had two. In addition, in Giza and Qalyubiya governorates, some areas of Greater Cairo are classified as rural, and these were divided into *marakiz* (rural districts), of which there were five in Giza and four in Qalyubiya.[7] Whether *ahya'* or *marakiz*, these local district units, which are purely executive, are extremely weak and are preoccupied mainly with building control and permit functions as well as dealing with day-to-day crises. Even so, the district chiefs, appointed by the Ministry of Local Development from a pool of largely ex-military and ex police officers for durations that rarely last more than a couple years, exercise considerable power and influence as the main conduit to the governor's office. The districts are largely staffed with low-level employees, who may not even show up to work, although in each there is at least a handful of surprisingly committed staff. District personnel have gained a reputation as being particularly corrupt, mainly because most of their functions relate to the control of building activities (and the inevitable bribes paid to look the other way, especially in informal areas), but there is no evidence that they are any more prone to corruption than other civil servants.

Elections, Popular Councils, and Representation

There are two levels of electoral representation in Greater Cairo. First, there are roughly thirty-five electoral districts in Greater Cairo, each of which selects two members every five years to the 444-seat national parliament.[8] This means that Greater Cairo is seriously underrepresented on a proportionate basis, with less than 10 percent of seats to represent some 22 percent of Egypt's population. Secondly, there is the system of *al-magalis al-mahaliya al-sha'biya* (local people's councils) found throughout Egypt, whereby there is an elected local council for each *hayy*, city, *markaz*, and village, with elections taking place every four years. Usually made up of ten to twenty persons, each of these lower-level councils in turn selects two representatives to sit on the local council at the level of the respective governorate. By law, these local councils are meant to act as the citizens' representation and oversight vis-à-vis their counterpart executive government bodies. In fact, local council members tend to be from influential families and functionaries of the ruling National Democratic Party in a particular area, and the councils' activities mainly involve the workings of patronage and favoritism. Few inhabitants of Cairo put any faith in the members of their local people's councils.[9]

As with the rest of Egypt, and as is endlessly recounted in both the local opposition and foreign press, democratic structures and processes in Greater Cairo are largely forms of window dressing that mask the real system of one-party authoritarian rule that disenfranchises the electorate from any effective voice. Here is not the place to go into details of all the faults of the electoral process, and the many ways in which the National Democratic Party ensures its dominance at all levels. But it should be pointed out that turnout is low even in parliamentary elections, and can be derisory for local council elections in urban areas, where by one estimate only 3 to 5 percent of the registered electorate bothered to vote.[10]

Even so, within Greater Cairo's districts there is a kind of personal and informal representative dynamic. As explained in Chapter 4, in informal settlements there is often pressure from citizens seeking missing services, and this may be articulated through local councils, the district, the governorate, or the National Democratic Party. Of course, special interests may distort the whole process, but the Egyptian government is very sensitive to criticism that it fails to extend services. And the Egyptian press, for all its faults, does keep the worst examples of government delinquency and negligence in the public eye, and is read by authorities who are very much preoccupied with enhancing their own ego-fueled images.

At this point one wishes it could be said that Greater Cairo boasts a vibrant grass-roots civil society, which has leapt into the vacuum and functions as an alternative means of citizen representation. Unfortunately, this is definitely not the case. Although the NGO movement in Egypt is very strong, it is largely an elitist phenomenon and, in Greater Cairo's massive popular areas at least, true 'community-based' organizations that articulate local needs and advocate rights and change are few and far between.

Governing or Muddling Through?

The style of local government in Greater Cairo is often described as "crisis management," day-to-day "muddling through," and lurching from one problem to the next with "insular, symbolic actions."[11] Trying to get ahead and to initiate processes and transformational strategies, or even simply to launch concrete projects, is something Greater Cairo's local administrations cannot seem to accomplish. One of the problems is the horrible lack of inter-agency coordination, and there is a constant and jealous ballet between governorates, the main infrastructure and service authorities, and the principal ministries. In most cases, even a minor local crisis slowly moves up the governorate structure until it lands on the governor's desk, and he needs to personally intervene, frequently more than once, for some response to be initiated.

The situation is further confused by mysterious orders that come from the highest levels of political power, which seem to have been instigated without the least logic or forethought but which are never questioned. The slaughter of all of Cairo's pigs in the summer of 2009, as a bizarre response to the swine flu threat, is only one of many glaring examples that "has exposed the failings of a government where the power is concentrated at the top, where decisions are often carried out with little consideration for their consequences and where follow-up is often non-existent . . . ."[12] Add to this the frequent phenomenon in Cairo of VIP visits and their accompanying security circuses, and of inspection tours by national-level officials, and it is no wonder that local administrators can never rise above the day-to-day.

So, how do things work at all? Can it be said that Cairo runs itself on a kind of enormous auto-pilot, with the government's role reduced to near irrelevance? It is clear from previous chapters that, in terms of planning, control of urbanization, traffic, housing, and large segments of the city's economy, the answer is yes. But there are certain urban functions where government has been and continues to be essential, and it is these that need a closer look.

The Minimalist City and Its Unsung Heroes

A large metropolis needs its underlying systems to function, at least on some basic level. The construction and improvement of main roads, the supply of potable water, the collection and disposal of sewage, the operation and extension of phone networks, and the provision of metered electricity: all are required. Today in Greater Cairo these essential systems run quite well and coverage extends throughout the metropolis. Such high levels of service are nothing less than remarkable when compared to similar systems in many large Third World cities, where for example water rationing and frequently interrupted power are common even in prime downtown areas. It is not that such systems in Greater Cairo are anywhere near perfect, and poor service levels are found in some informal areas and especially in parts of the peri-urban periphery. Also, the authorities that provide these systems have fundamental weaknesses common to all Egyptian government organizations, in that they are unlikely to win management excellence awards. But these systems are the minimalist conditions that allow Cairo to function and grow, as the following sections will show.

Potable Water

Access to water is considered a fundamental right in Egypt. Following three decades of concentrated investments, partly funded through international assistance, drinking water is now almost universally available throughout Greater Cairo, something few megacities in developing countries have achieved. For example, the 2006 Census reported that in Cairo Governorate, 99.2 percent of households were connected to a piped water system. The 2008 HSUE confirmed this near-universal coverage, with 96.7 percent of households in Greater Cairo proper reporting a water faucet within the dwelling.[13] Except for some small rural areas of Giza and Qalyubiya that rely on groundwater as a source, Greater Cairo is all supplied by the Greater Cairo Water Supply Company, a subsidiary of the national Holding Company for Water and Wastewater, which in turn is an affiliate of the Ministry of Housing.[14] This public-sector company takes water from the Nile, where it is purified and treated in a total of eighteen water treatment plants located near the Nile or the Ismailiya Sweetwater Canal.[15] Water is distributed through a huge network of water mains and booster stations, with twenty-one water districts east of the Nile and five west of the Nile.

Figure 9.1. Installation of water main by government to serve informal areas of Manshiyat Nasir, 2002. (Photograph by David Sims.)

In most areas water is usually available on a twenty-four hour basis. In fact, in the aggregate, water supply is very ample for consumer demand. For all of Greater Cairo, Nippon estimated in 2007 that daily water consumption by all users was 4.1 million cubic meters (of which roughly 20–30 percent was industrial consumption), compared to an estimated daily production capacity of 8.7 million cubic meters.[16]

However, the water picture in Greater Cairo is not all rosy. Water pressure throughout the city is rarely sufficient to reach upper floors even in upmarket parts of town, and in some areas, system water can become contaminated by infiltration of ground water. Many distribution networks are old, use asbestos cement pipes, and are under-designed for current demand loads. Also, the city's potable water systems are extremely wasteful. There are no domestic water meters, and water consumption charges are among the lowest in the world. (Even after tariff reform, domestic consumption rates were LE0.30 per cubic meter in 2007, compared to two to three Euros in European countries.) But this is somewhat academic, since without water meters actual consumption is unknown and standard practice is for lump-sum monthly fees to be charged for each building. It is thus no great surprise to find that USAID has estimated that Greater Cairo's actual per-capita domestic water consumption is 340 liters a day (a level similar to that in California!), and that of this total, 24 percent is lost in network leakage, 34 percent is wasted inside residences, and only 34 percent is actually used.[17] It is also no great surprise to discover that, in spite of endless lecturing by donor agencies, under current tariff rates the water authorities in Greater Cairo cannot even cover system operating and maintenance costs from water consumption revenues, and all system investments must come from the central government.

Whether or not institutional and tariff reform will proceed to make the city's water systems more efficient, many more water supply projects are planned for Greater Cairo, and by 2011, total production capacity is to be increased to 12.5 million cubic meters per day. By 2027, total water demand is estimated to be at most 10.5 million cubic meters per day, meaning that there is every likelihood that water supply will keep well ahead of demand.[18] However, of the total estimated demand in 2027, some 40 percent is expected to come from the eight new towns around Cairo, both for industry and for the very high water-consuming residential developments expected in these new towns.

Sewerage

In the 1970s the city's existing sewerage system, which had been designed for only two million inhabitants, was near total collapse, and none of the informal settlements that were springing up around the city had any drainage services. In 1978, a master plan was prepared to completely overhaul the system and provide wastewater coverage for over seven hundred square kilometers of Greater Cairo. Implementation of the Greater Cairo Wastewater Project started in 1984 and enjoyed considerable technical and financial assistance from both British and American aid. The result, as they say, is history. On the east bank of the Nile a main sewage collector was inserted under Port Said Street, running north through a main lift-pumping station at al-Amiriya to a new treatment plant at Gabal al-Asfar. With an internal diameter of five meters, this became what is claimed to be the largest sewage line in the world, serving most of central and northern Cairo. Another huge treatment plant was built on the east bank in Helwan, in this case with German assistance. On the west bank, a huge collector was built, extending out to a new treatment plant in the desert at Abu Rawash, and networks were included to serve most of Giza's residential areas, both formal and informal.

The Greater Cairo Sanitary Drainage Company operates the present sewerage system in Greater Cairo. As with the water sector, this company is a subsidiary of the Holding Company for Water and Wastewater, an affiliate of the Ministry of Housing. There are other public-sector authorities involved with the design and implementation of sewerage projects, and these also fall under the Ministry of Housing. Institutional reform in the wastewater sector is ongoing.

Today, Greater Cairo boasts very high coverage in sewerage services. In 2008 the HSUE reported that 98.0 percent of dwelling units in Greater Cairo proper had access to sewerage lines. There are a total of thirteen sewage treatment plants in and around Greater Cairo, the largest of which of is the Gabal al-Asfar plant, which alone accommodates almost 40 percent of Greater Cairo's total sewage discharge. Seven of the treatment plants are smaller units located in and serving particular new towns. According to Nippon, in 2007 the combined design capacity of all treatment plants was 4.6 million cubic meters per day, more than sufficient to meet an estimated sewage generation of 3.8 million cubic meters per day.[19]

Figure 9.2. Installation of local sewers and house connections: project financed by German Financial Cooperation, in 'Izbit Bikhit (Manshiyat Nasir), 2001. (Photograph by David Sims.)

Of course the system has its faults, and sewage overflows are experienced from time to time, especially in dense informal areas, where system capacities cannot cope with the increasing discharges. Also, many informal areas in the peri-urban fringes are still not at all served by the system, and in these areas inhabitants must rely on septic tanks that require frequent emptying by suction trucks. For example, the 2008 HSUE recorded that only 54.6 percent of dwelling units in peri-urban Greater Cairo had access to sewerage lines.[20] Furthermore, although actual user fees are minuscule (based on a 30 percent surcharge on a residential consumer's water bill, which rises to 70 percent for commercial consumers), the cost of house connections is quite high and involves bureaucratic hassles and often a tip or petty bribe. There are also systemic environmental issues. The outflow from the Gabal al-Asfar plant, supposedly completely treated but in fact only partly so, ends up in agricultural drains that discharge eventually into Lake Manzala. The effluent from the Helwan plant runs south through the al-Suf Canal, built to irrigate reclamation farms, but due to poor maintenance the plant cannot fully treat the effluent, and water that reaches the fields is sometimes heavily contaminated. And on the west bank, the Abu Rawash plant was never completed beyond primary treatment, and the effluent discharged into agricultural drains is of bad quality, at least for agricultural use. Furthermore, the sewerage systems must accept industrial effluent discharges, and practically no pre-discharge measures are taken by manufacturers to remove noxious chemicals and metals before they flow into the wastewater treatment plants.

Electricity

Electricity supply in Greater Cairo was, until the 1980s, pretty much a hit-or-miss affair, with cuts, voltage drops, and brownouts common even in central areas, and with power lines in peripheral areas and informal settlements that were either nonexistent or horribly overloaded. The city, and the country as a whole, has come a long way since then. First, the Ministry of Electricity (through the Egyptian Electricity Holding Company since 2000) has made huge investments in power-generation schemes, some of which were financed through World Bank and other international loans. These projects have increased generating capacities in Egypt severalfold, and more and more power stations are coming onstream, mostly fueled by Egypt's relatively plentiful supply of natural gas. As a result, in 2005/06 Egypt had 22,350 megawatts of installed capacity to meet peak loads of 17,300 megawatts.[21] There are eight power-generation plants in the Cairo area, the largest of which is the Shubra al-Khayma station, whose tall stacks are a familiar feature of Cairo's skyline. Second, tremendous investments have been made in power transmission and distribution networks. Greater Cairo is currently completely covered by two distribution companies, the North Cairo Electrical Distribution Company and the South Cairo Electrical Distribution Company.[22] In 2006 there was a total of 6.6 million metered customers of the two distribution companies, fed through 89,600 kilometers of mostly underground lines and some 28,000 distribution transformers. According to Nippon, the quality of service in terms of reliability, availability, and serviceability, was quite good throughout Greater Cairo.[23] The distribution companies aim to install a new connection within ten days of receiving a completed application.

Major Roads

As described in Chapter 8, Greater Cairo now enjoys a relatively good network of arterial roads, especially its outer radial highways, which provide entrances to the city and connect the capital to other parts of Egypt. These transport links take advantage of the opportunities provided by the city's unobstructed desert hinterland. Most of these highways have been planned and built by the Ministry of Transport's Roads and Bridges Authority.[24] As one moves progressively into the metropolis the situation is less satisfactory, but it is improving. The Ring Road (1987–2000) was a colossal project that radically improved Cairo's surface transport, as did the October Bridge with its many extensions. Other bridges, flyovers, arterial roads, and urban expressways have been added to the system in a somewhat slow and piecemeal fashion. These projects are said to be following an overall transport master plan, or rather, a succession of plans, although some seem to materialize in a decidedly ad-hoc manner. For example, the Twenty-Sixth July extension to the Alexandria Desert Road was not on anyone's plan, but it was designed and built in a remarkably short time following orders from the Presidency in 1999. In fact, most additions to Cairo's road system, and the priority they are given for implementation, seem to be initiated in mysterious ways. In any event, once a project is committed to, the whole affair, from land acquisition to clearances to rearranging affected roads and utilities to actual implementation, can be achieved in what is a remarkably short time. The Maryutiya Connector, a 5.7-kilometer elevated eight-lane monster, was opening in mid-2009 after just two short years of construction, although this 'missing link' to the ring road system had been under discussion for fifteen years.[25] Another elevated expressway some four kilometers in length, which slices through dense parts of Bulaq al-Dakrur, is presently under construction, even though few outside the transport fraternity have a clue as to why it is being built.

Unlike in other infrastructure sectors, donors have never helped fund roads and bridges in Cairo and it is the Egyptian government that has financed and continues to finance all such projects.[26] Partly for this reason, most projects are designed and implemented by Egyptian consulting and contracting firms, and foreign road engineers frequently criticize the results: poor geometric design and less-than perfect final surface treatment, not to mention a rather cavalier attitude in the placement of on- and off- ramps and the design of elevated highway interchang-es.[27] These criticisms may be more or less correct, but the fact is that projects do get built, structures do not collapse, traffic does flow, and bit by bit Greater Cairo's main arterial road systems are expanded and improved. In the author's opinion, a more valid criticism is that many of Greater Cairo's major urban corridor projects aim primarily to improve accessibility to the new towns rather than to improve surface transportation within the metropolis proper, where over 96 percent of the population lives.

Telecommunications

Many Cairenes will recall with a kind of perverse nostalgia the 1970s, when getting a dial tone on one's telephone, let alone completing a call, was considered a minor victory. It could take decades after submitting an application for a new telephone connection to be installed, and interna-tional calls had to be booked and paid for at least three days in advance.[28] In fact, telephone services were to all intents and purposes nil, and this was when Cairo had less than half the residents and businesses that it does today. Starting in the early 1980s (with assistance from USAID) the Arab Republic of Egypt Telecommunications Organization began a long process of revamping Cairo's telephone networks and switching stations, installing high-capacity cables and modern equipment. The result has been nothing short of a miracle: by the 1990s most of Cairo had a good telephone service, and national and even international direct calls could be made. And public telephone boxes that actually worked began to appear on Cairo streets. In 1996 the government let out the first private mobile phone license, and now there are three competing systems that provide universal coverage in Greater Cairo (and in most of Egypt) at call rates that are among the cheapest in the world. In 1998 Egypt Telecom was reformed into a state-owned private company, and a telecom regulatory agency was also set up. Starting in 2003 numer-ous private companies, under agreement with Egypt Telecom, began to offer ADSL Internet services over landlines, and there are now few corners of Greater Cairo where such a service cannot be easily provided. In addition, the mobile phone companies now offer comparable services over 3G wireless networks, all of which provides Cairo's inhabitants and businesses with a wide choice and, due to competition, very reasonably priced and fast Internet access.

Why Does the Minimalist City Work?

Why do the systems described above work relatively well in Greater Cairo and how are they able to continue to extend services? First, an important underlying factor is Greater Cairo's compactness and very high density of habitation. The fact that Greater Cairo is by some measures the world's most dense large city goes a long way toward explaining how Cairo's transport works in spite of everything (as shown in Chapter 8), and it also helps explain how its infrastructure systems can function remarkably well. Every such system is made up of lines, and the more people and businesses served by a given unit of line length, the lower the installation and operation costs and the lower the maintenance needs.[29] Second, most of the authorities that provide Cairo's basic services are national-level organizations, either ministries or their subsidiaries. Thus their budgets are more or less assured and each enjoys considerable autonomy.[30] (The downside of this is, of course, an almost total lack of inter-agency coordination.) Third, these authorities tap into Egypt's large and experienced engineering and contracting sector—most of which is private—for studies, designs, and execution of system elements. For large civil works projects, authorities will usually contract out engineering feasibility and design and supervision to Egyptian consulting firms, often teamed up with foreign bureaus, and for implementation international bids are usually solicited, which will bring in Egyptian/foreign consortiums to compete for business. Fourth, many of Egypt's infrastructure authorities have been or are currently adopting organizational and tariff reforms (albeit grudgingly and at a snail's pace), giving them more viability and cost-effectiveness.

None of these infrastructure systems attempts to get ahead of urbanization and extend services to newly settled areas. The one exception is in the new towns around Cairo, whose advance servicing, as seen in Chapter 6, is very expensive and underutilized and, in addition, carries huge economic costs. In effect, urban system extensions throughout most of Greater Cairo are slowly *following* and reinforcing urban growth and extending services to the people and businesses wherever they can be found. Of course some areas are served more quickly and better than others. But overall one could call this a kind of 'post-facto municipal service extension' that is efficient and very logical.

10

Summing Up: Cairo Serendipity?

I n this book an attempt has been made to understand Cairo and to show
that, in spite of everything, the metropolis functions moderately well
and has not become the urban nightmare prophesied by so many. The
preceding chapters have made this point and also have tried to uncover
and explain the modes or logics, internal to the city itself and its people,
which are operating to make Cairo, at least compared to many megacities
in the developing world, a kind of success story.

And success story, with qualifications, it certainly is. Greater Cairo
has not collapsed under its own weight, as often predicted. And it is
a near miracle that such a huge agglomeration has been able to grow
from four to seventeen million inhabitants in less than fifty years *on its
own*, so to speak, counter to government intentions and plans, while
that same government has stubbornly put all its faith, and most of its
resources, in the chimera of modernist development out in the desert.
This 'auto-development' has generated efficient neighborhoods where
two-thirds of all Cairenes live and almost half of them work, where
housing is minimally acceptable and quite affordable, and where 'basic
services,' which only government can provide, are surprisingly not bad.
Moreover, transport in the metropolis works (up until now at least),
small enterprises flourish, and a majority of inhabitants can live modestly respectable lives.

One obvious explanation for this success of Cairo as a megacity is its
high density. Not only does this compactness allow the city's otherwise
creaky transport to function, but it makes the extension of infrastructure
cost-efficient and allows the legions of informal businesses to find nearby
markets and customers. It is more than ironic that such high density is

perceived by government as a root evil, and is used by it to justify the imperative of moving out to the desert.

Informality Is the Key

For lack of a better word, Cairo's success can be attributed to the operation of informal processes, all of which are proscribed by law. It is informal urban development that has created the high densities that the metropolis enjoys. Land is subdivided, housing is built, properties are exchanged, businesses operate, and public transport moves in the shadows of illegality. Informal processes are autonomous and individualistic; they rely on personal relations, trust, and petty bribes, and they are the antithesis of modern corporate modes. They have allowed people to get on with their lives, in spite of formalistic modern norms that would have been disastrous had they been applied with any vigor.

One should not overromanticize the concept of informality and pretend there is some miracle guiding hand embodied in it. The word 'suboptimal' development, so popular among economists, comes to mind. And Cairo has not been completely on autopilot. A certain minimalist government has been an essential ingredient in Cairo's relative success. Funds are allocated, moneys are spent. Roads and bridges are built, transport systems are created, and utilities are provided, however tardily or haphazardly.

Why is the Informal City So Prominent?

The standard answer to this question, found throughout the copious literature on urban development in developing countries, is that informal urban development is a negative response, due only to a lack of enough affordable public housing, or a lack of appropriate urban plans and housing programs, or a lack of appropriate economic assistance packages to help the poor, or a lack of regional development strategies to stem the drift to the cities, or all of the above. In other words, the state has not done enough. It has not performed its 'high-modernist' function. Such an explanation is insufficient, at least for Cairo. We would advance the opposite: informal life in all of its aspects would exist even were government policies and budgets 'appropriate' and realistic. Perhaps the scale and pervasiveness of informality would have been less, but there is no government that could have met the challenge of the megacity such as Cairo represents. Governments in developing countries are just not that omnipotent, even if they were somehow able to set aside a whole canon of prejudices in favor of control and modernity and give priority to the simple needs of the majority. And even if that were possible, governments like Egypt's have their inevitable fellow-traveling business elites who will constantly redirect policies back to western, modernist-corporate paradigms.

It follows that informal city-building should best be seen as normative. The state can only add layers and tinker at the margins. It may be able to assert control if cities are small, and urban growth is of a scale and tempo where government can get ahead of the game. But to the extent that Third World governments succeed in controlling and diverting the phenomenon into more or less legal channels, it is rare for that to happen except at the expense of the poor. If there is a message in all of this, it is that informal urban development is a new form of urbanization, one for which governments are ill-prepared, even with—and in spite of—all the advice bestowed upon them.

The same could be said for the informal urban economy. A huge unregulated sector of urban enterprise and marginal self-employment is not simply caused by the failure of the state to stimulate the modern private sector to generate enough formal jobs and opportunities. Such a task in the face of the demographic avalanche is impossible. The Egyptian government could have done much more to create equitable market conditions and to ease the entry of enterprises into formal status, but the fact would remain that there is no way to absorb the ever-growing, young, and ill-prepared labor force into the modern city economy.

Cairo Serendipity

Standing back, one can say that Cairo has been blessed, both by geography and, ironically, by the state's misguided approach to it. Geographically, Greater Cairo is unique as a megacity. How many large city hinterlands have the stark dichotomy of huge tracts of publicly owned desert land upon which to expand, and simultaneously intensive small-farm agriculture and dense rural settlements arrayed along the immediate urban fringe?

Egypt is certainly fortunate in having a desert hinterland. This has allowed Greater Cairo's expansion to bifurcate: practically all new industries over the last thirty years have been located in the desert, avoiding the common land-use and environmental conflicts associated with metropolises whose expansion on all directions must confront a rural hinterland. Also, land-hungry modern corporate development, with its speculative subdivisions, gated communities, business parks, and megamalls, all can find a home in the desert. So can huge government establishments, such as those needed for defense, security, and utilities, as well as garbage disposal and other noxious activities. Cairo's desert is a case of a near-perfect match between huge amounts of land and land-wasteful development, all of which is sanctioned and encouraged by the state.

By shunting off large-scale formal urban development to the adjacent deserts, the rural fringes have been left to 'silently' absorb people and the dense and small-impact informal residential neighborhoods they create. It wasn't at all planned that way. The rural hinterland was supposed to freeze as it was, and practically all population growth was to occur in the deserts. But the economics of housing and livelihoods for the mass of inhabitants has prevailed, and as a result, over a few short decades the rural fringes of Greater Cairo have now been transformed, house the majority of the city's inhabitants, and represent, in a real way, the future of the city. The incremental and informal mode of settlement expansion in these fringe urban areas is dense and efficient, minimizing the loss of the agricultural land that surrounds them and making their (eventual) servicing straightforward and cost effective. There are certainly many problems in these areas, but they relate mostly to the lack of sufficient state investments in infrastructure and public services to keep up with population growth. A reprioritization of government budgetary allocations could make these areas much better, and at little cost.

Here is where true ironic serendipity comes in. Informal urban development on a massive scale, with all of its logic as laid out in this book, could not have occurred had the government *not* adopted and stubbornly pursued its wholesale desert development strategy and *not* tried, however unsuccessfully, to proscribe all development on the rural plain. The reasoning is as follows.

Consider what would have happened had the government not pursued desert development as the future of Greater Cairo. What if it had, sometime in the 1960s or 1970s, instead encouraged Cairo to grow out logically into the agricultural plain? It is sobering to think. Master plans would have set the parameters for urban extensions. High-standard subdivision and building regulations would have been imposed. Progressively, agricultural lands would have been bought up and assembled by companies and entrepreneurs. Cairo's rural hinterland would have been ripe for scattered upscale housing estates, commercial strip development, and industrial parks, extending and leapfrogging in all directions, mixed in with many stalled and speculative projects. Existing rural settlements would have been confined to only the smallest and most miserable expansion, and sky-rocketing land values would preclude any affordable informal residential development. Authorities would be wrestling with serious land-use conflicts and environmental disasters. One has only to look at the fringes of Jakarta or Delhi or practically any metropolis of the industrializing world to imagine what would have been Greater Cairo's fate.

Instead, practically all of these developments have been shunted off into the desert, leaving the near fringes of Cairo to develop in a people-oriented way. And here is the second serendipity or irony. Had the state not tried to prevent such informal development, it would have generated another kind of massive urban sprawl. Ever-seeking cheaper land prices, families and informal developers would have bought land in more and more remote locations, and today one could imagine Cairo's rural hinterland as one amorphous and chaotic sprinkling of small informal settlements, individual housing, and speculative overbuilding stretching far beyond what we see today. Serving these areas with utilities, roads, and services would have been a nightmare, even were government so inclined. 'Fortunately,' the government proscribed all building on agricultural land. But given the soft nature of the Egyptian state, it could only at best slow such development and confine it to progressive accretions onto existing agglomerations and villages.

Thus, in a sense, Cairo ended up with the best of all worlds. The informal dynamic was left to operate, but constrained into a form of organic spatial growth and consolidation. This dynamic could thus provide well-located housing affordable to the masses, create neighborhoods that could easily be supplied with basic infrastructure (however tardily), and generate its own economy and services. All of these new areas were created, for the most part, without any polluting factories or other non-conforming land uses nearby, and without the remaining agricultural land and settlements being subject to the frequently predatory behavior of formal, large-scale and well-connected developers.

The Nature of the Egyptian State and Its Modernist Delusions

Some political analysts have advanced the idea that the Egyptian government and its associated elites have recognized informality as the best way to keep Cairo's masses inert and marginally satisfied with their lot. This rather convoluted theory posits that somewhere in the highest corridors of power there is a quiet, conscious strategy to let the informal dynamic work as a safety valve to preclude any real political empowerment that could threaten the state. It may be articulated only behind tightly shut doors, but it is one way to explain how the informal has become such a huge presence in Cairo.

This theory is hard to swallow. It is more plausible that the rise and dominance of the informal, and the inability of the government to deal with it, to channel it, or even to extract positive elements from it, is due to continued self-delusion. There appears to be a pervasive and studied ignorance of reality, even when such reality is stark and visible, as is the case of the informal city. It is as if such facts are invisible since they do not conform to a continued belief in the state as agent of modernization. Decision makers, business elites, and even Cairo's intelligentsia seem to be engaged in a long love affair with modern technology and imported urban models, and this has been the case for decades.

Part of this delusion is an inability to recognize that Egypt's people and economy simply cannot afford all the shining paraphernalia of western city living. Few of Cairo's inhabitants are living in grinding poverty, but likewise only a few are lucky enough to enjoy the levels of consumption that the modernization imperative would dictate.

Another part of this delusion is the belief that the state can actually be effective, that it can intervene and has the ability to transform society and the economy. Although time and time again government programs have been spectacularly unsuccessful, there is still a stubborn faith that somehow the agents of government (and the armies of dispirited and self-serving government employees) will actually, finally achieve something. This is only too evident in the desert city, not to mention the many stillborn 'city beautiful' initiatives. The mechanistic, social engineering approaches of high modernism that have led to so many failures in the past seem to be very much favored still.

Lessons Learned

It would be edifying to be able to say that this investigation into understanding Cairo has uncovered some universal truths applicable not only to Cairo but to metropolises in other parts of the industrializing world. Unfortunately this is not the case. As has been explained, Greater Cairo is in many ways unique, and its 'success' can at least partly be ascribed to a kind of serendipity. Even so, it is hoped that one message has come across: a serious understanding of a city, and how it works, is a prerequisite for moving forward. Understanding means taking a jaundiced look at glib generalizations and especially at attempts to squeeze a city into some paradigm or global truth. It means that statistics and numbers and maps do count, as long as they are treated with a very critical eye. It means asking questions and trying to uncover why certain processes, in particular those that develop organically out of the activities and desires of the majority of city dwellers, can succeed in spite of government irrelevance.

Postscript: Revolutionary Cairo One Year On

This book originally went to press in December 2010, just a month before the Egyptian Revolution. Like most people, this author was taken by surprise by the cascade of events that led to the resignation of President Mubarak on 11 February 2011. Passing through Midan Tahrir on the morning of 25 January (Police Day no less!) and seeing the barriers, the serried ranks of thousands of anti-riot security troops, the officers with their squawking radios, and the scores of police vans parked around the corners, it seemed inconceivable that the demonstrations called for that day would end in anything but the usual violent repression, wholesale arrest, and swift dispersal. How wonderfully wrong I was!

It is now twelve months since Mubarak stepped down. Much has changed, more change is expected, and much more change is still needed. The Egyptian Revolution is certainly still a work in progress, but it is useful to try to sum up how the city of Cairo has fared in the last year. My postscript attempts to answer this by briefly revisiting the main themes found in the first edition of *Understanding Cairo*. Has the imaging of the city changed? What are the current plans and dreams for Cairo? How is the enormous informal city coping and changing? What is happening in the housing sector? What is the fate of the new towns around Cairo? What can the recent parliamentary elections tell us about the politicization of Cairo and the intentions of the Islamic majority toward the city? Is the former governing style of muddling through still in vogue? And finally, what does all this mean for the future, and can a better understanding of Cairo serve as a guide?

Imaging Cairo

In terms of imaging Cairo, Tahrir Square and the revolution have certainly given Cairo's image a huge alternate spin, and for once it is a positive one. The global media has focused at great length on the democratic and social justice movements among millions of ordinary Egyptians. This outpouring of commentary in articles, books, television programs, and Internet sites has given the city, much maligned in the past as the epitome of urban ills, a shining face and made it a symbol of how a people can lose their fear and unite to overthrow a sclerotic authoritarian regime.

All of this only covers the city's image with a general gloss. In attempts to explain the groundswell that rapidly discarded Mubarak and his cronies, a number of commentators have pointed to the gross inequities between the haves and have-nots in Egypt, and in Cairo in particular. Certainly the inequities in Egyptian society were (and are still) manifest, and the cavalier co-option of the country's wealth by a tiny elite was (and still is) striking. But to ascribe the underpinnings of the revolution to a grass-roots upheaval of the disenfranchised is wide of the mark. Those who braved the security troops and took part in demonstrations came from all walks of life, but they were and still are mobilized mainly by educated youth, the intelligentsia, and organized political factions. As we will see in subsequent sections, inhabitants of Cairo's huge informal areas made their contributions, and demands were heard for addressing the needs of the poor, but nowhere has this yet been translated into political or development programs that tackle the spatial dimension of inequality across the landscape of the metropolis.

Many of the misconceptions and prejudices about Cairo (amply catalogued in Chapter 1) continue unabated. Amusingly, totally overblown estimates of the population of the City of the Dead continue, and it seems that a figure of 1.5 million 'tomb dwellers'—over one hundred times the actual number—remains fixed in the minds of some commentators.[1] Another misconception that continues unabated is that the informal areas of Cairo, which are taken to be vast slums, house millions in subhuman conditions. In a contribution to the online newspaper *Egypt Independent* in August 2011, Safaa Marafi writes: "Little effort was put to resolve the deteriorating problems of Egypt's slums, which suffer from lack of sewerage . . . , lack of electricity, and lack of water—the basic needs for any human being."[2] She seems unaware that numerous studies, including the Census, show that in urban Egypt, electricity connections reach over 99 percent of households, water connections 97 percent, and sewerage connections over 80 percent.

It should be added that a number of books and other treatments of Cairo as a city have appeared recently. In early 2011, UN-Habitat released a glossy report entitled *Cairo: A City in Transition*.[3] It repeated much of the information contained in the first edition of *Understanding Cairo*, and visited the same themes. It pinned its authority on a 2007/2008 household survey commissioned from the American University in Cairo (AUC) Social Research Center. This survey generated much data, disaggregated into somewhat confusing classifications of high-, medium-, and low-quality residential zones; and it used an equally puzzling "area based physical deprivation index." However, the analysis covered Cairo Governorate alone (which contains only about half the population of Greater Cairo), and furthermore, no maps were presented to allow one to locate these special zones.

Another book, entitled *Le Caire: réinventer la ville*, appeared in April 2011.[4] This anthology, sponsored by a number of French research and development institutes, assembles the thoughts of some twenty mostly Egyptian 'pioneers' and 'reformers' who have ideas on how to turn Cairo into an open, inclusive, and sustainable city.

Another treatment of the city appeared in March 2009 as a radio program and video by the Australian Broadcasting Corporation. It was entitled *Cairo, A Divided City* and it zeroed in on just that—the large divide between the privileged few living in gated communities in the new towns, and the rest of the population crammed into the existing agglomeration.[5] This same theme was further explored in a photojournalistic effort that first showed at the Townhouse Gallery in January 2012 called *Cairo Divided*. One of the authors writes about the new towns around Cairo: "The advance of private capital is marshaled by an aggressively retreating state, gated compounds for the elites are re-imagined as inclusive national projects, isolation gets marketed as community, and plush green golf courses can rise miraculously from some of the most arid land on earth."[6]

Finally, just out is a book by the well-known Anglo-Egyptian novelist Ahdaf Soueif called *Cairo: My City, Our Revolution*.[7] It is the diary and personal story of the revolution over the January–November 2011 period that "unlocks the historical and emotional background of a city."[8]

Unfortunately, her 'city' is, as is often the case, a limited view of the well-known downtown and older upscale areas, as well as the city's elitist cultural milieu.

Plans, Projects, and Dreams for Cairo

Since the revolution, there has been a near total silence about plans, projects, and development schemes for Cairo. The main reason is twofold. First, the transitional government, currently led by Prime Minister Kamal al-Ganzouri (a retread from the 1990s) lacks legitimacy and, moreover, is fearful of making mistakes that might land ministers in jail. For lack of other models, he and his cabinet seem to be generating little more than the same kinds of reassuring if irrelevant pronouncements that had been a hallmark of governments under Mubarak. Secondly, the state is on a downward slide to bankruptcy, and the moneys that had in the past propped up government interventions in Cairo have mostly evaporated. As is well reported in the press, the budget deficit has mushroomed, foreign direct investment and tourism have almost vanished, and as a result foreign exchange reserves more than halved in 2011. The many promises of funds from countries sympathetic to Egypt and its revolution have so far failed to materialize. The government must meet an ever-expanding wage bill (having had to raise the salaries of protesting government employees), fund expensive subsidies (which continue to be enjoyed as much by the well-to-do as the poor), and meet a growing debt (resulting from increasingly desperate and expensive government bond sales).

The upshot, as will be seen at several points in the following paragraphs, is that there are practically no funds for capital investments anywhere in Greater Cairo. The Ministry of Finance is scrambling to save money here and there, and the austerity ax falls first on large projects in the pipeline.

However, hopes and dreams, which cost almost nothing, are still to be found. A vision and strategy for the metropolis, called 'Cairo 2050,' first came out in 2008 and was much criticized in 2009 and 2010 (see also Chapter 3). Unknown to most, it continues to be developed by the General Organization for Physical Planning (GOPP), and a first volume called the *Greater Cairo Region Urban Development Strategy, Volume One, Vision and Strategic Directions*, is set to be released any day. Volume Two, which contains details of project proposals, is expected to be finished later in 2012. It is curious, and an indication of GOPP's isolation, that the organization and its parent, the Ministry of Housing, continue with this work in spite of mounting criticism from both Egyptian and foreign quarters. It will be interesting to see if Cairo 2050, which originally called for huge megaprojects across the city, the relocation of millions of inhabitants as well as most cemeteries, and a remake of Cairo into an ultramodern mirror image of Dubai, will have been at least toned down. Whatever form it takes, in the current climate in Egypt, Cairo 2050 is likely to be completely irrelevant.

The Informal City, More Triumphant than Ever

Chapters 3 and 4 catalogued the overwhelming dominance of informal housing and informal settlements on the landscape of the metropolis. It was estimated that almost two-thirds of the current population live in these areas, which are absorbing some 75 percent of all population increase in Greater Cairo. Although it seems hardly possible, this dominance is set to increase further, and for a period that remains completely open ended. Probably the single most striking physical result of the January Revolution has been the frenetic increase in informal housing construction across the city, mainly in and around informal settlements on the agricultural fringe. No one can put numbers to the spurt in construction, but virtually all observers of Cairo agree it is rampant. A short newspaper article appeared on 2 March 2011, only five weeks after the revolution started, in which it was said that there were 12,831 cases of illegal construction on agricultural land inventoried by the Administrative Prosecutor, and that these needed to be prosecuted and the buildings demolished, in some cases with help from the Armed Forces.[9] The article implied that most of these violations were the result of citizens exploiting the chaotic situation that prevailed in Egypt. Of course these are nationwide figures, but it can be assumed that many were within Greater Cairo. Field inspections by the author, carried out in the summer and fall of 2011 in peripheral informal areas of Greater Cairo, confirm that there is wholesale new construction on what had been agricultural land (see Figure 11.1). This is attributable to the disappearance of agents of the state who should prohibit the phenomenon (mainly district and *markaz* housing directorate officials, and agricultural directorate inspectors). These agents were always only partially effective, but now they are largely absent, and for a large segment of society the current situation presents a golden opportunity to begin construction. Even the business press, which normally ignored the informal sector, has noted the phenomenon of massive 'unlicensed' housing construction. Iman Ismail, managing director of the Egyptian Mortgage Refinance Company, was quoted as saying, "demand is being met through unlicensed building. . . . It is a functioning market, they have their services, there is real supply and demand and there is a home equity market. There is actually something there to emulate."[10] These are very true words, but they are unlikely to have any impact.

There have been no studies of this accelerated informal housing construction around Cairo. However, anecdotal information and field observations show that most construction is the classic informal mode of reinforced concrete frame and red brick infill, small building footprints, and progressive, floor-by-floor and even room-by-room construction. Absent from the current phenomenon are the one-off residential high-rises that had begun to pepper informal areas in the preceding ten years (see Chapter 4). Perhaps such speculative construction, spawned in a murky world of collusion between investors, lawyers, fix-it men, and local officials, is just too risky in revolutionary Cairo. On the other hand, the individual informal owner-builder, who never relied on the state, avoided its bureaucracy at all costs, and relied on personal and community ties, feels no risk.

Since the revolution there has been a certain uptick in efforts to help people in the more deprived informal areas or 'slums' of Greater Cairo. There was always a certain amount of charitable work aimed at uplifting the downtrodden, mainly steered by important personalities (*shakhsiyyat bariza*), not the least of whom were the First Lady and her coterie. Although she and her organizations have been discredited, others continue to take on the mantle of good works. Some efforts are sincere, down-to-earth, and effective, but these tend to be modest and unpublicized.[11] Others are definitely in the limelight. Most prominent is a weekly talk show aired by Amr El-Leithy on Dream TV called *Wahid min al-nas*, which started in 2009 and continues to run. It hosts various political figures and celebrities, and also highlights the problems of those living in 'slums' and conducts fund-raising campaigns. Dramatic visits to slums (always the most deteriorated neighborhoods that can be found) with celebrities in tow are standard fare for the program. Just after the revolution another project was started under the supervision of El-Leithy called 'Hamlat al-Milyar li-Nuhud al-'Ashwa'iyyat' (The Billion Campaign to Develop Informal Areas). This campaign is supported by the well-known actor Mohamed

Figure 11.1. Informal construction in north Giza, October 2011. (Photograph by David Sims.)

Sobhy, actress Hanan Turk, televangelist Amr Khaled, as well as others, and money is being raised by volunteers from Egyptians both at home and abroad. It is not exactly clear what is intended, but the general idea is to fund new houses for slum inhabitants from the worst areas of Cairo and other cities. It is said that the project also plans to send psychologists and medical caravans to treat those suffering in these areas![12] Through an associated NGO called 'Ma'an,' headed by Mohamed Sobhy, the aim is to fund five new settlements in five Egyptian cities on lands donated by the governorates, including infrastructure, schools, hospitals and factories, to rehouse slum dwellers, and to teach them to be productive workers. This approach mimics exactly a number of older government programs that were mainly expensive public relation exercises and that benefited only a precious few.[13] The AUC seems to see no problem with this patronizing, unsustainable, and media-hyped scheme. The university provost has announced its intention to form an association with "these worthwhile endeavors" of Ma'an through a memorandum of understanding.[14]

Far from talk shows and funding drives, an extremely positive and welcome development in informal areas of Greater Cairo is the spontaneous appearance of popular committees (*ligan sha'biya*). During the insecurities of the revolution, these committees initially performed 'neighborhood watch' functions all across Cairo. In many informal areas they have remained, expanded, and metamorphosed. For once, these are truly grass-roots organizations. Many of them have started to engage in addressing community needs such as garbage collection, organization of traffic, protection of citizens and businesses, the reconciliation of disputes, social and health awareness, price controls and distribution of subsidized bread and *butagas* (butane gas), repair of utilities, and the securing of vacant land for service needs. Several alliances have been formed among popular committees in different areas. One of them is the Federation of Popular Committees in Informal Settlements, which was founded in February 2011 by popular committees from Duweiqa, Dar al-Salam, Bulaq al-Dakrur, Imbaba, Maspero, al-Gamaliya, Qal'at al-Kabsh, Ard al-Liwa, and al-'Umraniya. Their intentions are even wider. Some aim at recovering land in and close to informal areas, which had been assigned to failed investors, for use by much-needed community services; others the rehabilitation of utilities and roads; and still others lobby for the right to social and health insurance for all residents in informal settlements, particularly workers, craftsmen, and the unemployed.

The most active popular committees are made up of mostly young people who are highly critical of established institutions, political parties, and even NGOs. Cooperation between local NGOs and popular committees exists in some areas, but this seems to be the exception, since most development NGOs working in poor neighborhoods are not staffed by volunteers, are not dynamic or flexible, and are governed by paternalism and the management logic of the external funding source upon which they depend. Members of political committees may participate as volunteers in campaigns, but not as integral parts of these NGOs. Many political committees prefer, therefore, to work on their own and to cooperate with a range of organizations on a case-by-case basis. Cooperation in some cases exists with government entities, political parties, and businesses, and the links usually depend upon known and credible local personalities. In Giza, popular committees have an office in the governorate, and in Cairo several meetings have taken place with the governor. A wide range of youth, including non-politically affiliated, secular, leftist, and Muslim Brotherhood, are involved with popular committees in many areas. Salafis seem to be more reluctant to cooperate or engage with popular committees but undertake similar activities on their own, for example, in controlling distribution of subsidized bread and *butagas*.

To summarize: since the revolution, informal areas of Greater Cairo have seen a much accelerated pace of construction, the appearance of popular committees, and much more community solidarity and action. But has anyone in the transitional government, or even in the concerned professions and in universities, taken notice? Has the need to upgrade these neighborhoods and improve the lives of their millions upon millions of inhabitants been at least articulated, as social justice and other values of the revolution would dictate? To date, there has been an almost deafening silence. There is an initiative currently being undertaken by the World Bank to mobilize all parties to look seriously at a comprehensive upgrading program for informal areas of Greater Cairo. However, it remains to be seen if this initiative will succeed in awakening the interest of the incoming elected government, given the difficult financial position the country finds itself in.

Housing in the Metropolis

In revolutionary Egypt little has changed in terms of housing policies. There have been no fundamental legal reforms or innovative schemes to address housing affordability and pro-poor market issues, which some might have expected to follow on from revolutionary rhetoric. More than ever, most housing in Greater Cairo (and almost all affordable housing) is being produced 'out of sight' by the informal sector, as mentioned above. As yet the post-revolutionary governments have continued the old regime's approach to these areas—neglect, marginalization, and failed proscription. Government housing schemes have stagnated, and the only ongoing construction is related to the completion of projects of the old National Housing Program (NHP) in the new towns around Cairo. As will be seen below, some of the programs of the main political parties participating in the recent elections call for affordable housing for the poor, but these are vaguely worded and imply that all needed housing will somehow be provided by the government.

One dimension of housing that saw more activity directly after the revolution is human and housing rights NGOs, who became more vocal in defending disadvantaged residents, and tenants under threat of eviction. These are national in scope but tend to concentrate on Cairo neighborhoods. A manifesto was drafted by a number of organizations as early as February 2011,[15] and in July 2011 a workshop on housing rights in Egypt was sponsored by a number of NGOs, with themes that included housing rights, housing legislation, the role of the media, violations of housing rights, campaigns and networks, and so on.[16] Since this event, little has been heard of these initiatives, and their relative silence may be due to the fact that most of these civil society groups are associated with outside affiliates and/or obtain funding from abroad, something that is definitely frowned on in post-revolution, military-guided Egypt.

Another change relating to housing, which mirrors the Egyptian political scene as a whole, is the number of direct actions by those who see themselves as wronged by the state. These may take the form of forcibly occupying vacant government housing units, demonstrating in front of government offices, or both. The residents of Duweiqa, who, after the rock slide and subsequent clearances three and a half years ago, have still not received their promised housing units, are a good example. They were foremost among the multi-cause sit-ins in front of the prime minister's office, until the most recent riots in December (2011) forced them out.

In terms of government housing pronouncements, there has been a startling revolution-connected development. The story is as follows: before the revolution, the Ministry of Housing had begun preparing for the second National Housing Program (NHP), which, like the first one launched in 2005, was to produce, over a period of six years, some five hundred thousand 'affordable' social housing units in Egypt (about half of which would be in and around Greater Cairo). As with the first program, this new one was timed to coincide with the presidential term, and in fact most Egyptian officials referred to the NHP as *wa'd el-ra'is*, or "the President's promise," as they had to the first program.

This second NHP had reached an advanced stage of planning, and like the first it was to involve a mix of housing unit types (including the popular *ibni baytak* program), a mix of implementers (including the New Urban Communities Authority (NUCA), the Ministry of Awqaf, governorates, and private companies), and a strong obligatory mortgage finance system covering over half of the units, backed by a World Bank loan and technical assistance to the various Egyptian players in the mortgage scene. After the revolution in January it was obvious that the new NHP could not continue along its original track, which was completely associated with President Mubarak.[17] Also, the Ministry of Investment, which was a strong partner in the mortgage side of the NHP, had been abolished as being too friendly to big businessmen.

So what happened? On 11 April 2011, only two months after the fall of Mubarak, the minister of international cooperation sent around to donors a proposal for a 'National Social Housing Program.' This new program called for building a colossal amount of low-cost housing—some one million units in six years, at an estimated program cost of $3.34 billion per year. The Ministry of Housing, the Housing Development Bank, and the NUCA would be the implementing agencies. Housing projects would be mostly in the new towns as well as in governorates, with perhaps half of the total in the Greater Cairo region. The minister called for international donors to contribute some 50 percent of total costs, equaling a total commitment over the life of the program of over $8 billion. Such a level of donor involvement would contribute an astounding amount, several times more than any previous donor-financed program in Egypt. And it would completely eclipse all previous donor support for the housing sector.

Why would the 'new' government think a proposal for such a colossal housing program would fly? Its parameters were much the same as the first NHP, which had been roundly criticized in donor assessments—and to which no donors had contributed. The justification, which came in the first paragraphs of the proposal, was as follows:

> This project resembles part of a rescue/stimulus package to help put the Egyptian economy back on track. Young Egyptians who attracted the admiration of the whole world need to feel that their revolution is not coming to their detriment. They need jobs and homes (shelters). This project utilizes the construction sector of Egypt—which is known to spur other economic sectors—to provide these young Egyptians with just that: jobs and homes/shelters.[18]

In April 2011, the donors huddled together and came up with a politely dissenting response that called first for a national housing strategy, which would set the parameters for any subsequent housing programs. The fact that the National Social Housing Program would repeat and even exacerbate the problems of the earlier NHP—being very expensive, financially unsustainable, ill-targeted, and creating thousands of units in remote new-town locations that would remain mostly empty—could be read between the lines.

In any event, the new National Social Housing Program has remained a government priority, even though there is no significant source for the enormous funds required. In October 2011, at a conference entitled "Stimulating Growth and Investment during Transition," Fayza Abul-Naga, the minister of international cooperation and planning, asserted in her opening speech that the government was currently implementing procedures to help achieve social justice, including the creation of job opportunities, enhancement of small and medium enterprises, and the provision of one million housing units at reasonable prices over the coming five years.[19]

Another parallel government initiative appeared in October, with the announcement by the minister of housing of a program to release one hundred thousand plots of land in new towns "for those of limited income."[20] Plots average from two to three hundred square meters, and up to four floors can be built. Prices for plots range from LE60,000 to LE150,000, and can be paid over three years. Many controls are to be put in place to force construction and dampen speculation and resale. But where will all these plots be located? After all, we are talking about some ten thousand hectares of land that will be required and provided with infrastructure. Very small numbers are available in some new towns around Cairo—al-Badr, al-Shuruq, Fifteenth of May, and Tenth of Ramadan—and most are located in the least successful of the new towns in Upper Egypt. (Note that no plots are available in the most popular new towns in Greater Cairo, such as Sixth of October and New Cairo.) Practically any citizen can register (group applications of four for one plot are allowed), and evidently the demand is high.

It is absurd to call this program "land for those of limited income," considering that the outlay for land alone can exceed LE100,000, that a single apartment unit will cost at least LE175,000 to build, and that they are in locations that require private vehicles (something only 11 percent of households in Greater Cairo possess). But it is an indication that the government desperately needs to be seen as active in the housing sector; and since the funding for the new National Social Housing Program is nonexistent, the carving up of some unserviced desert land, which now costs almost nothing, was seen as a brilliant intermediate solution. In fact, in December 2012 it was announced that this program would be expanded from one hundred thousand, to two hundred and fifty thousand plots!

The Desert City, Sour Land Deals, and the Real Estate Bubble

In Chapter 6, the Desert City (the huge and continuing effort of the state and its corporate clients to develop the new towns around Cairo) and the multiple visions of these desert developments as the future of Greater Cairo, were described in some detail. What has happened in the new towns in the year that has passed since the revolution?

After January 2011 there emerged a cascade of accusations of land manipulation and sweetheart land deals implicating a number of leading figures in the Mubarak government, as well as prominent businessmen associated with the old regime. Most such land deals were located in the desert around Cairo, where the opportunities for outrageous profit were greatest. Some of those implicated went to trial and, as everyone knows, there are ministers and prominent businessmen who are still on trial or have been convicted of fraud or 'wasting state finances.' Actually, the accusations had started even in the year leading up to the revolution,[21] but without the protection of Mubarak's cronies, what had been a couple of isolated cases soon mushroomed into scores of scandals. The case of Palm Hills and its extremely profitable 'land bank' is a particularly revealing example of the marriage of politics and business, nepotism, and the favoring of the well connected.[22]

Such embarrassing events had an immediate and negative impact on the wider corporate real-estate market. Further undermined by perceptions of insecurity and political turmoil, this market rapidly deflated. Right up to January 2011, the modern property sector, mainly devoted to high-end, luxury housing and an astonishing rollout of new multipurpose compound projects in Cairo's new towns, had seemed to be booming and unstoppable. At least, this is what appeared to be the case, based on ever more glowing pronouncements coming from the major real-estate corporations, their media commentators, and even government officials.

There was no sudden market collapse, with prices plummeting and a cascade of bankruptcies. But quickly there was an almost total freeze on new purchases. The upper classes, and Egyptians working in the Gulf (always an important demand segment) decided to wait and see. Obviously, this factor rapidly forced firms to delay existing construction and cancel or postpone projects in the pipeline. Even worse, demand in the secondary market (housing and commercial units offered for resale) began to dry up. Few owners of these units could bring themselves to dramatically reduce their asking prices, but as time went on, the more desperate—especially those with other debts that needed to be covered—began to knock down prices.

This has not stopped real-estate corporations from continuing to advertise and promote their projects. Billboards and television spots still extol the modern, exclusive, luxurious, and spacious living to be had in these gated communities. But even the real-estate cheerleading media has begun to pose embarrassing questions. In July 2011, only six months after the revolution, an article in *Al-Ahram Weekly* summarized the real-estate scene as bleak. Even though summer was usually a time when property-market demand peaked, in 2011 the reverse was the case. Noting that real-estate developers focusing on high-end property for Cairo's wealthy elites have been most effected, the article quoted Ayman Sami of Jones LaSalle as saying, "We consider 2011 a lost year for the real estate market," adding that no improvement is expected until "the dust settles."[23]

Further on, in October 2011, it was reported that the Credit Suisse brokerage saw continued weaknesses in the real-estate market, with significant delays in project completions and shrunken earnings for big players in the new towns around Cairo such as Palm Hills Developments and Sixth of October Development and Investment Company (SODIC). These publicly traded companies have seen their stock prices tumble.[24]

Very recently, in January 2012, Orascom Development Holding and Madinet Nasr Housing decided to scrap a large 320-hectare project located near Cairo airport called Tigan, a mixed luxury housing and office/commercial complex. Orascom said in a statement that the decision was made "in light of the recent changes in the real-estate industry and the unsuitable timing to launch a huge and luxurious housing project." It did not provide further details.[25]

These examples show that the property downturn, especially that for upscale and luxury housing, is serious and not likely to reverse anytime soon. Even so, the real-estate sector, never one to admit defeat, is forging ahead with plans for a bigger-than-ever exhibition in February

2012. Called Next Move—Cityscape Egypt, the exhibition expects all the big developers to attend, such as SODIC, Talaat Moustafa Group, Palm Hills, Ocean Blue, Moharram Bakhoum, DAMAC, Al-Futtaim Group, Emaar Misr, Rooya Group, Tiba, Orascom, and so on. One commentator was credited with the tired old phrases that "market fundamentals remain strong" and "the growing demand on housing will restore confidence in the sector."[26]

The new towns outside Cairo are run by the NUCA, and up until January 2011 this semiautonomous government entity was seen as extremely powerful due to its large vacant land holdings, some of which were being sold for huge profits. Not only was it financially powerful, it was run by ex-generals, it allotted land parcels to friends of the regime, and it had a business culture that was extremely opaque. After the revolution, NUCA's financial surpluses largely evaporated as the transitional government, desperate for cash, appropriated huge chunks.[27] And almost all prime land sales were halted (although not land subdivisions for low-cost housing programs, as discussed above). Interestingly, some seventeen private developers who had acquired large land parcels from the government have agreed to return all of the lands that are still lying unused, or for which the allocations were of a dubious nature.[28]

What is the current scene on the ground in the most prominent new towns such as Sixth of October, New Cairo, and al-Shuruq? This is very difficult to say, but from residents and passersby, one gains the impression that development has slowed considerably. Yes, the occasional new mall or private school is opening, but other businesses are closing, almost all construction has ground to a halt, and there is more of a feel of emptiness. Yet these new towns continue to make the major contribution to Greater Cairo's traffic mess (see below), so in this sense at least it can be said that there is still life in the new towns.

Transportation and Traffic
Traffic in Cairo became more messy and anarchic than usual directly following the revolution, mainly due to the abrupt withdrawal of all the traffic police, who abandoned key intersections and junctions, and no longer provided even the smallest restraint to erratic driving behavior. But as the weeks passed and the police trickled back to work, the traffic jams seemed to continue and even become worse. There have been no traffic studies since the revolution, but practically everyone (including

taxi drivers, who should know!) agrees that the situation continues to get worse. Most weekdays the congestion mounts steadily from noon, until by two or three all major arteries are clogged and traffic flows at a snail's pace, if at all. This state continues well into the evening. Even on weekends (Friday and Saturday, typically days when the traffic used to be quite thin) there is now the same rising congestion in the afternoon and blockages in the evening, especially on the main roads. The Ring Road and the connections to the new towns suffer particularly, and two- and three-hour journeys out or back from these satellite towns are said to be common. No one knows why things are so bad.

If traffic congestion in Cairo is reaching crisis point, is the government doing anything about it? As with other government responsibilities, there is a budgetary crisis, and this is said to have stalled the Rod al-Farag connector (to serve the western new towns) and other proposed links and flyovers. Moreover, there appears to be a kind of paralysis in any traffic initiatives, except in rerouting traffic off Qasr al-'Aini Street and other arteries around Tahrir Square. The love affair with physical barriers continues, and lumps of concrete force long detours and U-turns.

More fundamentally, nothing seems to be in train to improve public transport. In Chapter 8 it was underlined that only some 11 percent of households in Greater Cairo own private cars, yet the private car makes up about 60 percent of all traffic on the roads, and with random parking is the main culprit for clogging many streets. Obviously, the solution would be dramatically improved public transport that is separate from the general traffic or receives priority over it. The metro system, although expensive, should be an urgent national project. However, construction on the third metro line continues at a snail's pace. In October 2011 its first stage, from 'Ataba to al-'Abassiya, some 4.3 kilometers and four stations, was opened after four years of work. Work on the second stage along Shari' al-'Uruba continues. Given that the total length of the third line is some forty-six kilometers comprising twenty-six stations, it is plain that the completion of this line, at the present pace, will take decades!

As far as is known, there are no other public transport priority projects in the works. The World Bank's Urban Transport Infrastructure Development Project, conceived in 2009, called for a system of six exclusive bus ways to run on sections of the Ring Road and also connecting to the new towns both east and west of Cairo proper. There has been no movement on this project, and the alleged reason is that the Egyptian government cannot agree on which ministry should be responsible for project implementation.[29] In addition to this hung-up project, the concept of a super tram (a light rail link) connecting Heliopolis with New Cairo and the AUC campus, was announced by the then minister of transport with great fanfare in December 2010, just before the revolution. This project's feasibility study was completed, the length was forty-four kilometers, and it was to cost some LE5 million (of which LE1.4 billion were to come as a loan from the World Bank) with construction due to start immediately.[30] Nothing has been heard of this project since. This is just as well, since although much of the line would pass through the heavily populated Madinat Nasr, its extension all the way to the AUC campus would have been laughable. It would have been serving rich students, who anyway all own cars. But such was the arrogant 'subsidize the rich' approach of the latter days of the Mubarak regime.

It should be noted that there are still no systems planned for on-street or off-street parking, no ideas for limiting the use of the private car in the center of Cairo, or of how to improve the organization of minibuses, and, in particular, no measures to accommodate the long-suffering pedestrians in what must be, as was pointed out in Chapter Eight, the least pedestrian-friendly city on earth.

The Elections in Greater Cairo

Egypt's first free parliamentary elections in some sixty years have been completed, and the final results, which gave an amazing two-thirds of seats to Islamist parties, were announced at the end of January. How did voting fare in Cairo, and can this give us any indication of the politicization of the city and the intentions of the Islamist majority toward its development?

First, attempts to analyze voting patterns by electoral district were largely defeated by the complicated voting system for both individual candidates and party lists. It had been hoped to trace voting patterns by rich areas compared with inner-city poor and fringe informal areas. Cairo is composed of many police districts (the smallest electoral unit), but the party or individual vote-counts are not available by these police districts, even on the excellent official Higher Judicial Election Commission website.[31] Even the results that are broken down by specific electoral districts (of which there are nine in Cairo Governorate, spanning neighborhoods both poor and rich, old and new) only gave the names of individual winners and not their vote count. The only hard numbers for parties come from the party-list zones, of which only four in Cairo Governorate, and one in parts of Giza Governorate, are included in Greater Cairo. The results from these show that in Cairo Governorate the Egyptian Bloc (a coalition of secular and leftist parties) did remarkably well, at least compared to national averages, capturing between 25 and 32 percent of the vote and outperforming the Salafis in three of four zones. In Giza the Egyptian Bloc gained only 10 percent of the vote. Of course, in all zones the Freedom and Justice Party (the political party with strong ties to the Muslim Brotherhood) gained by far the most votes, usually between 40 and 50 percent. All this shows is that, in Cairo Governorate, there are fewer voters than the national average who lean toward the more extreme Islamists, and more who lean toward the liberal and secular parties.

In the run-up to the elections, to what extent did the major parties articulate development programs, and did any talk about housing and urban development? According to newspaper accounts in November 2011,[32] salient features were as follows: the Free Egyptians Party (part of the Egyptian Bloc coalition) called for the state to be committed to provide housing to all citizens, by (1) preventing the state from trading in real estate; (2) amending laws to end monopoly in housing-related industries, such as cement and steel; and (3) providing housing units for people with limited resources. Al-Nour Party (part of the Islamist Bloc coalition) called for the provision of cheap housing for newly married couples and citizens living in slums, and in impoverished areas across the country. The Freedom and Justice Party (part of the Democratic Alliance coalition) promoted redirecting the subsidies given to housing-related goods and industries into direct subsidies given to citizens to fund their housing. The party also called for restructuring the slum areas to make them habitable for their residents. And the Socialist Popular Alliance Party (the Revolution Continues coalition) proposed large-scale, national, and nonprofit projects to provide housing for youth and the poor, at affordable prices. It also proposed restructuring slums, and preventing forced evacuations unless the government provided immediate alternative housing.

All of these party programs have a populist tilt and call for more equitable housing policies, mainly through the provision of subsidized housing. However, they are very short on details, and it could be said that there are only small differences from what the former regime espoused. Only the Freedom and Justice Party and the Revolution Continues coalition-specifically call for the restructuring of slums (presumably meaning *'ashwa'iyyat*). And 'restructuring' could mean almost anything. Finally, none of the prominent parties even mentions Greater Cairo and its problems, nor urban problems in general (such as transport, pollution, solid waste, and so on). Only time will tell how the parties that form large blocs in the new parliament will address these issues, if at all.

Governing Cairo

In Chapter 9, the governing of Greater Cairo was described as largely an exercise in muddling through, with the governorates in a state of eternal crisis management, but, luckily, with the basic utilities—power, telephones, water, and wastewater—functioning quite well if in a 'minimalist' mode. Not much has changed since the revolution, except that muddling through has reached new heights, and the phrase 'automatic pilot' comes to mind more than ever.

Still, there have been a couple of actions that are very welcome. In April 2011 the 2008 decrees that created the new governorates of Helwan and Sixth of October, and reduced the size of Giza and Cairo Governorates, were cancelled, meaning that these absurd administrative boundary changes were no longer around to confuse everyone. Secondly, in April 2011 the local popular councils in all local-government units of the country were dissolved, including those of the governorates and districts of Greater Cairo. These mechanisms of patronage and favors, which had paralyzed local representation and were simply vehicles for the special interests of the former ruling National Democratic Party, will not at all be missed. It remains to be seen what will eventually take their place.

Summing Up: The Revolution Has a Long Way to Go

While the partial removal of the self-serving political structure in Egypt is a cause for celebration, it is not at all certain that the revolutionary spirit will continue and extend to issues that matter to the majority of Cairo's citizens. It is precisely this entirety of the population of the metropolis that should be carefully counted, and much could be corrected by the simple device of measuring government actions by the benefit they bring to the largest number.

It is still early days, and perhaps it is unfair to bemoan the lack, up to now, of any articulation or steps that would give priority to the interests of the majority—such as the ever increasing majority of the population that lives in informal areas, and the large majority that relies on public transport. Such fundamental shifts will require the wholesale redirecting of state budgets. But in these times of austerity there is precious little discretionary state budget to redirect.

At least, policies toward state land could be easily and immediately changed. There are still large amounts of unused government land found in the deserts east and west of the metropolis, as well as numerous underutilized parcels within the city belonging to various state organizations and enterprises, including the military and police. And there are more large land parcels that could be repossessed by the state from numerous failed business ventures. If the current paralysis in government decision-making can be overcome, it is very feasible to assign such land for affordable housing (especially self-built by the residents themselves, as is most of Cairo), for workshop clusters and enterprise zones, and for a range of urban projects that would benefit Cairo's youthful majority and not just the thin crust of the upper classes. Ironically, most well located undeveloped land is in the hands of the military. A great opportunity thus exists to develop these tracts through planned and transparent land allocations, should the military become a partner.

These are just some of the measures that could be taken to reorient Cairo's development away from inefficient and wasteful grandiosity, toward the needs of its inhabitants and toward efficient and sustainable economic growth. Many more can be identified. Is there a chance that they will materialize in the new, revolutionary Egypt?

First, by no means has the state got rid of all of its self-serving land grabbers and allied business elites. A few examples have been made of some ministers and businessmen, but three decades under Mubarak have created a very entrenched mafia at multiple levels, oiled by corruption that will not easily be flushed out. The revolutionary spirit so far is focused on changing national political structures, and there is no guarantee that manipulators and opportunists, so prominent in the past, will not still find fertile ground. Another, more complicated revolution is needed for fundamental reform of ministries and governorates, the courts, and economic authorities, so that real accountability and transparency begin to dominate urban development.

Second, a sea change in attitudes is needed. Cairo's academic, media, and professional circles are, with few exceptions, still bewitched by the shining hope of a modern Egypt that will somehow materialize, simply, with more and more concrete. Elitism, arrogance, *and* ignorance are still alive and well. That most Egyptians are poor, that the economy remains stagnant, and that mundane needs must first be met are inconvenient truths that the educated classes ignore or, at best, perceive as a call for more top-down patronizing. The hope is that Egypt's youth and the new representative parties do not buy into this, and that new attitudes will prevail which sweep away the pompous posturing of the older professional elites whose models for Cairo are Los Angeles, Singapore, or Dubai.

However, the record after one year does not show that attitudes have changed much. Certainly there is more criticism of the government's Cairo 2050 plan, but this is an irrelevant and easy target. Where are the more pertinent criticisms of past land assignments, such as those for Uptown Cairo or New Giza, where huge tracts of land, which could have been used for a number of social-cum-housing development projects (and still made a profit) have instead gone for a pittance to private developers who cannot think beyond sumptuous villas and exclusive lifestyles that are affordable to only the top 5 percent of households? Where is the criticism of NUCA, which remains in control of most remaining developable land in Greater Cairo, assigns land in complete opacity, clings to ridiculously high planning and building standards, and is run as a secret society? For that matter, where is the call for transparent state budgets that show where the nation's money has gone and is going, both in Greater Cairo and throughout the country?

Thus it could be said that Egypt's revolution still has a long way to go, at least as far as the metropolis of Cairo is concerned. Much work still needs to be done. The people of Cairo in their millions and millions do matter, and they deserve better treatment and better opportunities than they have had in the past.

February 2012

Notes

Notes to the Introduction

1   Nippon Koei Co. Ltd. and Katahira Engineers International, *Strategic Urban Development*, 2–9. The ranking of the sizes of the world's megacities by population is a slippery exercise, and other sources put Greater Cairo lower down the scale. See for example http://www.e-geopolis.eu. In any event, the Cairo agglomeration is extremely large and getting larger.

2   Mehta, *Maximum City*.

3   *Lagos/Koolhaas*. A much delayed book on Lagos, a collaboration between Koolhaas and Harvard University, which is said to be an in-depth effort of several volumes, will hopefully present the city in a more detailed light. As of late 2009 it had not, however, appeared in published form.

4   Roy, *City Requiem*. As in many urban academic studies, the actual fieldwork and data sources date back several years, in this case to 1997.

5   Abu-Lughod, *Cairo: 1001 Years*, and Abu-Lughod and Attiya, *Cairo Fact Book*. Both studies focused on the then known extents of Cairo including the urbanized areas of Giza and exhaustively analyzed the *shiyakhat* population data for 1947 and 1960, the most recent available at the time.

6   Clerget, *Le Caire*. Although Clerget was only in Cairo for a total of eight years in the 1920s, he managed to produce a work of over eight hundred pages in two volumes, replete with maps and even aerial photos, on the urban geography and history of what at the time had become a dualist city, with an emerging modern, even European sector standing in stark contrast to an insalubrious and mainly poor traditional city.

7   Sutton and Fahmi, "Cairo's Urban Growth," 135–49.

8   A short seven-kilometer walk from Ramsis Square along 26th July Street through Zamalek and Mohandiseen and along the *mihwar* puts one in the middle of cultivated fields west of al-Mu'tamidiya Village. This evokes the saying attributed to Cyril Connolly: "No city should be too large for a man to walk out of in a morning" (quoted on the jacket of the Yusuf Islam CD, *An Other Cup*, Ya Records/Polydor Records).

9   'Extralegal' is another word used more or less synonymously with 'informal.' As Ananya Roy states: "What is useful about the concept of extralegality is that it shows how informality is at once an outcome and a process. The significance of this process lies in the inherent ambiguities of the informal, and it is this that creates a dynamics of constant negotiation and negotiability." Roy, *City Requiem*, 140.

10   See for example Roy and AlSayyad, *Urban Informality*.

11   Abu-Lughod, *Cairo: 1001 Years*, v.

12   See for example, the works of the eminent urban economist Alain Bertaud, found in http://www.alain-bertaud.com.

13   As pointed out by the Marxist geographer David Harvey, it is easy "to criticize texts for what they leave out rather than appreciate them for what they accomplish" (David Harvey, *The Limits to Capital*, 1982, quoted in Castree and Gregory, *David Harvey*, 9).

14   Nippon Koei Co. Ltd. and Katahira Engineers International, *Strategic Urban Development*, 2008.

15   It should be a relief to readers that the understanding of Cairo as advanced in this book is free from academic ax-grinding. There is no convoluted hypothesis to test, no need to advance the frontiers of some arcane niche discipline, and, especially, no need to leap into a bewildering, self-referential, and jargon-loaded debate that only a handful of academics even claim to understand.

16   CAPMAS, in collaboration with CEDEJ, compiled quite accurate digital maps of all *shiyakha*, *qarya*, *qism*, and *markaz* boundaries in most of Greater Cairo, based on the 1996 Census. See *Century Census Egypt 1882–1996*.

Notes to Chapter 1

1   Authors such as Gamal al-Ghitani, Gamal Hamdan, and others have written books about Cairo, but they invariably tend toward the historical and do not take up the subject of modern Cairo. At least two technical books about informal or slum areas of the contemporary city have been written: see al-Wali, *Sukkan al-ahshash*, and Rayan, *'Amaliyat al-irtiqa'*.

2   Another entertaining book on Cairo, also mainly historic, appeared some forty years ago (see Aldridge, *Cairo*). Even further back in time, Clerget's opus on Cairo was published in 1934. Huge segments of this book were also devoted to Cairo's pre-modern development.

3   Raymond, *Cairo*, 351.

4   Raymond, *Cairo*, 377.

5   Rodenbeck, *Cairo*, 267.

6   Rodenbeck, *Cairo*, 277 and 286.

7   Rodenbeck, *Cairo*, 288.

8   Golia, *Cairo*, 7.

9   Golia, *Cairo*, 7, 8.

10 Golia, *Cairo*, 92, for all quotes in this paragraph.

11 Abu-Lughod, *Cairo: 1001 Years*, vi.

12 Examples include works by Cynthia Myntti, Samir Raafat, and Mercedes Volait. (See Volait, *Fous du Caire*.)

13 Sometime in the late 1990s *Nisf al-dunya* magazine published an undated special issue of over three hundred pages of photographs and articles on the life of Farouk (see *Faruq: zaliman wa mazluman*).

14 See Denis, "Cairo as Neoliberal Capital?," 50.

15 Attallah, "Cairo 1990," 97.

16 A draft law called *al-tanzim al-sukkani* was prepared by a former governor of Cairo for submission to Parliament, which would have forbidden anyone from outside the Greater Cairo region to take up residence there. See *al-Ahram*, 17 May 1992, 3: "al-Qahira, li-l-basr hudud."

17 Golia, *Cairo*, 21.

18 These descriptors are taken from the back cover of Davis, *Planet of Slums*.

19 Davis is a popular leftist writer on urban and environmental subjects. His book *Planet of Slums* has been criticized as being "anti-urban and overly apocalyptic." See *Wikipedia* article "Mike Davis (scholar), Criticisms and reviews."

20 Davis, *Planet of Slums*, 19.

21 Davis, *Planet of Slums*, 17.

22 A much more sympathetic if journalistic treatment of urban squatters in the Third World is to be found in Neuwirth, *Shadow Cities*.

23 Abhat et al., "Cities of the Future," 2.

24 Abhat et al., "Cities of the Future," 3

25 Praise by the *New Statesman* (quoted inside cover of Davis's book).

26 Singerman and Amar, eds., *Cairo Cosmopolitan*.

27 Singerman and Amar, eds., *Cairo Cosmopolitan*, 9.

28 Singerman and Amar, eds., *Cairo Cosmopolitan*, 3.

29 Singerman and Amar, eds., *Cairo Cosmopolitan*, 3. Presumably this term was modeled on the Chicago school of urban sociology, which became prominent in the 1950s and 1960s.

30 Singerman and Amar, eds., *Cairo Cosmopolitan*, 18.

31 Singerman and Amar, eds., *Cairo Cosmopolitan*, 19.

32 One of the authors gets a bit carried away with vocabularies. Writing about the Giza Pyramids area, that epitome of international tourism, Petra Kuppinger manages to mention 'global' or 'globalized' sixteen times in two short paragraphs of her article (Kuppinger, "Pyramids and Alleys," 314).

33 Vignal and Denis, "Cairo as Regional/Global Economic Capital?," 99–153.

34 Singerman, ed., *Cairo Contested*.

35 See Dorman, "Of Demolitions and Donors," and Deboulet, "The Dictatorship of the Straight Line."

36   Singerman, "Introduction," 6.

37   Singerman, "Introduction," 4.

38   Dorman, "Politics of Neglect."

39   Dorman, "Politics of Neglect," 3.

40   Waterbury and Richards, *A Political Economy of the Middle East*, 298, n. 20.

41   Sadowski, *Political Vegetables?*, 22.

42   World Bank, *Poverty Alleviation and Adjustment in Egypt*, 30.

43   Le Gac, *L'Envers des Pyramides*, 60.

44   Horwitz, *Baghdad without a Map*, 99.

45   Stewart, *Old Serpent Nile*, 15.

46   Mitchison, "Photographer on the Run."

47   "CNN Makes Egyptians Suspicious," 7.

48   Quoted in El Kadi and Bonnamy, *Architecture for the Dead*, 255; translated from the Arabic by El Kadi.

49   Heba Fatteen Bizzari,"Feature Story: City of the Dead," http://www.tour-egypt.net/featurestories/city.htim

50   *al-Ahram*, 18 May 1992, 3.

51   El Kadi and Bonnamy, *Architecture for the Dead*.

52   El Kadi and Bonnamy, *Architecture for the Dead*, 265.

53   Soliman, "Legitimizing Informal Housing," 187.

54   http://www.cairostreetchildren.com.

Notes to Chapter 2

1   The *A. R. E. Statistical Year Book 2008*, 97, reports that in 2001–2005 the total cultivated area of the 'old lands' was 6.6 million feddans, including the Fayoum. The cultivated area of the 'new lands' due to desert reclamation was 1.7 million feddans.

2   *A. R. E. Statistical Year Book 2008*, 39. This figure excludes some three to four million Egyptians resident outside the country.

3   *A. R. E. Statistical Year Book 2008*, 68.

4   The population growth problem has recently been highlighted by the creation of a separate ministry for population in 2009 and the need to redouble population control measures.

5   *A. R. E. Statistical Year Book 2008*, 114. In a recent World Bank report, somewhat different figures are given. In the rural Delta 43 percent of family landholdings are more than three feddans in size, and in rural Upper Egypt 18 percent of land holdings are over three feddans. In any event, both sets of statistics point to very small land holdings in Egypt (World Bank, "Arab Republic of Egypt: Upper Egypt—Challenges and Priorities," 14).

6   *A. R. E. Statistical Year Book 2008*, 28.

7   It is a rare event for CAPMAS to redraw or reclassify census areas, and the Ministry of Local Development is even less likely to decree new urban areas for administrative purposes. Changing a rural administrative area into an

urban one commits the government to provide higher levels of services and to make changes in representation in Parliament.

8   Bayat and Denis, "Who is Afraid of Ashwaiyyat," 185–99.

9   Census of Egypt 1996: *Ijmali al-jumhuriya al-juz' al-awwal* [Table 20].

10   Census of Egypt 1996: *Ijmali al-jumhuriya al-juz' al awwal* [Table 20].

11   Shorter, "Cairo's Great Leap Forward."

12   United States Agency for International Development (USAID), *Housing Study for Urban Egypt*, 53. According to the Census of Egypt 2006, [Table 1], for all of Egypt 'marriage' was the reason for changing residence for 30.4 percent of cases, and 'accompanying others' 29.0 percent of cases. 'Work' was the reason in 22 percent of cases.

13   *al-Ahram*, 28 December 2006, 17.

14   Deutsche Gesellschaft für Technische Zusammenarbeit (GTZ), *Cairo's Informal Areas*, 151.

15   United States Agency for International Development (USAID), *Housing Study for Urban Egypt*, 11.

16   Sims, "South Sinai Development Profile."

17   According to Wikipedia, a primate city is the leading city in its country or region, disproportionately larger than any others in the urban hierarchy. The 'law of the primate city' was first proposed by the geographer Mark Jefferson in 1939. He defines a primate city as being "at least twice as large as the next largest city and more than twice as significant" (http://www.en.wikipedia.org/wiki/Primate_city).

18   GOPP PowerPoint presentation, 2005: *Ru'ya mustaqbaliya li-iqlim al-Qahira al-Kubra fi du' al-tahaddiyat al-numuw al-'umrani* [Future vision of the Greater Cairo Region in the Light of Urban Growth Challenges].

19   Vignal and Denis, "Cairo as Regional/Global Economic Capital?," 130–31.

20   Vignal and Denis, "Cairo as Regional/Global Economic Capital?," 136–37.

21   Over the 1994–2007 period the average increase of Egypt's labor force was 590,000 persons per year. However, in the most recent years, 2004–2007, the reported increase was 996,000 per year (*A. R. E. Statistical Year Book 2008*, 75). Labor force data is often distorted due to the definitions used and should thus be treated with extreme caution.

22   *Egypt Human Development Report 2005.*

23   *A. R. E. Statistical Year Book 2008*, 87.

24   *A. R. E. Statistical Year Book 2008*, 45.

25   Al Khamissi, *Taxi*, 162–63.

26   *A. R. E. Statistical Year Book 2008*, 45.

27   *A. R. E. Statistical Year Book 2008*, 278.

28   *A. R. E. Statistical Year Book 2008*, 86.

29   *A. R. E. Statistical Year Book 2008*, 82.

30   *A. R. E. Statistical Year Book 2008*, 63. Curiously, the reported infant mortal-
      ity in 2006 in urban areas was significantly *higher* than the rate in rural areas
      (24.0 per thousand versus 16.3 per thousand). This may be due to under-
      reporting of infant deaths in rural areas.
31   *A. R. E. Statistical Year Book 2008*, 67 and 527–34.
32   *Household Income, Expenditure, and Consumption Survey, 2004–2005.* The full
      survey is carried out every five years, and the last survey had a sample of
      48,000 households in both urban and rural areas. Since it used a sample
      frame that was based on the 1996 Census, there was probably an under-
      representation of newer informal urban areas and thus also an underrepre-
      sentation of the urban poor.
33   *A. R. E. Statistical Year Book 2008*, 490–94.
34   Consumption items are relatively inexpensive in Egypt and basic foods,
      particularly bread, are partly subsidized by the state. However, the purchas-
      ing power parity ratios applied to the Egyptian pound ($1=LE2.57) have
      not been adjusted for the steep rises in the cost of living in the 2006–2009
      period in Egypt. In any event, 'purchasing power parity' is a slippery con-
      cept and allows for only very rough cross-country comparisons of purchas-
      ing power.
35   World Bank, *Arab Republic of Egypt: A Poverty Assessment Update*, iv.
36   The most recent country-specific gini coefficient estimates, made by the
      UN in 2008 for 142 countries, show a maximum of 74.3 (Namibia) and a
      minimum of 24.7 (Denmark). Egypt's gini coefficient is reported at 34.4.
      That of the United States was 46.1 and rising (http://www.wikipedia.org/
      wiki/List_of_Countries_by_Income_Inequality).
37   United States Agency for International Development (USAID), *Hous-
      ing Study for Urban Egypt.* The survey included a sample of 21,500 urban
      households and used the Census of Egypt 2006 sample frame. Results show
      slightly lower income and expenditure figures than the *Household Income,
      Expenditure, and Consumption Survey, 2004–2005.* For example, the median
      urban family income was calculated at LE1,000 per month, which is almost
      exactly the same as reported by the *Household Income, Expenditure, and Con-
      sumption Survey, 2004–2005* for *all* of Egypt. Since it is well known that
      rural incomes are significantly lower than urban incomes (in 2004–2005,
      CAPMAS reported that the average or mean urban household income was
      LE16,170 per year versus LE11,080 for rural households), this could mean
      that the results of 2004–2005 are inflated, that those of 2008 are deflated,
      that Egyptian urban incomes declined in the 2005–2008 period, or all of
      the above!
38   See Sabri, "Poverty Lines."
39   World Bank, *Arab Republic of Egypt: A Poverty Assessment Update*, iv. These
      figures are based on analysis of CAPMAS's *Household Income, Expenditure,
      and Consumption Survey 2004–2005* results. But there are queries on the

assumptions used, and many observers have calculated higher incidences of poverty. Even this World Bank report includes an estimate of the "near poor," which was 21 percent of the population in 2005 in addition to the 19.6 percent considered "poor."

40   The boundaries of these governorates are pre-2008. See Chapter 3 for an explanation of the geographic breakdown of Greater Cairo and Chapter 5 for a discussion of the 2008 HSUE.

Notes to Chapter 3

1   Some urban observers would say that it is necessary to go further back in history, at least to the beginning of the twentieth century, in order to understand how what is now the core of Cairo gained structure and form. Early expansion both into the agricultural plain and out into the near desert represented precedents that were to be formative features of the city's explosive expansion in the post-1950 period. However, this earlier history is well covered by Abu-Lughod, *Cairo: 1001 Years*, and Clerget, *Le Caire*.

2   The annual rate of population increase in Cairo was reported to be an amazing 6.4 percent per year in 1945 (Nippon Koei Co. Ltd. and Katahira Engineers International, *Strategic Urban Development*, 2–32).

3   These northern axes, which Janet Abu-Lughod called the Northern City, contained almost half of Cairo's population by 1960 and "could claim with a fair degree of accuracy to have become the real Cairo" (Abu-Lughod, *Cairo: 1001 Years*, 179).

4   In particular, Laws 51 and 52 of 1940. Most subdivision development up to this time was undertaken by private companies, many of which were under non-native management and all of which employed European professionals or Egyptians with European training backgrounds, and adherence to regulations was near-universal. It had yet to be discovered that enforcement was a relative concept.

5   Abu-Lughod, *Cairo: 1001 Years*, 180.

6   *Century Census Egypt 1882–1996*, Cairo Governorate section, years 1947 and 1960. These person-per-room rates are calculated by counting all rooms except kitchens and baths. Also, the definition of a 'room' is quite wide and includes entrees, living rooms, and reception areas, however small, as well as bedrooms. Thus the actual number of persons per usable room is higher than reported in the census.

7   The Mohandiseen scheme reveals a number of misconceptions and ironies. The project was conceived in 1944, thus predating the 1952 revolution by a long shot. The plans foresaw the complete disappearance of the traditional villages found in the area, such as Mit 'Uqba and Agouza, but these clusters are still there sixty years later and are doing very well. It is ironic that some of those professionals and urban elites who bemoan the loss of agricultural land around Cairo due to informal urbanization live or work in

Mohandiseen, itself built entirely on very productive agricultural land. It is amusing, seeing the area today with its huge apartment towers, to recall that the original *tanzim* plans specified a maximum building height of only ten meters, or three floors, for all of the scheme except the main boulevards (Volait, *Architectes et Architectures*, 344–45).

8   Abu-Lughod, *Cairo: 1001 Years*, 179.

9   For details on the Masakin al-'Ummal project in Imbaba, see Volait, *Architectes et Architectures*, 338–41. Today the area is a pleasant, quiet, and tree-shaded neighborhood, with most of the original structures having been altered and building heights increased dramatically through individual initiatives. It is ironic that this 'town house' form of public housing, which allowed residents to expand and improve their units as circumstances permitted and thus is extremely suitable to the Egyptian urban family, has never been repeated in any of the hundreds of subsequent public housing projects scattered throughout Cairo and indeed Egypt.

10   Abu-Lughod, *Cairo: 1001 Years*, 231.

11   Three luxury public housing blocks were built in the mid-1960s in al-'Abbasiya and intended for ranking army officers, but following Egypt's defeat in the 1967 war these buildings were turned into government offices.

12   United States Agency for International Development (USAID), *Review of Egyptian Subsidized Housing Programs*, Annex B.

13   United States Agency for International Development (USAID), *Housing Study for Greater Cairo*, 25. This figure may be on the low side, since older respondents in the survey may have inherited or been gifted government units. For comparison, over the 2003–2008 period a total of 10.3 percent of households in Greater Cairo moved into units that were government-built (pages 38–39). In peri-urban Greater Cairo, this figure falls to 1.1 percent. (United States Agency for International Development (USAID), *Housing Study for Peri-urban Areas*, 25.)

14   The population of upscale Zamalek, which had recorded small losses from 1966 through 1996, registered a slight upturn in the 1996–2006 period, and its 2006 population was enumerated at 16,900 inhabitants.

15   United States Agency for International Development (USAID), *Housing Study for Greater Cairo*, 19.

16   This scheme, *al-hayy al-hukumi*, is described in Chapter 6.

17   The definition of 'informal' urban development is given below in Chapter 4.

18   Abu-Lughod, *Cairo*. Her book was not published until 1971. It included a postscript based on rapid revisits to Cairo in 1968 and 1969, but even at this late date, she observed only small informal developments in al-Basatin and Dar al-Salam.

19   The 1:5,000 map series prepared by the Institut Géographique National (IGN).

20 El Kadi, *al-Tahaddur al-'ashwa'i*, 297–303. Galila El Kadi noted that there were only nine land subdivision companies registered in 1973; these had multiplied to number thirty-five by 1982. Around Greater Cairo these companies were most active in al-Matariya (forty-five out of seventy-eight land subdivision projects in Greater Cairo).

21 The core of 'Izbit al-Haggana has been said to have started much earlier with the settlement of border-patrol policemen (see Soliman, *A Possible Way Out*, 186). However, the area only began to take off in the late 1970s, as can be seen from 1977 IGN maps.

22 See Abt Associates Inc., with Dames and Moore Inc., *Informal Housing in Egypt*. This study was able to arrive at such a conclusion because integral to it was a large, representative sample household survey carried out by the USAID consultants in Greater Cairo in 1981.

23 An exercise using SPOT satellite images carried out by the technical assistance team of Institut d'Aménagement et d'Urbanisme de la Région d'Ile-de-France (IAURIF), in association with GOPP in 1990.

24 For an early commentary on the decrease of migration to Cairo, see Shorter, "Cairo's Great Leap Forward."

25 These self-help efforts were frequently of dubious quality given the lack both of technical supervision and sufficient funding. Many of the leakages and overflows found today in some informal areas result from the deficiencies and undercapacities of these secondary lines, and most require complete replacement.

26 For a description of the insertion of services as well as bureaucratic control into al-Munira al-Gharbiya, and the resulting political changes and alliances, see Haenni, "Cousins, Neighbors, and Citizens," 309–29.

27 Sims, "Informal Residential Development in Greater Cairo," 25.

28 Denis and Séjourné, "ISIS Information System," 12.

29 See World Bank, *Arab Republic of Egypt: Urban Sector Note*, vol. 2, Section 3.

30 Dorman, "Politics of Neglect," 87. The 1969 Master Plan also called for the construction of a ring road that would create a physical barrier and prevent further city expansion on agricultural land.

31 Madbouli, "Background Paper on Urban Planning," 59.

32 Reported in *Al-Ahram Weekly*, 14–20 November 1997, 2.

33 Many of these conferences were organized by the International New Towns Association (INTA) based in the Hague. Interestingly, INTA changed its name to the International Urban Development Association in 2006, reflecting a need to be more relevant internationally.

34 According to gossip at the time, the site of Tenth of Ramadan was chosen personally by Sadat. He was in his helicopter flying over the Ismailiya Desert Road, and at a certain point he was said to have pounded the floor with his walking stick, and his accompanying ministers had to try to figure out just where this act should be pinpointed.

35   PADCO Inc., "National Urban Policy Study," 1982.

36   For more details on the study and reactions to it, see Dorman, "Politics of Neglect," 192–94.

37   In 1996 an *Aramco World* article on Cairo reported: "Salah al-Shakhs, who headed the government's Division of General Planning in the late 1960s, maintains that despite the overly optimistic early projections, the new cities are bound to fill up. He points out that it took more than 20 years for Brasilia, Brazil's new capital city, to become popular. 'Now it has twice as many people as it was supposed to,' he says. 'It just takes time.'" (Doughty, "Cairo: Inside the Megacity.")

38   There are a number of micro studies and reports that confirm the shockingly high level of housing vacancies within Cairo's new towns. A study in 2006 sampled different kinds of housing in New Cairo and found that vacancy rates were 60 percent for subsidized government youth housing, 68 percent for resettlement public housing, 60 percent for the Qattamiya Heights gated community, and 100 percent for private residential blocks. And it should be pointed out that the areas of New Cairo sampled were the more mature, western neighborhoods. In Sheikh Zayed gated communities, the same study reported a vacancy rate of 53 percent. (Fahmi and Sutton, "Greater Cairo's Housing Crisis," 277–97.). Very high vacancies were also reported for public housing projects in Cairo's new towns in United States Agency for International Development (USAID), *Review of Egyptian Subsidized Housing Programs*, Annex B. Various investigative articles appear in the local press about ghost cities from time to time. See for example "Min yaqul inn fi azmat al-iskan?".

39   Dorman, "Politics of Neglect," 209.

40   Dorman, "Politics of Neglect," 198.

41   In 1947 the Census of Egypt reported 2.1 million inhabitants for Cairo governorate (then *mudiriya*), 268,000 for Giza *qism* and Imbaba, and 41,000 for "Cairo suburbs" in Qalyubiya. See *Century Census Egypt 1882–1996*, Cairo Governorate section, year 1947.

42   See the discussion of "large informal areas" in Chapter 5.

43   The Japanese calculate an area of 404 square kilometers for the "main agglomeration" and 125 square kilometers for "villages and small towns," which together equal existing Greater Cairo (Nippon Koei Co. Ltd. and Katahira Engineers International, *Strategic Urban Development*, 2–10 for population estimates and 2–14 for density estimates, allowing a calculation of surface areas).

44   It is interesting to note that of this huge area the Japanese calculate that in 2007 only 96 km² of the new towns were 'built-up,' or a minuscule 7 percent of the total planned area (Nippon Koei Co. Ltd. and Katahira Engineers International, *Strategic Urban Development*, 2–10 and 2–14).

45   Nippon Koei Co. Ltd. and Katahira Engineers International, *Strategic Urban Development*, 3–9 to 3–14.

Notes to Chapter 4

1   A certain flow of information on various aspects of informality in Cairo (and Egypt in general) is coming from 'ashwa'i upgrading projects such as those supported by German Cooperation (Manshiyat Nasir, Bulaq al-Dakrur, and the Participatory Development Programme in Urban Areas). GOPP in 2009 and the Ministry of Planning in 2000–2002 are some of the government organizations that have superficially studied aspects of 'ashwa'i areas. Over the years academic work has led to articles with particular interest. Also, some information on informal housing, tenure, and extralegality in Greater Cairo has resulted from the work of Hernando DeSoto and the Institute for Liberty and Democracy (Lima, Peru) with the Egyptian Center for Economic Studies over the 2000–2004 period).

2   Just after the cliff disaster in Manshiyat Nasir (Duweiqa) in September 2008, which caused a media storm, a newcomer to Cairo went around the office of his engineering consulting firm, one of the largest in Cairo, asking Egyptians if anyone could locate the disaster on Google Earth. Not one of a score of professionals could even come close, even though the site is less than half a kilometer from the Autostrad, one of Cairo's main inner arteries.

3   Al Khamissi, *Taxi*, 161, 162.

4   Nkrumah, "Living on the Edge," 1.

5   Singerman, "The Siege of Imbaba."

6   al-Alaily, "Kayf natanawal qadiyyat 'ashwa'iyyat al-'umran."

7   For example, as late as 2009 the minister of economic development was quoted as saying: "What we need to do is to redefine and recategorize informal settlements and to focus on dealing with them within the framework of a comprehensive program" (Deutsche Gesellschaft für Technische Zusammenarbeit (GTZ), *Cairo's Informal Areas*, 201).

8   Urban residential areas that started or were consolidated before 1950 are not considered informal, even if they exhibit considerable informal characteristics. The year 1950 is convenient for a number of reasons: it represents the beginning of the tremendous postwar expansion of Cairo, and it follows the introduction of the first stringent urban planning laws, in particular the subdivision laws of 1940.

9   Interestingly, interpretation of satellite images shows that when informal settlements first began to appear in the 1960s on agricultural land, there seemed to be some attempt to lay out street grids. Examples include neighborhoods in al-Matariya and parts of Imbaba. But this early organized parcellation soon gave way to truly random subdivisions of agricultural parcels. Using satellite images it is possible to discern the old farm field ownership patterns in the present-day urban fabric of these later and more common subdivisions.

10 GTZ has estimated that informal areas of Greater Cairo proper cover 132 square kilometers, which "is four times the area that official authorities have

previously acknowledged as being informal." (Deutsche Gesellschaft für Technische Zusammenarbeit (GTZ), *Cairo's Informal areas*, 211. Another seventy-three square kilometers of informal areas are estimated to have been found in peri-urban Cairo, based on Nippon Koei Co. Ltd. and Katahira Engineers International, *Strategic Urban Development.*

11   El Kadi, *al-Tahaddur al-'ashwa'i*, 107, 125, and 134.

12   Shorter, "Cairo's Great Leap Forward."

13   Institute for Liberty and Democracy and Egypt Center for Economic Studies, "Preliminary Assessment of Residential Informality in Egypt," 1997 (unpublished working paper).

14   Sims, "Informal Residential Development in Greater Cairo."

15   Denis and Séjourné, "ISIS Information System." Due to limited satellite image coverage, not all of Greater Cairo could be analyzed.

16   The Wilson Center map, prepared for USAID, appears in El Kadi, *al-Tahaddur al-'ashwa'i*, 59. The GTZ map appears in Deutsche Gesellschaft für Technische Zusammenarbeit (GTZ), *Cairo's Informal Areas*, 16, 28. In 2002, an article appeared in an academic journal that produced a series of maps of Greater Cairo, using 1996 Census results by *qism* (district), including one that sketches out "informal developments" and "squatter settlements" (Harris and Wahba, "Urban Geography of Low-Income Housing," 58–79. The map referred to is found on page 67).

17   It is interesting that the Japanese, who recently carried out the most extensive cartographic exercise on Greater Cairo to date for GOPP, never tried to map informal areas and in fact studiously avoided the use of informal nomenclature (Nippon Koei Co. Ltd. and Katahira Engineers International, *Strategic Urban Development*).

18   For a courageous attempt to catalog and compare the confusing government data sets on informal areas in Egypt, see Sabri, "Egypt's Informal Areas," 29–34. Also, a 1997 article refers to conflicting estimates by GOPP and the Ministry of Local Administration of the populations of informal areas of Greater Cairo (see Singerman, "The Siege of Imbaba," 143, n. 1).

19   Sims, "Informal Residential Development in Greater Cairo." This study is now rather dated, and the author, who carried it out, is the first to admit that it was less than perfect, given the information base at the time.

20   In the past, and to avoid these fees, it was quite common for groups of neighbors to band together to install their own local sewage collectors, inspection chambers, and house connections through *guhud zatiya*. However, the quality of these works was frequently poor and undersized, resulting in frequent blockages and sewage overflows.

21   United States Agency for International Development (USAID), *Housing Study for Urban Egypt*, 29. Breakdowns of this data were not available for informal areas of Greater Cairo separately, but the same high coverage rates can presume to apply, at least for Greater Cairo proper. However, it should

be pointed out that while overall water and electricity coverage was near universal in peri-urban Greater Cairo, for sewerage connections to public sewers the overall rate was only 54 percent. (United States Agency for International Development (USAID), *Housing Study for Peri-urban Areas*, xviii.)

22 According to a complaint filed by the school manager and members of *al-maglis al-mahalli* (the local popular council) of Saft al-Laban, a large informal area of Giza, the Saft Primary School had in excess of 110 pupils per class, and the school building was over sixty years old and full of cracks. Several previous letters to the education authorities about the problem had been ignored (*al-Misri al-yawm*, 22 November 2007, 3).

23 Sims, "Cairo, Egypt," 7.

24 The understandable reluctance of government authorities to use coercive power to clear slums is described by Dorman in "Of Demolitions and Donors," 269–90.

25 To get an idea of the copious international literature on the subject, simply type into Google the keywords 'insecure tenure urban.'

26 Sims, "What is Secure Tenure in Urban Egypt?"

27 A considerable amount of demolition of informal buildings was necessary to build the Ring Road, but both building owners and occupiers were compensated with cash payments. This was a slow process, carried out by the Jihaz Ta'mir al-Qahira al-Kubra (Greater Cairo Development Authority), an executive arm of the Ministry of Housing.

28 For a detailed account of a small rural community's struggle against eviction in Greater Cairo, see Gerlach, "al-Qorsaya Island," 91–95.

29 After the cliff collapse in Duweiqa in 2008, there was a veritable scramble by residents as well as pure opportunists to acquire one of the nearby public housing units made available for victims of the disaster. In an earlier slum clearance in the same area in 2002, most families were resettled in government housing units, but since the resettlement rule is "one family for one unit, regardless of the household size," some extended families felt they should have received more than one unit and held out in the rubble for months, much to the delight of the local media.

30 Thus, 16 percent of informal households were in the fifth or richest national urban quintile, 23 percent in the fourth, 22 percent in the third, 22 percent in the second, and 17 percent in the first and poorest quintile. For comparison, the national urban household income distribution places an equal 20 percent of households in each income quintile. (United States Agency for International Development (USAID), *Housing Study for Greater Cairo*, 8.)

31 For peri-urban families living in informal areas, 8 percent of informal households were in the fifth or highest national urban quintile, 15 percent in the fourth, 22 percent in the third, 29 percent in the second, and 25 percent in the first and poorest quintile. (United States Agency for International Development (USAID), *Housing Study for Peri-urban Areas*, 5.)

32 Manshiyat Nasir's illiteracy rates are extremely high, reflecting its reputation as the poorest large informal area of Cairo. In other large informal
   areas such high rates are unknown. Thus, for example, in Bulaq al-Dakrur
   the 2006 Census records illiteracy at 17.8 percent and in Imbaba at 21.2
   percent, compared to an average in urban Giza of 19.5 percent.

33 Deutsche Gesellschaft für Technische Zusammenarbeit (GTZ) and Cairo
   Governorate, "Manshiet Nasser Guide Plan," 6.4.

34 He or she may employ a local contractor who is skilled in both the technical
   aspects of construction and, especially, in the ways of bypassing or otherwise
   dealing with local authorities, and this is becoming more common.

35 Perhaps the best, if rather dated, description of the informal owner-builder
   process is found in el-Hadidi et al., "Informal Communities in Cairo."

36 Madbouli and Lashin, "al-Manatiq al-'ashwa'iya."

37 However, these rents relate to rental contracts made in the five year period
   2003–2008 and thus do not fully reflect the huge inflation Egypt has
   recently experienced. Anecdotal information suggests that 2009 rents in
   informal areas might be significantly higher.

38 These figures refer to all informal areas in urban Egypt. The breakdown for
   Greater Cairo is not available.

39 Deutsche Gesellschaft für Technische Zusammenarbeit (GTZ), *Cairo's
   Informal Areas*, 68–69.

40 For a further discussion of advantages to be found in informal areas of
   Greater Cairo, which to some might seem overly romantic, see Shehayeb,
   "Advantages of Living in Informal Areas," 35–43.

41 It should be added that most informal buildings are not well insulated,
   mainly because to keep construction costs down it has become the norm for
   external walls to be as thin as possible, usually only half a brick thick. This
   means internal rooms quickly become hot in summer and cold in winter.

42 Madbouli and Lashin, "al-Manatiq al-'ashwa'iya."

43 These densities are gross densities, and include nonresidential land uses,
   main roads, and open spaces found inside each agglomeration. Net residential densities, which exclude these items, would be much higher.

44 This informal conurbation straddles the borders of Cairo and al-Qalyubiya
   governorates and includes the informal parts of al-Khanka City and the
   shiyakha of al-Salam al-Sharqiya, as well as all of the village of al-Qalag and
   the *shiyakhat* of al-Salam al-Gharbiya and Gabal al-Asfar.

45 'Izbit al-Haggana is a good example of how population estimates for informal areas can be contradictory and how absurdly high estimates can be generated. The Census of Egypt 2006 preliminary results reported a population
   of 59,000 for the area. GTZ has made an estimate of 213,000 based on 2007
   satellite imagery, by counting buildings and by assuming there were 25 persons per building. (Deutsche Gesellschaft für Technische Zusammenarbeit
   (GTZ), *Cairo's Informal Areas*, 31.) Ahmed Soliman estimates amazingly

high populations for the area and at the same time manages to contradict himself. In Soliman, *A Possible Way Out*, 131, he states that 'Izbit al-Haggana had at least one million inhabitants, but on pages 181 and 183 he states that the area had a population of 400,000. No substantiation is given for these estimates, other than that they were based on Soliman's field surveys. Evidently Soliman's highest and totally erroneous estimate has gained a kind of legitimacy, as a recent UN report mentions 'Izbit al-Haggana as having "more than one million inhabitants." See Feature Stories at http://www.unfpa.org/news/news.cfm.

46   *al-Ahram*, 6 August 2006, 14.

47   The failure of these schemes is discussed in Chapter 4. Very recently the Ministry of Housing has launched the *ibni baytak* (build your own house) program in some of the far-flung new towns around Cairo, and this subsidized scheme, in which citizens can acquire small plots for building apartment units, has become quite popular. However, this very bureaucratic program can hardly be seen as a means of harnessing the informal dynamic, nor as an alternative to continued informal development on the agricultural plain.

48   For the Imbaba experience see Rayan, *'Amaliyat al-irtiqa'*.

49   For a description of the current activities of GTZ's Participatory Development Programme in Urban Areas, see Deutsche Gesellschaft für Technische Zusammenarbeit (GTZ), *Cairo's Informal Areas*, 211–13.

50   "In a short statement delivered at the inauguration Mrs. Mubarak stressed that Zeinhoum, like similar projects that aim to provide housing for the millions of Egyptians who live on the outskirts of major cities, was central to efforts seeking to combat a host of social ailments." *Al Ahram Weekly*, 21–27 May 2009, 2.

51   This project was steered by the First Lady's Integrated Care Society and also involved GTZ. The Secretary General of the Society calls it a "holistic" and "participatory approach" and considers it the Society's "most noteworthy accomplishment." (Deutsche Gesellschaft für Technische Zusammenarbeit (GTZ), *Cairo's Informal Areas*, 158.)

52   As is frequently the case, population figures become inflated, and in the press the area is said to contain "more than one million inhabitants." ("Imbaba tantazir al-tatwir," *al-Misri al-yawm*, 4 October 2009, 17.)

53   It is laughable that there should be such a concentration of these outlets in Zamalek, the wealthiest district in all of urban Egypt and with a population of only 16,000, whereas in the informal area of Manshiyat Nasir, with well over half a million inhabitants, there is only one such outlet, whose range of goods is limited to dusty cans of sardines and powdered detergent.

54   Exceptions of course exist. For example, some quite active religious *gam'iyat* are said to exist in Ard al-Liwa. See Néfissa, "Cairo's City Government," 187–90.

55   Piffero, "What Happened to Participation?"

56   World Bank, *Arab Republic of Egypt: Urban Sector Note*, vol. 1, 34.

57   Nippon Koei Co. Ltd. and Katahira Engineers International, *Strategic Urban Development*, 2–35.

58   This is not to say that the loss of prime agricultural land in the Nile Valley due to construction is not an issue, but the main culprit is not Greater Cairo's expansion. Rather, it is the incessant expansion of the thousands of villages and small towns found throughout the Nile Valley and Delta.

59   The Unsafe Area Development Fund and its activities in twenty-nine urban areas were announced by the Prime Minister in July 2009 as an integral party of the government's strategy toward developing informal areas (*al-Misri al-yawm*, 1 July 2009, 1).

60   World Bank, *Arab Republic of Egypt: Urban Sector Note*, vol. 1, 16.

Notes to Chapter 5

1   It is interesting that the lead sponsor of the affordable housing finance conference, Rooya Group, which claims to provide "elegance, uniqueness, and innovation in property development," actually gained its experience developing tourist resorts on the Red Sea. In fact, many of the companies now prominent in Cairo's corporate housing sector are ones whose main activities originally were (and sometimes still are) resort tourism. This is hardly the kind of expertise that would seem to fit with affordable, low-cost urban housing.

2   The study, the *Housing Study for Urban Egypt*, was carried out as part of USAID's Technical Assistance for Policy Reform II project, and Bearing-Point Inc. was the main contractor. Individual local and international consultants were hired, and Zenati Associates, Cairo, undertook the surveying of some 21,000 households in urban Egypt in May and June 2008, using the 2006 CAPMAS sample frame to ensure statistical representation. In total, six reports were produced, one for each of the following regions: Greater Cairo, peri-urban Greater Cairo, the Delta, Alexandria, the Canal cities, and Upper Egypt. Another report was produced on the methodology of the survey. The author was the Senior Housing Specialist in the study and lead author. (United States Agency for International Development (USAID), *Housing Study for Urban Egypt*, and associated reports.)

3   USAID's Egypt Financial Services project started in 2005 and was executed by Chemonics Inc.

4   See Chapter 1 for a discussion of the Census of Egypt and its flaws.

5   Greater Cairo proper is made up of all of Cairo Governorate, plus Shubra al-Khayma City in Qalyubiya Governorate, plus Giza City in Giza Governorate, plus the new towns associated with Cairo, Giza, and Qalyubiya governorates. In the sampling of the new towns there were so few households that the sample size was too small to be of any significance, since the 2006 population of these seven new towns amounted to only 450,000 inhabitants.

It should be noted that the terms used in this definition relate to administrative divisions that were in use prior to the changes in May 2008 that created the two new governorates of Helwan and Sixth of October.

6   Much of Cairo's residential housing is built progressively a floor at a time, and this figure presumably refers to the age of the first floor.

7   In peri-urban Greater Cairo, the figure for crowding was slightly higher, at 1.27 persons per room.

8   Also in Mumbai, 73 percent of families lived in only one room, according to the 1990 Census of India. (Mehta, *Maximum City*, 452.) In Lagos in 1976 the rate was reported to be 4.1 persons per room (Paccionne, *Problems and Planning*, 134). The U.S. Department of Housing and Urban Development defines overcrowding as more than 1 person per room (see Rubenstein, "Housing and Urban Development").

9   Census of Egypt 1966, reprinted in *Century Census Egypt 1882–1996* (Cairo Governorate section, 1960 Census).

10   Abu-Lughod, *Cairo: 1001 Years*, 164.

11   A quintile represents 20 percent of total households. Thus the first income quintile represents the poorest 20 percent of households per capita, the second income quintile represents the second poorest fifth of total households, and so on. Ranking households according to per capita income is carried out to avoid the distortions caused by differing household size and thus to arrive at a better measure of living standards relating to income.

12   Erroneously, most people believe that rent controls were instituted as one of Nasser's socialist projects, whereas they predate his rule by almost ten years.

13   In 1996 a law was passed that allowed between 25 and 100 percent increases in rental values depending on the date of the rental contracts, but since the base rents were so tiny, the increases did not at all bring rents in line with market realities.

14   The actual number of households residing in government-supplied units is probably higher, since some of these units have been rented or sold to third parties, households that would not be picked up in the survey as living in government-supplied units.

15   This tiny percentage includes apartments rented furnished to foreigners, often by those holding fixed-rental contracts on the units, and who enjoy huge windfall profits. There are apartments in upscale areas, stuffed with 'Louis-Farouk' furniture, boasting all modern conveniences, and sometimes even with a Nile view, where the fixed rent on a unit will not exceed LE50 per month, whereas the same unit is rented out by the tenant to a foreigner for thousands of dollars.

16   The average length of a rental contract in Greater Cairo proper was five years, advance payment on rents was paid in over one-third of cases, and annual rental increase clauses were found in 32 percent of contracts.

17 An important caveat is necessary here. Most of the information on housing supply and markets from the 2008 *Housing Study for Urban Egypt* relates to housing exchanges over the five-year period from the beginning of 2003 to mid-2008. Starting in 2005, Egypt began to suffer very steep and continuing inflation, which, based on anecdotal information, has also hit housing markets. Thus current (2009) average housing prices and rents in Greater Cairo may have risen significantly.

18 And it should be remembered that Greater Cairo proper includes a proportionate representation of occupied housing in the associated new towns, where both government and the private sector are very strongly represented in housing production.

19 It is perhaps not so surprising that housing exchange is localized, since in urban Egypt most people move locally if at all. In Greater Cairo proper, 73 percent of households who moved in the previous five years did so *within* the same *qism* or neighborhood.

20 Up until recently, those wishing to register a property transfer also had to pay a hefty official fee of 6 percent of the declared value, but this amount was reduced to a small flat fee in 2006.

21 Menelaws, "Property and Registration Law in Egypt.", 1.

22 Egyptian Center for Economic Studies and Institute for Liberty and Democracy, "Formalization of Egypt's Informal Real Estate Sector," 17, 18.

23 Menelaws, "Property and Registration Law in Egypt," 2.

24 Most of the information in this section comes from United States Agency for International Development (USAID), *Review of Egyptian Subsidized Housing Programs*, which was written by the author.

25 Cairo Governorate's Muqattam housing estate, constructed in the late 1980s, is a case in point. A couple of thousand units built on the middle plateau were found to be structurally unsound due to soil problems and have remained abandoned until the present.

26 Donor-supported pilot housing schemes have introduced some innovative designs (such as the Helwan New Communities project of USAID), but these have never been adopted and generalized. Similarly, sites and services targeted at low-income households have been piloted only by donor-supported efforts. By far the largest and most successful of such schemes were developed in the late 1970s and 1980s in Ismailiya, with UNDP and British aid support. Unfortunately, such an approach (small plots and eventually services, with full cost recovery coming from land sales) has never been replicated at any scale by either local or national government agencies.

27 United States Agency for International Development (USAID), *Review of Egyptian Subsidized Housing Programs*, Annex B.

28 Collective efforts to landscape and otherwise upgrade public housing estates have been marginally successful in some neighborhoods of Madinat Nasr, mainly where there are high concentrations of middle-level government

employees who can exercise a certain influence with municipal authorities. In 1991 the Unit for Housing and Urbanization at Harvard University's School of Graduate Design collaborated with the Institute of National Planning and 'Ain Shams District in training district staff in managing improvements in public spaces, mainly in public housing estates. One pilot was undertaken in the Ehlal estate, but little remains today from this effort. In this and other efforts, keeping up community interest has proven difficult. (United States Agency for International Development (USAID), Office of Environment and Urban Programs, "Community-based Development," 42–51.)

29   United States Agency for International Development (USAID), *Review of Egyptian Subsidized Housing Programs*, 29.

31   As discussed in Chapter 9, in Greater Cairo as a whole, only 11 percent of households own a private vehicle (and this includes taxis and trucks).

32   Proposals for such measures aimed at improving the general housing market have been made in a recent World Bank study. See World Bank and United States Agency for International Development (USAID), "A Framework for Housing Policy Reform in Egypt."

33   In developed countries with efficient urban housing markets, vacancies rarely exceed 5 or 10 percent of the housing stock.

34   In the 1980s the concept of a tax on vacant land was introduced in some governorates, but the application of the tax proved difficult and eventually such a tax was declared unconstitutional.

Notes to Chapter 6

1   Denis, "Cairo as Neoliberal Capital?," 49.

2   *Ayoub*, 1984, directed by Hani Lashin, produced by Mamduh El Laithy, and loosely based on a story by Naguib Mahfouz.

3   There is a ninth new town that has been on GOPP maps for years—al-Amal, some forty-five kilometers east of Cairo on the 'Ain Sukhna Road—but this one has yet to see the light of day.

4   Because one of the new towns, Fifteenth of May, is a grafting onto a part of existing Cairo rather than a geographically independent unit, it can be considered a simple urban extension to the metropolis rather than a new town *per se*. Another, Tenth of Ramadan New Town, is so remote from the Cairo agglomeration that it is functionally separate from Greater Cairo. Thus, were these two cities to be excluded from the list of new towns that form part of Greater Cairo, then the new towns' combined demographic weight within the metropolis would be even less than what was recorded by the Census of Egypt 2006, that is, down to 2.4 percent from an already feeble 3.7 percent.

5   Figures on total investments made by government in the new towns are extremely hard to come by. One dated government publication mentions

that over the Fourth Five Year Plan (1997/98 to 2001/02), 22 percent of all of MHUUD's investments were in Egypt's new towns, and many think that the current levels are much higher. (World Bank, *Arab Republic of Egypt: Urban Sector Note*, vol. 1, 61.)

6   Government planners seem to have a penchant for odd angles for the layout of road intersections and public housing blocks, thirty and sixty degrees being preferred. This results in a lot of awkward and unusable land segments, which, for lack of any better solution, are designated for yet more open space and, on plans at least, are verdant. A simple grid layout of streets, by far the most efficient, is rarely adopted in the new towns.

7   All of the new towns around Cairo are located on elevated desert plateaus where no shallow water tables exist, thus even hardy indigenous palm trees cannot survive without continuous watering. Even worse, most water consumed in the new towns, both for irrigation and for urban use, is lost forever since the desert locations are far from the Nile Valley and do not recharge the underground Nile Valley aquifers.

8   Very early on, in 1982, a NUCA announcement called on investors to purchase industrial plots in Sixth of October for LE20 a square meter, requiring a 25 percent down payment (printed announcement from NUCA dated 27 November 1982).

9   Madbouli, "Background Paper on Urban Planning," 60.

10 For those who are unfamiliar with Egypt's recent history, it should be pointed out that the sixth of October commemorates the start of the war with Israel to liberate Sinai in October 1973. Tenth of Ramadan is that same date according to the Islamic calendar. Fifteenth of May commemorates Sadat's 'corrective revolution' of 1972.

11 Media Production City, or 'Hollywood East,' obtained a large site along the southern entrance to Sixth of October. The land was assigned at no cost to the Ministry of Information, which then created a joint venture with private capital to provide film and television studios and support services. The land value was calculated as the ministry's (controlling) share in the joint venture.

12 If Sheikh Zayed New Town is considered part of Sixth of October, the combined 2006 population rises to 187,000 inhabitants.

13 The Census of Buildings includes, in its dwelling unit count, units that may be unfinished, and thus vacancy rates throughout urban Egypt seem high (averaging almost 30 percent for Greater Cairo as a whole). Even so, the vacancy rates in Sixth of October and in other new towns around Cairo are remarkably high.

14 Singerman, "Introduction," 14.

15 GOPP optimistically estimated the population of New Cairo at 300,000 in 2005, but this was presumably based on registered housing units rather than actual population.

16   Starting in late 2009 the pace of development in this part of New Cairo
      has accelerated, particularly south of the central spine where a number of
      individual apartment buildings are being finished and inhabited, private
      gardens and parked cars are appearing, and even a few lights can be seen
      at night. Some commercial services and office blocks have begun operating
      along the spine and many more are under construction. Yet this part of New
      Cairo can be considered the most vibrant and successful of all neighbor-
      hoods in all the new towns around Cairo, anchored as it is on one side by
      al-Tagammu' al-Khamis and on the other by the American University in
      Cairo campus. In fact, there is an immense prestige in real estate marketing
      terms to be able to say a scheme is near either.

17   The Extension of Municipal Services project, a study financed by the World
      Bank, aimed to create expansion zones for poorer inhabitants in the deserts
      both east and west of Cairo, with extensive use of sites and services zones to
      attract the informal housing dynamic. See also Chapter 4.

18   GTZ's three-year exercise is an interesting side story. At considerable
      expense, attempts were made to introduce a sites-and-services approach for
      residential neighborhoods with the aim of attracting the informal housing
      dynamic to al-'Ubur, which included detailed layouts of small plots and
      semi-public spaces and simple building regulations.

19   United States Agency for International Development (USAID), *Review of
      Egyptian Subsidized Housing Programs*, Table A5.

20   In the early 1990s there were attempts to relocate the hundreds of noxious
      and mostly small leather curing and processing firms out of the inner-city
      area of Fumm al-Khalig to al-Badr, over fifty kilometers away. Since such
      a move would spell the death of all but the largest of these enterprises and
      result in the unemployment of thousands, the issue rightly disappeared off
      anyone's agenda at a time of tough economic policies of structural adjust-
      ment. However, in 2008 the same concept for relocation of these firms to
      al-Badr reared its head again, this time with backing for the study from the
      European Commission's Industrial Modernization Project. To date nothing
      has materialized.

21   Details of the National Housing Program can be found in United States
      Agency for International Development (USAID), *Review of Egyptian Subsi-
      dized Housing Programs*, chapter 9.

22   A full-page article on housing in the new towns appeared in *al-Ahram* in
      2004, in which it was reported that some public housing, especially Muba-
      rak Youth Housing, is only occupied "25 percent at best" and that residents
      are fleeing in large numbers because of the many problems. *Al-Ahram*, 11
      December 2004, 13.

23   In the past few years such stipulations have been relaxed for the older
      worker-housing areas of Sixth of October, and the result is the wholesale
      conversion of ground-floor units in public housing blocks into a wide range

of small shops and services. However, this much more 'liberal' policy has not yet extended to other new towns around Cairo.

24   Refer to Chapter 8 for an analysis of Cairo's transport systems and the transport problems of the new towns.

25   There are of course exceptions to this, and in some smaller compound developments a well-known developer may not need to advertise, relying on friends and word of mouth to line up buyers.

26   For example, the central commercial spine of the original city core remains, but twenty years after parcels were allocated, only 30 percent have developed (and many of these structures are vacant).

27   In the late 1990s a 1.1-kilometer strip was added to the city core on the north (on what was originally the city's green belt/buffer zone). This area of 1,170 hectares has hardly developed at all, with the exception of a Mubarak Youth Housing estate and one private housing compound. Even so, the city has designed another further huge 'northern extension' on over 1,500 hectares and the land there has almost all been allocated, although not a single project has started. And city planners have designed and allocated most land in yet another extension to the east, a colossal area of 2,100 hectares, which currently has three scattered projects under construction on less than 2 percent of the land.

28   As recently as June 2008 the grace period for successful applicants under the *qur'a* system to make land payments and obtain building permits in the new towns was extended "for the last time." See *al-Misri al-yawm*, 21 June 2008, 1.

29   World Bank, *Arab Republic of Egypt: Urban Sector Note*, vol. 2, 69–70. A review of these superblocks using 2008 satellite images and visits in 2009 shows that there has been considerable additional construction activity in the intervening three to four years, at least in the older neighborhoods, due to pressures from the authorities. But actual occupancy remains extremely low.

30   GOPP PowerPoint presentation dated 2008 prepared by Space Consultants.

31   This land was understood to have been assigned for free, but the developer is supposed to provide his own infrastructure and also to build some public housing units for NUCA whose value is equal to 7 percent of the total cost of Madinaty. This land assignment, which like so many in desert Cairo, materialized as a decidedly untransparent and uncompetitive *fait accompli*, has been challenged in the courts by a group of citizens, but it is exceedingly unlikely that it will be overturned. See *al-Misri al-yawm*, 23 November 2008, 1.

32   Nippon Koei Co. Ltd. and Katahira Engineers International, *Strategic Urban Development*, 2–152 and 2–153.

33   Due to the political importance of the new towns, securing water sources and transmission rights of way has not been a problem. Also, NUCA has

imposed water consumption charges in the new towns that, although still subsidized, are three to five times those at present in Greater Cairo proper. And it may well be that water has to date been amply available simply because real populations, and thus actual water consumption, have been only a fraction of the wildly optimistic estimates made by NUCA.

34	At between 150 and 300 meters higher than the Nile, these areas are much more costly to supply with water than Greater Cairo proper, where 5 to 15 meters is the maximum difference.

35	World Bank, *Arab Republic of Egypt: Urban Sector Note*, vol. 1, 23.

36	Here is not the place to delve into the confusing mechanisms of public land management and the political and patronage interests involved in the disposal public land in Egypt. Readers might want to refer to World Bank, "Arab Republic of Egypt: Egypt Public Land Management Strategy."

37	In a long overdue recognition that these developments represent windfall profits for their owners, it is reported that a 'urban conversion' fine of up to LE100,000 per feddan is to be charged by the Ministry of Agriculture post-facto for such conversions of what were to have been agricultural reclamation schemes. See *al-Misri al-yawm*, 10 January 2008, 1.

38	GOPP PowerPoint presentation dated 2008 prepared by McKinsey Associates.

39	Not to be outdone, the newly created governorate of Helwan announced in July 2009 the signing of a memorandum of understanding with foreign investors and government ministries to create four megaprojects located around the Helwan suburb on a total of 2,000 hectares: 'Avenues Egypt' will be an integrated development of offices, a shopping mall, commercial and recreational areas, and hotels; 'Traders City' will offer logistical services for commercial and trade companies; 'Helwan International Medical Park' will be a destination for a range of health care and curative facilities and businesses; and 'Degla Safari Park' is expected to be "the world's largest open zoo." Reported in *Al-Ahram Weekly*, 16–22 July 2009, 4.

40	The 2008–2009 global financial crisis dampened demand for land and property in desert Cairo, and there are reports of prices sliding by 15 to 20 percent. But observers do not see anything like a price collapse since, as one put it, those holding properties will simply keep them off the market rather than incur what they perceive as disastrous losses. This is probably true because so many property holdings are speculative, were purchased with family capital, and do not need to be liquidated at any price to repay loans and debts. See *al-Misri al-yawm*, 13 September 2009, 10. Demand for real estate in Greater Cairo is greatly strengthened by a particular market segment: the millions of Egyptians working abroad, whose savings and remittances frequently go into property investments, either real or speculative.

41	New towns are currently exempt from the *'awayid* (property taxes), and there are no monthly or annual fees imposed on built property in the new towns. Under the new (2008) property tax law these properties are to be taxed, but the allowed exemptions are such that only a small portion will fall under the new tax regime, if and when it is up and running.

42   The reader may ask why property owners in the new towns do not rent out their units rather than leave them empty? First of all, demand for rental housing, especially for the large units typically found in new towns, is very weak, and market rents are very low. Secondly, throughout Egypt, renting is viewed by many owners as problematic, especially when it comes to ensuring that the renter will vacate the unit at the end of the lease. For a discussion of the rental markets and vacancies in Greater Cairo, see United States Agency for International Development (USAID), *Housing Study for Urban Egypt*.

43   A citizen can apply for and purchase a plot of land in the new towns under the *qur'a* (lottery) system, and turn around and resell it almost immediately, often at a handsome profit. Property sections of the national newspapers are dominated by announcements of land and property sales in Cairo's new towns.

44   In 1995 the Council of Ministers took a decision to stop land sales in New Cairo, worried about oversupply of new land and the high costs of servicing this land. However, the minister of housing at the time ignored this decision and continued to sell land parcels, and in 2000 the government reversed its policy and announced the resumption of land sales throughout the whole of New Cairo. See "Runaway Sales" in *Al-Ahram Weekly: Beyond* (quarterly supplement), Summer 2007, 4.

45   Unlike exclusive communities in many industrializing world capitals, the need for security is not deemed to be a large draw factor for residential compounds in Cairo's desert.

46   Starting in 2006 the MHUUD adopted a new policy whereby prime 'investor' land in Cairo's new towns would be sold by open auction. In May 2007 many Egyptians were startled to find that some prime lots in New Cairo were sold to Arab investors for a whopping total of $3.1 billion. (Peterson, *Unlocking Land Values*, 56–60.) And in June 2009 NUCA announced it was floating an international bond valued at LE4.6 billion using land as collateral and guaranteed by the Ministry of Finance, with another tranche to be floated in September 2009. Presumably these bonds are to finance more investment in new towns, although not necessarily those around Cairo. (See "Bank Consortium Wins Bonds Management Bid," *Daily News Egypt*, 30 September 2009, http://www.thedailynewsegypt.com/article.aspx?ArticleID=24841.)

Notes to Chapter 7

1   A Web page entitled "Cities of the World—Cairo" states the following: "Cairo is the economic center of Egypt, with two-thirds of the country's gross national product generated in the greater metropolitan area"

(http://www.city-data.com/world-cities/Cairo-economy.html). Just how this estimate is calculated is not mentioned, and since there are no regional product accounts in Egypt, one presumes this is a guess, hopefully an educated one.

2   *A. R. E. Statistical Year Book 2008*, 87, 88. These figures do not include persons employed in state-owned public sector enterprises, whose total for all of Egypt in 2007 was 700,000 (according to the *A. R. E. Statistical Year Book 2008*, 89) and of whom between one-quarter to one-third can be assumed to work in Greater Cairo.

3   Colossal is a term not used lightly. The public sector in Egypt is estimated to employ between 29 and 35 percent of the nation's labor force, versus 17 percent for Europe and the U.S., 8 percent for Latin America, and 6 percent for Asia. (Chen, "Business Environment," 7). Guaranteed employment for secondary school and university graduates was law from 1964 to 1978, and the hiring of the educated unemployed continued well into the early 1990s.

4   There are more than forty different laws and fifty-five decrees said to regulate pay for government employees. Amazingly, the minimum official wage for government employment remains LE35 per month (set in 1984 and never changed). There are a host of bonuses, annual increases, allowances, and incentive structures. Thus the entry-level grade six employee's base monthly salary was LE35 per month in 2008, but with allowances and added bonuses his or her pay reached LE289. Finally, it has been noted that government pay bonuses—or promises of pay bonuses—tend to coincide with years in which presidential elections are held. (Abdelhamid and el Baradei, "Reforming the Pay System.")

5   Vignal and Denis, "Cairo as Regional/Global Economic Capital?," 131.

6   Extrapolated by figures on factories and industrial employment in Egypt's new towns in Barada, "The Egyptian New Cities Program."

7   Nippon Koei Co. Ltd. and Katahira Engineers International, *Strategic Urban Development*, 2–140 and 2–141.

8   World Bank and International Finance Corporation, *Doing Business in Egypt 2008*, 2. The survey carried out in this study only looked at limited liability companies in Alexandria, Cairo, and Asyut. According to the results, Cairo showed the best improvement across 178 economies, excelling in starting a business, dealing with licenses, registering property, getting credit, and trading across borders.

9   Census of Egypt 2006: volumes for Qalyubiya, Cairo, and Giza governorates.

10   Chen, "Business Environment," 4.

11   Egyptian Center for Economic Studies and Institute for Liberty and Democracy, "Business Formalization Study."

12   The list of legal requirements for forming and operating an enterprise in Egypt is very long. An operating license is required (usually from municipal

authorities), and firms must comply with social security laws, commercial registry laws, tax laws, labor laws including the employment of children, and health and safety laws. In addition, particular businesses may need permits from the ministries of health, tourism, and internal trade and industry.

13 Chen, "Business Environment," 5.

14 el-Mahdi, *Towards Decent Work*, 10.

15 Various organizations use different terminology. For some, 'SME' means small and medium enterprises. The Ministry of Trade and Industry uses 'M/SME' which stands for micro, small, and medium enterprises.

16 Census of Egypt 1996 (Census of Establishments, volume for Cairo Governorate). Similar breakdowns of establishments by size for 2006 were not yet available as of November 2009.

17 In one GTZ project helping to formalize plastics manufacture in 'Izbit al-Nakhl, an informal area in northern Cairo, workshops were inventoried and a list was submitted to the district authorities to help obtain temporary licenses. To the chagrin of the GTZ project, inspectors promptly used the list to go out and collect bribes. (From a lecture entitled "Notes on Formalization, Focus on the Egyptian Plastic Recycling Case," presented by M. Siebert and W. Sabry at the GTZ Seminar Series, 20 January 2009.)

18 Meyer, "Survival Strategies."

19 Sims, "Assessment of Selected Concentration Zones."

20 el-Mahdi and Powell, "Small Entrepreneurs," 8–12.

21 According to the Ministry of Foreign Trade (now the Ministry of Industry and Trade) in 1998 there were 1.2 million self-employed in all of Egypt, of whom over 60 percent were engaged in trade, 15 percent in manufacturing, and 9 percent in transport. (Ministry of Foreign Trade, *Profile of M/SMEs in Egypt*, March 2003, 10.)

22 If the size of the street children phenomenon in Cairo is measured by the recent interest shown in them, then this would seem to be Egypt's main social problem. Just type 'street children in Egypt' into Google's search engine. The figure of one million street children comes from http://www.cairostreetchildren.com. The United Nations Office of Drugs and Crime cites 'experts' who estimate the number at between 200,000 to one million in 2009 (http://www.unodc.org./newsletter/perspectives/. A good if slightly dated article on the subject is Iman Bibars, "Street Children in Egypt: from the Home to the Street to Inappropriate Corrective Institutions," *Environment and Urbanization* 10 (1) (1998): 201–16.

23 Meyer, "Survival Strategies," 11.

24 Meyer, "Survival Strategies," 12.

Notes to Chapter 8

1 Ominously, traffic jams and tailbacks have begun appearing in places and at times that are unexplainable and unpredictable. Many taxi drivers, whose

knowledge of the city's flows and bottlenecks is remarkable, frequently find that their lore is useless in the face of jams that appear without any seeming logic.

2 World Bank, *Arab Republic of Egypt: A Poverty Assessment Update*, 4.

3 Nippon Koei Co. Ltd. and Katahira Engineers International, *Strategic Urban Development*, 2–14. These calculations even include Cairo's desert new towns as part of Greater Cairo, where densities of even the built-up areas are far below seventy persons per hectare.

4 Bertaud, "Spatial Organization of Cities," 9.

5 McClure, *Egypt Almanac*, 42; Arab Republic of Egypt, Ministry of Transport, *Greater Cairo Transportation Planning Study*, 2–30.

6 Pacific Consultants International, "Transportation Master Plan," 2–17.

7 Metge, *World Bank Urban Transport*, 31.

8 Metge, *World Bank Urban Transport*, 46.

9 Arab Republic of Egypt, *Greater Cairo Transportation Planning Study*, 1–7 to 1–9.

10 "Car Sales in Egypt Rise Year on Year," *Daily News Egypt*, 26 April 2007.

11 Another factor boosting car sales was the sharp reduction in 2004 on customs duties for imported cars with motors of 1.6-liter capacity and less.

12 The Information Decision Support Center of the Egyptian government reported there were 1.6 million passenger cars in Egypt in 2004. See Al-Baaly, "Cairo: The Future Amsterdam of the Middle East?," 7. Nippon reported a total of 1.01 million registered vehicles in the three governorates of Cairo, Giza, and Qalyubiya in 2005. See Pacific Consultants International, "Transportation Master Plan," 4–36.

13 United States Agency for International Development (USAID), *Housing Study for Urban Egypt* (from raw survey frequency results for Greater Cairo and peri-urban Greater Cairo).

14 There are some in Cairo who do not own a car but have the private use of company, ministry, or military vehicles. Thus private car use is slightly higher than private car ownership.

15 Cairo's roughly 80,000 taxis and 30,000 minibuses add somewhat to traffic flow volumes, and do cause flow disruption due to their frequent stops, but at least they are circulating and do not clog arteries as do parked private cars.

16 Galal Amin has devoted a whole chapter to the private car in Cairo and the conspicuous consumption of cars as a form of class prestige (Amin, *Whatever Happened to the Egyptians*, chapter 9).

17 Nippon Koei Co. Ltd. and Katahira Engineers International, *Strategic Urban Development*, 4–37.

18 Arab Republic of Egypt, Ministry of Transport, *Greater Cairo Transportation Planning Study*, 1–6.

19 Cook, "Transport Problems in Cairo," 174.

20 United States Agency for International Development (USAID), *Housing Study for Urban Egypt* (from raw survey frequency results for Greater Cairo).

21 Al-Baaly, "Cairo: The Future Amsterdam of the Middle East?," 8.

22 Huzayyin, "Evolution of Cairo Transport," slide 6.

23 The suffering of the Cairo taxi driver at the hands of the police is well and amusingly documented in Al Khamissi's book, *Taxi*.

24 United States Agency for International Development (USAID), *Housing Study for Greater Cairo*, chapter 2.

25 United States Agency for International Development (USAID), *Housing Study for Peri-urban Areas*, chapter 2.

26 *al-Misri al-yawm*, 21 January 2009, 1.

27 *al-Misri al-yawm*, 12 January 2009, 1.

28 World Bank, "PHRD Grant," 4.

29 Paradoxically, this meant that extremely heavy traffic would be forced to pass along the Maryutiya Canal corridor, bringing air pollution and vibrations to within seven hundred meters of the Pyramids, compared to the three-kilometer distance of the canceled Ring Road segment.

30 World Bank, "Preparatory Grant Assistance," 5.

Notes to Chapter 9

1 According to Dorman, "lame Leviathan" is "characterized by durable autocracy and state incompetence." Neglectful rule entails "state-society disengagement; patrimonialism and clientelism; and risk avoidance" (Dorman, "Politics of Neglect," 247). 'Political vegetables' comes from Sadowski, *Political Vegetables?*, 7.

2 Myrdal sees manifestations of the "soft state" as "deficiencies in legislation and in particular law observance and enforcement, a wide-spread disobedience by public officials on various levels to rules and directive handed down to them, and often their collusion with powerful persons and groups of persons whose conduct they should regulate. Within the concept of the soft state belongs also corruption . . . .These several patterns of behavior are interrelated in the sense that they permit or even provoke each other in circular causation causing cumulative effects." (Myrdal, *Challenge of World Poverty*, quoted in Sadowski, *Political Vegetables?*, 90–91.)

3 Slackman, "Egyptians Lament Lack of Government," 1.

4 In 1993, the president agreed on the formation of a committee, to be chaired by the prime minister, to oversee development projects throughout Greater Cairo. The president himself was to attend this committee's meetings, but as far as is known it has never met (*al-Ahram*, 11 March 1993, 3). In May 2008 the chairman of GOPP announced that a coordinating council for the Greater Cairo region would be established, which would function as a single administration for the five governorates of the metropolis, but that the nature

of this council was still being studied (*al-Ahram*, "Tahqiqat al-jum'a," 16 May 2008, 11). More recently, it was announced by the chairman of GOPP that a ministerial committee had been formed to draft a new "capital city law" that would bestow upon at least part of Greater Cairo a unique legal nature, radically different from the traditional governorate structure. The boundaries of this 'capital city' are yet to be defined (*al-Misri al-yawm*, 18 October 2009, 1).

5   UCLG Country Profiles: Arab Republic of Egypt 2007 (http://www.cities-localgovernments.org/gold/Upload/country_profile/Egypt.pdf).

6   These subdivisions apply only to the governorate jurisdictions. There are many other ways Greater Cairo is sliced up geographically, and only a few of these coincide to any degree with any others. The census has its own subdivisions, as do the courts, the electoral districts, the property registration offices, the traffic zones, and so on. And it is rare to find the boundaries of these different subdivisions mapped, nor do those who work within these administrations always know where the boundaries lie.

7   In *marakiz*, local administrations may be further divided into small towns with city councils and into village administrative units.

8   According to the Egyptian State Information Service website (http://www.sis.gov.eg), there are twenty-five parliamentary districts in Cairo Governorate, fourteen in Giza Governorate, and nine in Qalyubiya Governorate. However, in the last two governorates not all parliamentary districts fall within the boundaries of Greater Cairo.

9   According to one national survey in 2005, some 52 percent of respondents were ignorant of the very presence of these councils, and ignorance was even more acute in urban areas (Néfissa, "Cairo's City Government," 185). This survey is said to have been undertaken by the Information and Decision Support Center, but there is no reference given.

10   Blaydes, "Electoral Budget Cycles," 12.

11   See Deutsche Gesellschaft für Technische Zusammenarbeit (GTZ), *Cairo's Informal Areas*, 216.

12   Slackman, "Belatedly Egypt Spots Flaws in Wiping Out Pigs."

13   United States Agency for International Development (USAID), *Housing Study for Greater Cairo*, 23. Only 1.3 percent of households had no access to running water.

14   The Holding Company was established in 2004, part of extensive and ongoing institutional reforms in the sector. The Greater Cairo Water Supply Company is itself undergoing restructuring, and separate companies are being formed for Giza and Qalyubiya (and now presumably for the new governorates of Helwan and Sixth of October).

15   Some would say treatment is overdone, and the distinct taste of chlorine in the water is a common complaint.

16   Nippon Koei Co. Ltd. and Katahira Engineers International, *Strategic Urban Development* 2–157.

17   Nippon Koei Co. Ltd. and Katahira Engineers International, *Strategic Urban Development*, 2–160.

18   Nippon Koei Co. Ltd. and Katahira Engineers International, *Strategic Urban Development*, 2–158 to 2–159.

19   Nippon Koei Co. Ltd. and Katahira Engineers International, *Strategic Urban Development*, 2–177.

20   United States Agency for International Development (USAID), *Housing Study for Peri-urban Areas*, 23.

21   Hydropower from the High Dam at Aswan, once the main source of power in Egypt, now only accounts for less than 10 percent of the nation's power generation.

22   These two companies also serve Cairo's new towns, except for Tenth of Ramadan, which is covered by the Canal Zone Electrical Distribution Company.

23   Nippon Koei Co. Ltd. and Katahira Engineers International, *Strategic Urban Development*, 2–208 and 2–209.

24   Some of these highways have also been constructed by the army and the New Urban Communities Authority.

25   The local roads underneath the connector are still a complete mess, and residents in the area suffer from water and power failures due to this project.

26   In 1990 the then minister of housing formally requested USAID to fund the two Nile bridges required to complete the Ring Road. After an extensive internal debate, USAID declined to finance the two projects, justifying its refusal partly on the erroneous assumption that the two bridges, and the Ring Road in general, would benefit mainly car-owning elites. Another decidedly non-technical reason was due to pressure from congressmen who were worried that the approaches to the Munib Bridge would necessitate the partial removal of the Jewish cemetery in al-Basatin.

27   An exception to this is the al-Azhar Tunnel, completed in 2001, but this was a project of the National Tunnels Authority, an agency well versed in the use of foreign expertise and funding.

28   One story has it that in the 1980s a middle-aged housewife was totally amazed to find the telephone people at her door ready to hook up a new line. She had to have it explained that it was her father, with considerable foresight, who had made the application in her name at the time of her birth. Compare this anecdote to one in October 2009. Someone had just rented a flat in one of the new informal tower blocks in a chaotic fringe neighborhood of Bulaq al-Dakrur and applied for a phone line on a Wednesday. He was told it would be installed in three days and, presto, by Saturday the line was hooked up and working.

29   In 2007 the minister of housing bemoaned the high cost of serving dense informal areas. He claimed that serving these areas with infrastructure costs society four times what it would cost in planned areas (that is, in the new

towns). Maybe he was talking about costs per hectare rather than costs per capita, since otherwise such a statement is clearly false. (See Singerman, "Introduction," 27.)

30 The main infrastructure services vary as to their ability to recover all costs. Power and telecommunications are financially nearly going concerns, whereas water and wastewater can only at best recoup running costs from their customers. And roads are totally dependent on state budgets.

Notes to the Postscript

1 See for example an opinion piece by the prominent Algerian political commentator Omar Benderra, "Le Caire dans l'oeil du cyclone," Palestine Solidarité website, http://www.palestine-solidarite.org/analyses.Omar_Benderra.250611.htm, dated 25 June 2011. He states: "La tristement célèbre ville-cimetière du Caire, dont les tombes abritent 1,5 million de déshérités bien vivants."

2 Safaa Marafi, "Living in Slums . . . A Historic Dilemma that Needs to be Resolved," *Egypt Independent*, 28 August 2011. http://www.egyptindependent.com/node/490426.

3 *Cairo: A City in Transition*. Cities and Citizens Series: Bridging the Urban Divide, Study 2.

4 Barthel and Monqid, eds., *Le Caire: réinventer la ville*.

5 The video, prepared from the audio by Andrew Turner and Hagar Cohen, can be seen at www.youtube.com/watch?v=EaXcmaAzm1A; and the audio file and transcript of the Australian Broadcasting Corporation radio program, first broadcast on 1 February 2009, can be downloaded from http://www.abc.net.au/radionational/programs/backgroundbriefing/cairo-a-divided-city/3178362.

6 *Cairo Divided* is both a photographic display (Jason Larkin) and an essay (Jack Shenker); see http://www.markdearman.com/cairodivided/.

7 Soueif, *Cairo: My City, Our Revolution*.

8 From a blurb on *Cairo: My City, Our Revolution* in the *Guardian* newspaper's Bookshop web page, http://www.guardianbookshop.co.uk/BerteShopWeb/viewProduct.do?ISBN=9780747549628.

9 Marwa Hythem, "al-Niyaba al-idariya tuhaqqiq fi 12,831 halat ta'adi 'ala al-aradi al-zira'iya," *al-Ahram*, 2 March 2011, 3.

10 This is quite a startling admission by one of the main players in Egypt's formal housing market (see Dina Zayed, "Egyptians Build, Shop for Homes Despite Downturn," *Daily News Egypt*, 29–30 October 2011, 3). Also http://www.masress.com/en/dailynews/133732.

11 Examples of these small but effective NGOs include *The Spirit of Youth Association*, oriented toward environmental improvements, especially in solid waste. It is based in Manshiyat Nasir but has recently extended its activities to other informal and also some poor formal areas. Sohbit Kheir

Association is a Greater Cairo NGO that focuses on vocational training and job placement. This NGO is working in the five informal settlements of Stabl 'Antar, 'Izbit Khayrallah, al-Hagara, Batn al-Baqara, and al-Kharta.

12 Marafi, "Living in Slums."

13 This charity initiative brings to mind the Telal Zeinhoum project, described in Chapter 4.

14 E-mail from AUC Provost Medhat Haroun to AUC faculty and staff, dated 10 January 2012.

15 Center for Development Services, Building Common Grounds Project, Promoting Transparency and Good Governance in Urban Planning and Housing in Egypt, "Urban Planning: Priority Areas to be Included in DAG (Donor Assistance Groups) Agenda," 24 February 2011.

16 This was the Workshop on Urban Policy in Egypt ("Warshat 'Amal hawl Mashari' al-Tatwir al-Hadari wa Huquq al-Nas ba'd Thawrat 25 Yanayir"), held on 13–14 July 2011 under the umbrella of the Housing and Land Rights Network and Habitat International Coalition.

17 Mubarak's picture was *de rigueur* on all NHP announcements and project advertisements. It was a rare image of him, jacketless, in just a shirt and tie, presumably to show his hands-on involvement in program details. Ahmed Maghrabi, the then minister of housing (now in jail on corruption charges), was seen hovering in the background.

18 Arab Republic of Egypt, Ministry of Housing and Utilities and Urban Development: "National Social Housing Program," project proposal, 31 March 2011, 1.

19 See *Al-Ahram Weekly*, 27 October–2 November 2011, 7. The conference was organized by the Federation of Egyptian Industries, the Egyptian Junior Business Association, and the European Bank for Reconstruction and Development.

20 *al-Misri al-yawm*: "al-Iskan: tarh 100 alf qita' aradi li-mahdudi al-dakhl bidayat 2012," 23 October 2011, 4.

21 Most notably the Talaat Mustafa Group (Madinaty), Palm Hills, and Egyptian Resorts.

22 See Salma El-Wardani and Salma Hussein, "Palm Hills: Engine of Growth or Example of Crony Capitalism?" *ahramonline*, 17 December 2010. http://english.ahram.org.eg/NewsContent/3/12/1861/Business/Economy/Palm-Hills-engine-of-growth-or-example-of-crony-ca.aspx.

23 See Nesma Nowar, "Real Estate Slow Down," *Al-Ahram Weekly*, 28 July–3 August 2011, 5.

24 "Credit Suisse still cautious on Egyptian real estate sector," *Daily News Egypt*, 7 October 2011, 3.

25 See Dina Zayed, "Egypt's Orascom, Nasr City Scrap Tigan Cooperation," *Daily News Egypt*, 16 January 2012. http://www.thedailynewsegypt.com/egypts-orascom-nasr-city-scrap-tigan-cooperation.html.

26 "Cityscape Egypt Gears Up for February Real Estate Exhibition," *Daily News Egypt*, 23 January 2012, 3.

27 It is said that NUCA cash was used to purchase the new fleet of German ambulances so prominently seen around Tahrir Square, as well as the new red Cairo Transport Authority buses. (Private communication with Ministry of Housing officials.)

28 "Egypt Seeks to Settle Land, Other Contract Rows," *Reuters Africa*, 1 September 2011. http://af.reuters.com/article/topNews/idAFJOE7800IC20110901.

29 For basic information on this project (in Arabic) see the World Bank document at: http://web.worldbank.org/external/projects/main?pagePK=642 83627&piPK=73230&theSitePK=40941&menuPK=228424&Projectid= P115837.

30 See Khair Ragheb, "Egypt to Launch Cairo–AUC Supertram by 2015," *Egypt Independent*, 27 December 2010. http://www.egyptindependent.com/node/280969.

31 Intikhabat Misr: al-Mawqi' al-Rasmi li-l-Lajna al-Qada'iya al-'Ulya li-l-Intikhabat. http://www.elections2011.eg.

32 "Highlight: Political Party Programs in Focus," *Daily News Egypt*, 27 November 2011. http://www.thedailynewsegypt.com/egypt-elections-2011/highlight-political-parties-programs.html.

Glossary

ahwash	see *hawsh*
ahya'	see *hayy*
ahyad	see *hod*
amin al-shurta	special police
'ashwa'iyyat	informal urban areas
'awayid	property taxes
awqaf	religious endowments
bawwab	doorman of residential building
bayarat	soakaway pits for domestic sewage
da'wa sihha wa-nafadh	petition for execution of a contract
fakhr	luxury
fardi (adj.)	individual
feddan	area of land equivalent to 4,200 square meters
fuq mutawassit	above the average
gam'iyat	informal revolving credit groups, or community associations
guhud zatiya	self-help
hawsh (pl. *ahwash*)	tomb courtyard
hayy (pl. *ahya'*)	urban administrative district
al-hayy al-hukumi	government zone

331

al-hayy al-mutamayyiz	upscale (tourist) zone
hirafi	artisanat
hod (pl. *ahyad*)	small irrigated agricultural plot
ibni baytak	Build Your Own House (housing program)
ikramiyyat	small bribes or considerations
infitah	Open Door policy
iskan iqtisadi	economic or affordable housing
istimarat	application forms
al-magalis (sing. *maglis*) *al-mahalliya al-sha'biya*	local People's Councils
Maghrib	western Arab countries
maglis al-madina	city council
al-manatiq al-'ashwa'iya	informal areas
al-manatiq al-gheir mukhattata	unplanned areas
markaz (pl. *marakiz*)	rural district
masakin iwa'	governorate emergency housing
Mashriq	eastern Arab countries
al-mihwar	literally 'the corridor,' the name given to the axis roadleading to Sixth of October City
mufakkirin	intellectuals
Mugamma' al-Tahrir	central government services complex in Midan Tahrir, downtown Cairo
mugamma'at 'umraniya gadida	new urban settlements
muhafaza (pl. *muhafazat*)	governorate
muklifa	private agricultural landholding
mulid	traditional annual festivals celebrating the birthdays of holy men or women
munadi	informal car parker

muqawil (pl. muqawilin)	contractor
mutawassit	average or middle level
qanun al-igar al-gadid	New Rent Law
qarya (pl. qura)	village administrative and census unit
qirat	area of land equivalent to 175 square meters
qism (pl. aqsam)	urban census (and police) district
qura	see *qarya*
qur'a	lottery
raba'	single-story courtyard housing with individual rooms
al-ri'aya al-ula	'basic care'
samasira (pl.)	see *simsar*
sha'bi	'of the people,' 'common,' or 'lower-class'
shahr al-'aqari	property registration office
shawish	police sergeant
shirka musahima	limited liability share company
shiyakha (pl shiyakhat)	smallest urban census enumeration district
al-sigill al-'ayni	individual deed properties
al-sigill al-shakhsi	title deed properties
sihha wa-nafadh	see *da'wa sihha wa-nafadh*
sihhat tawqi'	contract signature confirmation
simsar (pl. samasira)	informal real estate broker
al-Tagammu' al-Khamis	the Fifth Quarter (district of New Cairo)
tahzim	belting or containment
tamlik	freehold ownership
al-tansiq al-hadari	urban harmony

tanzim	urban control
tawkil (pl. *tawkilat*)	power of attorney
tuk-tuk	three-wheeled auto-rickshaw
'urfi	traditional or common law (contract)
wust al-balad	downtown
zabbalin	garbage collectors and sorters
al-zahr al-sahrawi	desert backyard

Bibliography

Abdelhamid, Doha, and Laila el Baradei. "Reforming the Pay System for Government Employees in Egypt." Working Paper No. 151. Cairo: Egyptian Center for Economic Studies, 2009.

Abhat, Divya, Shauna Dineen, Tamsyn Jones, Jim Motavalli, Rebecca Sanborn, and Kate Slomkowski. "Cities of the Future: Today's Megacities Are Overcrowded and Environmentally Stressed." *Emagazine* 16, no. 5 (2005), http://www.emagazine.com/?issue=122&toc (accessed 7 October 2010).

Abt Associates Inc., with Dames and Moore Inc. *Informal Housing in Egypt.* Cairo: United States Agency for International Development, 1982.

Abu-Lughod, Janet. *Cairo: 1001 Years of the City Victorious.* Princeton: Princeton University Press, 1971.

Abu-Lughod, Janet, and Ezz el-Din Attiya. *Cairo Fact Book.* Cairo: American University in Cairo, Social Research Center, 1963.

al-Alaily, Sameh Abdallah. "Kayf natanawal qadiyyat 'ashwa'iyyat al-'umran fi Misr?" Unpublished paper presented at the international symposium, Exchanging Global and Egyptian Experience in Dealing with Informal Areas within the Wider Urban Management Context, Deutsche Gesellschaft für Technische Zusammenarbeit Participatory Development Programme in Urban Areas, Cairo, 14–15 October, 2008.

Aldridge, James. *Cairo: Biography of a City.* Boston: Little, Brown and Company, 1969.

Amin, Galal. *Whatever Happened to the Egyptians?* Cairo: American University in Cairo Press, 2000.

Arab Republic of Egypt. Central Agency for Public Mobilisation and Statistics. *Household Expenditure, Consumption and Income Survey.* Cairo, Egypt: CAPMAS, 2004–2005.

Arab Republic of Egypt. Central Agency for Public Mobilisation and Statistics, and Centre d'Études et de Documentation économiques et juridiques. *Century Census Egypt 1882–1996*. CD ROM, 2003.

Arab Republic of Egypt. Ministry of Transport. *Greater Cairo Transportation Planning Study*. Paris: RATP-SOFRATU, 1973.

A. R. E. Statistical Year Book 2008. Cairo, Egypt: Central Agency for Public Mobilisation and Statistics (CAPMAS), 2008.

Attallah, Mursi. "Cairo 1990." *al-Ahram al-iqtisadi*, 28 March 1990, 97.

Al-Baaly, Mohammed. "Cairo: The Future Amsterdam of the Middle East?" World Bank Essay Competition, 2005, http://www.essaycompetition.org/docs/essays2005/al%20baaly.pdf (accessed 6 October 2010).

Barada, A. "The Egyptian New Cities Program, a Critical Review," 2005. http://www.scribd.com/doc/6603387/ (accessed 3 October 2010).

Barthel, Pierre-Arnaud, and Safaa Monqid, eds. *Le Caire: réinventer la ville*. Collection Villes en Mouvement. Paris: CEDEJ/Éditions Autrement, April 2011.

Bayat, Asaf, and Eric Denis. "Who is Afraid of Ashwaiyyat?" *Environment and Urbanization* 12, no. 2 (2000): 185–99.

Bertaud, Alain. "The Spatial Organization of Cities; Deliberate Outcome or Unforeseen Consequence?," 2004. http://alain-bertaud.com (accessed 3 October 2010).

Bibars, Iman. "Street Children in Egypt: from the Home to the Street to Inappropriate Corrective Institutions." *Environment and Urbanization* 10, no. 1 (1998): 210–16.

Blaydes, Lisa. "Electoral Budget Cycles under Authoritarianism: Economic Opportunism in Mubarak's Egypt." Unpublished paper presented at the annual meeting of The Midwest Political Science Association, Chicago, 20 April, 2006.

Cairo: A City in Transition. Cities and Citizens Series: Bridging the Urban Divide, Study 2. Nairobi: United Nations Human Settlement Programme, 2011. http://www.unhabitat.org/pmss/listItemDetails.aspx?publicationID=3136.

Castree, Noel, and Derek Gregory. *David Harvey: A Critical Reader*. Oxford: Blackwell Publishing Limited, 2006.

Census of Egypt 1996. al-Jihaz al-Markazi li-l-Ta'bi'a al-'Amma wa-l-Ihsa'. *al-Ta'dad al-'am li-l-sukkan wa-l-iskan wa-l-munsha'at* [Census of Population, Housing, and Establishments 1996]. Cairo, Egypt, 1998. [The set comprises (1) *al-Nata'ij al-niha'iya li-ta'dad al-sukkan* (Final Results for the Census of Population); (2) *al-Nata'ij al-niha'iya li-l-zuruf al-sakaniya* (Final Results for Housing Conditions); (3) *al-Nata'ij al-niha'iya li-ta'dad al-mabani* (Final Results for the Census of Buildings); and (4)

Ta'dad al-munsha'at (Census of Establishments). Separate volumes of each are published for the governorates of Cairo, Qalyubiya, Giza, and the rest of Egypt.]

Census of Egypt 1996. al-Jihaz al-Markazi li-l-Ta'bi'a al-'Amma wa-l-Ihsa'. *al-Ta'dad al-'am li-l-sukkan wa-l-iskan wa-l-munsha'at. al-Nata'ij al niha'iya li-ta'dad al-sukkan. Bayanat makan al-iqama al-hali wa-l-milad wa-l-sabiq, ijmali al-gumhuriya.* Cairo, Egypt, 1998. [Special volume on location of current residence, birth, and former residence, all of Egypt]

Census of Egypt 2006. al-Jihaz al-Markazi li-l-Ta'bi'a al-'Amma wa-l-Ihsa'. *al-Nata'ij al-awwaliya li-l-ta'dad al-'am li-l-sukkan wa-l-iskan wa-l-munsha'at.* Cairo, Egypt, 2007. [Preliminary results of the Census of Population, Housing, and Establishments: volumes for the governorates of Cairo, Qalyubiya, and Giza.]

Census of Egypt 2006. al-Jihaz al-Markazi li-l-Ta'bi'a al-'Amma wa-l-Ihsa'. *al-Ta'dad al-'am li-l-sukkan wa-l-iskan wa-l-munsha'at.* Cairo, Egypt, 2007. Unpublished preliminary results, headcounts for Census enumeration districts (*shiyakhat* and *qura*) of Cairo, Qalyubia, and Giza governorates.]

Chen, Martha. "The Business Environment and the Informal Economy: Creating Conditions for Poverty Reduction." Unpublished draft paper for the Conference on Reforming the Business Environment, Cairo, November, 2005.

Clerget, Marcel. *Le Caire, Étude de Geographie urbaine et d'Histoire économique.* Cairo: Impr. E. et R. Schindler, 1934.

"CNN Makes Egyptians Suspicious of Foreigners Loitering in the Streets." *Egyptian Gazette,* 27 September 1994.

Cook, David. "Transport Problems in Cairo." *The Expanding Metropolis: Coping with the Urban Growth of Cairo* (Seminar Proceedings, 11–15 November), 152–57. Cairo: Aga Khan Award for Architecture, 1984.

Davis, Mike. *Planet of Slums.* London: Verso Books, 2006.

Deboulet, Agnès. "The Dictatorship of the Straight Line and the Myth of Social Disorder: Revisiting Informality in Cairo." In *Cairo Contested: Governance, Urban Space, and Global Modernity,* edited by Diane Singerman, 199–234. Cairo: American University in Cairo Press, 2009.

Denis, Eric. "Cairo as Neoliberal Capital? From Walled City to Gated Communities." In *Cairo Cosmopolitan; Politics, Culture, and Urban Space in the New Globalized Middle East,* edited by Diane Singerman and Paul Amar, 47–71. Cairo: American University in Cairo Press, 2006.

Denis, Eric, and Marion Séjourné. "ISIS Information System for Informal Settlements." Unpublished draft report for the Participatory Urban Management Programme. Arab Republic of Egypt Ministry of Planning, Deutsche

Gesellschaft für Technische Zusammenarbeit (GTZ), and Centre d'Études et de Documentation économiques et juridiques (CEDEJ), 2002.

Deutsche Gesellschaft für Technische Zusammenarbeit (GTZ). *Cairo's Informal Areas: Between Urban Challenges and Hidden Potentials: Facts, Voices, Visions.* Cairo: Participatory Development Programme in Urban Areas, 2009.

Deutsche Gesellschaft für Technische Zusammenarbeit (GTZ), and Cairo Governorate. "Manshiet Nasser Guide Plan, Analysis of the Existing Situation." Unpublished report by the Participatory Urban Development of Manshiet Nasser Project, 2001.

Dorman, W. J. "Of Demolitions and Donors: The Problematics of State Intervention in Informal Cairo." In *Cairo Contested: Governance, Urban Space, and Global Modernity*, edited by Diane Singerman, 269–90. Cairo: American University in Cairo Press, 2009.

———. "The Politics of Neglect; the Egyptian State in Cairo, 1974–98." Unpublished doctoral thesis. London University School of Oriental and African Studies, 2007.

Doughty, Dick. "Cairo: Inside the Megacity." *Aramco World*, March–April, 1996.

Egyptian Center for Economic Studies, and Institute for Liberty and Democracy "Business Formalization Study." Unpublished draft report, 2002.

———. *Egyptian Real Estate Formalization Study*. Main Report and Annexes 1–3. Cairo: Egyptian Center for Economic Studies, and Institute for Liberty and Democracy (Lima, Peru), 2000.

———. "Formalization of Egypt's Urban Informal Real Estate Sector: Institutional Reengineering Stage, Situation Analysis Report." Unpublished paper, 2000.

Egyptian State Information Service. http://www.sis.gov.eg.

Fahmi, Wael, and Keith Sutton. "Greater Cairo's Housing Crisis: Contested spaces from inner city areas to new communities." *Cities* 25, no. 5 (2008): 277–97.

Faruq: zaliman wa mazluman. Nisf al-dunya special issue. 2nd printing [undated; late 1990s].

Gerlach, Julia. 2009. "al-Qorsaya Island: A Struggle for Land." In Deutsche Gesellschaft für Technische Zusammenarbeit (GTZ), *Cairo's Informal Areas: Between Urban Challenges and Hidden Potentials: Facts, Voices, Visions*, 91–95. Cairo: Participatory Development Programme in Urban Areas.

Golia, Maria. *Cairo: City of Sand*. London: Reaktion Books Ltd, 2004.

el-Hadidi, Hagar, Linda Oldham, and Hussein Tamaa. "Informal Communities in Cairo: The Basis of a Typology." *Cairo Papers in Social Science* no. 10 (1987): Monograph 4.

Haenni, Patrick. "Cousins, Neighbors, and Citizens in Imbaba; The Genesis and Self-Neutralization of a Rebel Political Territory." In *Cairo Contested: Governance, Urban Space, and Global Modernity*, edited by Diane Singerman, 309–30. Cairo: American University in Cairo Press, 2009.

Harris, R., and M. Wahba. "The Urban Geography of Low-Income Housing: Cairo (1947–96) Exemplifies a Model." *International Journal of Urban and Regional Research* 26, no. 1 (2002): 58–79.

Horwitz, Tony. *Baghdad without a Map, and Other Misadventures in Arabia.* New York: Penguin Books/Plume, 1992.

Huzayyin, Ali. "Evolution of Cairo Transport and Land Use and of their Effects on Energy & Environment; Problems, Solutions, and Potentials." Unpublished Powerpoint presentation at Seminaire régional sur les déplacements urbains en méditerranée, Skhirat, Morocco, 22–23 January, 2008. (See http://www.europmedia.org.)

El Kadi, Galila. *L'Urbanisation spontanée au Caire.* Tours: URBAMA & ORSTOM, 1987.

———. *al-Tahaddur al-'ashwa'i.* Translated from the French edition of 1987 by Minha al-Bitrawi. Cairo: al-Markaz al-Qawmi li-l-Targama, 2009.

El Kadi, Galila, and Alain Bonnamy. *Architecture for the Dead: Cairo's Medieval Necropolis.* Cairo: American University in Cairo Press, 2007.

Al Khamissi, Khalid. *Taxi.* Translated by Jonathan Wright. Laverstock, Wilts.: Aflame Books, 2008.

Kuppinger, Petra. "Pyramids and Alleys: Global Dynamics and Local Strategies in Giza." In *Cairo Cosmopolitan; Politics, Culture, and Urban Space in the New Globalized Middle East*, edited by Diane Singerman and Paul Amar, 313–44. Cairo, Egypt: The American University in Cairo Press, 2006.

Lagos/Koolhaas. Film directed by Bregtje van der Haak, distributed by Icarus Films, 2003. http://icarusfilms.com/new2003/lag.html (accessed 7 October 2010).

Le Gac, Daniel. *L'Envers des Pyramides: L'Egypte au quotidien.* Paris: S.F.I.E.D., 1984.

Madbouli, M. "Background Paper on Urban Planning, Management and Administration." Unpublished paper, United Nations Common Country Assessment in Egypt, United Nations Programme for Human Settlements (UN-Habitat), 2005.

Madbouli, M., and A. Lashin. 2003. "al-Manatiq al-'ashwa'iya fi-l-Qahira al-Kubra: dirasat al-hala al-qa'ima fi Bulaq al-Dakrur." Unpublished working paper for the GTZ Participatory Urban Management Program, Egypt, 2003.

el-Mahdi, Alia. *Towards Decent Work in the Informal Sector: The Case of Egypt.* Geneva: International Labour Organization, 2002.

el-Mahdi, Alia, and K. Powell. "Small Entrepreneurs in Greater Cairo Community." Unpublished paper for the Social Research Center of the American University in Cairo, 1999.

McClure, Mandy, ed. *Egypt Almanac: The Encyclopedia of Modern Egypt.* Wilmington, DE: Egypto-file Ltd., 2003.

Mehta, Suketu. *Maximum City: Bombay Lost and Found.* New York: Vintage Random House, 2005.

Menelaws, Dougal. "Property and Registration Law in Egypt: Current Operations and Practice." Unpublished working paper for Financial Services Project, Chemonics International, 2005.

Metge, Hubert. *World Bank Urban Transport Strategy Review: The Case of Cairo Egypt.* Edition 3 November 2000, Ref. 3018/SY5-PLT/CAI/709-00. Washington, D.C.: World Bank, 2000.

Meyer, Guenter. "Survival Strategies of Small-scale Manufacturing in the Informal Settlements of Greater Cairo: Results of a Long Term Study." Unpublished paper submitted to International Symposium Exchanging Global and Egyptian Experience in Dealing with Informal Areas within the Wider Urban Management Context. Cairo, 14–15 October, 2008.

"Min yaqul inn fi azmat al-iskan?" *Majallat al-shabab*, no. 349, 1 August, 2006.

Mitchison, Amanda. "Photographer on the Run." *Independent Magazine*, 29 December, 1990.

Myrdal, Gunnar. *The Challenge of World Poverty.* New York: Vintage Books, 1970.

Néfissa, Sarah Ben. "Cairo's City Government: The Crisis of Local Administration and the Refusal of Urban Citizenship." In *Cairo Contested: Governance, Urban Space, and Global Modernity*, edited by Diane Singerman, 177–98. Cairo: American University in Cairo Press, 2009.

Neuwirth, Robert. *Shadow Cities: A Billion Squatters, A New Urban World.* New York: Routledge, 2005.

Nippon Koei Co. Ltd., and Katahira Engineers International. *The Strategic Urban Development Master Plan Study for Sustainable Development of the Greater Cairo Region in the Arab Republic of Egypt, Draft Final Report.* Vol. 1: *Strategic Urban Development Master Plan.* Cairo, Egypt: Japan International Cooperation Agency, 2008.

Nkrumah, Gamal. "Living on the Edge." *Al-Ahram Weekly*, 11–17 September, 2008.

Paccionne, Michael. *Problems and Planning in Third World Cities.* Beckenham, UK: Croom Helm Ltd., 1981.

Pacific Consultants International. "Transportation Master Plan and Feasibility Study of Urban Transport Projects in Greater Cairo Region in the

Arab Republic of Egypt." Unpublished report of the Cairo Regional Area Transportation Study and A. R. E. Higher Committee for Greater Cairo Transportation Planning, 2001.

PADCO Inc. "The National Urban Policy Study: Final Report." Unpublished report prepared for the Advisory Committee for Reconstruction, Ministry of Development, Arab Republic of Egypt, vols. 1–2, 1982.

Payne, Geoffrey, ed. *Land, Rights and Innovation: Improving Tenure Security for the Urban Poor*. London: Intermediate Technology Development Group Press, 2002.

Peterson, George. *Unlocking Land Values to Finance Urban Infrastructure*. Washington, D.C.: World Bank Public-Private Infrastructure Advisory Facility, 2009.

Piffero, Elena. "What Happened to Participation?: Urban Development and Authoritarian Upgrading in Cairo's Informal Neighborhoods." Unpublished doctoral thesis. Universita di Bologna: Dottorato di Ricerca, Ciclo XXI, 2008.

Rayan, Ghada. *'Amaliyat al-irtiqu' bi-l manatiq al 'ashwai'ya fi fa'aliyat tanfiz al-mukhattatat*. N.p., 2008.

Raymond, André. *Cairo: City of History*. Cairo: American University in Cairo Press, 2001.

Rodenbeck, Max. *Cairo: The City Victorious*. London: Picador Macmillan, 1998.

Roy, Ananya. *City Requiem, Calcutta*. Minneapolis: University of Minnesota Press, 2003.

Roy, Ananya, and AlSayyad, Nezar, eds. *Urban Informality: Transnational Perspectives from the Middle East, Latin America, and South Asia*. Lanham, MD: Lexington Books, 2004.

Rubenstein, Edwin. "Housing and Urban Development: Immigration Fiscal Impact Statement." *Social Contract Journal* 18, no. 2 (2007–2008): 130–33.

Sabri, Sarah. "Egypt's Informal Areas: Inaccurate and Contradictory Data." In Deutsche Gesellschaft für Technische Zusammenarbeit (GTZ), *Cairo's Informal Areas: Between Urban Challenges and Hidden Potentials: Facts, Voices, Visions*, 29–34. Cairo: Participatory Development Programme in Urban Areas, 2009.

———. "Poverty Lines in Greater Cairo: Underestimating and Misrepresenting Poverty." *International Institute for Environment and Development Working Paper* no. 21 (2009). http:www.iied.org/pubs/display.php?o=10572IIED (accessed 18 October 2010).

Sadowski, Yahya. *Political Vegetables? Businessman and Bureaucrat in the Development of Egyptian Agriculture*. Washington. D.C.: The Brookings Institution, 1991.

Shehayeb, Dina. "Advantages of Living in Informal Areas." In Deutsche Gesellschaft für Technische Zusammenarbeit (GTZ), *Cairo's Informal Areas: Between Urban Challenges and Hidden Potentials: Facts, Voices, Visions*, 35–43. Cairo: Participatory Development Programme in Urban Areas, 2009.

Shorter, Frank. "Cairo's Great Leap Forward: People, Households, and Dwelling Space." *Cairo Papers in Social Science* no. 12 (1989): Monograph 1, iv.

Sims, David. "Assessment of Selected Concentration Zones: Are They Representative of Business Concentration in Cairo?" Unpublished paper for the Business Formalization Study. Cairo, Egypt: Egyptian Center for Economic Studies and Institute for Liberty and Democracy (Lima, Peru), 2002.

———. "Informal Residential Development in Greater Cairo: Typologies, Representative Areas, and Causal Factors." Unpublished report for the Egyptian Real Estate Formalization Study under the auspices of the Egyptian Center for Economic Studies and the Institute for Liberty and Democracy (Lima, Peru), 2000.

———. "South Sinai Development Profile." Unpublished report for the South Sinai Environmental Action Plan under the auspices of the Egyptian Environmental Affairs Agency, Support for Environmental Assessment and Management Programme, 2003.

———. "What is Secure Tenure in Urban Egypt." In *Land, Rights and Innovation: Improving Tenure Security for the Urban Poor*, edited by Geoffrey Payne. London: Intermediate Technology Development Group Press, 2002.

Sims, David, with contribution from Monika El-Shorbagi and Marion Sejourne. "Cairo: Egypt." In UN-Habitat, *Global Report on Human Settlements 2003. The Challenge of Slums*, 2003. http://www.ucl.ac.uk/dpu-projects/Global_Report/cities/cairo.htm (accessed 7 October 2010).

Singerman, Diane. "Introduction: The Contested City." In *Cairo Contested: Governance, Urban Space, and Global Modernity*, edited by Diane Singerman, 3–38. Cairo: American University in Cairo Press, 2009.

———. "The Siege of Imbaba, Egypt's Internal 'Other,' and the Criminalization of Politics." In *Cairo Contested: Governance, Urban Space, and Global Modernity*, edited by Diane Singerman, 111–44. Cairo: American University in Cairo Press, 2009.

———, ed. *Cairo Contested: Governance, Urban Space, and Global Modernity*. Cairo: American University in Cairo Press, 2009.

Slackman, Michael. "Egyptians Lament Lack of Government." *International Herald Tribune*, 1 March 2007, 1.

———. "Belatedly, Egypt Spots Flaws in Wiping Out Pigs." *New York Times*, 20 September 2009, City Ed., A1.

Soliman, Ahmed. "Legitimizing Informal Housing: Accommodating Low-income Groups in Alexandria." *Environment and Urbanization* 8, no. 1 (1996): 183–91.

———. *A Possible Way Out: Formalizing Housing Informality in Egyptian Cities.* Lanham, MD: University Press of America, 2004.

Soueif, Ahdaf. *Cairo: My City, Our Revolution.* London: Bloomsbury, 2012.

Stewart, Stanley. *Old Serpent Nile: A Journey to the Source.* London: Flamingo, 1991.

Sutton, Keith, and Wael Fahmi. "Cairo's Urban Growth and Strategic Master Plans in the Light of Egypt's 1996 Population Census Results." *Cities* 18, no. 3 (2001): 135–49.

UCLG Country Profiles: Arab Republic of Egypt 2007. http:// www.cities-localgovernments.org/gold/Upload/country_profile/Egypt.pdf (accessed 20 September 2009). [Website of United Cities and Local Governments.]

United Nations Development Programme, and Arab Republic of Egypt, Ministry of Planning and Local Development. *Egypt Human Development Report 2005. Choosing our Future: Towards a New Social Contract.* Cairo, Egypt: Institute of National Planning, 2005.

United States Agency for International Development (USAID). *Housing Study for Greater Cairo.* Final, 2 November 2008. Technical Assistance for Policy Reform II. Authors: David Sims, Hazem Kamal, and Doris Solomon. Washington, D.C.: USAID/Egypt Policy and Private Sector Office, 2008.

———. *Housing Study for Peri-urban Areas Around Greater Cairo.* Final, 24 December 2008. Technical Assistance for Policy Reform II. Authors: David Sims, Hazem Kamal, and Doris Solomon. Washington, D.C.: USAID/Egypt Policy and Private Sector Office, 2008.

———. *Housing Study for Urban Egypt.* Final, 2 December 2008. Technical Assistance for Policy Reform II. Authors: David Sims, Hazem Kamal, and Doris Solomon. Washington, D.C.: USAID/Egypt Policy and Private Sector Office, 2008.

———. *Review of Egyptian Subsidized Housing Programs and Lessons Learned.* Final Report, April 15, 2007. Technical Assistance for Policy Reform II. Washington, D.C.: USAID/Egypt Policy and Private Sector Office, 2007.

United States Agency for International Development (USAID), Office of Environment and Urban Programs. "Community-Based Development: Experience Across Cities." Working Paper PN-ABU-443 presented at the Forum on Enabling Sustainable Community Development, Second World Bank Conference on Environmentally Sustainable Development, 1994.

Vignal, Leïla, and Eric Denis. "Cairo as Regional/Global Economic Capital?" In *Cairo Cosmopolitan: Politics, Culture, and Urban Space in the New Globalized Middle East*, 99–153. Cairo: American University in Cairo Press, 2006.

Volait, Mercedes. *Architectes et Architectures de L'Égypte Moderne (1830–1950): Genèse et Essor d'une Expertise locale*. Paris: Maisonneuve et Larose, 2005.

———. *Fous du Caire: Excentriques, Architectes, et amateurs d'art en Égypte 1867–1914*. Montpelier: L'Archange du Minotaure, 2009.

al-Wali, M. *Sukkan al-'ahshash wa-l-'ashwa'iyyat*. Cairo: Naqabat al-Muhandisin al-Misriyin, 1993.

Waterbury, John, and Alan Richards. *A Political Economy of the Middle East: State, Class, and Economic Development*. Boulder CO: Westview Press Inc., 1990.

World Bank. "Arab Republic of Egypt: Egypt Public Land Management Strategy." Vol. 1, Finance, Private Sector and Infrastructure Group, Middle East and North Africa. Unpublished draft policy note, April 2006.

———. *Arab Republic of Egypt: A Poverty Assessment Update*. Vol. 1: Main Report. 39885-EGT. Washington, D.C.: World Bank Social and Economic Development Group, Middle East and North Africa Region, 2007.

———. "Arab Republic of Egypt: Upper Egypt—Challenges and Priorities for Rural Development." Unpublished final draft for World Bank Water, Environment, Social and Rural Development Department, Middle East and North Africa Region, 2006.

———. *Arab Republic of Egypt: Urban Sector Note*. Vol. 1: *Urban Sector Update*. Report no. 44506-EG. Washington, D.C.: World Bank, Sustainable Development Department, Middle East and North Africa Region, 2008.

———. *Arab Republic of Egypt: Urban Sector Note*. Vol. 2: *Towards an Urban Sector Strategy*. Report no. 44506-EG. Washington, D.C.: World Bank, Sustainable Development Department, Middle East and North Africa Region, 2008.

———. "PHRD Grant for Preparation of Greater Cairo Development Project." Unpublished aide mémoire of World Bank Mission to Egypt, 29 January to 7 February 2008, TF-057140, 2008. World Bank, and International Finance Corporation. *Doing Business in Egypt 2008*. Washington D.C.: World Bank and International Finance Corporation, 2007.

———. *Poverty Alleviation and Adjustment in Egypt*. Vol. 2: Main Report. Washington, D.C.: World Bank, 1990.

———. "Preparatory Grant Assistance for Greater Cairo Metropolitan Development Strategy and City-wide Upgrading." Unpublished cities alliance proposal of the World Bank, 2007.

World Bank, and United States Agency for International Development (USAID). "A Framework for Housing Policy Reform in Egypt: Developing a Well Functioning Housing System and Strengthening the National Housing Program." Unpublished draft policy note, May 2008.

Index

al-'Abbasiya, 50
Abdel Nasser, Gamal, 12, 13, 61
'Abdin, 46, 55
above the average *(fuq mutawassit)*, 51
Abu-Lughod, Janet, 2, 4, 14, 21, 59
Abu Qatada, 61
Abu Rawash, 73
Abu Rawash hills, 26
Abu Za'bal, 214; growth of, 135;
    population, 128
Abu Za'bal desert, 183
Abul-Naga, Fayza, 286
access to state land, 159
administration of Greater Cairo, 252–53
administrative districts *(ahya')*, 254
affordable housing, 49, 139, 187. *See also*
    housing
"Affordable Housing in Challenging
    Times," 139
agents *(samasira)*, 126
agricultural land, development of, 112–15
agriculture, 26, 29
Ahmad 'Urabi Agricultural Land
    Reclamation Cooperative, 81, 183
al-Ahram, 22
al-Ahram al-iqtisadi, 15
al-Ahram newspaper, 33, 93, 94, 170
ahwad (small irrigated agricultural
    plots), 113
ahya' (administrative districts), 254
'Ain al-Sira: leather industries, 59;
    slums in, 107
'Ain Shams, 53, 62
'Ain Shams University, 38
'Ain Sukhna Road, 59

airlines, 214
'ala bab Allah (at God's gate), 112
Alexandria, 26, 30; desert cities near,
    76; growth, 74; migration, 32;
    population, 35; rent control in, 146
Alexandria Desert Road, 57, 203,
    243, 246
'Ali al-Maqrizi, Ahamd ibn, 10
Allied Force armies, 45
allocation of land, 192, 193, 194, 196
amenities in informal Cairo, 105–107
American University in Cairo (AUC),
    178, 179, 277, 282, 291
amin al-shorta (traffic officer), 238, 241
al-Amiriya, 260
al-Amiriya al-Gadida, 76
amusement parks, 176, 194
analysis, mapping, 66
apartments, 103, 146, 205, 237.
    See also housing
applications *(istimarat)*, 158
aqsam (districts), 21, 22, 49, 55, 106
'Arab al-Walda, 131
Arab Contractors, 200
Arab Republic of Egypt Telecommunica-
    tions Organization, 264
*Architecture for the Dead: Cairo's Medieval
    Metropolis*, 22
Ard al-Liwa, 61, 92
artisanat *(harafi)*, 155
'ashwa'i, 92, 93
assignments of land, 200, 202
Aswan, migration, 32
at God's gate *('ala bab Allah)*, 112
authoritarianism, 18, 20

347

authorities, housing, 158. *See also* Ministry of Housing
automobiles, 234–38, 248. *See also* transportation
Ayoub, 170
al-Azhar, 61, 228
al-Azhar Park, 190
al-Azhar tunnel, 56
al-Azhar University, 38

Bab al-Sha'riya, 50, 55, 220
al-Badr, 7, 79, 185–86
Badrashayn, 7, 70
al-Badr New Town, 59
Baghdad Without a Map, 21
Bahariya Oasis road, 75
Bahtim, 52
banks, 214
al-Basatin, 52, 62, 84, 92; access to central Cairo, 121; average household sizes in, 112; Jewish cemetery, 22
al-Bashtil, 64
basic care (*al-ri'aya al-ula*), 162
bathrooms, 143
bawwabs (building owners), 166, 237
bayarat (soakaway pits), 114
Bayat, Asef, 12
bedrooms, 144
Begam, 64
belle époque (1870-1925), 14, 15n14
belting (*tahzim*), 137
beltway enterprises, 208
Beni Suef, 31
Beverly Hills, 194
bicycles, 237
bidonvilles, 107. *See also* slums
Bilbis desert road, 183
Billion Campaign to Develop Informal Areas, 280
birth rates, 28. *See also* population
bribes, 126, 152
brick, 103
British International School, 181
bubbles, new urban development paradigm, 207–209
budgets: governmental, 252; governorates, 254
building codes, 59, 62, 144, 164
building owners (*bawwabs*), 166, 237
building permits, 68, 126, 129, 188
buildings in informal Cairo, 99–105

Build Your Own House program (*ibni baytak*), 163, 285
Bulaq, 46, 50, 55, 56
Bulaq al-Dakrur, 13n6, 61, 62, 84; access to central Cairo, 121; GTZ projects in, 134; metro, 233; public transportation in, 230; roads, 263; vehicular access, 122; al-Zumur Street, 240
bus fleets, 160, 173, 189, 227, 229–34. *See also* transportation
business sector jobs, 214–17

Cable News Network (CNN), 22
Cairo 2050, 278, 279, 295
Cairo: Airport, 73, 190; comparison to other cities, 84–88; demographics, 86; future of, 88–89; historical dimension of, 10–14; history of modern, 45; informal, 91. *See also* informal Cairo; Master Plan (1956, 1969), 74; Master Plan (1983), 78; migration to, 15–16; nostalgic view of, 14–15; overview of success of, 267–73; peri-urban, 85; population, 50n8; rent control in, 146; rents and housing prices in, 148–49; slums in, 16–17; view of, 9
Cairo: City of History, 10
Cairo: City of Sand, 10
Cairo: The City Victorious, 10
Cairo: 1001 Years of the City Victorious, 2
Cairo Contested: Governance, Urban Space, and Global Modernity, 19
Cairo Cosmopolitan, 18
Cairo Governorate, 6, 252. *See also* government; construction of public housing, 50, 55; loss of population, 55; Madinat al-Salam project, 55
Cairo Ring Road, 56, 69, 178, 190, 204, 232, 243, 246, 290
Cairo School of Urban Studies, 18
"Cairo's Great Leap Forward," 96n12
Cairo Stadium, 53
Cairo Transport Authority, 189, 229, 245. *See also* Cairo Transport Authority
Cairo University, 38, 61, 94, 190
Cairo University Lecturers' City, 93
Cairo 2050 vision, 88
Camp David peace negotiations (1977), 52
Canal Zone, 26
capitalism, 18

cars, 234–38, 248. *See also* transportation;
    car parts, 219; car repair workshops,
    removal of, 57
cartography, informal Cairo, 96, 98
cement factories in Helwan, 52
cemeteries, 22. *See also* tomb dwellers
Census (1996), 97
Census (2006), 5, 7, 79, 85
census districts *(aqsam)*, 21
Census of Buildings, 165, 166
Census of Establishments (2006), 216
Census of Population, 165
Central Agency for Public Mobilization and
    Statistics (CAPMAS), 7, 39–41, 141, 212
children, street, 223
City of the Dead, 21n40, 276
City Requiem: Calcutta, 2
City Stars, 56, 206
civil service, 252
classic informal housing, 103
Cleopatra cigarettes, 214
Clerget, Marcel, 2
clothing, 219
collapses, building, 100
commercial areas, 173
community associations *(gam'iyat),* 133
Companies Law, 216n9
conditions, housing, 149–50
congestion, 228
construction: on agricultural land, 113;
    building permits, 129. *See also* building
    permits; of desert towns, 78; govern-
    mental control of, 122–26; in informal
    Cairo, 95; of public housing, 50; roads,
    263–64; Sixth of October, 175; styles
    of, 105
containment *(tahzim),* 137
contemporary city (1920–1960), 14
contractors *(muqawilin),* 126
contracts: signature confirmation *(sihhat
    tawqi'),* 153; *'urfi* sales, 114
control, 3
Cooperative Housing Authority, 187
core city, 196
corporate offices, 214
corridor *(al-mihwar),* 189, 249
credit, 118–19
crime, 3, 5, 120
crowding rate, 145
current strategies for new towns in Cairo,
    199–200

DAMAC, 289
Dar al-Salam, 19, 62, 84
al-Darb al-Ahmar, 55; slums in, 108
al-Darrasa, 50, 61
Davis, Mike, 16, 17
da'wa sihha wa-nafadh (petition for execu-
    tion of a contract), 153
days, length of work, 213
dead property, 167
Deboulet, Agnès, 19
debt, 200
decline in population, 10
Deed Law *(al-sigill al-shakhsi),* 152
deltas, 25
demand for housing units, 105
demographics, 28. *See also* population;
    Cairo, 86; new towns in Cairo, 192;
    spatial, 28–31
Denis, Eric, 19, 35, 97
'desert backyard' initiative *(al-zahr
    al-sahrawi),* 33
desert cities, emergence of, 73–84; real-
    estate land deals in, 287–89
deserts: development on, 115–18, 287;
    Greater Cairo, 7; migration to, 34
Desoto, Hernando, 69, 217
deteriorated slum pockets, 107. *See also*
    slums
Deutsche Gesellschaft für Technische
    Zusammenarbeit GmbH (GTZ), 97
development. *See also* new towns in
    Cairo: of agricultural land, 112–15;
    on desert land, 115–18; land, 197;
    New Cairo, 178; new urban develop-
    ment paradigm, 207–209; over
    the 1936–92 period, 10;
    residential, 202; suburban,
    203; urban, 66
distribution jobs, 213. *See also* jobs
distribution process, housing units, 158
districts *(aqsam),* 21, 22, 49, 55, 106
districts *(marakiz),* 7, 30, 32
documentation of property claims, 110
Dokki, 56, 61, 85
Dorman, W. Judson, 19, 20
dormitory suburbs, 78, 177
down payments for housing, 158
downtown, 45. *See also* Khedivial Cairo
Dreamland, 194, 195
driving tests, 238. *See also* cars;
    transportation

Duweiqa, cliff collapse (2008), 93, 136, 284; government public housing programs, 155, slums in, 108
dynamics of internal migration, 32–34

early revolutionary period (1952–62), 14
earthquakes, 100
Eastern Company for Tobacco, 214
East Gate, 169
economic or affordable housing *(iskan iqtisadi)*, 50, 51, 283, 284, 292, 294, 295
economies, 4; liberalization, 169; urban, 16
education in Egypt, 37–39
Egypt, 25–43; dynamics of internal migration, 32–34; education in, 37–39; Greater Cairo, 35. *See also* Greater Cairo; labor force, 36–37; living standards in, 39–42; Nile Valley, 25–27; population, 25, 27–28; spatial demographics, 28–31
Egypt Housing Finance Conference (2009), 139
Egyptian Electricity Holding Company, 262
Egyptian Environmental Affairs Agency, 58, 254
Egyptian Railways Authority, 245
Egyptian Red Crescent, 130
Egyptian Survey Authority, 152
Egypt Iron and Steel Company, 214
elections, 255–56; post-revolution parliamentary, 284, 291–93
electricity, 105, 262
El Kadi, Galila, 22, 96n11
Emaar Misr, 140, 289
emergency housing *(masakin iwa')*, 108, 109
emerging small towns, 31
Empain, Baron, 196
employment, 121, 211–12; formal business sector jobs, 214–17; formal manufacturing jobs, 213–14; future of, 224–25; generation of, 223–24; government jobs, 212–13; labor force, 36–37; in Nile Valley, 34; self-employment, 218, 221–23; small and micro enterprises, 217–19; small manufacturing workshops, 219–20
establishments, distribution and concentrations of, 220–21
Euromoney Conferences, 139
eviction, protection against, 110
exchange of property, 3

expenditure distribution, 40
Extension of Municipal Services Project, 82, 181n17
extremism, 92

fabric, 58
facades, 198
factories, 128, 173; jobs, 40. *See also* jobs; private-sector jobs; small manufacturing workshops, 219–20
fakhr (luxury), 51
fardi (individual), 216
fares, bus, 230. *See also* transportation
Fatimid Cairo, 61
Fatimid era, 10
Fayoum Road, 80, 200
feddans (land, 4,200 square meters of), 26
Federation of Popular Committees in Informal Settlements, 282
fertility, 28. *See also* population
Fifteenth of May, 7, 76; housing, 182; new towns in Cairo, 182–83; population, 182
financing housing, 118–19, 152n21
flats, 146. *See also* housing
flood plains, Nile River, 112
floor plans, 122
food, 219
footwear, 219
formal business sector jobs, 214–17
formal city, 46–59
formal housing, 140. *See also* housing
formal manufacturing jobs, 213–14
fraud, mortgage-based, 153
Freedom and Justice Party, 292
freehold ownership *(tamlik)*, 115
French occupation (1798), 10
fuq mutawassit (above the average), 51
furniture, 219
al-Fustat, 12
Fustat plateau, 64, 115
Al-Futtaim Group, 289
Future City, 179, 200
Future Foundation, 130
future of Cairo, 88–89

Gabal al-Asfar, 260, 261
al-Gamaliya, 50, 55, 56, 108, 220
Gam'at al-Duwal al-'Arabiya Street, 233
gam'iyat (community associations), 133
gam'iyat (informal revolving credit groups), 119

al-Ganzouri, Kamal, 278
garbage collection, 106
garbage collectors (zabbalin), 133
gardens, water for, 201
gas companies, 216
gated communities, 15, 17
General Organization for Physical
    Planning (GOPP), 79, 86–87, 95,
    246, 254, 278
geometric patterns of housing blocks, 154
al-Gharbiya, 31
Giza, 45, 46, 49, 281, 283, 292; demolition
    campaign, 69; expansion in core vil-
    lages, 64; governorates, 254; al-Haram
    Street, 214; pyramids, 80; transporta-
    tion, 247
Giza City, 6, 7
Giza Governorate, 292; reactions to infor-
    mal settlements, 130; size of, 6, 293
Giza Plateau, 26
Giza pyramids, 10
globalization, 17–20
golf courses, 177, 201
Golia, Maria, 10, 13
Google Earth, 7, 118
government, 251; administration of
    Greater Cairo, 252–53; continu-
    ing functions of, 265; elections,
    255–56; governorates and their local
    units, 253–55; infrastructure needs,
    257–64; jobs, 38, 212–13; overview of
    operations of, 251–52; public housing
    programs, 153–62; style of, 256–57;
    zone (al-hayy al-hukumi), 204
governorates (muhafazat), 252
Grand Egyptian Museum, 82
graves, 20. See also tomb dwellers
Greater Cairo, 5. See also new towns in
    Cairo; access to Central Cairo, 121;
    accelerated informal settlement after
    Egyptian Revolution, 279–83; admin-
    istration of, 252–53; budget deficit,
    278; Census (1986), 78; comparison to
    other cities, 84–88; deserts, 7; desert
    towns, 82; electricity, 262; employment
    in, 212; government public housing
    programs, 154, 284, 285; Greater Cairo
    Proper, 6–7; housing, 142–46; Housing
    Study for Urban Egypt (HSUE), 142;
    informal cities in, 96, 280, 282, 283;
    infrastructure services, 106; migration,

32; Nile River, 26; peri-urban Greater
    Cairo, 7; population, 10, 35–36, 68, 72,
    86–88, 277, 279; private cars in, 122,
    229, 235, 236, 248, 290; profile of aver-
    age household in, 42–43, 277; public
    transportation, 230, 290; real-estate
    transactions, 148–49, 287–89; rents
    in, 120; Sanitary Drainage Company,
    260; security of tenure, 147; sewerage,
    260–62, 277; slums, 16–17, 93–94,
    107–10, 276, 280, 292; style of govern-
    ment, 256–57, 278, 282–86, 291–93;
    Transport Planning Study, 236; types
    of informal areas in, 97–99; university
    students in, 39; urban development of,
    91, Wastewater Project, 260; Water
    Supply Company, 258
Gross Domestic Product (GDP), 218, 252
ground water, 26. See also water
growth, 12; Abu Za'bal, 135; of business
    sector, 214; expansion of core villages
    in Giza, 64; of informal settlements,
    33; al-Khanka, 135; al-Marg, 135; in
    new towns in Cairo, 187–92; peri-
    urban frontier, 69–73; population,
    80, 219; of population, 27–28. See also
    population; types of, 84
GTZ projects, 134
guhud zatiya (self-help), 68

Hada'iq al-Ahram, 80
Hada'iq al-Qubba, 56
al-Hakim, Athar, 170
Hanna, Milad, 93
Haram City, 169
al-Haram Street, 214
al-Hawamidiya, 7, 70
hayy (urban administrative district), 126
Hayy al-Ashgar, 194
al-hayy al-hukumi (government zone), 204
al-hayy al-mutamayyiz (upscale or 'tourist'
    zone), 195
health centers, 95, 159
Heikastep camp, 73, 82
Heliopolis, 45, 49, 55, 100; emergence of
    desert cities, 73; housing, 140; Tram
    Company, 245; urbanization, 197
Helwan, 45, 50. See also new towns in
    Cairo; cement factories in, 52; Census
    (1986), 78; development in, 118; indus-
    trial zones, 214; informal settlements

in, 131; iron and steel complex in, 51; new towns in Cairo, 173; wastewater treatment, 262
Helwan University, 38
high-speed Internet services, 264
highways, 189, 227. *See also* transportation
Hikr Sakakini, slums in, 107
Hilmiya, 50
Hina maysara (When Fate Calls), 92
hirafi (artisanat), 155
historical dimension of Cairo, 10–14
history of modern Cairo, 45
Holding Company for Water and Wastewater, 258, 260
home ownership, 120. *See also* real estate transactions
Horwitz, Tony, 21
hospitals, 169, 205
hotels, 214
Household Expenditure, Consumption and Income Survey of 2004–2005 (HECIS), 39
household incomes, 39–42
housing, 139–41; arrangement of blocks, 154; authorities, 158; conditions, 149–50; Fifteenth of May, 182; financing, 118–19. *See also* real estate transactions; government public housing programs, 153–62, 283–86; Greater Cairo, 142–46; *Housing Study for Urban Egypt (HSUE)*, 141–42. *See also Housing Study for Urban Egypt (HSUE)*; National Housing Program (NHP), 162–63, 283, 284, 285, 286; New Cairo, 177; New Rent Law, 146–48; prices, 148–49; projects in the new towns of Cairo, 187, 278–79, 283–85, 287–88; real estate transactions, 150–51, 287–88; registered property titles, 152–53; security of tenure, 146–48; Sixth of October, 176; vacancies, 165–67
Housing Development Bank, 187, 285
Housing Promise, 140
Housing Study for Urban Egypt (HSUE) (2008), 41, 42, 55, 106, 120, 166, 241, 261
hutments, 107. *See also* slums
hypercites, 16

ibni baytak (Build Your Own House) program, 163, 285

illiteracy, 37, 112
Imbaba, 7, 45, 49, 70, 84, 92; access to central Cairo, 121; Airport, 131, 245; government reaction to informal settlements, 130; Masakin al-'Ummal project in, 50; metro, 233; public transportation in, 230
immigration, 15–16
incomes: household, 39–42; rent and housing prices in Cairo, 148–49
Independent magazine, 21
individual *(fardi)*, 216
industrial areas, 76
industrialization, 51
industrial zones, 173; al-Badr, 186; Helwan, 214; manufacturing jobs, 213–14; New Cairo, 177; Sixth of October, 176, 195; small manufacturing workshops, 219–20; Tenth of Ramadan, 182
infant mortality rates, 39
infitah (Open Door policy), 52, 64, 74, 85, 233
inflation, effect on rent, 146
informal Cairo, 91; advantages and disadvantages of, 119–22; amenities in, 105–107; community participation in upgrading projects, 133–34; descriptions of, 95–97; development of agricultural land, 112–15, 279; development on desert land, 115–18; effects of revolution on, 279–83; future of, 134–37; governmental control in, 122–26, 279; government approaches to, 129–33; images and attitudes toward, 92–95, 276–77, 280–82; large informal areas, 126–29; means of financing housing, 118–19; population, 96, 111–12; quality and types of buildings in, 99–105, 280; popular committees, 282–83; security of tenure in, 109–10; slums, 107–109; types of in Greater Cairo, 97–99
informal city, 59–70
informal minibuses, 229. *See also* minibuses
informal real estate broker *(simsar)*, 114, 151
informal revolving credit groups *(gam'iyat)*, 119
informal settlements, growth of, 33
informal urban areas *('ashwa'iyyat)*, 19
Information Decision Support Center (IDSC), 97

information technology (IT), 227
infrastructure, 105; funding of, 20; needs,
  government capacity to fill, 257–64;
  new towns in Cairo, 208; post World
  War II, 45; services, 12
Institute for Liberty and Democracy
  (ILD), 69, 217
Integrated Care Society, 33
Internet services, high-speed, 264
Investment Authority, 77
investments, land as, 167
Iran-Iraq War (1980s), 66
iron and steel complex in Helwan, 51
irrigation, 25, 173. *See also* water
iskan iqtisadi (economic or affordable hous-
  ing), 50, 51, 283, 284, 292, 294, 295
islands, Nile River, 88
Ismailiya, 34, 173
Ismailiya Desert Highway, 76
Ismailiya Desert Road, 73, 81, 183, 204
istimarat (applications), 158
'Izbit al-'Arab, 58
'Izbit al-Haggana, 64; development on,
  115; styles of construction in, 105
'Izbit al-Nasr, 64
'Izbit al-Walda, 131
'Izbit Bikhit, 93
'Izbit Khayrallah, 64, 108

Jahin, Bahaa, 22
Japan International Cooperation Agency,
  228
jobs, 35, 121, 199. *See also* employment;
  business sector, 214–17; distribution
  and concentrations of establishments,
  220–21; future of, 224–25; generation
  of, 223–24; government, 212–13; manufacturing, 213–14; self-employment,
  221–23; small and micro enterprises,
  217–19; small manufacturing workshops, 219–20
June 1967 war, 52

Kadi, Galila El, 64
Kafr al-Gabal, 64
Kafr al-Taharmus, 64
Al Khamissi, Khaled, 37, 93
al-Khanka, 7, 70; growth of, 135; populat-
  ing, 128
Khedivial Cairo, 45
Khusus, 70, 84, 128

King Farouk, overthrow of (1952), 14
al-Kirdasa, 64
kitchens, 143
Kitkat, 61
Koolhaas, Rem, 2

labor force, 173; education of, 38; Egypt,
  36–37; formal business sector jobs,
  214–17; government jobs, 212–13;
  manufacturing jobs, 213–14; self-
  employment, 221–23; small and micro
  enterprises, 217–19; small manufacturing workshops, 219–20
labor laws, 213
Lagos, 2n3
Lagos/Koolhaas, 2
Lake Manzala, 261
land: access to state, 159; allocations,
  159, 192, 193, 194, 196; assembly, 82;
  assignments, 200, 202; development,
  197; development of agricultural,
  112–15; development on desert,
  115–18; as a family investment,
  167; *feddans* (4,200 square meters of
  land equals), 26; incorporation, 175;
  land-use planning, 254; *muklafa* (agricultural land holding), 29; National
  Housing Program (NHP), 164; New
  Cairo, 178; nonresidential, 128;
  oversupply of, 206–207; reclamation
  projects, 74; state ownership of deserts, 202; taxes, 167
land-claim conflicts, 183
land-disposal policy, 79
landlines. *See* telephone service
landscaping, 156
Law no. 59 of 1979, 77
Law no. 114 of 1946 (Deed Law), 152
Law no. 142 of 1964 (Title Law), 152
leather industries, 59
*Le Caire: Étude de Géographie urbaine et
  d'Histoire économique*, 2, 2n6
Le Gac, Daniel, 21
l'Envers des Pyramides, 21
levels of urbanization, 28–31
liberalization of economies, 169
ligan sha'biya (popular committees), 282–83
lights, traffic intersection, 238
limited liability share company (*shirka
  musahima*), 216
living standards in Egypt, 39–42

loans, 118–19
local people's councils (al-magalis al-mahaliya al-sha'biya), 126, 255
loss of population, 55
lottery (qur'a), 198
lower-class (sha'bi), 145
Lower Egypt population, 28
lower-income families, 42
luxury (fakhr), 51
luxury flats, 146. See also housing

Maadi, 45, 64, 73, 140
Ma'an, 281, 282
Madinat al-Awqaf. See Mohandiseen-Agouza
Madinat al-Haram, 162
Madinat al-Mustaqbal, 200
Madinat al-Nahda, government public housing programs, 160
Madinat al-Salam, 53, 73, 85, 155, 160
Madinat Nasr, 52, 53, 57, 85, 100, 179, 189, 291; City Stars, 206; housing, 140; Muqattam, 73
Madinaty, 169, 200
magalis (local popular councils), 126
al-magalis al-mahaliya al-sha'biya (local people's councils), 255
al-Maghrabi, Ahmed, 198
Maghreb-Machrek, 22
maglis al-madina license plates, 243
Mahalla al-Kubra, 31, 32
major roads, repair and construction, 263–64
Mamluks, 12, 61
al-manatiq al-gheir mukhattata (unplanned areas), 95
Manshiyat al-Bakari, 129
Manshiyat Nasir, 58, 61, 84, 220; access to central Cairo, 121; average household sizes in, 112; development on, 115; GTZ projects in, 134; population, 128; redevelopment plans, 136; slums in, 108, 109; styles of construction in, 105
manufacturing: jobs, 213–14; small manufacturing workshops, 219–20
mapping: analysis, 66; informal Cairo, 96, 98
marakiz (districts), 7, 30, 32
marakiz (rural districts), 254
marakiz (zones), 70
al-Marg, 64, 84; growth of, 135; metro, 233; population, 128

Marg al-Qibliya, 62
markets: housing, 150–51. See also housing; modern real estate, 165–67
Maryutiya Connector, 263
Masakin al-Amiriya al-Ganub, 62
Masakin al-'Ummal project in Imbaba, 50
Masakin al-Zilzal, government public housing programs, 160
masakin iwa' (emergency housing), 108, 109
Ma'sara, 64
al-Matariya, 62, 112, 220
Maximum City: Bombay Lost and Found, 2
median area of housing units, 142
Media Production City, 176n11
Mehta, Suketu, 2
metal items, 219
metered electricity, 105
metro, 204, 242. See also public transportation; transportation; planning for, 233, 290; underground metro system, 232, 245
metropolis, 186n20, 227
MHUUD, 118, 162, 183, 199
microbuses, private, 229–34
micro enterprise jobs, 217–19
Midan al-Rimaya, 80, 82
middle (mutawassit), 51
middle class, 42
migration: to Cairo, 15–16; dynamics of internal, 32–34
al-mihwar (the corridor), 189, 249
military: use of deserts, 73–74; use of desert towns, conversion of, 82
minibus fleets, 173, 189, 229–34
minister of housing, 195, 286
minister of international cooperation, 285, 286
Ministry of Agriculture, 81
Ministry of Awqaf, 50n7, 285
Ministry of Education, 253
Ministry of Electricity, 262
Ministry of Finance, 278
Ministry of Housing, 77, 131, 201, 258n14, 260, 279, 284, 285; and Reconstruction, 57; Utilities, and Urban Development, 171
Ministry of Interior, 238, 243, 253
Ministry of Investment and the Mortgage Finance Authority, 139
Ministry of Justice, 152
Ministry of Local Development, 97, 255

Ministry of Reconstruction, 75, 77
Ministry of Trade and Industry, 214
Ministry of Transport, 233
Misr al-Qadima, 49, 55, 107
Mit 'Uqba, 49
modern Cairo, 169, 170–86
modernization, 19
modern real estate markets, 165–67
Mohandiseen, 61, 85
Mohandiseen-Agouza, 50
Moharram Bakhoum, 289
mortgages, 118–19, 152n21
motorbikes, 237. *See also* transportation
Mubarak, Hosni, 12, 74
Mubarak Police City, 177
Mubarak Youth Housing Program (1997 to
    2003), 156, 157, 158
mufakkirin, 94
Mugamma' al-Tahrir, 14
mugamma'at 'umraniya gadida (new settle-
    ments), 177
muhafazat (governorates), 252
muklafa (agricultural land holding), 29
munadis (self-appointed car parkers), 237
al-Munira al-Gharbiya, 61, 62, 68, 240, 246
Muqattam, 26, 50, 57
muqawilin (contractors), 126
al-Muski, 55, 56
Muslim Brotherhood, 283, 292
al-Mu'tamidiya, 64
Myrdal, Gunnar, 252

al-Nahda, 55, 183
National Democratic Party, 255, 256, 293
National Housing Program (NHP), 80, 140,
    157, 162–64, 187, 283; new (second)
    National Housing Program, 284–86
National Social Housing Program, 285,
    286, 287
The National Urban Policy Study, 77, 82n39
neglect, 122
neo-colonialism, 18
neoliberalism, 19
Next Move—Cityscape Egypt, 289
New Cairo, 7, 78, 79, 286, 289, 291; hous-
    ing, 177; industrial zones, 177; land
    incorporation, 175; new towns in
    Cairo, 177–81; population, 179; strate-
    gies for, 199
New Communities Law (Law no. 59 of
    1979), 77

New Giza, 295
New Kingdom, 12
New Rent Law, 120, 146–48, 150–51, 164,
    166
new settlements *(mugamma'at 'umraniya
    gadida)*, 177
New Towns Authority, 82
new towns in Cairo, 170–86. *See also* specific
    new towns; al-Badr, 185–86; al-Shuruq,
    185; al-'Ubur, 183–85; building permits,
    188; current strategies for, 199–200;
    distances between, 190; Fifteenth of
    May, 182–83; New Cairo, 177–81; new
    urban development paradigm, 207–209;
    oversupply of property, 205–206; popu-
    lation, 171, 187–92; Sheikh Zayed, 181;
    Sixth of October, 175–77; as the specu-
    lative frontier, 206–207; as successful
    real-estate ventures, 192–98; Tenth
    of Ramadan, 181–82; urbanization,
    201–205; water in, 200–201
New Towns Program (1977), 171
New Urban Communities Authority
    (NUCA), 77, 79, 171, 187, 193, 198,
    207, 254, 285, 289, 295
new urban development paradigm,
    207–209
NGOs, 133, 281, 282, 284
Nile River: flood plain, 112; Greater Cairo,
    26; islands, 88; water supply from, 258
Nile Valley, 25–27; dynamics of internal
    migration, 32–34; employment in, 34;
    growth, 74
1952 Revolution, 12
1967 war, 73
Nippon study (2008), 249, 259,
    260
nonresidential land, 128
North Cairo, 49, 61
North Cairo Electrical Distribution
    Company, 262
Northern City, 50, 62
nostalgic view of Cairo, 14–15
al-Nuzha, 53, 57, 73, 85, 140

October 1973 War, 52, 74
oil companies, 216
Old Serpent Nile, 21
one-off towers, 104
Open Door policy *(infitah)*, 52, 64, 74,
    85, 233

open space, 197
Orascom, 140, 288, 289
Orascom Hotels, 162
oversupply of property, 205–206
ownership of private cars, 235. *See also*
    private cars; transportation

Palm Hills, 287, 288, 289
paper products, 219
parking in Cairo, 237
parks, recreational, 88
parliament, 126, 255
Participatory Development Programme in
    Urban Areas, 134
passengers, competition among minibuses,
    231
payment arrangements, 194. *See also* real
    estate transactions
pedestrian-friendly, Cairo as, 228, 291
peri-urban Cairo, 85, 241
peri-urban frontier, 70–73, 85
permits, building, 68
petition for execution of a contract *(da'wa
    sihha wa-nafadh)*, 153
Piffero, Elena, 134
Planet of Slums, 16
planning: master plans, 3; for the metro
    system, 233
plastic products, 219
police, 275; brutality and corruption, 2, 93,
    239; housing for, 82; protection, 200;
    traffic police, 122, 227, 289, 238–41,
    248
policies: government housing, 162–64;
    transportation, 248–49
Political Vegetables, 21
politics, leadership, 3, 291–95
pollution, 58, 238. *See also* transportation
popular committees *(ligan sha'biya)*, 282–83
popular councils, 255–56
population, 2; Alexandria, 35; Cairo, 49–50,
    50n8, 78; Cairo Governorate loss of,
    55; density in Cairo, 228; dynamics
    of internal migration, 32–34; educa-
    tion levels of, 38; Egypt, 25, 27–28;
    Fifteenth of May, 182; formal city, 59;
    Greater Cairo, 7, 10, 35–36, 68, 72,
    86–88; growth, 80, 84, 187–92, 219,
    279; informal Cairo, 96, 111–12, 279,
    293; large informal areas, 128; Lower
    Egypt, 28; New Cairo, 179; new towns

in Cairo, 171; overburden of infrastruc-
    ture services, 106; peri-urban frontier,
    72; al-Shuruq, 185; Sixth of October,
    175; Tenth of Ramadan, 75, 181; al-
    'Ubur, 183; Upper Egypt, 28; urban, 29
Population Institute, 17
Port Said, 30, 34, 52
Port Said Street, 260
post World War II infrastructure, 45
potable water, 105, 258–59. *See also* water
Potemkin neighborhoods, 198
poverty, 17, 39–42
powers of attorney *(tawkilat)*, 153, 161
prices, housing, 148–49
Prince of Imbaba, 68
private cars, 234–38, 248. *See also* transpor-
    tation
private compounds, 181, 194
private microbuses, 229–34
private-sector jobs, 37, 40
private universities, 176
processed food, 219
production: capacity of water supply, 259;
    levels, National Housing Program
    (NHP), 164
productivity, 38
professional job market, 217
profit margins, private minibuses, 231
property, 152–53. *See also* housing; real
    estate transactions; claims, documenta-
    tion, 110; exchange of, 3; oversupply
    of, 205–206
public housing. *See also* housing: construc-
    tion of, 50; programs, 153–62
public-sector jobs, 38
public services: in informal Cairo, 95
public transportation, 189, 190, 214, 230.
    See also bus fleets; transportation
purchases, housing, 150–51. *See also* real
    estate transactions
Pyramid Gardens, 80
pyramids, 26, 73; Giza, 10, 80, 81

al-Qalag, populating, 128
Qalyub, 7, 70
Qalyub City, 247
Qalyubiya, 46, 254
Qalyubiya Governorate, 70
al-Qanatir al-Khayriya, 7, 70
qanun al-igar al-gadid. See New
    Rent Law

Qasr al-Nil, 55
Qattamiya Heights, 177, 178
Qaytbay, 22
qirat (175 square meters), 113
quality and types of buildings in informal
    Cairo, 99–105
quality-of-life indicators, 39, 41
qur'a (a kind of lottery draw), 158
qur'a (lottery), 198

al-Rabwas, 194
radical Islamic movements, 68
rail lines, 227. *See also* transportation
rainfall, 25
Ramses Square, 128, 228, 247
rapid industrialization, 51
rapid light rail, 245, 291
Raymond, André, 10, 12
real-estate, 114; agencies, 214; demand,
    208; financing housing, 118–19;
    Greater Cairo, 148–49; housing,
    150–51; modern real estate markets,
    165–67; new towns in Cairo, 192–98;
    oversupply of property, 205–206
reclamation projects, land, 74
recreational parks, 88
red brick, 103
redrawing governorates, 252
Red Sea, 26
registered property titles, 152–53
regulations: building codes, 61, 62; limita-
    tions on population growth, 187
al-Rehab City, 169, 178, 194
religion, 12
rent: control, 14, 54, 110; New Rent Law,
    120, 146–48, 150–51, 164, 166; prices,
    148–49
repayment schedules, 162
representation, 255–56
residential developments, 202
residential property, 158. *See also* property
restaurants, 214
restricted access points, 173
retail destinations, 206
retail stores, 214
Revolution (1952), 146
al-ri'aya al-ula (basic care), 162
al-Rif al- Urubi, 203
Ring Road. *See* Cairo Ring Road
roads, repair and construction, 263–64
Rod al-Farag, 45, 49, 56, 107

Rodenbeck, Max, 10, 12, 13
rooms per units, 142. *See also* housing
Rooya, 140, 289
routes, bus, 229. *See also* bus fleets
Roy, Ananya, 2
rural districts *(marakiz)*, 30, 254
rural migration to Cairo, 33n14. *See also*
    migration

Sabri, Sarah, 42n38
Sadat, Anwar, 12, 80; desert cities, 75; *infi-
    tah* (Open Door policy), 52, 64, 74, 85,
    233; October Paper (1974), 74
Sadat City, 57, 76
Sadowski, Yahya, 21
Saft al-Laban, 64, 93
al-Sahel, 56
Salah Salim Street, 233
al-Salam, 58, 183
salaries, 213, 216. *See also* employment; jobs
samasira (agents), 126
Sayyida Zaynab, 46, 55, 130
schools, 37, 95, 159. *See also* education
security of tenure, 143; housing, 146–48; in
    informal Cairo, 109–110
Séjourné, Marion, 97
self-appointed car parkers *(munadis)*, 237
self-employment, 218, 221–23
self-help *(guhud zatiya)*, 68
Semiramis Intercontinental Hotel, 139
septic tanks, 261. *See also* sewerage
settlement patterns, 26
sewerage, 260–62, 276, 277
sewers, 105, 114
sha'bi (lower-class), 145
shacks, 108
shahr al-'aqari offices, 152
shantytowns, 107. *See also* slums
al-Sharabiya, 50, 61
Sharif, Omar, 170
Sharqiya, 173
shawish (police sergeant), 238, 241
Sheikh Zayed, 7, 78, 79; new towns in
    Cairo, 181; strategies for, 199, 200
Shibin al-Qanatir, 7, 70
shirka musahima (limited liability share
    company), 216
shopping malls, 204
shortages, water, 201
Shorter, Frank, 32, 96
Shubra, 45, 49, 55

Shubra al-Khayma, 6, 52, 58, 64, 84, 214; metro, 233; populating, 128
al-Shuruq, 7, 79, 200, 286, 289; new towns in Cairo, 185; population, 185
shuttle-bus services, 191. *See also* public transportation
al-sigill al-'ayni (Title Law), 152
al-sigill al-shakhsi (Deed Law), 152
sihhat tawqi' (contract signature confirmation), 153
simsar (informal real estate broker), 114, 151
Sixth of October, 7, 75, 76, 79, 162, 195; Census (1986), 78; construction, 175, 289; conversion of military use, 82; Haram City, 169; industrial areas, 173; industrial zones, 195; land allocation, 196, 286; land incorporation, 175; new towns in Cairo, 175–77; population, 175; strategies for, 199; superblocks, 198
Sixth of October Bridge, 52
sleeping rooms, 144
slums, 94; al-Badr, 186; in Cairo, 16–17; informal Cairo, 107–109
small and micro-enterprise (SME) sector, 218
small enterprise jobs, 217–19
small irrigated agricultural plots *(ahwad)*, 113
small manufacturing workshops, 219–20
small towns, emerging, 31
Smart Village, 203
soakaway pits *(bayarat)*, 114
Social Fund for Development, 38
social housing, 14
socialism, 14
SODIC, 140, 288, 289
Soliman, Ahmed, 24n53
Soueif, Ahdaf, 277
South Cairo Electrical Distribution Company, 262
spatial demographics, 28–31
speculation, housing, 165–67
speculative frontier, new towns in Cairo as, 206–207
speculative one-off towers, 104
spontaneous urbanization of agglomerations, 31
square footage of informal housing, 103
squatters, 20, 108, 131. *See also* tomb dwellers
Stabl 'Antar (Fustat Plateau), 19n35, 136

standards, housing, 142. *See also* housing
state enterprises, 159
state ownership of desert land, 202
state-subsidized building materials, 78
Statistical Year Book (CAPMAS, 2007), 212
Stewart, Stanley, 21
Strategic Urban Development Plan for Greater Cairo, 135
strategies for new towns in Cairo, 199–200
street carts, employment, 223
streets, 227. *See also* transportation; in informal Cairo, 95; traffic, 235. *See also* traffic
subdivisions, 59, 198
subsidies: public housing, 187–88; for public housing, 157, 158; public transportation, 189
suburban developments, 203
Suez, 30, 34
Suez Canal, 62, 181
Suez Desert Highway, 79
Suez Desert Road, 73
Suez Road, 64, 186, 200
al-Sulimaniya, 203
Sunduq Tatwir al-Manatiq al-Ghayr Amina (Unsafe Area Development Fund), 136
superblocks, 156, 198
supply and demand, real estate, 149
swimming pools, 201, 204

Tahrir Square, 14, 276, 290
tahzim (belting or containment), 137
Talaat Moustafa, 140
Talaat Moustafa Group, 169, 179, 200, 289
tamlik (freehold ownership), 115
al-Tansiq al-Hadari ('urban harmony') division, 15
tanzim (urban control), 254
tawkil (power of attorney), 153
tawkilat (powers of attorney), 161
taxes, 167, 217n11, 219
Taxi, 93
taxis, 235. *See also* transportation
Telal Zeinhoum, 109, 130
telecommunication, 264
telephone service, 264
Tenth of Ramadan, 7, 75, 76; Census (1986), 78; industrial areas, 173; industrial zones, 182; new towns in Cairo, 181–82; population, 181

tenure of security, 109–11, 143, 146–48
terrorism, 92
textiles, 52, 219
Title Law *(al-sigill al-'ayni)*, 152
titles to registered property, 152–53
toilets, 143
toll roads, 243
tomb districts *(aqsam)*, 22
tomb dwellers, 20–24
al-Tonsi, 22
tourism, 34
Tourism Company, 162
tourist zones, 195
towers, one-off, 104
traffic, 12; laws, 243; management, 238–39;
    private cars, 234, 235
traffic officer *(amin al-shorta)*, 238, 241
tram stations, 245
transactions, real-estate, 114. *See also*
    real–estate
transportation, 173, 227–29; future of,
    211–18; options for the majority of the
    population, 240–43; policies, 248–49,
    290; private cars, 234–38; private
    microbuses, 229–34; public, 189; roads,
    263–64; traffic management, 238–39,
    289, 290; trucking, 243–44
travel agencies, 214
treatment: wastewater, 260; water, 201
trends: global, 18; migration, 33
trucking, 243–44
tuk-tuks, 122, 191, 223, 242. *See also* trans-
    portation
Tulumbat 'Ain Shams, 62
Tunnels Authority, 245
Tura, 52, 214
Twenty-Six July: Corridor, 92; flyover, 233

al-'Ubur, 7, 75, 243; industrial areas, 173;
    new towns in Cairo, 183–85; popula-
    tion, 183
al-'Umraniya, 62, 84
underground metro system, 232, 245
UNESCO, 248
UN Habitat Report (2003), 107
Unified Building Code, 164
United States Agency for International
    Development (USAID), 64, 66, 77
universities: American University in Cairo
    (AUC), 178; Cairo University, 190;
    private, 176

university education, 38. *See also* education
unplanned areas *(al-manatiq al-gheir
    mukhattata)*, 95
upper class, 42
Upper Egypt, 26, 247; one-off towers, 104;
    population, 28
upscale zones, 195
Uptown Cairo, 295
urban administrative district *(hayy)*, 126
urban agglomeration (congestion), 228
urban control *(tanzim)*, 254
urbanization, 1, 91; Heliopolis, 197; infor-
    mal, 130; levels of, 28–31; new towns
    in Cairo, 201–205; new urban develop-
    ment paradigm, 207–209
urban places, definition of, 31
urban planners, 66, 75
urban population, 29, 30, 84
'urfi contracts, 114, 153, 161
Usim, 7, 70
utilities, 105, 262. *See also* infrastructure

vacancies, housing, 165–67
vehicles. *See* cars; transportation
vehicular access, 122
Vignal, Leïla, 19, 35
villages, 29; peri-urban frontier, 85; village-
    style informal structures, 100
violent crime, 3
voting, 256n10

Wadi al-Nakhil, 203
wages. *See* salaries
Waraq, 84
Waraq al-'Arab, 64
warehousing zones, 173
War of Attrition, 52
al-Waseet free marketing paper, 170
wastewater, 262. *See also* infrastructure;
    sewerage
water, 105; irrigation, 173; in new towns in
    Cairo, 200–201; sewerage. *See* sewer-
    age; supply, 258–59; treatment, 201
Waterbury, John, 21
al-Wayli, 45, 49, 56, 61, 107
wealth, 3, 42. *See also* poverty
weeks, length of work, 213
welfare programs, 212n3
Western Desert, 26
westernization, 19
West Gate, 169

When Fate Calls *(Hina maysara)*, 92
Wilson Center, 97
workforce, 121
World Bank, 64, 247, 262, 283, 285, 291
World Bank Urban Transport Infrastructure
    Development Project, 290
World Bank Report, 216n8

youth centers in informal Cairo, 95
youth clubs, 159

zabbalin (garbage collectors), 133
al-Zahir, 55
Zahra' al-Maadi, 57, 73
Zamalek, 132
al-Zawya al-Hamra', 50, 61, 62
al-Zeitoun, 50
zones: containment *(tahzim)*, 137;
    marakiz, 70